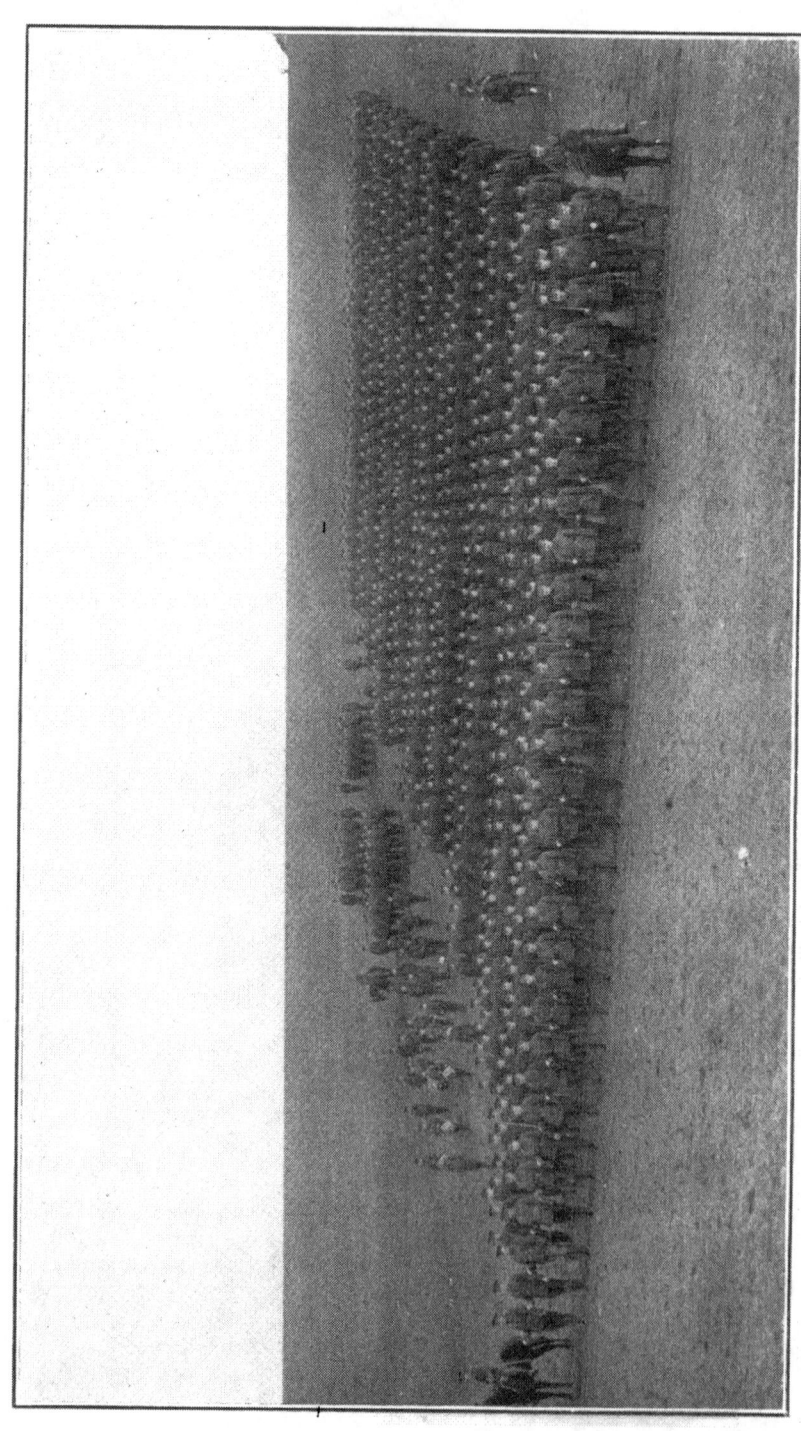
The Royal Montreal Regiment—West Down South—Salisbury Plain, November, 1914

The Royal Montreal Regiment

14th Battalion, C.E.F.

1914 - 1925

Edited and Compiled

By

R. C. FETHERSTONHAUGH

The Naval & Military Press Ltd

Published by

The Naval & Military Press Ltd
Unit 10 Ridgewood Industrial Park,
Uckfield, East Sussex,
TN22 5QE England

Tel: +44 (0) 1825 749494
Fax: +44 (0) 1825 765701

www.naval-military-press.com
www.nmarchive.com

In reprinting in facsimile from the original, any imperfections are inevitably reproduced and the quality may fall short of modern type and cartographic standards.

IN·THE·FIELDS·OF
FRANCE·&·FLANDERS
SLEEPS·A·BATTALION·OF
THE·ROYAL·MONTREAL
REGIMENT
1,192 STRONG

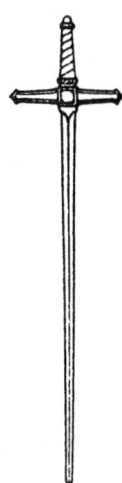

TO ITS MEMORY
THIS BOOK IS
DEDICATED

PREFACE

IN preparing this narrative history of The Royal Montreal Regiment (14th Battalion, C.E.F.), the author received assistance which it is his duty and pleasure to acknowledge.

From the beginning the book has owed much to the Regimental History Committee, under the chairmanship of Lieut.-Col. C. B. Price, D.S.O., D.C.M., with Lieut. L. W. Taylor as Honorary Secretary. This Committee, including at one time or another more than twenty officers, met frequently for over a year, to discuss problems and to provide the author with information supplementing the official Battalion Diary. Other members of the Regiment, and relatives of many who were killed, granted interviews, or lent letters and diaries, which shed light where most needed. To all these the author desires to express his sense of deep obligation.

This preface also affords opportunity for expression to Sir Andrew Macphail, Kt., O.B.E., of the Regiment's, and the author's, indebtedness for scholarly advice, which polished the manuscript in many places. Similarly, the Regiment and the author desire to acknowledge invaluable assistance given by the Historical Section, General Staff, Department of National Defence, and by the Records Section of the Department. Under the directorship of Col. A. Fortescue Duguid, D.S.O., the Historical Section checked the manuscript and verified, or corrected, the text as required. From data supplied by Col. F. Logie Armstrong, O.B.E., Director of Records, the appendices of this book were compiled. To the courtesy of the Directors and Staffs of the Historical and Records Sections, therefore, the book owes a large share of any merit it may possess.

R. C. F.

MONTREAL, February 1st, 1927.

In the preparation of this work the Department of National Defence has allowed the author free access to official diaries, orders, messages, maps and other documents.

FOREWORD

By LIEUT.-GENERAL SIR R. E. W. TURNER,
V.C., K.C.B., K.C.M.G., D.S.O.

THE author's work stands on its own merits and needs no introduction, as, in every way, it is admirable; but when my old comrades asked me to write a foreword, I could not refuse.

The 14th Canadian Battalion, designated "The Royal Montreal Regiment" by special warrant — authority of H.M. the King — and recruited in August, 1914, from three Montreal units of the Canadian Active Militia,

> 1st Regiment, Canadian Grenadier Guards,
> 3rd Regiment, Victoria Rifles of Canada,
> 65th Regiment, Carabiniers de Mont-Royal,

was one of the four battalions in the Third Canadian Infantry Brigade. As I had the honour of commanding the Brigade from the beginning of the Great War until September, 1915, I can speak from personal knowledge of the Regiment.

From the outset it was composed of both English and French, and illustrated more than any other battalion in the 1st Canadian Division the spirit of unity between those two great races. When the Regiment landed at St. Nazaire in February, 1915, the French people, as I well remember, were amazed and delighted to find Canadians in British uniform speaking French as their mother tongue.

Like other Canadian troops, most of the members of this Regiment had their first experience of war conditions at Valcartier Camp and on Salisbury Plain. Like others, they cheerfully accepted sunshine and rain, comfort and discomfort, as part of the day's work. Even before they reached France, they began to learn that in modern warfare discipline and training are essential; and that nothing must be left to chance when men's lives are at stake.

I shall not attempt to tell over again the story of the many gallant deeds done by the Battalion. Mr. Fetherstonhaugh has described the fighting; also in Chapter VI and elsewhere he has shown how little real rest our fighting men had in the war. Among events in the Regiment's history that came under my own notice were:—The winning by Stretcher-Bearer Drake, at Sailly-sur-le-Lys, of the first Distinguished Conduct Medal in the Canadian Division; the winning of the Victoria Cross by the Medical Officer, Capt. Scrimger, at Ypres; the stand made at Ypres by Williamson and his machine guns; and the assisting in bringing in wounded under shell fire by Bugler Ginley, a lad of 15 years, at Festubert.

Later, as history shows, the record so begun was continued by such men as Beaton, Topham, Pelletier, Jobel, Lepine, Woodward, and Wilson; by Brewer in the Buissy Switch; by McKean, who won in succession the Military Medal, the Victoria Cross, and the Military Cross; and by Patterson, who returned to the Battalion after being five times wounded. The magnificent team work of Worrall, Price, and MacRitchie, and the gallant conduct of other senior officers, such as Meighen, Burland, Fisher, Clark, McCombe, Frost, and McKenna, are also a matter of record.

From the first, by its union of French and English, the Royal Montreal Regiment helped to promote Canadian esprit de corps; now by its affiliation with the West Yorkshire Regiment, the old 14th Foot of the British Army, it also helps to bind Canada to the Motherland. It is gratifying to all who served in the Battalion during the war to know that the Regiment is part of the re-organized Active Militia of Canada—with its own fine armoury in Westmount—and that both the name of the Regiment and the record of the services loyally given for the Empire will thus be preserved for all time.

R. E. W. TURNER,
Lieut.-General.

QUEBEC, P.Q., January, 1927.

Contents

	PAGE
CHAPTER I.	
MOBILIZATION. July 24, 1914—September 28, 1914	3
CHAPTER II.	
THE FIRST CONTINGENT. September 28th, 1914—February 9, 1915	12
CHAPTER III.	
FROM SALISBURY PLAIN TO TRENCHES IN FRANCE. February 10, 1915—April 14, 1915	24
CHAPTER IV.	
THE GAS ATTACK AT YPRES. April 15, 1915—May 6, 1915	35
CHAPTER V.	
FESTUBERT, GIVENCHY, AND THE SUMMER OF 1915. May 6, 1915—August 4, 1915	52
CHAPTER VI.	
MESSINES. August 5, 1915—March 18, 1916	67
CHAPTER VII.	
BACK TO THE SALIENT. March 18, 1916—June 1, 1916	77
CHAPTER VIII.	
JUNE, 1916. June 2, 1916—June 30, 1916	84
CHAPTER IX.	
FROM THE SALIENT TO THE SOMME. July 1, 1916—August 31, 1916.	98
CHAPTER X.	
THE SOMME. September 1, 1916—October 15, 1916	106

Chapter XI.

Montreal Crater and Trench Raids. October 16, 1916—
March 31, 1917 124

Chapter XII.

The Taking of Vimy Ridge. April 1, 1917—May 5, 1917 . . 141

Chapter XIII.

Holding Vimy Ridge. May 6, 1917—July 13, 1917 . . . 152

Chapter XIV

The Battle of Hill 70. July 14, 1917—August 22, 1917 . . 160

Chapter XV

The Ypres Salient Again. August 23, 1917—November 11,
1917 172

Chapter XVI.

Winter on the Lens Front. November 11, 1917—March 18,
1918 185

Chapter XVII.

Germany's Great Effort. March 21, 1918—May 19, 1918 . 196

Chapter XVIII.

Army Reserve and Telegraph Hill. May 19, 1918—July 31,
1918 210

Chapter XIX.

Germany's Black Day. August 3, 1918—August 21, 1918 . 216

Chapter XX.

The Corps Strikes Again. August 21, 1918—September 24,
1918 230

CONTENTS

Chapter XXI.

Across the Canal du Nord. September 24, 1918—September 30, 1918 245

Chapter XXII.

The Armistice. September 30, 1918—November 11, 1918 . 254

Chapter XXIII.

Over the German Border. November 11, 1918—January 4, 1919 267

Chapter XXIV.

Huy, Bramshott and Montreal. January 5, 1919—April 20, 1919 278

Chapter XXV.

Re-organization. April 20, 1919—December 31, 1925 . . 286

APPENDICES

A—Honour Roll 296

B—Honours and Awards (Regimental) 309

C—Honours and Awards 314

D—Commissions 317

E—Itinerary 320

F—Statistics 334

Illustrations

	PAGE
THE BATTALION, WEST DOWN SOUTH, SALISBURY PLAIN, NOVEMBER, 1914	*Frontispiece*
HIS MAJESTY KING GEORGE V—BRAMSHOTT CAMP	10
FRONT LINE TRENCHES, FLEURBAIX, MARCH, 1915	30
OFFICERS OF THE BATTALION, CASSEL, FRANCE, MARCH, 1915	34
CLOTH HALL, YPRES, APRIL, 1915	36
THE CRATER, BIRDCAGE, PLOEGSTEERT WOOD, 18TH JULY, 1915	64
SCENE OF COUNTER ATTACK, 3RD JUNE, 1916	86
RAILWAY CUTTING, APPROACH TO HILL 60 TRENCHES, JUNE, 1916	94
BATTALION MEMORIAL, SOMME, 1916	122
SOUCHEZ	140
VIMY RIDGE, APRIL, 1917	148
COMMANDING OFFICERS IN FRANCE	160
MARCHING TO REST BILLETS AFTER HILL 70, AUGUST, 1917	172
PLATOON OF NO. 2 COMPANY, FREVILLERS, JULY, 1918	212
HANGARD WOOD, 8TH AUGUST, 1918	218
BEAURAINS, NEAR ARRAS, SEPTEMBER, 1918	242
ASSEMBLY POSITION, CANAL DU NORD, 27TH SEPTEMBER, 1918	250
PRESENTATION OF COLOURS, UNTER ESCHBACH, GERMANY, 4TH JANUARY, 1919	276
HOME-COMING, MONTREAL, 20TH APRIL, 1919	284
COMMANDING OFFICERS, AFTER REORGANIZATION	288
BATTALION V.C.'S: LT.-COL. F. A. C. SCRIMGER, V.C., CAPTAIN G. B. MCKEAN, V.C., M.C., M.M	292

Maps

(Specially prepared by Captain J. S. Brisbane)

THE SECOND BATTLE OF YPRES, APRIL 1915	42
3RD JUNE, 1916	84
SOMME, 1916	114
VIMY RIDGE, APRIL, 1917	146
AMIENS, AUGUST, 1918	232
CANAL DU NORD, SEPTEMBER, 1918	252

The Royal Montreal Regiment
14th Battalion C.E.F.
1914-1925

CHAPTER I

MOBILIZATION

> Once more we hear the word
> That sickened earth of old:—
> "No law except the Sword
> Unsheathed and uncontrolled."
> Once more it knits mankind,
> Once more the nations go
> To meet and break and bind
> A crazed and driven foe.
> —RUDYARD KIPLING.

I

"ARM and prepare to quit yourselves like men, for the hour of your ordeal is at hand." Speaking at Manchester, in 1912, Field Marshal Earl Roberts of Kandahar, V.C., used these words to warn the Empire of approaching war with Germany, but in spite of the solemnity with which the warning was uttered, and afterwards constantly repeated, few heeded it. The newspapers for the most part commented with respectful pity. It was a tragedy, they said, to see a fine old soldier showing signs of senile decay. Colonial wars still might occur; European war was utterly unthinkable.

This opinion was widely accepted in Canada, though individuals prepared for the coming storm, as is shown by a letter, dated in Winnipeg on August 3rd, 1912, and written by a young ex-private of the 3rd Regiment, Victoria Rifles of Canada:—"I joined the 90th the other night, for it seems to me that there's trouble coming very soon, and to my thinking every man who can march and shoot will be needed. There's no certainty, of course, but 'Qui vivra, verra'."

Canadians truly lived to see, though on July 24th, 1914, when the Austrian ultimatum to Serbia was made public, few were more than casually interested. Austria declared war on Serbia on July 28th, but still Canadians believed that the conflict would prove a "Balkan affair" of minor significance. Soon this unreasoning hope was shattered. On August 1st Germany declared war on Russia, and inevitably thereafter nation after nation was drawn into the abyss. France and Germany exchanged declarations of war on August 3rd, and all eyes turned to Britain. What part was the world's greatest empire to play in the world's greatest tragedy? Viscount Grey, then British Secretary of State for Foreign Affairs, describes in his memoirs the immense strain on all responsible ministers as the question of peace or war was discussed. Britain had guaranteed Belgian neutrality, which Germany was determined to violate. Accordingly, the British Army was mobilized and an ultimatum sent to Berlin, demanding a satisfactory reply by midnight on August 4th. On the evening of August 4th, Mr. Asquith, Sir Edward Grey, and a group of British Cabinet Ministers waited at 10 Downing Street for Germany's answer. Midnight struck; and no reply had come. England, therefore, was at war with Germany.

II

Perhaps the most amazing phenomenon of July and August, 1914, was the response of the British Empire. Without hesitation the Dominions joined the Mother Country in accepting Germany's challenge, a remarkable development in view of the fact that the Dominions were non-militaristic to a degree. Australia and New Zealand had never suffered invasion, or attacked a national foe, limited participation in the South African war marking the extent of their military effort up to this time. In Canada the situation was not widely different, for, though Canada had seen wars and invasions, these events had passed into history and the Canadian people had spent a century at peace, minor rebellions and the South African war having affected directly but a few thousand troops or civilians. Under a quiet surface, however, the blood of generations of fighting men ran true and strong. Britain was still "home" to thousands of Canadians, and was the "Old Country" to thousands more, commanding no small measure of love and loyalty. In Quebec, too, there was the call of the old land, deep ties of ancestry, race, language, and religion summoning the sons of French Canada to the side of France in her fight against the Teuton aggressor. Evidence of the spontaneity of the war spirit in Canada is found in the fact that the Militia Council met on July 30th and forthwith announced that, should war break out, Canada would send overseas a first contingent twenty-two thousand five hundred strong.

Without waiting to be informed of the Government's attitude, the regiments of the Canadian Militia took steps to prepare detachments for whatever service might be required of them. Included amongst the units so doing were the 1st Regiment, Canadian Grenadier Guards, the 3rd Regiment, Victoria Rifles of Canada, and the 65th Regiment, Carabiniers de Mont-Royal. These regiments, each with proud traditions of its own, had their respective armouries in Montreal, the

Guards on Esplanade Avenue, facing Fletcher's Field; the Victoria Rifles on Cathcart Street, west of University Street; and the Carabiniers de Mont-Royal on Pine Avenue, between Drolet and Henri Julien Streets.

When war was declared these armouries became the scene of intense activity as, under the leadership of Col. J. W. Carson, Lieut.-Col. W. W. Burland, and Lieut.-Col. J. T. Ostell, the three regiments recruited their overseas contingents. At first, each of the regiments wished to send its own battalion to the front, but the Department of Militia and Defence refused to permit this and ordered the three to combine forces.

Early in August conferences to this end took place and eventually an active service battalion was brought into being. Col. the Hon. Sam Hughes, Canadian Minister of Militia and Defence, bestowed on the new unit the title "Royal Montreal Regiment", and under this name the Battalion fought in France. Officially, warrant to use the royal prefix was granted by the King only after the Regiment had established its worth on a score of hard fought fields and returned in triumph to Canada. In the meantime the full title "Royal Montreal Regiment" was used to designate the Battalion in the Army List issued by the War Office.

On formation, command of the Royal Montreal Regiment was assumed by Lieut.-Col. F. S. Meighen, who had risen to the command of the 1st Battalion, 5th Regiment, Royal Highlanders of Canada, in 1906, and subsequently had transferred to, and served with, the 1st Regiment, Canadian Grenadier Guards. The post of Second-in-Command of the new Regiment was awarded to Lieut.-Col. W. W. Burland, Commanding Officer of the 3rd Regiment, Victoria Rifles of Canada, and Lieut. A. P. Holt, of the Grenadier Guards, was appointed Battalion Adjutant. Under the organization arrangements, recruiting for Nos. 1, 2, and 3 Companies of the Regiment was carried on by the Grenadier Guards; Nos. 4, 5, and 6 Companies were recruited by the Victoria Rifles; and Nos. 7 and 8 Companies were raised by the Carabiniers de Mont-Royal. Command of the eight companies was given respectively to Capt. J. N. Warminton, Capt. R. Steacie, Capt. P. R. Hanson, Capt. Gault McCombe, Capt. A. C. Shaw, Capt. V. G. Curry, Capt. Hercule Barré, and Capt. Emile Ranger.

During the days of early and mid-August these officers and their subordinates worked enthusiastically at the tasks which organization and recruiting presented, receiving much assistance from officers and men of the parent Militia regiments, many of whom, though unable to proceed overseas with the first contingents, planned to follow as soon as their obligations permitted. Major W. O. H. Dodds, of the Grenadier Guards, who crossed with the First Contingent as Adjutant of the 1st Brigade, C.F.A., rendered assistance which officers of the Royal Montreal Regiment gratefully remember.

In addition to organizing and recruiting, the three regiments trained conscientiously, both in the armouries and in such open spaces as Fletcher's Field, and the campus of McGill University. Probably the most important incident of this period was a review held one night on the Champ de Mars by the Minister of Militia, Col. the Hon. Sam Hughes. Thunder roared and lightning flashed during the parade, rain swept in sheets across the ground, and the troops, most of whom were still in civilian clothes and many of whom had drilled only for a day or two, manœuvred uncertainly, but with anxiety to do well, in mud and water ankle deep. From a military standpoint the review was a failure, as was the march through the city which followed, but, owing perhaps to the rain, the thunder, the lightning, and the mud, a strange grimness made itself felt, and that wild August night remains as the first occasion on which many of the men realized that days of bitterness and testing lay inevitably before them.

Following the review, independent company training was continued for a few days, then, on August 24th, at 10 a.m., the companies of the Guards, Victoria Rifles, and Carabiniers de Mont-Royal marched from their respective armouries to Fletcher's Field and combined for the first time in battalion drill. Separating again, the three detachments returned, each to its own armoury, and there put in a busy afternoon preparing for a move to the mobilization camp of the First Canadian Contingent at Valcartier.

That evening Montreal gave all its detachments a memorable farewell. The Royal Highlanders of Canada marched westward from their armoury on Bleury Street to entrain at Windsor Station, while the Guards, Victoria Rifles, and Carabiniers de Mont-Royal marched eastward from their respective headquarters to the Moreau Street Station of the Canadian Northern Railway. As was natural, the detachment from the 65th Regiment received an ovation in the French-speaking section of the city, but this same section also cheered the Guards and Victoria Rifles. No distinctions existed that night. Canadian troops were going on active service and the city wished them well. Each detachment was applauded and upon the men of each were showered cigarettes and sweets in token of good will. Men rushed forward to shake the soldiers' hands and women, too, broke the ranks repeatedly for a last word of farewell. Once or twice it seemed that enthusiastic wellwishers would sweep over a detachment completely, but somehow a measure of formation was preserved and eventually all three sections reached Moreau Street intact. Here colonist cars were waiting, entrainment was quickly carried out, and soon the Royal Montreal Regiment was on its way to Valcartier. Simultaneously, the vanguard of the British Army faced German forces near Mons, in Belgium. Speaking in the House of Lords on August 25th, Lord Kitchener, British Secretary of State for War, announced that the first clash had occurred. "Our troops," he said, "have already been for thirty-six hours in contact with a superior force of German invaders. During that time they have maintained the traditions of British soldiers and have behaved with the utmost gallantry."

III

At 7.30 o'clock on the morning of August 25th, the Royal Montreal Regiment detrained at Valcartier Mobilization Camp, situated on a sandy plain sixteen miles north-west of Quebec. When war broke out Valcartier had been an area of small farms, covered in part with low bush. On August 8, 1914, transformation of the district began; when the Royal Montreal Regiment arrived on August 25th, roads and railway sidings had been laid, three miles of rifle ranges constructed, water and drainage pipes installed, shower baths erected, electric light brought in from Quebec, a telephone exchange placed in operation, and a great camp brought into being.

Some thousands of troops had arrived before the Royal Montrealers and a number of these, who obviously considered themselves "old sweats", gathered to cheer ironically as the newcomers, under the watchful eye of the Regimental Quartermaster, Capt. H. H. Smith, struggled to erect tents. Progress was not as rapid as the Quartermaster, a veteran of the South African campaign, thought desirable, but at last the task was accomplished, whereupon some distant authority ordered the tents struck and moved a short distance away. Being new to the army, the recruits wondered at this order, which seemed purposeless. Old timers, however, soothed them with assurances that worse was to come, and these pessimistic prophets acquired honour when, the tents having been erected in the new locality, orders were received to move them back again.

For a few days after arrival at Valcartier the Royal Montreal Regiment was occupied with routine. As Sir Andrew Macphail in his official "Medical Services" has observed about Valcartier, "military training in a general sense was negligible." Thirty-three thousand men, drawn from over two hundred units of the Canadian Militia, assembled in the Camp and time was necessarily spent in " organizing and reorganizing, issuing clothing and equipment, examining and inoculating recruits, and preparing for reviews ". Work on the ranges was also a feature of Valcartier life, in spite of the prevailing shortage of rifles. The Royal Montreal Regiment possessed three hundred rifles only, but these were passed from squad to squad and kept in service, with the result that every man was taught how a rifle should be handled and cared for. Special attention was also given to the Machine Gun Section of the Battalion, which, throughout the month at Valcartier, trained diligently under the command of Lieut. R. de V. Terroux.

Before the end of the first week in camp the troops were inoculated against typhoid. In accordance with existing regulations, inoculation was referred to as a " voluntary " measure, but no officer or man was permitted to escape. The talented brain which conceived of a " voluntary " but inescapable inoculation was cursed by the troops, who suffered considerable discomfort. Ultimately they benefited, but during their temporary misery ultimate benefits were lost to sight, and some alarm was caused when, following the second inoculation, eight men fainted on parade and required medical attention.

By the end of August thousands of troops had poured into Valcartier and organization of a Canadian division was in process. After one or two tentative formations had been abandoned, the Royal Montreal Regiment, which for some time had been known as the 1st Battalion, R.M.R., was given the title, " 14th Battalion ", and placed in the 3rd Canadian Infantry Brigade, under the command of Col. R. E. W. Turner, V.C., D.S.O., a veteran of the South African War, who had won his primary distinction at Komati River, on November 7, 1900. With the 14th Battalion, Royal Montreal Regiment, in the 3rd Brigade were the 13th Battalion, Royal Highlanders of Canada, from Montreal; the 15th Battalion, 48th Highlanders, from Toronto; and the 16th Battalion, Canadian Scottish, composed of units from the Seaforth Highlanders (Vancouver), the Gordon Highlanders (Victoria), the Cameron Highlanders (Winnipeg), and the Argyll and Sutherland Highlanders (Hamilton). These units, commanded respectively by Lieut.-Cols. F. O. W. Loomis, J. A. Currie, and R. G. E. Leckie, caused the formation to be spoken of as the " Highland Brigade " and at one time it was suggested that the 14th should doff trousers and don the kilt. The incongruity of Grenadiers, Riflemen, and French-Canadian Infantry in kilts was pointed out, however, and the proposal definitely rejected.

To bring the battalions of the newly formed 3rd Canadian Infantry Brigade up to war strength, reinforcements were allotted as required. To the 14th Battalion drafts were allotted from the 45th Lindsay Regiment (Ontario), the 63rd Rifles (Halifax), and a small detachment from the Queen's Own Rifles (Toronto). Lieut.-Col. F. H. Hopkins, Commanding Officer of the 45th Lindsay Regiment, accompanied his men and became attached to the 14th Battalion for duty. This placed on the Royal Montreal Regiment's establishment two lieutenant-colonels, holding the posts of Commanding Officer and Second-in-Command, with a third attached, a situation which might have presented difficulties but for the co-operative spirit displayed by all concerned. As part of the reorganization at this time, a Base Company was established, under the command of Major H. J. Woodside, while additions to the personnel of the Battalion included Canon F. G. Scott, of Quebec, who joined as Protestant Chaplain; Capt. A. F. C. Winslow, who assumed the duties of Battalion Paymaster; and Capt. F. A. C. Scrimger, C.A.M.C., who relieved Capt. H. L. Pavey, C.A.M.C., as Battalion Medical Officer. Although it had been understood from the beginning that Capt. Pavey's connection with the Battalion was temporary, he had worked hard in examining recruits, inoculating the men, and attending to those who reported sick. It was with regret, therefore, that the Battalion bade him farewell.

Promotions amongst the non-commissioned officers took place at the same time as the changes mentioned above. Men who showed ability in the ranks were promoted whenever possible, and maintained in authority when the display of ability continued; when responsibility proved too much for them they were promptly reduced and others given a chance to do better. Typical of the fine spirit animating all ranks in regard to promotion was the action of Regimental Sergeant-Major C. B. Price, an officer of the Victoria Rifles, who had relinquished his commission to accompany the 14th overseas. Price learned that J. M. Stephenson, a regular soldier with wide experience, was serving in another unit as a sergeant. Realizing how valuable to the Regiment Stephenson would be as R.S.M., Price relinquished his post and became a colour-sergeant to permit Stephenson's appointment.

During the early days of September the Battalion drilled and practised at the rifle ranges. Much equipment was issued and many of the men were uniformed by September 6th, when H.R.H. the Duke of Connaught reviewed the Contingent in pouring rain. Cold rain continued for several days after the review and greatcoats, issued on the 8th, were welcome in consequence. Though the rain was far from pleasant, the troops used the resulting waters in a cheery little game played after dark. The rules of this sport have never been coded, but the object is to divert surface water from one's own tent into the tent of one's next door neighbour. This requires skill and an eye for contours. Speed with a shovel and ability to fade silently into the dark are also attributes of value. The game is undignified for authority, of course, and one officer, caught digging a ditch on a rainy night, claimed never to have heard of it. He was, he said, laying out a golf course.

On two occasions in September the Battalion took part in night outpost schemes during which rivalry was keen. Rumours of fists flying, black eyes, and missing teeth drifted back to Headquarters, but no official action was invited. Similarly, the authorities were "without information" one night when troops in the camp, annoyed by broken promises in regard to change of programme, cut the ropes of a "movie" tent and flopped the whole affair down on the owner's head. The wreckage took fire, flames lit up the sky, and all over the camp bugles sounded the alarm. Fortunately, the owner was rescued from under the blazing canvas without serious injury.

Issues of material and equipment continued through September, service uniforms gradually replacing the militia uniforms and mufti in which the troops had reached camp. As a result of these issues, the men presented a smart appearance when reviewed by H.R.H. the Duke of Connaught on September 20th. Departure of the Contingent was imminent by this time and many people were visiting the camp to wish the troops good-bye, among them being H.R.H. the Duchess of Connaught, H.R.H. the Princess Patricia, The Right Honourable Sir Robert Borden, and many of the heads of Church and State. The parade, therefore, was memorable, and improvement in the bearing of the troops was noted, particularly when the units marched past in columns of half battalions in line. The march past of thirty thousand men is always an impressive sight, but this occasion had special significance, as Canada's royal Governor-General was reviewing the First Contingent for the last time. Of all present, probably the Duke of Connaught was best fitted to judge what the men would have to face in European war. He knew something of Continental armies and knew that victory would exact the outpouring of endless blood and tears. With emotion, therefore, he bade the troops, "God speed".

H.M. KING GEORGE V. WITH LT.-COL. R. W. FROST, D.S.O.,
WATCHING THE CANADIAN TROOPS IN TRAINING
AT BRAMSHOTT CAMP

Though His Royal Highness had some impression of the hostilities which lay ahead, few of the men could visualize the shock of vast armies, and none contemplated the stalemate of trench warfare. Discussion of the probable course of events was endless and fascinating. One N.C.O., writing at this time, sums up the opinion held by his small group of friends. "All expect," he says, "two or three weeks in England, some time on lines of communication, and a winter of sieges of some fortress on the German frontier. Of course it may be quite different, but that is the general guess." Things were different; but only in the light of later knowledge is that letter fantastic. In September, 1914, after the victory of the Allied armies at the Marne, the forecast it contained seemed reasonable.

Following the Duke of Connaught's farewell review, re-attestation of the men for overseas service was expedited, as the day when the Contingent must sail was fast approaching. No sailing date was publicly announced, but all news from the camp was suddenly censored and this was correctly interpreted by the Canadian people to mean that the Contingent was on the move. For the 14th Battalion, which at this time numbered 46 officers and 1,097 other ranks, the move began on the afternoon of September 25th, when Nos. 1, 2, 3, 7 and 8 Companies, under Lieut.-Col. F. S. Meighen, proceeded by train to Quebec and boarded the Cunard liner *Alaunia*, which was also carrying the 13th Battalion, Royal Highlanders of Canada, the Headquarters of the 3rd Canadian Infantry Brigade, and A.S.C. Details (Divisional Train). Nos. 4, 5 and 6 Companies of the Battalion, and the Base Company, remained in camp till the morning of September 28th, when, under command of Lieut.-Col. W. W. Burland, they followed their comrades to Quebec and embarked on the S.S. *Andania*, together with the 16th Battalion, Canadian Scottish.

Both the *Alaunia*, commanded by Capt. Rostron, R.N.R., and the *Andania*, commanded by Capt. G. W. Melsom, R.N.R., swung into mid-stream once the troops were on board and, with other transports, lay beneath the walls of the towering Citadel awaiting orders to sail. Much of Canadian history those old walls had witnessed, as Frenchmen and Englishmen fought bitterly to possess them and, dying, gave to them undying fame. Now the descendants of those who had fought one another were united to fight a common foe. Perhaps the sailing of the First Contingent marked more significantly than any previous event the fact that the old wounds no longer smarted.

CHAPTER II

THE FIRST CONTINGENT

> And captains that we thought were dead,
> And dreamers that we thought were dumb,
> And voices that we thought were fled,
> Arise, and call us, and we come.
> —ALFRED NOYES.

I

LATE on the afternoon of September 30th the *Alaunia* and *Andania*, together with other transports, weighed anchor and slipped downstream. Crowds lined the Dufferin Terrace and storms of cheering swept from shore drawing answering cheers from the troops on deck. Bands played; and suddenly there thundered over the waters from the ships a mighty chorus of voices singing " O Canada " and "Auld Lang Syne." Soon, however, this chorus faded away as the ships gathered speed and headed for their secret destination.

Once Quebec had been left behind, the troops on both ships settled down to enjoy the comfortable quarters allotted to them. Rumours of a rendezvous at Father Point aroused keen interest, but in the morning Father Point was passed and at night the destination of the vessels was still unknown. Morning on October 2nd, however, disclosed the secret. Gaspé Basin had been chosen as a rendezvous for the ships carrying the Canadian Contingent and in this safe and beautiful harbour the *Alaunia* and *Andania* joined a great fleet of transports and men-o'-war. Attempts have been made to describe the gathering of the convoy in Gaspé Basin, but for the most part they have failed. All who witnessed the scene were impressed; but only a gifted tongue, or pen, could convey a sense of the majesty, power, pride, and dominion which emanated from the long lines of ships as they lay at anchor in the bright autumn sunshine, or in the dark shadows of the surrounding hills.

On October 2nd, and during the forenoon of the 3rd, the *Alaunia* and *Andania* lay quietly with the rest of the fleet awaiting the hour to sail. Col. the Hon. Sam Hughes visited both ships to bid the troops good-bye, and took away with him letters and postcards for the mail. These were not censored, indiscretion endangering the convoy being guarded against by the simple expedient of holding them until the Contingent had arrived in England.

On the afternoon of October 3rd the transports steamed from Gaspé Basin and formed up in three parallel columns, about a mile and three-quarters of water being maintained between columns and each ship occupying a position approximately a half-mile behind the one in front. All dispositions were effected under the supervision of Rear-Admiral R. E. Wemyss, C.M.G., M.V.O., who commanded a squadron, including at one time or another His Majesty's Ships *Charybdis, Diana, Lancaster, Eclipse, Glory, Majestic,* and *Talbot*. With this escort the troops feared no attack, though the speed of the convoy, governed by the slowest vessel, was little above 10 knots.

CONVOY OF THE FIRST CANADIAN CONTINGENT

As on 10th October, 1915

H.M.S. *Majestic*

	H.M.S. *Eclipse*	H.M.S. *Diana*	H.M.S. *Charybdis*	
H.M.S. Princess Royal	*Megantic*	*Monmouth*	*Scotian*	*H.M.S. Glory*
	Ruthenia	*Caribbean*	*Arcadian*	
	Bermudian	*Athenia*	*Zeeland*	
	ALAUNIA	*Royal Edward*	*Corinthian*	
	Ivernia	*Franconia*	*Virginian*	
	Scandinavian	*Canada*	**ANDANIA**	
	Sicilian	(Carrying 2nd Battalion, Lincolnshire Regt.)	*Saxonia*	
	Montezuma		*Grampian*	
	Lapland	*Manitou*	*Lakonia*	
	Cassandra	*Tyrolia*	*Montreal*	
	Florizel	*Tunisian*	*Royal George*	
	(Carrying Newfoundland Contingent)	*Laurentic*		

H.M.S. *Talbot*

On the whole the voyage of the Contingent was uneventful. Lifeboat drills were frequent and much time was devoted to physical training, boxing, signalling, and deck sports of all varieties. On the *Alaunia* a spy scare caused the arrest of two men, both of whom, at a later date, were publicly exonerated. On the *Andania* an event of the voyage was the appearance of a Regimental paper, "The Fourteenth Battalion Bugler". The two issues of this journal, edited by Private C. D. B. Whitby, late of the Montreal "Gazette", with the assistance of Private H. G. Brewer, late of the Montreal "Star", were creditably produced and enjoyed a flattering circulation. They contained, amongst other items, copies of the ship's log, challenges to men of the 16th Battalion for boxing and shooting matches, gossip of the voyage, verse, and a black bordered paragraph announcing the death of "Vic", a cheery pup of doubtful lineage who had served as the Victoria Rifles' semi-official mascot. In view of the talent displayed in producing "The Bugler," Private Whitby was requested to act as Regimental Historian and to preserve an unofficial record of the Battalion's adventures and vicissitudes on active service. Much to the Regiment's regret, Private Whitby died as a result of wounds received at the Second Battle of Ypres, the history he had so faithfully compiled being destroyed by shell fire during the same engagement.

On October 5th a supposed German collier was encountered by the convoy and two days later the *Glory* stopped a Scandinavian tramp with several shots across the bows. These vessels were suspected of supporting the German cruiser *Karlsruhe*, which was at large in the Atlantic, but, so far as the troops could gather, no proof was forthcoming. After a week at sea certain supplies ran short. On the *Andania* cigarette stocks were exhausted, and cheese was substituted for butter and jam. Flour, too, was lacking, but each day a fatigue party was told off to grind up a few bushels of wheat. The "flour" so manufactured could not be mistaken for the refined product of Canadian mills, but, as someone pointed out, the resulting bread, if not particularly palatable, was wonderful stuff to fight on, a recommendation which did much to popularize it with the troops.

On October 13th, when nearing the coast of England, one of the armed transports fired a few rounds to test the mounting of a gun, whereupon smoke appeared at a half dozen points on the horizon, as small craft of His Majesty's Navy searched for trouble. A more striking demonstration of the care with which the Contingent was being guarded and of the British control in home waters could hardly have been afforded. Land was sighted that evening and on the following morning the *Alaunia* steamed into Plymouth Sound. Arrangements had been made to dock the convoy at Southampton, but, to baffle German submarines, plans had been changed. The arrival of the *Alaunia*, therefore, was the first indication that the troops from overseas were to disembark at Plymouth. Much has been written of the arrival of the Canadians in England; too much could not be written of the warm welcome which Plymouth extended. A first greeting came from the historic wooden war vessels in the Sound, the training crews on board manning the sides and rigging and cheering as ship after ship steamed majestically into harbour. Cheering continued as the ships dropped anchor, or moved up the Sound to Devonport. Factory whistles then joined in the welcome and church bells gave to the occasion that solemn touch which has etched it deeply on so many memories. The arrival of the Contingent was an historic event, as Plymouth was well aware, but civic pride never prompted that demonstration, the fact being, according to local newspapers, that the old city experienced a thrill equal to the one it enjoyed when Drake shattered the Spanish Armada. The loyalty of Canada, indicated by the arrival of thrice ten thousand fighting men, touched England's heart, and Plymouth, representing England, bade the Canadians welcome.

The *Alaunia* reached Plymouth first of all the convoy, but the *Andania* was only a few hours behind and both ships anchored for the night in Plymouth Harbour. Here the troops were deeply interested in powerful searchlights, which flashed across the water, or sent their long, white beams groping into the blackness of the sky. After the ocean voyage, during which lights had been forbidden and vision at night dependent on the whim of the October moon, the brilliantly lighted transports, the searchlights, the constantly winking signal lamps, and the glow from myriad lights ashore afforded a spectacle fascinating in the extreme.

Morning brought new sights and interests. A great dreadnought lay at anchor not far from the *Andania*, provisioning and fitting for some special service; tugs and small craft darted about on urgent business; and one by one the Canadian transports were towed upstream to Devonport. Both the *Alaunia* and *Andania* were docked during the afternoon and without delay much dunnage was enthusiastically dumped ashore. This scandalized the dockyard authorities, who ordered the troops to carry all material back on board and to keep it there until word to land it was given officially.

While at Devonport the Royal Montreal Regiment landed on one occasion for a route march through the town. Everywhere the Battalion was accorded a magnificent reception, and gifts were showered on the men as during the farewell march through the streets of Montreal. On returning to the ships, the men were ordered not to go ashore without permission, nor in any case beyond the limits of the dockyard. Idleness and desire to see more of the town prompted disobedience, however, and a number of men were noticed by officers in the city streets. How these individuals had passed the dockyard sentries was a puzzle at first, but the secret was disclosed when an officer came into the yard just as a "military party," under an N.C.O., marched smartly out, apparently on the King's business. Curiosity as to the services which His Majesty might require prompted the officer to ask questions, his investigation revealing that the "military party" was composed of enterprising individuals who, yearning to sample more of the town's abundant hospitality, had combined forces to deceive the guardians of the dockyard gate.

When the Canadians arrived in England command of the Division was assumed by Lieut.-Gen. E. A. H. Alderson, C.B., a British soldier with a distinguished record gained in India, Egypt, and South Africa. This officer demonstrated his interest in his new command by visiting Devonport during disembarkation of the troops, meeting as many officers as possible, and exchanging a word with many of the men. Disembarkation of the 14th Battalion commenced on the evening of October 15th when Nos. 1, 2, 3, 7 and 8 Companies landed from the *Alaunia* and marched to Plymouth Railway Station. Entraining here, the companies travelled all night, detraining at Patney Station shortly after dawn on the 16th and marching for about three hours across Salisbury Plain to West Down South. Tented lines were ready at this spot and were gratefully occupied by the men, whom the long sea voyage had softened and who, in consequence, were weary after the night journey in cramped quarters and the ten mile pre-breakfast march across the Plain.

Meanwhile Nos. 4, 5 and 6 Companies and the Base Company of the Regiment remained at Devonport on the *Andania*. Disembarking at 9.30 p.m. on October 18th, these companies entrained at midnight and, reaching Patney Station early on the morning of the 19th, marched across the Plain to rejoin their comrades at West Down South. With the arrival of this detachment and of the Transport, which, under the command of Lieut. J. F. Adams, had crossed the ocean in the *Montreal*, the Battalion became a co-ordinated unit once more and settled down, together with the whole Canadian Division to train for service at the front. While the 14th was in camp on Salisbury Plain, Divisional Orders contained the announcement that the Right Honourable Lord Mount Stephen, G.C.V.O., had accepted appointment as the Regiment's Honorary Colonel. This post Lord Mount Stephen held during the entire period of the Battalion's overseas career.

II

Salisbury Plain, selected as the training ground for the Canadian Division in England, is a desolate region fifteen by twenty-five miles in extent. Devoid of fencing, or houses, it provides a magnificent area for summer manœuvres, or for practice by artillery, but Nature never intended it to be used as a camp for troops in winter. A thin, clay soil covers the Plain, and beneath this lies a stratum of chalk, impervious to water. During rain, therefore, the Plain becomes a quagmire of glutinous and squelching mud. The stay of the Canadian Division extended through the wettest winter England had experienced in over fifty years; consequently the troops endured hardships and misery which tested their courage and endurance to the utmost. That they came through the ordeal without losing morale speaks for the spirit which animated them.

Even before the arrival of the *Andania* contingent at West Down South, the 14th Battalion, Royal Montreal Regiment, suffered its first casualty on English soil when Private Hartley, batman to Major P. R. Hanson, dropped dead on a road near the Regimental lines. A coroner's inquest brought in a verdict of death from heart failure, and the body was buried on the 20th of the month in Shrewton Churchyard.

Fine weather prevailed for the first few days at West Down South and advantage of this was taken in every way possible. Lieut.-Gen. Alderson, the Divisional Commander, inspected the 3rd Brigade on October 21st, and afterwards, in a soldierly speech from horseback, introduced himself to the men, who cheered his announcement that at Salisbury the "wet" canteen system would prevail. At Valcartier, owing possibly to the strong prohibition beliefs held by the Canadian Minister of Militia, Col. the Hon. Sam Hughes, all canteens had been "dry," despite dissatisfaction among the troops.

Three days after General Alderson's inspection of the 3rd Brigade, the Canadian Division was reviewed by its Honorary Colonel, Field Marshal Earl Roberts of Kandahar, V.C. No British soldier was more popular than this veteran, and the troops endeavoured by the warmth of their welcome to prove that his services in South Africa and elsewhere had not been forgotten. Unfortunately, his review was somewhat marred by heavy rain.

Following Lord Roberts's visit, the 14th Battalion Diary states that company training was carried out, several long route marches took place, and, on one occasion, battalion manœuvres in extended order familiarized the troops with the mud which was to play such a part in their lives during the months still to come. On November 2nd the Canadian Division, drawn up in line of battalions in mass on both sides of the road from Bustard to West Down South, spent three hours practising for a review by His Majesty the King. Rain poured during the rehearsal and the men were drenched to the skin. All, however, were anxious to do well before the King and took the cold discomfort in good part.

In the 14th Battalion November 3rd was declared a holiday in order that the troops might dry their sodden clothes. No fires were possible and rain hindered the process, so that tunics and clothing were still damp on the following day when the Division paraded before the King, the Queen, Lord Roberts, Lord Kitchener, and their respective staffs. Glorious sunshine welcomed the King on this occasion, but the rain of the previous fortnight had left its mark on the troops, with the result that there was much coughing in the ranks. This was too much for the colour-sergeant of one company, who, as the King approached, turned on his men despairingly. "Shut up!" he hissed, "or the King will think you're a company of consumptives." Pride triumphed in response to this anguished appeal and, as the King eyed the rigid, motionless, and silent ranks, no suggestion of consumptive inferiority was conveyed to him.

In mid-November it was announced that Field Marshal Earl Roberts, V.C., Honorary Colonel of the Canadian Contingent, had died in France after an illness lasting but a few hours. On November 19th a memorial service for the dead Field Marshal was held in Salisbury Cathedral, the Royal Montreal Regiment, as a mark of respect, sending a detachment of 26 other ranks, under the command of Lieut. A. S. English, and Battalion Headquarters being represented by the Second-in-Command, Lieut.-Col. W. W. Burland. In view of Lord Roberts's visits to Salisbury and of the compliment he had paid the Contingent in becoming its Honorary Colonel, regret at news of his death was widespread and sincere.

Several night outpost schemes formed part of the Battalion's work in November, some friction resulting one night when a defending force held up a number of civilian motor cars, and some amusement on another occasion when a nervous sentry ordered an enemy party to advance and give the "Concordia," his side afterwards wondering how the enemy had learned the password and penetrated the defending lines. In addition to night outpost work, the November training included route marches, on one of which a Battalion bugle band made its first appearance; manœuvres, to instruct the troops in taking cover from enemy aircraft; and a Divisional field day, which General Alderson directed by signals sounded on a huntsman's horn. On November 29th and 30th little of interest can have happened, the Battalion Diary entry consisting in each case of the single word "Rain."

Bad weather continued during December and life in the flooded tents became miserable in the extreme. As one letter writer feelingly put it, "Things over here are not *pretty* wet, they are most blighted soaking." He might have added comment on the penetrating quality of the prevailing wind, which, another writer observed, made it "too cold to bathe outside," a disadvantage as it was also "too crowded to bathe in the tents." Such conditions, which interfered with all training and rendered outdoor recreation impossible, seriously endangered the health of the troops and eventually a move was made from the tents at West Down South to huts at Lark Hill. The 14th Battalion moved on December 21st, and no one was sorry to leave the soaking tents behind. The huts were not unduly commodious, but they were rain-proof and provided the men when off duty with shelter and a spot where they could partly dry their saturated clothes.

Meanwhile several events concerned the Battalion more or less directly. Early in the month General Alderson proposed to a group of senior officers of the 3rd Brigade that distinctive battalion badges in the Division should be eliminated and the troops permitted to wear battalion numerals only. This struck at traditions which many of the Canadian battalions valued, and Lieut.-Col. J. A. Currie, of the 15th Battalion (48th Highlanders), Toronto, presented the respectful protest of all officers present. Recognizing that he had stirred up a hornets' nest, General Alderson withdrew his proposal and the badges remained.

On December 17th the Royal Montreal Regiment prepared to move at short notice to an un-named point in England. German warships had shelled Scarborough and for some time the possibility of invasion was entertained. Soon, however, it became clear that the shelling was merely an expression of German "hate" and the stand-to order at West Down South was accordingly cancelled. On the day following this incident Lieut.-Col. Meighen temporarily assumed command of the 3rd Canadian Infantry Brigade, Col. Turner, the Brigadier, having suffered injury in a motor accident. During Lieut.-Col. Meighen's absence command of the 14th Battalion passed to Major A. C. Shaw, as Lieut.-Col. Burland, Second-in-Command, was on duty at Hayling Island.

After the move of the 14th Battalion to Lark Hill came the Christmas and New Year's holidays. Many officers and men were granted leave over one or other of the dates. Those remaining on duty decorated the huts, ordered parcels of special food and drink from London, organized sing-song hut parties, and endeavoured to forget for a few hours the constant rain, the all-pervading mud, and the endless digging and draining which the atrocious weather made necessary. Ordinary training during this period was impossible and recreation of any kind difficult to arrange. A few choice spirits on one occasion organized a broomstick rabbit hunt to relieve the appalling monotony. The pursuit led to trespass on private ground, whose indignant keepers obviously regarded the intrusion as a striking example of overseas lawlessness. Other landowners adopted a more friendly attitude and spared no pains to make the Canadians feel at home.

On Christmas Eve Capt. A. Sylvestre, Roman Catholic Chaplain of the Battalion, celebrated Mass in a hut occupied by the French-Canadian soldiers from the Carabiniers de Mont-Royal, and on New Year's Eve Major F. G. Scott, Protestant Chaplain of the Regiment, held a celebration of Holy Communion in Amesbury Parish Church. Each of these services was impressive, the former owing to the simple dignity with which Mass was celebrated in such strange surroundings, the latter because of the solemnity of the service and the hour. As the bells of the church rang out across the moonlit and frost-whitened fields, 1914 faded into history and the Empire faced its first New Year of the War.

III

On January 1st, 1915, and for some days thereafter, the Battalion Diary records " all available men on fatigues." As in December, training throughout the month was seriously hampered by rain, floods, and the heart-breaking mud, but, whenever outdoor work was quite impossible, lectures and instruction were substituted, Lieut.-Col. Burland lecturing to the officers on " Discipline "; General McCracken on " Active Service "; General Turner on " How to Combat Disease "; and Capt. E. W. Pope, of the 3rd Brigade Staff, on " Military Law." Other lectures were delivered, but particularly interesting to all ranks was a series of " Notes," with up-to-date information regarding the developments of trench warfare in France. Coming " hot from the battlefield," these notes were eagerly studied by officers and men alike.

During January the Battalion was reorganized on a four company basis. Once previously this reorganization had been effected, but, after a short trial, the old formation had been restored. Under the new system, now definitely adopted, the Battalion consisted of four companies instead of eight, each company being composed of four platoons, under a lieutenant, and each platoon of four sections, under an N.C.O. Command of the new double companies, Nos. 1, 2, 3 and 4, was given respectively to Major A. C. Shaw, Major P. R. Hanson, Major Gault McCombe, and Major Hercule Barré, who had as their seconds-in-command Capt. J. N. Warminton, Capt. R. Steacie, Capt. V. G. Curry, and Capt. E. Ranger. Major Shaw's company was formed by combining old Nos. 1 and 5, which had been recruited by the Guards and Victoria Rifles respectively; Major Hanson's company was made up from old Nos. 2 and 3, which were Guards units; Major McCombe's company was composed of old Nos. 4 and 6, from the Victoria Rifles; and Major Barré's company absorbed old Nos. 7 and 8, from the Carabiniers de Mont-Royal.

In mid-January Lieut.-Gen. E. A. H. Alderson, the Divisional Commander, visited the Battalion lines and assured the men that before long they would be on the way to France. This announcement was heartily cheered, as all ranks were weary of the mud of Salisbury Plain and eager to reach the front. Cerebro-spinal meningitis, a few cases of which had occurred previously, increased at this time and threatened for a while to hold the Division in England. Private J. K. Chandler, of the 14th, developed the disease on January 19th and died in hospital four days later. Corp. S. A. Randall died on January 30th. Meanwhile the huts where these soldiers had lived were rigidly quarantined, as were all affected huts throughout the Division. Altogether 39 cases occurred in the Contingent between December 13th and February 10th, 28 of these proving fatal.

On February 1st Lieut.-Col. F. H. Hopkins, who was attached to the Royal Montreal Regiment, transferred to the 17th Reserve Battalion. Next day Major H. Barré, of No. 4 Company, proceeded to France with an advance party from the 3rd Canadian Infantry Brigade, this move assuring the troops that a crossing of the Channel was really imminent, and further confirmation being provided by notice that His Majesty the King would come to Salisbury on February 4th to bid the Division farewell. On February 2nd Lieut.-Col. Meighen reconnoitred the ground where the review was to be held, and on the 4th, wearing greatcoats because of inclement weather, the Battalion paraded for the royal inspection. After walking down the line, the King took up station to receive the salute, and, following the march past, the troops lined the railway track to cheer the royal train. During the progress of the train through the ranks the King, at a window, acknowledged the cheers with his hand at the salute. It was obvious to those who could see his features that he was touched by the loyal demonstration accorded him.

Following the King's farewell, the Battalion prepared for the move to France. A number of men were found medically unfit for active service and transferred to reserve formations, a draft from the 17th Reserve Battalion being taken on strength to fill the vacant places. Adoption of the four company system had left the Battalion with a surplus of officers and on February 5th, greatly to their disappointment, Lieuts. W. M. Pearce, F. R. Heuston, G. W. Stairs, G. L. Stairs, W. C. Brotherhood, and E. Leprohon were ordered with the Base Company into reserve at Tidworth Barracks. Following the departure of these officers and the Base Company, Capt. A. P. Holt, the Battalion Adjutant, developed pneumonia and Lieut. H. A. Thompson was appointed Acting Adjutant in his stead, Lieut. Brotherhood being recalled from Tidworth to complete the establishment. On February 8th the Battalion received orders to be ready to move in 24 hours. With all dispositions effected, the Regiment stood by on the following day, Headquarters, the companies, and sub-formations being under the following officers, who were to command the unit in France.

Officers of the 14th Battalion, Royal Montreal Regiment
February 9th, 1915

Officer Commanding	Lieut.-Col. F. S. Meighen
Second-in-Command	Lieut.-Col. W. W. Burland
Acting Adjutant	Lieut. H. A. Thompson
Quartermaster	Capt. H. H. Smith
Machine Gun Officer	Lieut. G. M. Williamson
Medical Officer	Capt. H. A. Boyd
Paymaster	Capt. F. B. D. Larken
Protestant Chaplain	Major F. G. Scott

(Officially, Major Scott was attached to a medical unit.)

Roman Catholic Chaplain	Capt. A. Sylvestre

No. 1 Company

Major A. C. Shaw, Capt. J. N. Warminton, Lieuts. R. W. Frost, R. de V. Terroux, C. F. C. Porteous, and J. F. Adams (Transport Officer).

No. 2 Company

Major P. R. Hanson, Capt. R. Steacie, Lieuts. A. S. English, W. K. Knubley, W. C. Brotherhood, and K. L. McCuaig (Signalling Officer).

No. 3 Company

Major Gault McCombe, Capt. V. G. Curry, Lieuts. W. D. Adams, S. Grant, W. H. Draper, and E. A. Whitehead.

No. 4 Company

Major Hercule Barré (already in France), Capt. Emile Ranger, Lieuts. H. DesRosiers, R. DeSerres, R. Roy, and H. Quintal.

In Reserve

Lieuts. W. M. Pearce, F. R. Heuston, G. W. Stairs, G. L. Stairs, and E. Leprohon. Attached to British Units:—Lieuts. A. F. Major and W. A. Kirkconnell. Sick:—Capt. F. A. C. Scrimger (Medical Officer), Capt. A. P. Holt (Adjutant), and Lieut. W. K. de Kappelle.

CHAPTER III

FROM SALISBURY PLAIN TO TRENCHES IN FRANCE

> Broke to every known mischance, lifted over all
> By the light sane joy of life, the buckler of the Gaul;
>
> First to follow Truth and last to leave old Truths behind—
> France, beloved of every soul that loves its fellow-kind!
>
> Where did you refrain from us or we refrain from you?
> Ask the wave that has not watched war between us two!
> Others held us for a while, but with weaker charms,
> These we quitted at the call for each other's arms.
> —RUDYARD KIPLING.

BETWEEN the hours of 9 p.m. and midnight on February 10th, 1915, the 14th Battalion, Royal Montreal Regiment, paraded in full marching order at Lark Hill, and moved off in several detachments to Amesbury Station. Secrecy had been maintained as to the exact hour of departure and few spectators witnessed the unit's farewell to Salisbury Plain, but several officers, who had been transferred to reserve formations, were present to wish their comrades good luck and God-speed. Something of the regret with which these supernumeraries saw the Regiment leave for active service is reflected in the diary of a French-Canadian officer who writes, "Saw my dear Regiment march off to the front. How badly I feel to see them go and leave me here". Regret, however, was not the keynote of the occasion. Officers and men rejoiced that the weary months of training were over and that the Division was on the move, presumably to France, though even this was not certain. All of which the men felt sure was that they were proceeding to Amesbury Station, there to entrain for an unnamed destination.

Marching through the blackness of a cool, fine night, the detachments of the 14th reached Amesbury and entrained without incident, or misadventure, the trains moving out shortly afterwards and reaching Avonmouth Dock early on the morning of February 11th. At Avonmouth the Battalion embarked at once on the transport *Australind*, a captured German cargo and cattle steamer of some 4,000 tons, commanded by Captain Sidney Angell. With the 14th on board was the 1st Canadian Heavy Battery, under the command of Major F. C. Magee. Accommodation on the *Australind* was distinctly limited, officers occupying the few cabins that existed and the men, in the words of one diary, being "crowded into holds, hatchways, and empty horse stalls". "Gone", continues this record, "are the palatial quarters of the *Andania*. Here there is a smell of horses; dust is plentiful, and rats promenade on the pipes above our heads; but things like that bother us very little these days".

After lying all day and all night in dock at Avonmouth, the *Australind*, escorted by destroyers, sailed early on the morning of February 12th. The weather was fine at first and, after a short inspection by Lieut.-Col. W. W. Burland, those men not on duty were allowed to sleep, rest, or amuse themselves as they saw fit. Towards night a wind sprang up and this, increasing to a gale by the morning of the 13th, whipped up a wild cross-sea which pitched and rolled the boat to such an extent that few on board escaped severe sea-sickness. To add to the resulting discomfort, cold waves broke over the deck and poured onto the miserable men in the holds, while one of the horses, breaking loose from its stall, stumbled down an open hatch and crashed to its death on the deck below. No one was injured by the fall of this animal, but later a great wave broke over the ship, caught an artilleryman off guard on the upper deck, swept him along like a piece of matchwood, and killed him by dashing his head against an iron stanchion.

Warned by this misfortune, all men who had occasion during the remainder of the day to move about on deck did so with extreme caution. On February 14th the weather moderated and at noon the body of the unfortunate artilleryman was committed to the sea, Canon Sylvestre, Roman Catholic Chaplain of the 14th, reading the burial service, and military honours being paid by members of the dead man's unit and by officers and men of the 14th, who stood respectfully by.

That night the coast of France was sighted and early on the morning of February 15th French destroyers picked up the *Australind* and escorted her into the outer harbour of St. Nazaire, where the Canadian Division was to land. Shortly after noon, the *Australind* passed through a narrow lock into the inner harbour and docked at a wharf, opening with no barrier onto a street of the town. Naturally, the French city interested the men greatly, particularly as the townspeople welcomed the ship by tossing up onto the decks oranges, sweets, and other tokens of good will. Enthusiasm doubled when the good citizens found that a number of the men on board spoke French and were, actually, of French descent. The arrival in France of British troops who claimed France as the land of their forefathers was an event appealing to that sense of the dramatic which is the birthright of the Gaul. Unfortunately, or fortunately, perhaps, if one regards the matter from a military point of view, strict orders kept the troops from landing and accepting much proffered hospitality, and His Majesty's Transport regulations prevented the friendly citizens from bringing their offerings on board.

While docking, the men of the 14th caught sight of some blue-coated, red-trousered soldiers of France, who with long bayoneted rifles were guarding the docks, or, off duty, lounging about in the crowd. Were these the men who had fought those fierce frontier fights marking the first clash of the opposing armies, or were they the men who had, with the assistance of Sir John French's immortal "Contemptibles", hurled the Germans back from the Marne? Groups of the Royal Montrealers eyed the Frenchmen respectfully, noting their behaviour and bearing with the deepest interest. This interest was maintained until someone noticed a working group of German prisoners. In a moment the blue uniforms were forgotten and all eyes turned to study the men in grey. The Frenchmen were allies, which was important, but the prisoners represented those whom the Canadians were to fight *against*. Prisoners of war, poor devils, seldom appear impressive, and the group which the Royal Montrealers now studied so carefully provided no exception to the general rule. As a result the men of the 14th Battalion carried to the front a vivid recollection of the only German troops they had ever seen and a quiet, but definite, sense of superiority.

At about 3.30 p.m. unloading of the *Australind* began, numerous working parties of the 14th taking part in the consequent fatigues. In the evening goatskin trench coats, fingerless gloves, and mufflers were issued, and an advance party of 50 men, under Lieut. R. W. Frost, proceeded by train towards the front. Unloading continued throughout the night and was completed about dawn. Then, at 6 a.m., the Battalion paraded alongside the ship and marched a short distance to St. Nazaire railway station, entraining in box cars (the famous 40 hommes, 8 chevaux) at this point, and leaving for railhead shortly thereafter. One passenger coach, attached to the train, was reserved for the use of officers.

All day on February 16th, that night, and again on February 17th, the train trundled slowly forward, through Nantes, Rouen, Calais, Boulogne, and other towns of but slightly less importance. Stops were frequent, these being welcome to the troops, who appreciated any opportunity to stretch their cramped legs. At nearly every halt the French-Canadians of No. 4 Company surprised and delighted the townspeople, who kindly supplied refreshments, by singing those old French songs so beloved and so well known in the Province of Quebec. "Tipperary" and "Annie Laurie" the wayside Frenchman associated with the travelling British Army. "Alouette" and "En Roulant ma Boule", sung by men in khaki, touched his emotions and aroused his sympathies. Good wishes and blessings, therefore, showered on the Royal Montrealers as the train crept towards the front.

II

At 6 a.m. on February 18th the 14th Battalion detrained at Hazebrouck, picked up the advance party, under Lieut. R. W. Frost, and marched to Flêtre, passing the Headquarters of the 3rd Canadian Infantry Brigade in Caestre, and encountering H.R.H. Prince Arthur of Connaught, who rode along the column during one of its brief halts. Two features of this march are mentioned in many diaries and letters dealing with the time. On the march the Battalion suffered its first experience of the famous pavé roads of France. The word "suffered" is used advisedly, for the pavé blistered heels and toes to such an extent that many men were limping badly before the Battalion reached its destination. No complaints were recorded, however, as, during the march, a low, muttering, rumbling sound drifted back from some point far ahead. Unmistakably, it was the thunder of distant guns. Hearts leaped, and a shiver of excitement ran through the ranks. Who could complain of a blistered heel when guns were firing but a few miles over the horizon?

Arriving in Flêtre, the men of the 14th were billeted in the village, or in the barns and outbuildings of neighbouring farms. Battalion H.Q. was established in the Chateau de Wendigen and an Officers' Mess set up in the village inn. Night signal lamps were placed in the Chateau tower, Lieut.-Col. Meighen being able by means of these to communicate instantly with his outlying company H.Q's. The Battalion, though somewhat scattered, was thus ready for any emergency.

Five days were spent at Flêtre, the men accustoming themselves to life in billets and preparing for a move towards the front. On the 20th of the month Field Marshal Sir John French, Commander-in-Chief of the British Army in France, reviewed the 3rd Canadian Infantry Brigade in a field near Caestre and expressed satisfaction with the men's appearance and bearing. In a friendly speech he remarked that, if the Brigade could fight as well as it looked, he had some sympathy for the Germans who encountered it. At the Battalion's first church parade in France, held on the following day, Canon Scott officiated, his remarks being punctuated by the low throb of distant guns.

Two days after this service the 3rd Brigade paraded in Flêtre at 8 a.m. and marched by way of Meteren and Nieppe, to Armentières. On the march the Brigade passed Lieut.-Gen. Sir William Pulteney, commanding the 3rd British Army Corps, who scrutinized the Battalions with care and asked numerous questions. The men were unaware of the fact, but General Pulteney's interest was far from being academic, or impersonal. The Canadians were to be trained in trench warfare by units under his command and, although the reports of his brigadiers and front line battalion commanders would doubtless settle whether the new troops were ready to hold a line of their own, or not, much could be inferred by watching them during a long march over the hard, pavé roads. The 14th Battalion Diary records that, although the pavé troubled the men, there were no stragglers.

On arrival in Armentières, the 14th Battalion was attached for instruction to the 17th Brigade of British Infantry, commanded by Brig.-Gen. Harper. Battalion Headquarters, with Nos. 1 and 2 Companies, billeted in Armentières Asylum; Nos. 3 and 4 Companies occupied a large warehouse in the town; and the Transport and Quartermaster billeted in another building some distance away.

On the following day, February 24th, exactly six months after the Battalion had left Montreal, arrangements were made for several platoons to undergo a short period of instruction in the front line. One diarist mentions " great rivalry and wire-pulling to be allowed to go with the first lot into the trenches ", officers and men being keen for the honour of accompanying those detachments of the Regiment to come first under fire. Battalion Headquarters, as was fit and proper, moved up first and joined the 1st Battalion, The Prince of Wales's (North Staffordshire) Regiment, commanded by Lieut.-Col. de Falbe, in trenches opposite Pérenchies. Two platoons each from Nos. 1 and 2 Companies followed H.Q. and were attached for instruction to the same unit. Simultaneously, two platoons each from Nos. 3 and 4 Companies moved into the line at Chapelle d'Armentières to receive instruction from officers and men of the Rifle Brigade.

Remaining in the line for 24 hours, the platoons of the 14th Battalion were relieved on the night of the 25th without misadventure, other platoons of the Battalion taking their places. That night, at Chapelle d'Armentières, volunteers were called for a patrol in No Man's Land. Four men of No. 4 French-Canadian Company immediately offered themselves and were afterwards complimented by the company commander of the Rifle Brigade for the coolness and daring with which they carried out their work.

On the following night the platoons of the Battalion in the front line were again relieved by platoons of their comrades, these being replaced by still further platoons on the night of February 27th. On this date the Battalion suffered its first casualty, Pte. R. C. Eaton, of No. 1 Coy., being wounded. On the night of February 28th the front line platoons of the 14th were relieved and not replaced, as preparations were under way for the Canadian Division to take over an independent section of the line. During the tours in the trenches platoons of the Royal Montreal Regiment had, at one time or other, received instruction from various British units. In a semi-official document, compiled at the request of the Commanding Officer in July, 1917, Major Arthur Plow, then Adjutant of the Battalion, records the unit's appreciation of the warm welcome extended by these veterans. The willingness and painstaking care they displayed in imparting trench information furnished unmistakable evidence of good feeling and cemented those bonds of friendship which have since marked relations between Imperial troops and the Royal Montreal Regiment.

III

Previous to relief of the last platoons of the 14th Battalion in the line, Lieut.-Col. F. S. Meighen, Commanding Officer, Lieut.-Col. W. W. Burland, Second-in-Command, and Capt. A. P. Holt, Adjutant, accompanied Brig.-Gen. R. E. W. Turner, V.C., G.O.C. the 3rd Canadian Infantry Brigade, on a reconnaissance of trenches near Fleurbaix which the battalions of the 3rd Brigade were to take over from the British. Leaving Armentières at 4 p.m. on March 2nd, the 14th Battalion billeted at Bac St. Maur, where on the following morning the British Corps Commander warned the senior Canadian officers regarding what lay before them. "Gentlemen", he said, "you are about to face a cunning, cruel, and unscrupulous enemy. If you make a mistake you will not get a chance to make a second one." Later in the day Lieut.-Gen. E. A. H. Alderson, Commanding the Canadian Division, addressed the 14th Battalion, which was to take over a section of the line that night. In brief, he ordered the unit to hold its trenches come what might and regardless of cost.

Moving forward from Bac St. Maur after dusk, the Royal Montreal Regiment took over a section of the front line near the Rue Petillon (Fleurbaix Sector), opposite Fromelles, from a squadron of the Northumberland Hussars (Yeomanry) and from the 1st Battalion, Grenadier Guards, commanded by Lieut.-Col. Fisher-Rowe. The Guards, being veteran soldiers, had made themselves as comfortable as circumstances permitted, among their assets being three cows. These they presented with their compliments to Lieut.-Col. Meighen and the officers of 14th Battalion H.Q.

On relief of the Guards, Nos. 1, 2, and 3 Companies of the 14th occupied the front line, No. 4 Coy. taking up a position in support dugouts opposite Battalion H.Q., about 250 yards to the rear. Shelling each noon was a feature of this trench tour, and snipers, both by day and night, interrupted the construction and repair work on which the men of the 14th were employed, Pte. J. P. Rattigan being killed while at work on the roof of his dugout, and a man of a ration party from No. 4 Coy. being killed at a corner of the Sailly-Fromelles Road. These first dead of the Regiment were buried in a small military cemetery at Rue Petillon.

Relieved on the night of March 6th by the 15th Battalion (48th Highlanders), the Royal Montreal Regiment moved back to Brigade Reserve billets in Rue du Quesne, moving forward again on the night of March 9th and taking over the Rue Petillon trenches from the 15th. On this occasion Nos. 1, 2, and 4 Companies occupied the front line, No. 4 on the right, No. 2 on the left, and No. 1 in the centre. No. 3 Coy. remained in support.

On taking over the front line, the men of the Royal Montreal Regiment prepared to advance against the German line opposite. They were ordered to attack on the morning of March 10th if the Battle of Neuve Chapelle involved the British brigade on their immediate right. With the 16th Battalion on the left they would thus have taken part in the Battle of Neuve Chapelle had the attack proved successful. Unfortunately, it resulted in partial failure, and on the extreme left, where the British forces joined up with the 14th, no advance was called for, participation of the Royal Montrealers being confined to a demonstration in support.

Describing the work of the Regiment on this eventful morning, a private of the Battalion writes as follows: "Early on the morning of March 10, those of us who were fortunate enough to be asleep

Royal Montreal Regiment Front Line Trenches, Fleurbaix, March, 1915

were awakened by furious cannonading on our right. The British had let loose the whole force of their artillery on the German trenches. So many guns were massed along the line that it was impossible to hear individual reports. The sound came to us as a steady rumble of terrific volume and intensity. A little later the batteries of the 3rd Canadian Artillery Brigade, immediately in our rear, joined in. . . . The din was terrific—ordinary conversation was impossible, and orders had to be fairly shouted. While our men were speculating about the battle, down the line came the order 'Stand to!' Immediately the men dropped whatever they were doing and sprang to their allotted posts along the parapet. 'Open rapid fire!' came the next order, and the men stepped up to their firing positions, threw back the safety catches, and let drive. . . . Each man was firing twenty-five rounds a minute, so it was not long before extra bandoliers had to be served out. No. 3 Coy. was acting as reserve and all night long they had toiled, carrying up 100-pound boxes of ammunition to the trenches. It had been thought that 200,000 rounds would be ample for the Battalion, but apparently the rapid firing ability of some of the men had been under-estimated."

Continuing his letter, the writer mentions that, before very long a "Prepare to Advance!" order was received, whereupon the men "with fixed bayonets, stood to in light fighting order. Knapsacks were placed in the rear of trenches as superfluous weight, but of necessity each man carried 250 rounds of ammunition, full water bottle, and emergency iron ration. For more than an hour they remained on the alert, waiting for the command that would send them out across 300 yards of sloppy ground against the enemy trenches. But the gods of war did not favour them. The British division on the left remained passive, the roar of the big guns died down, and soon the men were resting quietly in the trenches." Casualties in the 14th Battalion during the engagement included Sergt. Thomas Moore, of No. 2 Coy., who had won the Distinguished Conduct Medal in China. Privates Hunt, Molt, and Coombes, of No. 2 Coy., were also killed, and several others badly wounded.

On the night of March 13th the 48th Highlanders (15th Battalion) relieved the Royal Montrealers, who moved back to billets in the Rue du Quesne. No parades, except rifle inspections, were held on March 14th, 15th, and 16th, the men being given a thorough rest, varied only by a few games of football on the afternoon of the 16th. At night on the 17th the Battalion moved up once more and took over the now familiar Petillon trenches from the 15th Battalion.

Previous to the move forward, Canon Scott held a Communion Service at a wayside shrine on the Rue du Bois, the communicants kneeling on the road at the feet of the silent figure on the Cross. This shrine, still standing at the end of the War, was the one which inspired Canon Scott's well known verses, beginning:—" O pallid Christ within this broken shrine ".

The three-day tour that followed was marked by appreciable activity, the enemy sniping persistently and shelling at intervals. One man was killed by a sniper on March 18th and three more by rifle fire on the 20th. In addition, nine men were wounded. Apart from rifle fire and shelling, the chief event of the tour was the appearance overhead of a German aeroplane. Enemy planes were destined to become familiar objects in the days that lay ahead, but this was the first the Royal Montrealers had seen. Unfortunately, it flew too high for rifle fire to be effective.

Following the tour in the line, the Battalion withdrew for three days to billets in the Rue du Quesne, then advanced once more to relieve the 15th Battalion in the front line, taking over the Rue Petillon trenches on the night of March 24th. The following day was quiet, but on the 26th the enemy showed marked activity, several men of the 14th being killed and approximately a dozen wounded. Previous to this activity, a patrol of the Royal Montreal Regiment in No Man's Land had been fired on by the enemy, Pte. A. S. Jones falling and one other man being wounded. On receiving a report from survivors of the patrol, a party of three men, under Sergt. Lang, went out to help Jones if he were still alive. They searched till dawn, but no trace of the fallen man could be found. Accordingly, on the Battalion records there was placed the entry:—" Private A. S. Jones—Wounded and Missing ".

During this same tour Stretcher Bearer Drake went out into the open to help a wounded man. Drake was himself wounded soon after leaving the protection of his trench, but in spite of his injury he pluckily bound up his comrade's wounds and remained with him, under fire, until further help was secured. For his courage on this occasion Stretcher Bearer Drake was awarded the first Distinguished Conduct Medal granted to a man of the Canadian Division. On the night of March 26th the 3rd Canadian Brigade was relieved by the 24th British Brigade, the 14th Battalion handing over to the 1st Battalion of the Worcester Regiment, commanded by Major Grogan. The relief on both sides was well carried out, the G.O.C. 24th British Brigade complimenting the 14th for the smartness with which the trenches were handed over. The 1st Worcester Battalion had participated in the Battle of Neuve Chapelle and had lost a great deal of equipment. The 14th, therefore, turned over a number of Very pistols and trench periscopes and a quantity of supplies. Authority to do this should, of course, have been sought from Brigade Headquarters, but, remembering the courtesy of the Imperial troops who had taught them the principles of trench warfare, officers and men of the 14th were glad of an opportunity to help the Britishers out of an awkward hole. Brigade asked questions, of course, and grumbled as a matter of form. No one, however, least of all Brigade, took the grumbling seriously.

When the Worcesters had taken over the Rue Petillon front, the Royal Montreal Regiment marched back to rest billets in Estaires. Here the Regiment spent eleven days, the time, after the men had visited the Divisional Baths and received clean underclothing, being devoted to training, with special attention paid to practice in bombing, entrenching, wiring, and attacking against wire. To provide diversion, a small stream, the Courant de Meteren-Becque, was dammed and the resulting swimming pool allotted to the companies at specified hours.

On April 2nd Lieut.-Col. Meighen and Lieut.-Col. Burland accompanied Brig.-Gen. Turner to Fauquissart to view a section of the German line where an attack was contemplated. The plan for this attack was eventually abandoned and on April 6th the units of the 3rd Brigade received orders for a move to Cassel. Marching from Estaires at 6 a.m. on April 7th, the Brigade proceeded through Neuf Berquin, Strazeele, and Caestre, and reached Cassel at approximately 3 p.m.

At Cassel, or rather in billets in the eastern outskirts of the town, the 14th Battalion remained for a week. Early in the stay a draft of 25 reinforcements was taken on strength from England, and a day or two later Lieut. G. W. Stairs reported for duty. An event which the Battalion witnessed in Cassel was the review of a French division by General Foch. The march past on this occasion was splendid, as the division was composed of veterans whose physique and bearing were of the finest. On April 10th the 3rd Canadian Infantry Brigade was inspected by Gen. Sir Horace Smith-Dorrien, G.O.C. the 2nd British Army, under whose command the Canadian Division had now passed. Sir Horace complimented the Brigade on the work accomplished at Fleurbaix and intimated that even sterner work lay ahead in that section of the line which the Canadians were about to take over. On the night of April 12th the Battalion Commanders of the 3rd Brigade, together with a group of company officers, joined Brig.-Gen. Turner on a reconnaissance of the new front. On their return it became known that the Brigade would move up to Ypres and take over from the French a section of front in the neighbourhood of Langemarck and St. Julien.

Officers 14th Battalion, Royal Montreal Regiment, 3rd Brigade 1st Canadian Division. Taken in Cassel, Flanders, France 12/4/15.

Back Row: Capt. R. W. Frost, Lt. W. K. Knubley, Lt. C. F. C. Porteous, Lt. W. D. Adams, Capt. and Quartermaster H. H. Smith. *Third Row:* Lt. G. M. Williamson, Capt. V. G. Currie, Major F. G. Scott (*Anglican Chaplain*), Lt. R. de V. Terroux, Capt. Gault McCombe, Major A. C. Shaw, Major H. Barré, Capt. R. W. Steacie, Capt. A. Sylvestre, (*Roman Catholic Chaplain*), Capt. E. Ranger. *Second Row:* Capt. H. A. Thompson, Capt. F. B. D. Larken, Lt. E. A. Whitehead, Lt.-Col. F. S. Meighen, Lt.-Col. W. Burland, Major P. R. Hanson, Capt. J. N. Warminton, Lt. W. C. Brotherhood. *Front Row:* Capt. and Adj. Andrew Hole, Lt. S. Grant, Lt. H. Quintal, Lt. H. Des Rosiers, Lt. R. de Serres, Lt. J. F. Adams, Lt. W. H. Draper, Lt. R. Roy, Lt. K. L. McCuaig, Capt. H. A. Boyd

CHAPTER IV

THE GAS ATTACK AT YPRES

> That day of battle in the dusty heat
> We lay and heard the bullets swish and sing
> Like scythes amid the over-ripened wheat,
> And we the harvest of their garnering.
> —JOHN McCRAE.

I

IN mid-April, 1915, the Canadian Division completed a short period of rest and moved forward into the Ypres Salient, taking over 4,250 yards of line, extending in a north-westerly direction from the Ypres-Roulers railway to a point just beyond the Ypres-Poelcappelle Road. Here the Canadian line connected with French troops, the point of contact and the line to the left being held by coloured soldiers (Turcos) of a French Algerian Division. The 3rd Canadian Infantry Brigade took over the left of the new line, adjoining the French; the 2nd Brigade moved into the right section, connecting up with British troops; and the 1st Brigade remained in Divisional Reserve.

The 14th Battalion began to move towards the new positions on April 15th, when, at 1.30 p.m., the unit marched from Cassel to Steenvoorde. On the following day the men experienced a thrill when motor busses carried them over the Belgian border and on towards Ypres. Even at this early date Ypres had acquired a sinister reputation, as a host of gallant soldiers had fallen there in the fierce fighting of the previous autumn. Now another host was marching into the Salient—a Canadian host, which asked only that, in any hour of trial, it might worthily uphold the proud traditions which the dead had established.

After halting at Poperinghe for lunch, the 14th Battalion marched through Vlamertinghe, around Ypres, and through St. Jean to a point north of Wieltje. At dusk French guides led the Battalion forward once more, Nos. 1, 2, and 4 Companies taking over the front line, and No. 3 Coy. moving into immediate support, about 300 yards to the left rear. As Major Barré and his officers spoke both English and French, No. 4 Coy. was placed on the flank, adjoining the French colonial troops. On the right flank no difficulty in regard to liaison existed, as the line there had been taken over from the French by the 16th Battalion, Canadian Scottish.

That the men of the 14th Battalion experienced a shock when daylight revealed the condition of their new trenches is stated in many diaries and letters covering the time. A parapet of sand bags stretched along the Battalion front, but this was flimsily constructed, was not bullet proof, and was broken by one gap approximately 100 yards wide. Some value attached to the parapet as a screen from view, but danger signs gave warning that the Germans sniped through the protection repeatedly. No parados had been built on the trench; few traverses existed, and no shell proof dugouts at all. Water, and bodies buried but a few inches beneath the surface, had rendered the construction of underground shelters impossible. Many bodies had been buried in the parapet of the trenches; scores lay unburied between the lines; large rats wandered everywhere; and sanitary arrangements were, from a Canadian point of view, inadequate. Consequently, the line was dangerous and possessed of the most sickening smell imaginable.

On taking over from the French, the men of the 14th Battalion were immediately put to work on repairs. This work continued while the Battalion occupied the line, being interrupted at intervals by successful sniping and less frequently by shell fire. On April 17th enemy planes were active overhead, and on the same date No. 4 Coy. reported that Germans were at work in a ruined house in No Man's Land. This news was sent to Brigade H.Q., who induced the artillery to give the house a few bursts of fire. At another point on the front, where the enemy trenches were within easy range, a group of enterprising individuals bombarded with tins of bully beef. Casualties may have resulted; certainly bad language suggested to the delighted Canadians that some important Hun had suffered humiliating injury.

On the night of April 17th, No. 4 Coy. extended beyond the Ypres-Poelcappelle Road and took over approximately 50 yards additional of front. On the following day the trenches were shelled to some extent, but the front line was peaceful compared to the spot where the Battalion Quartermaster had established his stores in Ypres. Here heavy shelling occurred in the morning and at intervals throughout the day. On April 20th this shelling was renewed with increased intensity, four men of the 14th Battalion being injured in addition to Capt. H. H. Smith, the Quartermaster, who was removed to hospital after being struck on the head by falling masonry.

CLOTH HALL, YPRES, AS THE BATTALION SAW IT ON 16TH APRIL, 1915, ON ITS WAY TO POSITIONS IN THE SALIENT

Copyright F. Wade Moses, Montreal

THE GAS ATTACK AT YPRES

Referring to the shelling of Ypres on April 20th, a Signaller of the 14th writes in his diary as follows:—" I went into the town during the bombardment to see what it looked like. Nearly all the buildings in the market place had already been destroyed and the café where I had breakfast this morning was spread all over the square. In a corner of the square a group of civilians and soldiers were loading wounded into ambulances. Close by another group were working feverishly with pick and shovel recovering bodies buried in the débris of ruined buildings. Here and there dead horses lay across the sidewalks and in the roadway. The few women I saw were all hysterical and running about like mad things. Later, in the evening, I went up again. An unnatural calm hung about the town. The civilians seemed awed and terrified, walking close to the walls, and crouching down every time a shell screeched overhead. It is difficult to describe that awful calm. The people seemed afraid to speak and every step they took they would put their feet down as if afraid to make the slightest noise. I hope I shall never see such a sight again ".

Meantime the companies of the Battalion in the front line had improved their trenches, and the men of No. 3 Coy. had toiled to construct a reserve line. Progress had been made on both these tasks when the Royal Montreal Regiment, which had suffered casualties amounting to 7 killed and 15 wounded, was relieved by the 13th Battalion. On completion of the relief, which occurred on the night of April 21st, Nos. 1, 3, and 4 Companies moved back to billets in St. Jean, No. 2 Coy. halting in St. Julien as a local reserve.

II

At about 3 o'clock on the afternoon of Thursday, April 22nd, 1915, the Germans opened a tremendous bombardment of Ypres, the roads leading from that city to the front line, and the trenches forming the rim of the Ypres Salient. Guns of all calibres joined in this drumfire, wrecking and devastating the lines of communication and tearing great gaps in the Ypres defences. Obviously such a bombardment heralded an attack on a major scale and the Allied forces stiffened to meet the blow. Little reply could be made to the German fire, however, owing to a pronounced shortage of guns and ammunition. In all France at this time the British Army controlled but 700 field guns and some 71 guns larger than 5-inch. The task of hurling back the German attack, therefore, fell to an overwhelming degree on the ever-willing and devoted infantry.

After two hours of intense shell fire, the Germans launched chlorine gas. Gas had been used on the Russian front in the previous January, but unsuccessfully, owing probably to extreme cold. This time, with the temperature ideal and with a favourable wind, the poison clouds rolled across the open fields and fell with disastrous effect on the trenches of the Turcos to the Canadians' left. Blinded, choking, and terror-stricken, the French coloured troops gave ground, while through the gaps torn in their front and subsidiary lines poured the grey-clad German infantry, destined, so their commanders hoped, to sweep victoriously through Ypres and on to Calais. The surprise was complete; all that remained was to exploit victory to the uttermost.

Up in the front line which the 13th Battalion, Royal Highlanders of Canada, had taken over from the 14th Battalion, Royal Montreal Regiment, on the previous night, Major D. R. McCuaig, who succeeded to command of the Highlanders' forward companies on the death of Major E. C. Norsworthy, felt the great danger to which the French retreat had exposed him and faced a section of his command square left to protect his threatened flank. All night on the 22nd, all day on the 23rd, and again that night, the Royal Highlanders clung with bravery and devotion to their bit of front, beating off a number of attacks and establishing a tradition for tenacity and courage which will for all time add lustre to the bright pages of Canadian military history. On the night of April 23rd, sadly depleted in numbers, they withdrew according to orders and formed a new line with other units of the Canadian Division, who, with a determination rivalling their own, had pushed forward to reinforce them.

When the attack opened on the afternoon of April 22nd, the 14th Battalion, as previously mentioned, lay in billets in St. Jean and St. Julien. No. 2 Coy., in St. Julien, formed part of a special reserve and came under the orders of Lieut.-Col. F. O. W. Loomis, Town Commandant of St. Julien, and Commanding Officer of the 13th Battalion. As soon as it became certain that the Germans had penetrated the French lines to the Canadian left, Lieut.-Col. Loomis ordered Major Hanson to take up a defensive position north of St. Julien and between the Steenbeek and the St. Julien-Keerselaere Road. Heavy fire was encountered during the move forward and after the position was occupied, Major Hanson, the Company Commander, and Lieut. W. K. Knubley suffering severe wounds and Capt Steacie, second-in-command, being killed. Command of the company thereupon devolved on Capt. W. C. Brotherhood, who dug in and linked up with Capt. R. Y. Cory, who commanded a half company of the 15th Battalion on the right. Later Cory sent to Brotherhood's support a party of approximately 200 French coloured troops, under a gallant subaltern, who were requested to dig themselves in on Brotherhood's left. The French troops were willing, but were discovered by a French senior officer, who sharply ordered them to the rear. This senior officer appeared dazed and was obviously lost, none the less the subaltern in command of the Turcos dared not disobey his explicit orders and the French troops accordingly withdrew.

As the position of No. 2 Coy. was vital to the safety of the troops on the forward flank, Lieut.-Col. Loomis gave orders that it must be held at all costs. In obedience to these orders, the men of the company prepared to hold on, come what might. Shell fire poured on the position throughout the night, halting occasionally to permit sharp attacks by battle patrols of the enemy. On April 23rd Lieut. G. W. Stairs, who had behaved most gallantly, was killed, together with many of the rank and file. All that day and all that night Capt. Brotherhood commanded the remnant of the company, encouraging the men by force of personal example to bear with courage the shelling and machine gun fire which harassed them sorely, the more so as, owing to shortage of ammunition, supporting fire was conspicuous chiefly by its absence.

At dawn on April 24th Capt. Cory, commanding the detachment of the 15th Battalion to the right, visited No. 2 Coy's. trenches and spoke to Capt. G. M. Williamson, of the 14th Battalion Machine Gun Section, who had a gun crew, composed of Sergt. Duffield, Pte. W. B. Lothian, Pte. R. Fletcher, Pte. R. Stewart, and Pte. R. Bremner, in position immediately to the left of the Poelcappelle Road. Returning later in the morning for further consultations, Capt. Cory was informed that all officers of No. 2 Coy. had fallen. He spoke to an N.C.O., who showed a cool grasp of the situation, and picked out a wounded man, Private Russell, whom he ordered to carry a written situation report to the rear.

Meanwhile, at approximately 11.30 a.m., Capt. Brotherhood notified Lieut.-Col. Loomis that some of his men had been shelled out of their trench and that enemy forces were advancing on his left and front. To this message he added that, should the enemy force him to retire to the right, he would contest every traverse of his trench. Somewhat later Capt. Brotherhood laid down his life in carrying out his promise. After his death, all officers having become casualties, command fell to Sergt. A. E. Hawkins, this N.C.O. leading back the remnant of the company when the order to retire was finally received.

Some conception of the work accomplished by No. 2 Coy. from April 22-24 is conveyed in a letter written by Major-Gen. Sir (then Lieut.-Col.) F. O. W. Loomis, who says:—" Capt. Brotherhood's action in defending this position to the death cannot be enhanced by anything I might say. It appears to me that a plain chronicle of the facts records as valorous a deed as men can achieve. The determined defence by Capt. Brotherhood and the officers and men of the 14th who were with him in front of St. Julien at that critical time was of vital importance to the tactical situation and of great comfort and assistance to me. I wish to record my full appreciation of their faithfulness and valour and do all honour to their glorious memory ".

Shortly after No. 2 Coy. of the 14th Battalion advanced on the afternoon of April 22nd, Nos. 1, 3, and 4 Companies were ordered to " stand to ", and soon afterwards to move forward. No. 1 Coy. at this time was commanded by Major A. C. Shaw, with Major J. N. Warminton as second-in-command and Lieuts. R. de V. Terroux and C. F. C. Porteous as junior officers; No. 3 Coy. was under the command of Major Gault McCombe, Capt. V. G. Curry, Lieut. W. D. Adams, Lieut. S. Grant and Lieut. E. A. Whitehead; and No. 4 Coy. was commanded by Major H. Barré, who had to assist him Capt. E. Ranger and Lieuts. H. DesRosiers, R. DeSerres, R. Roy, and H. Quintal. Before the advance of No. 4 Coy. began on the afternoon of the 22nd Major Barré was wounded, command of the company devolving on Capt. Ranger.

Even before the advance of Nos. 1, 3, and 4 Companies began, the men were aware that some disaster had overtaken the front line. Past their billets streamed a confused throng of soldiers and civilians, and to the left bodies of French troops, some in perfect order and others in the grip of panic, moved hurriedly to the rear. During the march up the St. Jean-St. Julien Road, evidence of disaster increased. "A steady tide of humanity—the most mixed and miserable lot of people I have ever seen ", writes an N.C.O., " moved by us in the direction of Ypres, leaving us barely room to squeeze through in the direction of the enemy. Most pitiful were the civilian population— mostly women and children—all utterly demoralized and passing in seemingly endless procession. In the village of St. Jean I saw a youth of sixteen carrying his aged grandmother on his back; and a little further on a child of five standing alone in the doorway of a deserted home, crying pitifully. And, of course, there were the wounded—

hundreds of them—and the main body of French colonial troops in retreat, some who had been gassed with yellow faces and gasping for breath".

Near the village of Wieltje, Lieut.-Col. Meighen, who had led the advance, took up a post at the side of the road and, with the assistance of his Adjutant, Capt. A. P. Holt, directed each company in turn to its position in what was known as "The G.H.Q. Line". This line stretched through Brigade H.Q. and roughly paralleled the old front. For the most part, it existed on maps and in imagination only. A few shallow trenches and pits had been dug, but these provided protection for individuals rather than for organized bodies of troops. Accordingly, Nos. 3 and 1 Companies were at once put to work digging trenches to the left of Brigade H.Q., while No. 4 Coy. established a sector between Brigade H.Q. and the Ypres-Poelcappelle Road. No. 1 Coy's. left was completely "in the air", the imaginary "line" stretching quite ungarrisoned as far as the Yser Canal.

Soon after taking up position in the G.H.Q. Line, No. 3 Coy. sent out two patrols, who discovered the enemy in strength some four or five hundred yards away. The first of these patrols, from No. 9 Platoon, consisted of Privates Boyd Symonds, C. D. B. Whitby, and B. R. Racey; the second, from No. 10 Platoon, was led by Corp. William Kirby, accompanied by Lance-Corp. Clifford and Private C. A. Harley. All of No. 10 Platoon's party were captured, as was Private Racey, who escaped from a German prison camp in July, 1916. Privates Symonds and Whitby eluded the enemy and returned with information as to the Germans' whereabouts. Shortly afterwards a riderless horse crashed into the Battalion lines and for a moment the men of the 14th thought that the enemy was upon them. Strict discipline prevailed, however, and the alarm did not cause the firing of a shot.

Meanwhile No. 1 Coy. on the left had sighted a body of troops moving in the open. Darkness prevented identification and Coy. Sergt.-Major C. B. Price with Private C. S. LeMesurier went out to discover whether the troops were English, French, or German. Approaching with caution, Price and LeMesurier established that the men were Germans, a fact which allowed No. 1 Coy. to open fire. Shortly afterwards LeMesurier went forward once more and challenged two individuals, who fired and wounded him. Price, who had followed LeMesurier, came up at this time and shot both the attackers. The two Canadians then made their way back to the G.H.Q.

Line. For the coolness and courage displayed on this occasion Coy. Sergt.-Major Price was awarded the D.C.M.

At about 11 o'clock that night, the 10th and 16th Canadian Battalions marched up the Ypres-Poelcappelle Road and, extending to the left, prepared to attack a wood held by the enemy. With these battalions was a bombing force, composed of some 128 men drawn equally from each of the 3rd Brigade battalions. Led by the bombers, the 10th and 16th Battalions, commanded respectively by Lieut.-Cols. R. L. Boyle and R. G. E. Leckie, drove their way through the wood, suffering heavily, but achieving their purpose of relieving the pressure on St. Julien, the fall of which would have uncovered the entire rear of the gallant battalions in the original front line.

Early on the morning of April 23rd a company of the Buffs arrived to occupy a position on No. 1 Coy's. flank. To reach this position it was necessary to cross a hedge gap which exposed each man to enemy fire. The first few men attempting to cross were shot down, No. 1 Coy. thereupon opening a covering fire in the general direction of the unseen enemy. At this juncture an officer of the Buffs took up a post in full view of the enemy and coolly directed his men to safety. He thanked the Canadians for their covering fire, but suggested that the ammunition had better be preserved. The daring of this officer and his splendid leadership aroused the Canadians' admiration, regret being felt when, just as his immediate task was completed, he fell, shot by a German sniper.

That same morning Nos. 3 and 4 Companies of the 14th were ordered to advance as far as possible, and dig in. At 8 o'clock the companies started forward, but immediately machine gun fire was opened from farm buildings on a ridge to the left and, after an advance of some hundreds of yards, the movement was definitely checked. During the advance Lieut. H. Quintal, of No. 4 Coy., was severely wounded. Casualties from machine gun and shrapnel fire continued and soon became so severe that a withdrawal was necessary.

At dusk that night Major McCombe led No. 3 Coy. forward to St. Julien and reported to Lieut.-Col. F. O. W. Loomis, Town Commandant. In St. Julien Major McCombe halted for about two hours, then Lieut.-Col. Loomis ordered him to move his company forward and report to Major V. C. Buchanan, Second-in-Command of the 13th Battalion, who, at the moment, was commanding the 13th Battalion's front line. Major McCombe's company carried forward in the subsequent advance food and water for the 13th, who had been on short rations for two days. The Royal Highlanders at this time

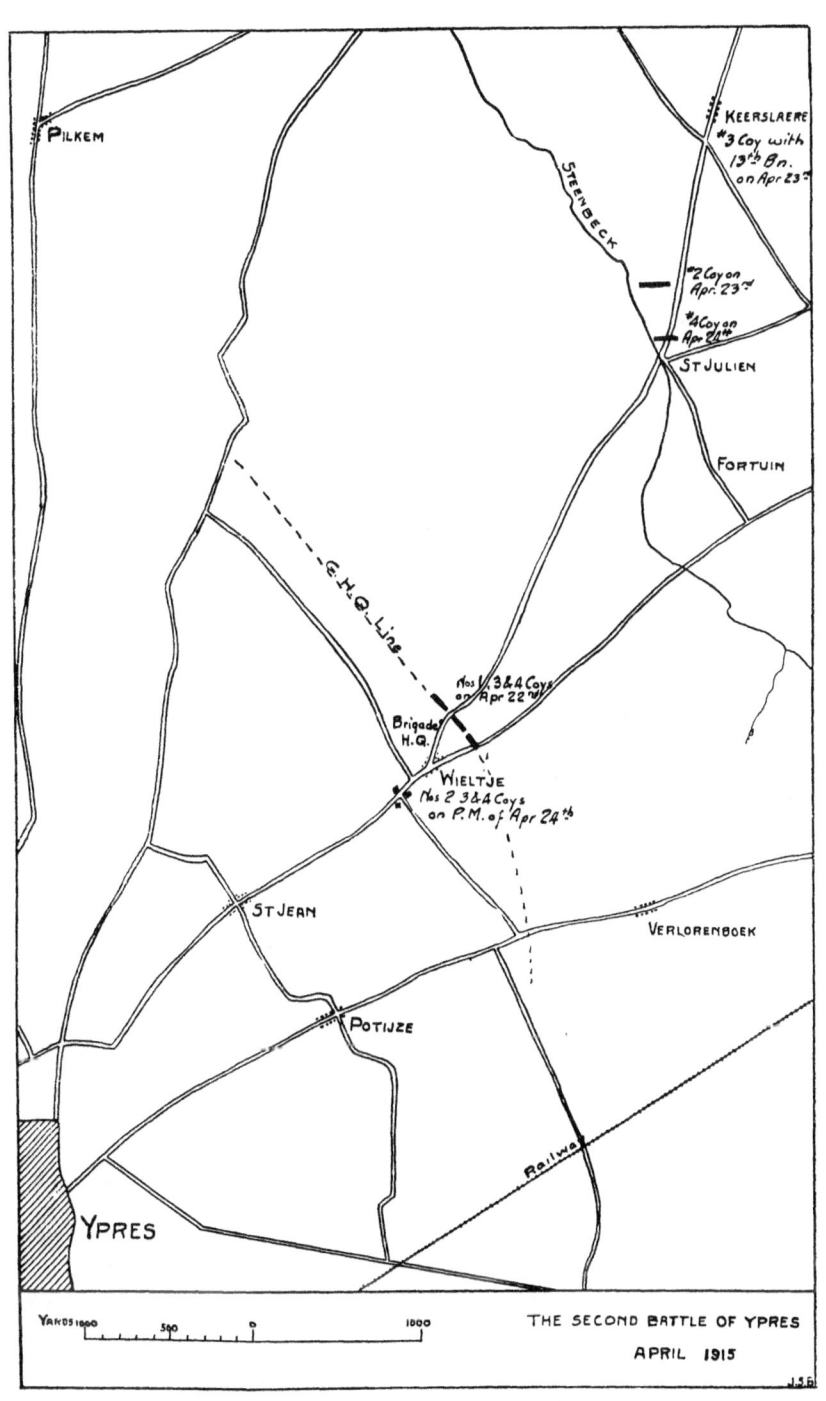

were pivoting on the left of the 15th Battalion, and throwing back their left flank to join with other units in forming a line across the gap which the gas attack had torn open. When Major McCombe reported to Major Buchanan the pivoting movement had been completed and the Highlanders were establishing their new line. A position in this was allotted to the Royal Montrealers, who, realizing that dawn was not far off, dug in as rapidly as possible.

Shortly after the advance of No. 3 Coy. on the evening of April 23rd, Lieut.-Col. Burland led No. 4 Coy. to a point near the St. Julien-Keerselaere Road, where contact was established with the remnants of No. 2 Coy. and with detachments of the 7th Canadian Battalion. Meantime other Canadian and Imperial units were moving up and entrenching further to the left, with the result that by dawn on April 24th a line—weak, and with gaps, it is true—stretched from the refused left of the 13th Battalion to a point on the west bank of the Yser Canal, or, in other words, across the great breach which the gas attack had opened.

Seeing the chance of victory slipping and realizing that a determined effort might still smash through the wearied Canadian lines, the Germans, at 3.30 a.m. on Saturday, April 24th, opened heavy fire with shrapnel and high explosive. Accurately directed, this fire wrecked the emergency trenches occupied by the Canadian battalions, inflicting heavy casualties, and preparing the way for an assault by the infantry. Amongst those in the 14th Battalion wounded at this time was Lieut. E. A. Whitehead, of No. 3 Coy., who received a bullet in the ankle. Although suffering severely, Lieut. Whitehead continued to command his platoon until he fainted from pain, fatigue, and loss of blood. In a brave effort to remove this wounded officer to a place of safety, Sergt. Arundel was shot and instantly killed. After several hours, shell fire rendered the line quite untenable and a retirement was ordered to a point on the forward side of a small ridge between the Poelcappelle Road and the Rue des Boches. Sullenly, the men obeyed the order to retreat, taking advantage of every ditch and fold in the ground to halt and open fire when the pursuing enemy failed to keep at a respectful distance.

At approximately 11 a.m., the Royal Montrealers, or rather what was left of them, were shelled out of their new positions and again forced to retire, this time to a series of disused trenches some 300 yards to the right rear. Following the retreat mercilessly and with unerring skill, the German artillery reached these trenches, which were also enfiladed by machine gun fire, and once more the Canadians were compelled to give ground. As previously, however, each foot of soil was yielded only after the enemy had paid a heavy price.

After retiring for some 200 yards, the men of Nos. 2, 3, and 4 Companies, together with their comrades of the 13th and other Battalions, occupied a line of ditches and natural folds in the ground. Here they remained till about 4.30 p.m., when they received orders to retire behind the G.H.Q. Line, their place being taken by Imperial troops who had pushed forward to take part in the great engagement. On relief, Nos. 2, 3, and 4 Companies moved into an open field east of St. Jean.

While the events just described were taking place, No. 1 Coy. of the 14th was holding its section of the G.H.Q. Line. A strong force of the enemy penetrated the Canadian front near St. Julien on the afternoon of April 24th and worked down towards 3rd Brigade H.Q. This force appeared about 350 yards in front of the G.H.Q. Line at approximately 3 p.m., and offered a target which the men of No. 1 Coy. at once accepted, rifle and machine gun fire inflicting such heavy casualties that the Germans retired hastily to their right rear. Shortly thereafter the enemy shelled a barn on the left flank and destroyed the company's reserve of ammunition.

For two days and two nights more No. 1 Coy., plus a platoon of No. 2 Coy., under Sergt. Dick Worrall, remained in the left section of the G.H.Q. trenches, exposed to constant rifle, machine gun, and shell fire, and suffering appreciably from a shortage of food and water. Ration parties worked to remedy this state of affairs, but, as they were forced to cross ground open to sniping in the daytime and swept by machine gun fire at night, their efforts were only partially successful. On one occasion Lance-Corp. H. Wright, under sharp fire, trundled a Belgian hand-cart full of food up the St. Jean-Wieltje Road almost to Brigade Headquarters. From this spot he dodged snipers and, reaching the G.H.Q. Line, told the men where food could be obtained. Volunteers, in extended order, then reached the cart and brought back rations for their comrades.

Meanwhile, at a farmhouse not far from Wieltje, the remnants of Nos. 2, 3, and 4 Companies of the Battalion had been assembled and reformed. During the various stands and retirements on the morning and afternoon of April 24th, it had been impossible to preserve company distinctions. In falling back, men dropped into the nearest trench and reported to the officer in charge. Thus, at one time, in a trench in front of St. Julien, men from the Canadian Engineers, 10th, 13th, 14th, and 16th Battalions fought side by side, intent only on checking the enemy's advance, and for this purpose yielding unquestioning obedience to any officer from one or other of the units who appeared on the scene. By dusk some 100 men of the 14th had gathered at the Wieltje farm and during the night this number was appreciably augmented.

On the night of Sunday, April 25th, Nos. 2, 3, and 4 Companies of the Royal Montreal Regiment were withdrawn behind the Yser Canal and for a while the men thought that their experiences in the Second Battle of Ypres were over. Reserves were too short, however, and on the morning of the 26th the companies were ordered forward to near St. Jean to support an attack being delivered by the French. Counter-attacks took place at several points on the front this day and the companies of the 14th suffered from the inevitable back lash of shell and rifle fire. Amongst the casualties from this fire was Major Gault McCombe, who was struck in the leg by a bullet, but remained at duty for several days thereafter. Eventually the bullet was extracted from the leg by Capt. Scrimger, the Battalion M.O.

On the night of April 26th No. 1 Coy. was relieved from the G.H.Q. Line and rejoined Nos. 2, 3, and 4 Companies, who were still near St. Jean. On the morning of April 27th, therefore, Lieut.-Col. Meighen once more commanded a four-company Battalion, under-strength as a result of casualties, and weary as a result of five days in the line, but a co-ordinated unit none the less, capable of marching, or fighting, as occasion should demand. During the day the reunited Battalion suffered approximately 15 casualties from shell fire.

That night the Battalion moved back to the Regimental Transport Lines, near Brielen, where, on the following day, Lieuts. W. M. Pearce, G. L. Stairs, E. Leprohon, and F. R. Heuston reported for duty from England. After dusk the Battalion moved into a poorly constructed line of trenches on the west bank of the Yser Canal.

All day on April 29th the Battalion lay in the Canal trenches. An occasional shell dropped nearby, but, on the whole, the day was quieter than any the men had experienced since the gas attack of the previous week. At dusk the 14th was ordered to the east side of the Yser Canal to establish a line facing the Pilkem-St. Julien Ridge, between trenches held by the 16th Battalion on the left and the King's Own Scottish Borderers (13th British Brigade) on the right. On arrival, it was found that space existed for but one company of the 14th and authority was accordingly sought from 3rd Brigade H.Q. to withdraw three companies of the Battalion to a position on the east bank of the Canal, where the men would not be under direct observation from higher ground. Permission for this move having arrived, No. 1 Coy. dug the trench between the 16th Battalion and the K.O.S.B.'s, Nos. 2, 3, and 4 Companies withdrawing as arranged.

April 30th was a warm day and the men of Nos. 2, 3, and 4 Companies enjoyed the novel experience of swimming in the Canal, under shell fire from enemy guns. At night, a rearrangement of dispositions having been effected, the companies moved forward to join No. 1 Coy. in the trenches facing the Pilkem-St. Julien Ridge. Fairly heavy shelling and scattered rifle fire were encountered during the move, Lieut.-Col. W. W. Burland receiving a severe shrapnel bruise and Lieut. S. Grant a bullet through the arm.

About 5 o'clock on the afternoon of May 2nd, a greenish cloud of poison gas, about 40 feet high, poured over the crest of the Pilkem-St. Julien Ridge and fell on the trenches of the Essex Regiment, which had replaced the King's Own Scottish Borderers on the 14th Battalion right. Three batteries of French '75's, which were in support, immediately lined the crest of the Ridge with shrapnel. This fire was beautifully placed and completely crumpled a strong attack which the German infantry attempted to deliver. After the attack had failed, the Essex Regiment reoccupied a front line trench, which the cloud of gas had rendered untenable. On sighting the gas the men of the 14th Battalion fastened small gauze pads over their faces for protection. These pads, soaked in chemicals, had been issued on the previous day, but, fortunately perhaps, a shift in the wind prevented their efficacy from being tested.

May 3rd was a quiet day, according to the official diary of the Battalion, although enemy aeroplanes were active. By this time the majority of the Royal Montrealers had cast aside their Ross rifles and equipped themselves with Lee-Enfields, a weapon better suited to meet the severe requirements of active service. Opening fire with these new rifles, and encouraged by Lieut.-Col. Meighen, who himself joined in the sport, the men of the 14th winged one plane which, however, managed to escape and land behind the enemy's line. Late that night the Battalion was relieved from the trenches and marched back to the Transport Lines near Vlamertinghe, passing May 4th in this position and marching at dusk, together with the other battalions of the 3rd Brigade, through Vlamertinghe, Ouderdom, and Locre, to Bailleul. At Bailleul the Brigade scattered, the men of the 14th, exhausted after the wearing experiences of the previous fortnight and the long night march, finding that another 3 kilometres were required of them. " It was a pretty sorry looking bunch that crept into Bailleul ", writes one diarist. "We were all footsore and weary, but we found that our billets were about two miles out of town. We managed to crawl that distance and reached our destination at dawn on the morning of May 5th. The march was the worst I ever experienced."

III

Although the foregoing account covers in outline the work of the 14th Battalion, Royal Montreal Regiment, in the Second Battle of Ypres, certain incidents remain to be recorded. At the outbreak of the battle Capt. F. A. C. Scrimger, the original Medical Officer of the Battalion, was in charge of an advanced dressing station at Wieltje, when French coloured troops poured back from the broken front line. A part of this stream halted at the dressing station where Scrimger was at work, and some of the poor Turcos, crawling on the floor, sought comfort by clinging to the M.O's. coat. Never before had Scrimger seen such terrible "mass fear". No attempt to pacify or reassure these individuals could be successful. Their morale was shattered, and weeks must elapse before it could be restored.

On the following day, Capt. H. A. Boyd, Medical Officer of the 14th Battalion, having been wounded, Capt. Scrimger was attached to his old unit and ordered to report for duty at 3rd Brigade Headquarters. That afternoon the vicinity of Headquarters was shelled and Capt. Scrimger, together with other medical officers present, was ordered to the rear. This order the M.O. of the 14th could not see his way to obey. Instead he proceeded to the G.H.Q. trenches, occupied by Nos. 1, 3, and 4 Companies of his Regiment, and there, under fire, dressed the wounds of five men who had been badly injured. Next day Brig.-Gen. R. E. W. Turner and officers of the 3rd Brigade Staff were standing in rear of their Headquarters farmhouse, studying a large map, when an aeroplane circled twice overhead. This plane bore Allied markings, but must have been a German, for a few minutes later Headquarters was blown to pieces. Shell after shell landed on the farmhouse and outbuildings, the ruins soon taking fire and blazing fiercely. Eventually the flames reached 350,000 rounds of small arm ammunition, the cartridges detonating individually, but in such rapid succession as to suggest a great roar of rifle fire. Some such impression must have been conveyed to a strong party of Germans, who approached under cover of the shelling. A half dozen men alone stood between this party and the capture of Brigade H.Q., but, when the cartridges started to explode, the Germans halted and dug in.

Numerous wounded lay in the farm stable when the shelling began and these, with the assistance of a small band of devoted stretcher bearers, under Sergt. Bethell, Capt. Scrimger removed to safety. Among the wounded was a staff officer, Capt. McDonald. Supporting this officer, who was helpless, Scrimger made his way out of the burning dressing station, only to run into shell fire. Refusing to abandon the wounded man, the Medical Officer lay with him at the side of a ditch, while some seventy-five 6-inch shells exploded around them. Five shells fell within fifteen feet of the lying men, who were dazed by the concussion and half smothered by the flying mud. Eventually, when the shelling subsided, Scrimger staggered with his wounded companion to safety. For his valour in effecting the rescue just described, and for his great devotion to duty throughout the period from April 22nd to April 25th, Capt. Scrimger was awarded the Victoria Cross. He was the first Canadian officer to win this most coveted of all distinctions in the Great War.

No account of the work accomplished by the Royal Montreal Regiment during those spring days of fiery trial would be complete without mention of Capt. G. M. Williamson and the men of the Battalion Machine Gun Section. When the 14th Battalion was relieved by the 13th Battalion on the night of April 21st, Capt. Williamson turned over one of his guns to the Highlanders. The remaining guns were mounted eventually in ruined houses on the outskirts of St. Julien and at different points in the new front line. On one occasion when the Germans drove against St. Julien, the machine guns caught the enemy in the open and inflicted heavy casualties. Later, guns were brought into action in the front line at a time when the Germans were pressing the Canadians sorely. Bravely served against great odds, the guns fought to the last, Capt. Williamson and many of his men laying down their lives, hoping that the sacrifice they made would assist in holding Ypres and preventing the Germans from sweeping through to Calais and the Channel. In a battle where disaster was evaded by a hair's breadth, who shall say that their sacrifice was made in vain?

While the companies of the 14th Battalion were engaged in the fighting at Ypres, Canon F. G. Scott, or to give him his military title, Hon. Major F. G. Scott, one-time Protestant Chaplain of the Regiment, wandered everywhere in the forward zones, bringing courage, good cheer, and religious consolation to all who stood in need. "The Canon", wrote one private of No. 3 Coy., "is known and loved by every man in the Regiment. He is one of the best and bravest men I have ever known. All through the campaign so far he has been with us, indefatigable, indomitable, and quite irrepressible. On the night of April 22nd, the Canon, hearing that the 14th Battalion was to counter-attack, hurried up from behind Ypres, right through terrific shell fire, and joined the 16th Battalion, which was on the way from reserve trenches. The Canon did not know where the 14th was located, so he stuck to the 16th, hoping to get in touch with his own Regiment. The reverend gentleman's description of his experiences is most amusing:—' We marched up the road and across a field ', he explains, ' and then there was considerable manœuvring about. I didn't know exactly what was in the wind until suddenly I found myself tearing across some fields in the moonlight with the boys of the 10th and 16th Battalions, who had fixed bayonets. It occurred to me that this must be a charge, and there I was with only a light walking stick as a weapon. The only thing that saved the situation was that a couple of poor fellows were badly wounded close beside me and I was able to go to their assistance ' ".

Characteristically, the Canon failed to mention the withering fire which greeted the attack of the 10th and 16th Battalions and through which he had passed, but made much of his fear that a rifle would go off while he was helping the wounded soldiers to cover. In a diary another private describes his feelings when, after a short period of rest, his company was again ordered into action. " I was greatly discouraged at this time and had it not been for the kind and cheerful words of encouragement given to me by our loved padre, Canon Scott, I am sure I could not have faced the new ordeal ".

Tribute to the work of senior officers of the Battalion is similarly paid in many letters and diaries. Writing a few days after the Ypres battle, a private observes:—" Col. Meighen, our Commanding Officer, was in constant touch with General Turner throughout the three-days' battle for St. Julien. I had an opportunity of observing the two commanders at Brigade Headquarters and, though I have never seen a man cooler under fire than General Turner, I don't think he had anything on our Colonel. Col. Meighen has been with us every minute since we got into action, sharing our fortunes and discomforts, and preserving a calm, unruffled demeanour, which undoubtedly has had a steadying influence on the men. As for Lieut.-Col. Burland, our Second-in-Command, he was right in the thick of the fight for St. Julien. He was with No. 3 Coy. when we were blown out of the trenches on Saturday morning and it was due in a large measure to his efforts that the remnants of the Battalion were quickly rallied and formed up for the rear-guard action after the first retirement ".

As men of the Royal Montreal Regiment were scattered during the Ypres Battle, it is impossible to follow the fortunes of all individuals who, through one cause or another, became attached to units other than their own. A few incidents, however, must be mentioned. Men of the 14th assisted Major W. B. M. King's battery to escape on the night of April 22nd, after it had fired over open sights into advancing bodies of the enemy less than 200 yards away. Lance-Corp. Fred. Fisher, of the 13th Canadian Battalion's Machine Gun Section, directed operations on this occasion and won a well-deserved V.C. The men of the 14th who assisted Major King moved forward under command of Lieut. G. W. Stairs, together with a number of men from the 15th Battalion, the whole party being despatched by Capt. Cory, of the 15th, who had visited Major King's position and seen how seriously it was threatened.

Some 30 men of No. 4 Coy. of the 14th, under Lieuts. Roy and DesRosiers, became attached to the 2nd Canadian Battalion, commanded by Lieut.-Col. David Watson, and helped to cover the retirement of this fine unit on the afternoon of April 24th. A Signaller of the 14th, who was in Ypres on the evening of April 22nd, received instructions to retire to Poperinghe. Distrusting the source of these orders, he "kept out of sight" for a time, then joined a party of Canadian Engineers, who worked all night, preparing two bridges across the Canal for destruction. "Three of us were still at it in the morning", this man writes, " though there were eight when we started. The other five had all been hit and two of them were dead. I don't know who my comrades of that night were. I never saw their faces clearly, not even in the early dawn of the following morning ".

Still other members of the Battalion acted as runners for Brigade Headquarters. One records in his diary that he was sent to St. Jean with a message for ambulances. " I located the ambulances and got them started on their way, following them on my bike. As I was nearing Wieltje a shell burst close to me, a piece cutting the rim of my front wheel in two and throwing me over the handle-bars. Leaving the wreck of the bicycle in the ditch, I finished my journey to Wieltje on foot ". Another private, acting as a runner for 3rd Brigade, was waiting for a message which General Turner was writing when a shell burst a few feet overhead. " Pretty close ", remarked the General, without lifting his head. " Nerve of that sort ", states the runner in his diary, " helped me a great deal ".

The stories of how the gallant 13th Battalion held the exposed left flank at Ypres; how the 10th and 16th charged against the wood at St. Julien; how the 15th Battalion suffered grievously from shelling and gas; and how the 1st and 2nd Infantry Brigades fought with superb valour and skill, are carved deep in the memories and hearts of the Canadian and British peoples. The 14th Battalion is proud to have shared with these and all other units of the Division in the distinction accorded by Sir John French of having by " a magnificent display of tenacity and courage—averted a disaster which might have been attended with the most serious consequences ". The Canadian Division had, indeed, at a cost of 5,000 casualties, upheld those traditions of sacrifice and valour which the " Old Contemptibles " had established at Ypres in the previous year.

CHAPTER V

FESTUBERT, GIVENCHY, AND THE SUMMER OF 1915.

O England of our Fathers and England of our Sons
Above the roar of battling hosts the thunder of the guns,
A Mother's voice was calling us, we heard it oversea,
The blood which Thou did'st give us is the blood we spill for Thee.
—FREDERICK GEORGE SCOTT.

I

WHEN the Canadian Division withdrew from the Ypres Salient early in May, 1915, it rested for some ten days and then moved south to take part in the Battle of Festubert. This engagement, which opened on May 15th, had as its immediate object the capture of Aubers Ridge, from which Lille and La Bassée could be dominated. Secondarily, the battle was fought to retain on the British front German forces which otherwise could have been used against the French Army attacking Vimy Ridge and Lens. By May 25th Sir John French realized that his plan had partly failed. Ammunition was running short by this time and gains in territory had been purchased at a disproportionate price in casualties. Accordingly, the engagement was brought to a close. On the Vimy front fighting continued for six weeks, heavy French losses, with no appreciable advantage gained, threatening for a time to bring about the downfall of General Foch, to whom General Joffre had entrusted the whole operation. Canadian participation in the Festubert offensive began on May 15th when Lieut.-Gen. E. A. H. Alderson, the Divisional Commander, moved his Headquarters to the southern section of the British line. The Canadian infantry brigades followed and the 3rd Brigade came into action on the afternoon of May 18th, when the 14th and 16th Battalions attacked to the east of Indian Village.

Previous to the move south the 14th Battalion lay for ten days in billets near Bailleul, resting and refitting after the Second Battle of Ypres. In that battle 4 officers of the Battalion had been killed and 8 wounded; amongst the other ranks 65 had been killed, 143 wounded, and 49 taken prisoner. To fill the gaps caused by these losses a draft of 275 men from the 23rd Reserve Battalion was taken on the strength of the Battalion on May 6th. Lieut. I. G. Robertson reported for duty from England at this same time, and on the 12th of the month commissions were granted to Coy. Sergt.-Major C. B. Price, of No. 1 Coy., Sergt. Dick Worrall, of No. 2 Coy., and Sergt. G. E. Leighton, all of whom had rendered conspicuous service at Ypres. Simultaneously, promotion was given to a number of N.C.O's. and men.

At Bailleul equipment was issued to the men to replace the losses of the previous fortnight, and the new officers strove to attain the high standard set by those who had become casualties. Similarly, the men of the new draft worked to equal their brothers-in-arms, whose deeds at Ypres commanded their unstinted admiration. Distinguished visitors during the ten days included Lieut.-Gen. Alderson, who inspected the Battalion and expressed pride in what it had accomplished; General Sir Horace Smith-Dorrien, who congratulated Lieut.-Col. Meighen and voiced agreement with the War Office statement that "the Canadian Division had undoubtedly saved the day"; Major-Gen. J. W. Carson, who brought greetings from the Canadian forces in England; and Brig.-Gen. R. E. W. Turner, V.C., who inspected the Battalion and satisfied himself regarding its reorganization.

A feature of the Bailleul period which many Royal Montrealers recall was provided by the issue of Irish butter. Butter had been scarce for some time and the men received the round, gold-lettered cans of "Guaranteed Finest Irish Butter", with unconcealed satisfaction. Buttered toast! Fried eggs and butter! Eagerly the cans were rushed to the cooks, who were ordered to waste no time in putting the contents to use. Meanwhile, an individual greedier, or perhaps it would be charitable to say, hungrier, than the rest, was digging at the cover of his can with a Lee-Enfield bayonet. Soon the point penetrated and simultaneously visions of golden butter faded. From the tin there escaped, like soda-water suddenly released, a sizzling fluid, foul smelling and horrible. "If that's Irish butter", remarked one N.C.O. disappointedly, "thank God we have no Irish cheese".

At 6.50 p.m. on May 14th the 3rd Brigade paraded in Bailleul and marched, by way of Estaires and Lestrem, to billets near Robecq. On this march the 14th Battalion, in rear of the Brigade, was halted by a G.S. wagon which broke down at a point where marsh prevented passage at the roadsides. When the obstruction was cleared, a Brigade guide led the Battalion astray, with the result that dawn found the men miles off their proper route. At daylight officers discovered the error, dismissed the humiliated guide, and themselves led the tired Battalion to billets at le Cornet Malo and Mont Bernenchon.

On May 15th and 16th the Royal Montreal Regiment rested at le Cornet Malo, marching thence at 5 a.m. on May 17th and reaching le Touret some three hours later. Here the Battalion moved into breastworks and trenches just south of the Bethune-Neuve Chapelle Road. Rain fell throughout the day, which was uneventful, except for the interest aroused by the sight of Gurkhas, with prisoners, moving back from the line, and the 4th Guards Brigade marching into action. The Guards, as always, afforded a splendid sight, and the Gurkhas, with their famous "kukris", aroused the Canadians' curiosity. The sacred "kukri" knife, rumour had stated, was never drawn without the shedding of blood, even if the owner had to nick his own person to satisfy the weapon's sanguinary honour. Alas! this fascinating legend soon faded into the limbo of abandoned beliefs, as several Gurkhas drew their kukris and unromantically proceeded to chop firewood. The brown men's reputation for being quick with the knife was maintained, however, when a Gurkha leaped at a German officer prisoner who had contemptuously refused a proffered cigarette. Prompt interference alone saved the German's life. Brig.-General Turner visited the Battalion at this time, apologetically explaining that he had been unable to arrange for a fight that day, but promising the men that they would see action on the morrow. Accordingly, at 9 p.m., the Battalion withdrew to Essars, billeting there, but prepared to advance on fifteen minutes' notice.

At 7 a.m. on May 18th the Royal Montreal Regiment moved into the trenches vacated the previous night. Here the Battalion remained until 2.30 p.m., when it advanced to old British trenches near Indian Village, east of the Rue de l'Epinette. Artillery fire was encountered during the move and, later, in assembly trenches, one shell caused 11 casualties. Reply to this fire was being made by a battery of Indian mountain guns, whose amazing mobility provided the Canadians with no little amusement. The battery would come into action, fire a few rounds, dismount the guns, transfer them to a spot some distance away, and come into action again just as German shells began to drop on the position vacated.

Soon after the 14th reached the assembly position, Brig.-General Turner summoned the Commanding Officers of the 3rd Brigade Battalions and explained the operation in which they were about to take part. The 14th and 16th Battalions had been chosen to advance on la Quinque Rue, northwest of a defended locality known as "The Orchard". The 14th Battalion was to attack with two companies

THE SUMMER OF 1915

and to hold two in reserve. The 16th Battalion was to attack on the right and the 14th Battalion on the left. To the left of the 14th was the 2nd Battalion, Grenadier Guards. The intent of the attack was to close up a gap in the British line and capture the Orchard, should this prove possible.

On the plan of attack being explained, Lieut.-Col. Meighen chose Nos. 1 and 3 Companies for the assault, the former under command of Major A. C. Shaw and the latter under Capt. V. G. Curry, who, though seriously ill, refused to be evacuated until the engagement had been fought. Major Shaw had as company officers Major J. N. Warminton, Lieut. R. W. Frost, and Lieut. C. B. Price; Capt. Curry had Lieuts. W. D. Adams, F. R. Heuston, and G. E. Leighton. Lieut.-Col. W. W. Burland was placed in command of the four attacking waves, which were to advance with 50 yards between waves and 5 paces separating each man from his neighbour to the right or left. A maze of intersecting ditches, trenches, and water-filled shell holes meant that direction would be maintained with difficulty, particularly as, in some cases, the ditches were too wide to jump and too deep to wade. Platoons in consequence would have to converge, cross on a single plank, and extend, only to repeat the manœuvre a few score of yards further on. British staff officers, however, intimated to the Staff of the 3rd Canadian Brigade that the advance, in their opinion, would not encounter serious opposition.

In preparation for the assault, Nos. 1 and 3 Companies advanced about 100 yards from the old British front line and took up a position in a German front line trench, captured a few days previously by men of an Imperial Brigade. From this position the companies of the 14th advanced at 4.20 p.m., the companies of the 16th Battalion on the flank following shortly thereafter. Unfortunately, the prediction of the British staff officers regarding opposition was not fulfilled, the men of the 14th encountering heavy fire as soon as they left their trenches. In spite of this fire, the attack progressed, though at one time it lost direction and swung to the right across the front where the companies of the 16th Battalion were coming up. Some time later this loss of direction was recognized and corrected, the 14th eventually digging in, after an advance of approximately 500 yards, and connecting up with the 16th Battalion on the right and the Grenadier Guards on the left. A line without a gap had accordingly been established, though capture of the Orchard had proved impossible.

Early in the advance of No. 1 Coy. Major A. C. Shaw was shot in the head, but continued to lead his men forward. Later he left the company and advanced with a runner, Private A. J. M. Craig, to reconnoitre his front. After progressing for several hundred yards and swimming some broad water-filled ditches, Pte. Craig's right arm was shattered and the pair took refuge in a large shell hole. Craig now realized that all was not well with his officer and attempted to restrain him. Major Shaw, however, would permit no interference. He scrambled from the shell hole and marched boldly forward. In spite of his own serious wound, Craig attempted to follow, but before he could clear the lip of the shell hole he saw Major Shaw reach the edge of a ditch, or trench, throw up his hands, and pitch forward. Soon afterwards Craig was shot through the lung. That night two Germans reached the wounded runner, and, thinking him dead, removed his papers and valuables. Later Craig struggled to his feet and made his way through mud and water back to the lines of the 16th Battalion. Here he collapsed from exhaustion and loss of blood, but recovered by an effort of will to give a clear report to Lieut.-Col. Burland, who had been summoned from the 14th lines. From the moment when Major Shaw fell forward into the ditch nothing has been heard of him. In his passing the 14th Battalion suffered the loss of a capable and gallant officer.

Late on the night of May 18th Nos. 1 and 3 Companies of the 14th Battalion were withdrawn from the advanced trenches, which were taken over by an extension of the Guards and the Canadian Scottish. On relief Nos. 1 and 3 Companies joined Nos. 2 and 4 Companies, who had taken position in the old German front line. During the advance of Nos. 1 and 3 Companies and the subsequent withdrawal casualties had totalled 67. Lieut. C. B. Price, D.C.M., had been severely wounded and 18 N.C.O's. had been killed or wounded. Coming so soon after the Ypres engagement, these losses were sharply felt, but the end was not yet.

From May 19th to May 22nd, the Royal Montreal Regiment lay in the old German trenches. On the 19th the Battalion suffered a severe loss when Major J. N. Warminton, who had succeeded to the command of No. 1 Coy., was killed by shell fire. Later the body of this officer was buried with full honours in the British Military Cemetery at the corner of the Rue du Bois and Rue de l'Epinette. Shell fire continued to take heavy toll after Major Warminton's death, the Battalion between the 19th and 22nd of the month losing 75 other ranks killed and wounded, bringing the total for the engagement up to 143.

On May 19th a draft of 25 men arrived from the 23rd Reserve Battalion in England and a few days afterwards Lieuts. R. Godwin, J. H. Richardson, and J. F. Sumption reported for duty, Lieut. Godwin later taking over command of the Machine Gun Section, vice Lieut. W. M. Pearce, who was wounded while temporarily attached to the 13th Battalion.

Throughout the stay of the 14th Battalion in the old front line trenches, burial parties were frequent, as the whole area was strewn with the bodies of those who had died in the fighting of the previous fortnight. Altogether, the men of the 14th saw to the burial of hundreds of British and German dead. The horror of life in such surroundings can with difficulty be exaggerated. One man writes in his diary:—" I crawled back on the first night and got some water from a shell hole to make tea. We boiled it and enjoyed our hot drink. Next morning I went back to the same shell hole and was about to fill my tin when I saw the dead face of a German soldier looking up at me through the water ".

While the British and German dead were being buried by parties of the 14th, Capt. Scrimger, who had established a dressing station at Indian Village, was caring for the wounded. The Medical Officer of the 13th Battalion was sick at this time, and accordingly Capt. Scrimger, Capt. Taylor, M.O. of the 15th Battalion, and Capt. Gillies, M.O. of the 16th Battalion, had placed upon them the medical work of the whole Brigade. The task of collecting the wounded at night, amid the complicated maze of trenches, mud, and watery ditches already described, was exhausting in the extreme. Capt. Scrimger was slightly wounded on one occasion and, during an attempt to reach the forward area on another, became lost and spent "two hours of falling into shell holes and water-filled ditches ". No rest was possible on his return, however, as the wounded required constant attention.

The devotion to duty practised by the Medical Officer during these trying days and nights undoubtedly stimulated the Battalion stretcher bearers, who, throughout the engagement, toiled unsparingly at their task. But the stretcher bearers were not alone in their effort to help the wounded. On the night of May 18th Bugler Anthony Ginley, aged 15, twice made his way back from the front of No. 3 Coy. to guide stretcher bearers up through heavy shelling to a spot where wounded men were waiting. The daring of this young soldier and the uncanny skill with which he picked his way over the difficult ground were held by all ranks of the Regiment to be worthy of the highest commendation.

II

At 9 p.m. on May 22nd the 4th Canadian Battalion relieved the Royal Montreal Regiment, which marched to billets in le Hamel, situated on the Rue du Bois between le Touret and Bethune. Here four uneventful days were passed, the Battalion marching forward at 7 p.m. on May 26th and relieving the Royal Canadian Dragoons (Seely's Detachment) in trenches southeast of the Orchard at Festubert, and northwest of Givenchy lez la Bassée. Trenches to the right of this position were held by a Territorial battalion of the London Regiment, and on the left was the 16th Battalion, Canadian Scottish. During the tour that followed Nos. 2 and 3 Companies of the 14th occupied the front line, the former under command of Capt. A. S. English and the latter under Capt. W. D. Adams, the two combined being directed by Lieut.-Col. W. W. Burland, Second-in-Command of the Regiment. Nos. 1 and 4 Companies, meanwhile, were in close support, No. 1 commanded by Capt. R. W. Frost and No. 4 under Capt. H. DesRosiers. The Battalion, as in every engagement up to this time, was commanded by Lieut.-Col. F. S. Meighen.

Relief was difficult on this occasion owing to scattered posts comprising the front line. One post, in an isolated trench, was completely overlooked until nearly midnight. A messenger then reported existence of the post to H.Q. and relief was arranged. When the men of the 14th Battalion took over from the Dragoons, they found, as during the previous tour, evidence of the fierce fighting which the area had witnessed not long before. Hundreds of dead bodies lay in the trenches and round about. "The position", writes one diarist, "is the most horrible place I have ever been in", and another adds, "We had to walk over dead bodies and sleep beside them". Amongst the bodies found and buried by a party of the 14th, under Pioneer Sergt. Baker, was that of an officer, whom the Germans had apparently strangled. A rope had been twisted around this officer's neck, all means of identification had been removed, and, from the condition of his clothing, it seemed that he had been dragged about until he died. This body, which bore no wound, was buried, together with that of an officer of the 5th Canadian Battalion, on the field where death had been encountered.

Dawn on May 27th revealed that a point, known as K5, was in possession of the enemy, though supposedly in the line held by the 14th. A bombing party occupied and consolidated this point without resistance, further reconnaissance to the left failing to locate a definite enemy line. Knowing, however, that the Germans held a position named L8, a party from the Royal Montreal Regiment advanced along a trench towards this post, the enemy retiring promptly to the north. The accommodating attitude of the Germans was probably explained by the fact that the trench was mined. Fortunately, this was discovered and the wires cut, before the mine could be blown. Two wounded Germans, captured during the advance of the 14th party, were sent back for medical attention. During the operations Lieut. R. Roy and Corp. Langelier accomplished valuable work.

On occupation of the trench between K5 and L8, the 14th Battalion established two blocks, about 150 yards apart. At night the men were withdrawn from between the blocks, owing to bad conditions there existing. Shortly before daylight a German party climbed the first block and took possession of the trench whence the men of the 14th had been withdrawn. This could not be tolerated and a platoon of No. 2 Coy. proceeded to dislodge them, the Germans throwing a few bombs, which exploded harmlessly, and then retreating as far as L8.

During the operations mentioned above the Signal Section of the Royal Montreal Regiment laid telephone lines to the outlying posts and maintained communication between the companies and Battalion H.Q. On one occasion Signallers Hazelgrove and Bickley were detailed to lay a wire to advanced Headquarters by way of a roundabout communication trench. The straight line across the open, though dangerous, seemed more practicable to the pair, who started to lay their line accordingly. Half way across the open they stumbled into a deserted German trench and found a machine gun with some sixty boxes of belted ammunition. Continuing, they brought their line to its destination and established connection with H.Q., just as an abandoned Germen trench some yards further forward was blown up by mines. This trench was ungarrisoned at the time, though the Germans probably imagined otherwise. During this same operation, Signaller Barltrop and a companion were at work one night in No Man's Land, when footsteps squelched in the mud a few feet away. Then a figure appeared and the Signallers challenged, " Halt! Who goes there? "

A moment's silence, then, " British officer ", came the reply.

" Name and regiment?" demanded the Signallers, keeping the halted figure covered.

" Barltrop is my name ", came the answer. " I'll name my regiment when I know more of yours. Who are you anyway?"

" Personally ", replied Signaller Barltrop of the 14th, " I'm your brother ".

And so it proved; whereupon Lieut. Barltrop explained that he had been sent from the London Regiment on the flank with a message to 14th Battalion H.Q. and had lost his way, little thinking that it would be pointed out to him by a brother whom he had not seen for years.

At night on May 28th the enemy attacked the barricade erected by the men of the 14th at L8. Bombing and counter-bombing followed, the attackers achieving not even a measure of success. Later that night when the 14th Battalion was relieved by the 13th Battalion, a working party of 100 men, under Lieuts. Dick Worrall and J. H. Richardson, remained to establish a line, previously reconnoitred by Sergt. H. G. Brewer, between K5 and the Post Office Rifles on the right. Some time after the relief Stretcher Bearer Lee, of the 14th, went into No Man's Land to the assistance of a wounded German who called for help. Reaching the German, Lee fell wounded, whereupon two stretcher bearers of the 13th volunteered to bring him in. These bearers were in turn wounded, but before dawn all the fallen men, including the German, were brought in to the Canadian lines by Capt. W. H. Clark-Kennedy and two stretcher bearers, all of the 13th Battalion. The assistance given to Stretcher Bearer Lee on this occasion was appreciated by officers and men of the 14th and served to strengthen the comradeship between the Royal Highlanders of Canada and the Royal Montreal Regiment. From the front line, stretcher bearers carried Lee to Indian Village, the ground being so difficult that four hours were taken to cover the few hundred yards. Unfortunately, Lee's wounds were severe and he died after being evacuated from the Battalion Dressing Station.

Following relief by the Royal Highlanders, the 14th Battalion moved to reserve trenches south of the Rue du Bois and west of Rue de l'Epinette, where four days were passed, the Regimental Diary recording that these were quiet, except for occasional German shells. At midnight on May 31st the Battalion left the reserve trenches and marched to rest billets at Oblinghem north west of Bethune. Here, a few days later, commissions were granted to Sergt. John Howe and Private Philippe Chevalier.

After resting and refitting at Oblinghem, the Royal Montreal Regiment paraded at 5.30 p.m. on June 6th and relieved the 5th Canadian Battalion (Lieut.-Col. G. S. Tuxford) in trenches at Givenchy, on the bank of the La Bassée Canal. Reaching this position after an exceedingly hot march, Nos. 1 and 2 Companies moved into the front line, with Nos. 3 and 4 Companies in support and reserve. The trenches in this area had been constructed by the Brigade of Guards, under the supervision of Major Russell Brown, R.E., and were quite the finest the Canadians had seen, although the actual front consisted not of a continuous fire trench, but of strong redoubts connected by communication trenches. On taking over the front, the Royal Montreal Regiment began construction of a fire trench, completing the work some days later.

During the tour in the line the enemy shelled at intervals and sniped, and on the left flank, at a position known as the "Duck's Bill", bombers on both sides were active. On the right flank at night, German fixed rifles and machine guns swept the bank of the La Bassée Canal, the enemy evidently considering that random fire might there prove effective. In reply, Lieut. Godwin, of the 14th Battalion Machine Gun Section, fired on a road some thousand yards behind the German line. His fire, it seemed, was accurate, as German wagons were heard galloping away.

After the Second Battle of Ypres, the men of the Canadian Division were always on guard against poison gas. A weathercock was accordingly mounted at Battalion H.Q. and the direction of the wind carefully observed. The Regimental Diary states that this was the first weathercock so used by a Canadian battalion.

One night a patrol from No. 1 Coy. investigated a suspected German machine gun post, finding no enemy above ground, but hearing sounds which strongly suggested a mine beneath. A report of this discovery was promptly forwarded to Brigade Headquarters. On the afternoon of June 9th the Royal Montreal Regiment handed over the front line to the 13th Battalion and moved to reserve trenches near the Canal. Large working parties were supplied to the Engineers that night and on the following afternoon, after relief by the 3rd Canadian Battalion (Lieut.-Col. Rennie), the Regiment marched to billets on the north bank of the Canal at Bethune.

There the Battalion remained for nine days, the men drilling and, in the intervals of training, swimming and carrying out aquatic sports in the Canal. On the day of the first water sports, a native gallery gathered to watch the fun, the good women of the town taking a frank interest in events, though puzzled by the embarrassment of the swimmers, who had counted on absence of clothing to keep the women away. That night Battalion Headquarters emphasized its modesty by ordering all swimmers in future to wear adequate bathing suits. Bathing suits on active service! The men were dismayed, for nothing of the kind was obtainable, but soon some enterprising individual cut holes for his legs in a sandbag and the problem was solved.

On June 13th it was announced that the Lee-Enfield rifle would replace the Ross as the authorized weapon of the Canadian forces. Most of the men had foreseen this change and quietly equipped themselves from Imperial casualties. The minority now turned in their Rosses and formally received Lee-Enfields from stores. From the 15th to the 18th of the month the Battalion " stood to ", pending the result of operations being carried out by the 1st Canadian Infantry Brigade. On June 19th, during a move of the Battalion to reserve billets at Beuvry, Lieut.-Col. F. S. Meighen, the Commanding Officer, left the unit in obedience to immediate orders which recalled him to Canada for special duty. Brigadier-General's rank was given to him and, at a later date, he was appointed a Companion of the Order of St. Michael and St. George. In addition, his name was twice brought to the notice of the Secretary of State for War. When his period of service in Canada and later in England was completed, Brig.-Gen. Meighen voluntarily reverted to the rank of lieutenant-colonel to command the 87th Battalion, Canadian Grenadier Guards, in France. Throughout these transfers and in his new commands, he was followed by the good wishes of all ranks of his original battalion. On his departure, command of the Royal Montreal Regiment was assumed by Lieut.-Col. W. W. Burland.

On the night of June 22nd, 1915, the 14th Battalion moved forward to reserve trenches (Givenchy Sector), and there passed two quiet and uneventful days, being relieved at 8 p.m. on the 24th by the 2/6th Battalion, Gordon Highlanders, and returning to billets at Beuvry. On the following day the Battalion was inspected by Brig.-General Turner, who announced that the Distinguished Service Order had been awarded to Lieut.-Col. W. W. Burland and that, for bravery and devotion at the Second Battle of Ypres, Capt. F. A. C. Scrimger, Medical Officer of the Battalion, had been granted the Victoria Cross. Rain fell during the inspection, but failed to dampen the enthusiasm of the troops, who cheered heartily. Obviously the honours gained by the Commanding Officer and the Medical Officer were approved by all ranks of the Battalion.

III

Following the engagements on the Festubert-Givenchy front, the Canadian Division turned once more towards the north, the 14th

Battalion marching from Beuvry at 6.30 o'clock on the evening of June 26th and reaching Neuf Berquin at 4 o'clock on the following morning. Rain fell that day, but the men were comfortably billeted and not inconvenienced, except at night when the Battalion marched from Neuf Berquin to Outersteene. At Outersteene the first passes for leave to England were granted. After nearly five months of active service these were welcomed by the recipients and hardly less by those others who felt that their turn would soon come.

On June 29th the Battalion paraded at 2.30 p.m. and marched three miles to near Steenwerck, following this move by another short march on June 30th to billets near la Crêche. Four days were spent at la Crêche, the Battalion marching on the evening of July 5th and relieving the 4th Canadian Battalion in trenches in front of Ploegsteert Wood.

On the way forward to the "Plug Street" trenches the men of the Battalion, passing through Ploegsteert Wood, were much interested in the board walks bearing the names of London streets; in field batteries hidden in attractive surroundings; and in Headquarters huts, which reminded them of log cabins in the sugar bushes at home. On taking over the trenches from the 4th Battalion, Nos. 1, 2, and 4 Companies of the 14th moved into the front line, with No. 3 Coy. in support. The positions occupied by all companies were clean and comfortable, except for the presence in dugouts of an abnormal number of huge rats. The right of the front was not entirely a pleasant spot, however, as underneath a knoll, held by No. 4 Company, the Germans were supposed to have dug a mine. Some compensation for the tension of living over a potential volcano was supplied at this point by the presence of a great catapult, similar to those used in the days when Caesar's legions were over-running Gaul. Bombs were fired at intervals from this dangerous contraption, also a few tins of bully beef. Probably the enemy regarded the beef as some particularly obnoxious Canadian poison. As ammunition the tins would otherwise fail to impress him.

Snipers were active throughout the tour, four men of the 14th being hit and many others escaping by narrow margins. On July 6th British forces to the right feinted an attack to draw enemy troops into an area where artillery could deal with them, the 14th Battalion "standing to" during this operation, and No. 3 Coy. reinforcing the front line. Unfortunately, a Canadian battery fired short during the "stand to", several shells crashing into the Royal Montrealers' front line and inflicting casualties.

Apart from the " stand to ", the chief work of the Regiment during the tour was carried out by large parties who assisted the Engineers in fortifying the Ploegsteert front and strengthening the defences of the famous wood. Such parties were not popular, as the work was hard and dangerous without compensating glory or excitement. Moreover, the troops considered that, when in the front line, routine construction and repair of their own trenches was all that should be asked of them, and that ordinary working parties should be provided by units in reserve. Despite this belief, the men worked well with the Engineers and satisfactorily carried out the heavy tasks assigned to them, one party, under Lieut. Johnston, rendering specially good service in carrying forward under fire black powder and high explosive for a trench mine.

On July 8th Lieut.-Col. F. W. Fisher, who had crossed from Canada in command of the 23rd Battalion, arrived in France to act as Lieut.-Col. Burland's Second-in-Command. On the following night the 13th Battalion took over the Ploegsteert trenches, the 14th Battalion marching back to Brigade Reserve in the Piggeries. The Piggeries, situated in rear of Ploegsteert Wood, was a large building in which the King of the Belgians had kept a fine breed of swine. Inside were two rows of concrete sties, providing a hard bed, but one free of rats and vermin and for that reason acceptable to the troops. For five days the Battalion remained at the Piggeries, supplying working parties to the Engineers each day and night. These parties, consisting of 3 officers and 150 men, worked on various forts and reserve trenches, passes to Ploegsteert affording diversion when the toil of the day, or night, was over.

Meanwhile, in the front line, the 13th Battalion had occupied and consolidated the craters of several mines, blown under a position known as " The Bird Cage ". This German position, situated only ten yards from the Canadian line, derived its name from wire netting which protected its garrison from bombs. As it had proved a trouble centre during their previous tour in the line, the men of the 14th heard that it had been blown up with distinct satisfaction, in no way diminished by the fact that they were due to take over the front once more. Moving forward on the evening of July 14th, the Royal Montreal Regiment occupied the crater frontage. Heavy rain fell during the night and again on the 15th, interfering to some extent with work in the craters, where sniping had become exceedingly active. On the 15th Pte. F. W. Heather was fatally wounded in one of the craters, and several additional casualties occurred before the tour was com-

The Crater, Birdcage, Ploegsteert Wood, 18th July, 1915. Lieut. R. Roy in Foreground

pleted on the night of July 18th, amongst the wounded being Corp. L. W. Taylor. Pte. Heather, who fell in a spot exposed to both rifle and machine gun fire, was gallantly carried to shelter by Capt. W. G. Turner, acting Battalion M.O.

On being relieved in the front line, Nos. 1 and 4 Companies of the Royal Montreal Regiment took over a defended locality in Ploegsteert Wood from a battalion of the Berkshire Regiment, and Nos. 2 and 3 Companies proceeded to reserve billets in La Grande Munque Farm. Working parties occupied much of the time on July 19th and 20th, though at night on the latter date the Battalion " stood to " for an hour and a half, pending the outcome of some operation further forward. At 10.45 p.m. the " stand to " order was cancelled and the men dismissed. On July 21st the 3rd Canadian Infantry Brigade paraded for inspection by Lieut.-Gen. E. A. H. Alderson, C.B., who was accompanied by H.R.H. Prince Arthur of Connaught, the Right Hon. Sir Robert Borden, Prime Minister of Canada, and Brig.-Gen. R. E. W. Turner, V.C. Following the inspection, the 14th Battalion marched to Kortepyp Huts, near Neuve Eglise, there to pass a week in Divisional Reserve.

While at Kortepyp Huts drill, sports, and working parties occupied the men's time, the week also being marked by the return to duty of Regimental Sergt.-Major J. M. Stephenson, who had been wounded at Ypres, and the taking on strength of a draft from the 23rd Reserve Battalion. The men of this draft had received a measure of instruction in trench warfare when, on July 29th, the 14th Battalion moved forward through Ploegsteert Wood and relieved the 4th Canadian Battalion in the front line.

July 30th was a quiet day on the front, though some trouble was caused by enemy trench mortars. At night a patrol, under Capt. W. D. Adams, moved into No Man's Land and returned with valuable information. Later the enemy opened rapid fire, as if fearing an attack, or planning to launch one. Nos. 1, 3, and 4 Companies of the 14th " stood to " during this demonstration, which died down shortly before dawn. That evening British artillery bombarded trenches and the ruins of a village to the 14th Battalion's right, the Royal Montrealers commanding a magnificent view of proceedings and agreeing that a bombardment of someone else's trenches provided a spectacle thrilling in the extreme.

On August 1st Major Gault McCombe, who had been wounded at the Second Battle of Ypres, returned to the Battalion and took over command of No. 3 Coy. Enemy grenade throwers and rifle grenadiers were active on this date, the Battalion losing several men wounded, among these being Sergt. Jock Walker, in charge of Battalion snipers. On the following day Brig.-General Turner inspected the trenches with care, and at night the 14th Battalion handed over the front to the 13th Battalion and proceeded to familiar billets in the Piggeries. From this spot working parties moved forward regularly to the front and reserve lines; and here the Battalion passed August 4th, the first anniversary of Britain's war declaration against Germany.

CHAPTER VI

MESSINES

> It isn't the foe that we fear,
> It isn't the bullets that whine,
> It isn't the business career
> Of a shell, or the burst of a mine;
> It isn't the snipers who seek
> To nip our young hopes in the bud;
> No, it isn't the guns,
> And it isn't the Huns,
> It's the mud, mud, mud.
>
> —ROBERT SERVICE.

I

IN mid-August, 1915, Brig.-Gen. R. E. W. Turner, V.C., C.B., D.S.O., left the 3rd Canadian Infantry Brigade to assume command of the 2nd Canadian Division, in England. General Turner had led the 3rd Brigade for a year and had directed operations at all times in a manner which commanded the admiration of his battalions. News of his departure, therefore, was received with regret, tempered only by satisfaction at his promotion and by a feeling that in Lieut.-Col. R. G. E. Leckie, of the 16th Battalion, the Brigade had secured a leader worthy to follow in the original commander's footsteps.

For eight months after Gen. Turner left, the battalions of the 3rd Brigade held trenches on the Messines front, carrying out routine duties of an arduous nature, suffering not infrequently from sharp artillery fire, and constantly from snipers, machine guns, and rifle fire. At first the line was dry and comfortable, but, with the advent of winter, the River Douve overflowed its banks, flooding trenches, communication trenches, dugouts, strong posts, and billets and rendering the life of the men miserable in the extreme, so much so that, in speaking of Messines, a soldier will mention rain, water, mud, and cold more frequently than bullets, bombs, or shell fire. The human enemy was almost forgotten in coping with water and mud.

On August 6th, 1915, the 14th Battalion took over the reserve position supporting trenches 135-138, the men occupying tents and bivouacs and Battalion Headquarters being established in Red Lodge. Major-Gen. Sir Sam Hughes and Staff visited this position on the following day and the Battalion paraded for inspection. Unfortunately, the occasion was marred by a salvo of 4.1-inch shells which burst some distance away. Being unwilling to subject General Hughes to avoidable risk, Lieut.-Col. Fisher dismissed the men, who returned to routine occupations.

Three days after Sir Sam's visit, 200 men of the Battalion and all officers not on duty marched to 2nd Brigade Headquarters where, under the supervision of the Divisional Commander, Lieut.-Gen. E. A. H. Alderson, C.B., gas helmets were tested. Donning the helmets, which had been issued a short time previously, the men passed through chlorine gas concentrated in a trench. On the whole the test demonstrated to the doubting men that the helmets afforded protection, though incipient confidence was shaken when Lieut. E. Leprohon's helmet proved defective. After recovering in Canada from the effects of the gas inhaled on this occasion, Lieut. Leprohon was promoted to the rank of lieutenant-colonel and appointed to the Conducting Staff of the Canadian Transport Service. On July 2nd, 1918, he was in command of 18 officers and 1,313 men on board the *S.S. City of Vienna*, outward bound from Montreal, when that vessel was wrecked on Black Rock, not far from Halifax. Owing in no small measure to the good discipline which Lieut.-Col. Leprohon maintained, all troops were removed from the wrecked vessel in safety.

At 9 p.m. on August 10th, the 14th Battalion moved a short distance into Divisional Reserve. On the 12th the companies paraded and marched in order to new Divisional Baths on the Neuve Eglise Road. Working parties, 150 strong, featured the next four days, and on the 18th of the month Field Marshal Earl Kitchener of Khartoum, British Secretary of State for War, inspected the Battalion on the Bailleul Road. From August 19th to 23rd the Royal Montreal Regiment occupied Trenches 135-137. On the 20th of the month the Germans planted a sign board in No Man's Land with news of Teutonic successes in Russia. This was brought in by a Canadian patrol, the men of the 14th replying by various hastily constructed signs, broadly humorous and generally satiric in nature.

Following relief by the 13th Battalion, the 14th Battalion occupied reserve positions in Ploegsteert Wood, furnishing working parties of 150 men to the Engineers each day and night, and moving forward into Trenches 135-137 again on the night of August 29th. During the five-day tour that followed rain called forth many repairing parties, No. 1 Coy. also working on the deepening of Currie Avenue communication trench. Night patrols were frequent and listening posts were established to check the enemy's movements. On the 31st of the month Ration Farm and Battalion Headquarters at La Plus Douce

Farm were shelled, among the casualties being Regimental Sergt.-Major J. M. Stephenson, who a few weeks previously had rejoined the Battalion after recovering from a wound received in the Second Battle of Ypres. Following Stephenson's evacuation, Sergt. W. A. Bonshor became Regimental Sergt.-Major.

On the night of September 3rd the 13th Battalion took over Trenches 135-137, the Royal Montreal Regiment moving back to spend five days in Divisional Reserve at Kortepyp Huts. Here a draft of 250 men strengthened the Battalion, which, on the 7th, was inspected by Gen. Plumer, who was accompanied by Lieut.-Gen. Alderson and Brig.-Gen. R. G. E. Leckie, G.O.C. the 3rd Canadian Brigade. Previous to this inspection improved tube gas helmets had been issued. These, the men professed, were issued to afford protection during the concluding remarks which Gen. Plumer would deliver. "Gas", however, could not be detected in the soldierly speech with which the General brought his inspection to a close.

From September 8th to 13th the Battalion occupied Trenches 135-137, working and repair parties keeping the men extremely busy. On relief, the unit moved to Brigade Reserve positions at Courte Dreve Farm, a fine old place, surrounded by a moat, in which swam scores of gold and silver fish. These fed, so far as could be judged, on a green water-cress, which, at a distance, gave the moat the appearance of being coated with unattractive scum. In a chapel attached to the farm-house Canon Scott on one occasion held an early morning celebration of Holy Communion for the men. On hearing of this at breakfast, Lieut.-Col. Burland expressed regret that he and Lieut.-Col. Fisher had not been invited to attend. Canon Scott listened gravely, smiled, and quietly remarked, "I'm sorry. I shall hold a special service for you at five to-morrow morning". And he did. After three days in the shell-battered neighbourhood of Courte Dreve Farm, the 14th Battalion was relieved by King Edward's Horse and moved to Kortepyp Huts and Westhof Farm, remaining there until 6.30 o'clock on the morning of September 21st, when it marched to Locre.

Three days were spent at Locre, these being marked by the arrival of the 24th Battalion (Victoria Rifles of Canada) of the 2nd Canadian Division. With the arrival of General R. E. W. Turner's 2nd Division in France there came into existence that formation since famed as the "Canadian Corps". Lieut.-Gen. E. A. H. Alderson was promoted from command of the 1st Canadian Division to command the new

Army Corps, and was succeeded in his former post by Major-Gen. A. W. Currie, C.B., who had won advancement by skilful leadership of the 2nd Canadian Infantry Brigade. Following the arrival of the 24th Battalion at Locre, the 14th Battalion moved forward on September 24th and relieved the 13th Battalion in the front line (Lindenhoek Area), Headquarters being established at Tea Farm. Immediately on taking over the trenches the men of the 14th were ordered to carry kerosene-soaked bags of straw into the front line. A smoke and artillery demonstration on a wide front had been planned for the morning of September 25th, but, on the 3rd Brigade front, the wind was unfavourable and the demonstration cancelled. Elsewhere it took place, the men of the 14th, from high ground, enjoying the impressive sight as several miles of smoke cloud rolled forward from trenches to the south. The demonstration on the whole front coincided with the opening of the Battle of Loos. This engagement continued until October 8th, rendering support to General Foch's attack against Vimy and to the greater offensive which General Joffre was conducting in Champagne, but failing to achieve the measure of success at first expected. During the course of the engagement, however, the British captured approximately 3,000 prisoners and 26 field guns.

On the night of September 25th the 29th Canadian Battalion relieved the 14th, relief being completed at 3.10 a.m. and the Royal Montrealers reaching billets at Kortepyp Huts and Westhof Farm some two hours later. After resting all day, the men of the 14th paraded at 6.45 p.m. and moved forward once more into the front line, taking over Trenches 113-120 from a battalion of the Berkshire Regiment and establishing H.Q. at Rifle House. Seven days were spent in this position, during which instruction in trench warfare was given to platoons of the 11th Battalion, Cheshire Regiment, and to the 4th Canadian Mounted Rifles. On September 30th commissions were granted to Sergts. H. G. Brewer and R. C. MacKenzie, these dating as from September 23rd. At 9 o'clock on the night of October 3rd the 11th Battalion, Cheshire Regiment, took over the front, the Royal Montreal Regiment proceeding to Aldershot Camp and moving thence on the following afternoon to Brigade Reserve billets at Courte Dreve.

During the remainder of October the 14th Battalion alternated with the 13th Battalion in reserve billets and the front line. When in reserve the Battalion occupied Courte Dreve Farm, or Kortepyp Huts; when in the line it held Trenches 135, 136, 137, and usually 138. Battalion Headquarters, during the trench tours, was located at Plus Douce Farm, which, incidentally, bore on its walls sketches by a previous occupant, Lieut. Bruce Bairnsfather, whose "Fragments from France" were outstanding amongst British cartoons of the war. On October 13th the Canadian Divisional Artillery opened fire on the enemy trenches and shortly thereafter the infantry simulated a gas attack, smoke bombs, made by the men of the 14th Battalion Grenade Section, under Capt. G. L. Dobbin, proving most useful. During a later tour in Trenches 135-138, the 14th Battalion took into the line for instruction four platoons of the 42nd Battalion, Royal Highlanders of Canada. This Montreal battalion, which eventually became part of the 7th Brigade, 3rd Canadian Division, had recently arrived in France and, together with the Royal Canadian Regiment, the Princess Patricia's Canadian Light Infantry, and the 49th Edmonton Battalion, was serving as Corps Troops. On October 17th, following an inspection by Brig.-Gen. Leckie, the Royal Montreal Regiment carried out for the 42nd a demonstration of battalion in attack.

On October 26th a German plane fell in the 14th Battalion lines and a group of Royal Montrealers found that the pilot had been killed and his observer severely wounded. On closer inspection the Canadians discovered that the plane carried Colt Machine Gun No. 1449, a weapon which the 14th Battalion had brought over from Canada and which had been lost during the Second Battle of Ypres. Now, after six months in enemy hands, the gun dropped from the clouds into the trenches of its original owners, who welcomed it and fought to retain it against the unromantic red tape which ordered it into stores. To the men of the Machine Gun Section "1449" was a comrade escaped from captivity, and the idea of yielding the gun to stores none would contemplate. All instructions from distant powers were accordingly "misunderstood", and the gun remains in the Regiment's possession to this day.

On October 28th Lieut.-Col. W. W. Burland, D.S.O., left the Royal Montreal Regiment to become Commandant of the Canadian Military School at Shorncliffe. At a later date he received a Staff appointment with the Imperial Army and returned to France. Lieut.-Col. Burland had commanded the 14th Battalion for nearly five months, had previously served as Second-in-Command, and had received the D.S.O. following the Second Battle of Ypres. He had commanded the attacking waves at Festubert and had at all times worked unsparingly. All ranks, therefore, bade him farewell with regret and appreciation of his services. With him he took to England Capt. A. P. Holt, the Adjutant, who had served the Battalion from the time of its organization and became Staff Adjutant of the School at Shorncliffe. On

Lieut.-Col. Burland's departure, Lieut.-Col. F. W. Fisher assumed command of the Regiment and Capt. E. A. Whitehead, who had recovered from the wound received during the Second Battle of Ypres, succeeded Capt. Holt as Adjutant.

In many ways the work of the Battalion in November, 1915, duplicated the work accomplished during October. Four trench tours, totalling 16 days, took place, the Battalion in each case relieving, and being relieved by, the 13th Battalion. Trenches 135-138 were occupied during three of these tours, but for the fourth three companies moved into the front line and took over Trenches 136-141. When out of the line the Battalion occupied billets in Kortepyp Huts, Courte Dreve Farm, or Red Lodge.

On November 9th the Royal Montreal Regiment moved up for a tour in the line. Rain had fallen continuously for some days and more fell during the tour, with the result that the River Douve overflowed its banks and flooded the adjoining system of trenches. Battalion Headquarters at Plus Douce Farm was inundated at 5 o'clock on the morning of November 13th and was moved to Brigade Battle Headquarters behind Hill 63. Writing of the flood during this tour in the line, an officer of the Battalion states: "Practically continuous rain for the past ten days has converted our front into a labyrinth of canals. This morning the waters of the River Douve rose to such a height that No. 4 Coy., in support, was compelled to evacuate its position and retire behind No. 2 Coy. in reserve. The water rose so rapidly during the night that many of the men had to run for it, leaving all equipment, even their rifles, behind. An officer's servant, sleeping on a table in the Mess, wakened to find chairs and benches floating around him in two feet of water. At Battalion Headquarters matters were even worse. Col. Fisher ordered a ditch dug to protect the officers' dugouts. This was a success insofar as it temporarily diverted the water from 14th Battalion H.Q., but, unfortunately, 15th Battalion H.Q., situated on lower ground, got the full benefit. The rain continued and the protective ditch failed. H.Q. was flooded and officers' equipment reposed under four feet of icy water. The Colonel escaped with one top boot and they are still grappling for the other. Quartermaster-Sergeant F. Lukeman rescued the papers and records from the Orderly Room dugout by getting in through the roof. A Signaller, asleep in an upper berth in a dugout, awoke to find the place aflood and the low entrance blocked by four feet of dirty water. He dived and swam for it, without awaiting developments. In the front line mud and water are knee deep; in communication trenches the water in places reaches one's waist. Sleep is impossible, as every man is working day and night on parapets. All reliefs must now pass overland to the front line. In spite of these handicaps, however, the men are well fed and most of the time they are too busy to worry about the hardships ".

In addition to floods, this particular tour in the line was marked by the accidental wounding of Regimental Sergeant-Major W. A. Bonshor, who was struck in the leg when a nose cap, brought from the front line by Capt. DesRosiers, was exploded at Battalion Headquarters by rifle fire. Another incident was the arrival from England of Capt. T. R. MacKenzie. Later in the month Sergt. J. K. Nesbitt was awarded a commission and appointed to No. 1 Coy., and Capt. J. P. Killoran joined as Roman Catholic Chaplain. On the 26th of the month five corporals were wounded during a bombardment, which, possibly, was a part of enemy retaliation for the daring of the 5th and 7th Canadian Battalions, who ten days previously had carried out a raid on the enemy lines, capturing prisoners, killing many Germans, and destroying much material. Later in the war such operations were not uncommon. At this time a raid represented a new form of hostilities, or rather a form elaborated and improved since first used by Indian troops on the la Bassée front in the autumn of the previous year.

Including the losses caused by the enemy shelling on November 26th, the casualties of the 14th Battalion up to this time totalled 22 officers and 614 men. Four officers and 84 other ranks had fallen in action; 39 other ranks had died of wounds; 3 other ranks had died of illness; 16 officers and 402 other ranks had been wounded; 53 other ranks had been taken prisoners of war; and 2 officers and 33 other ranks were listed on the Battalion rolls as "missing". In the 1st Canadian Division the grand total of all casualties at this same date amounted to 11,915; the 2nd Canadian Division had not yet gone through a heavy engagement, but, from trench warfare alone, had suffered a loss of approximately 1,100 men.

Throughout December the 14th Battalion continued to alternate with the 13th Battalion in billets and the front line. At noon on December 19th Sir Douglas Haig took command of the British Armies in France, vice Sir John French, who was recalled for duty in the British Isles. Changes in the higher command mean little in the life of a battalion, the men being more immediately concerned with changes and promotions nearer at hand. On December 21st Lieut. W. E. Beaton arrived from England and was posted to No. 1 Coy., and a little later Lieut. Dick Worrall was appointed Battalion Scout Officer and placed in command of all patrols. Previously patrols had been under the direction of the different companies. Immediately on taking over his new duties Lieut. Worrall started to establish Canadian superiority in No Man's Land. A sharp encounter between patrols occurred on the night of December 22nd, the patrol of the Royal Montreal Regiment suffering several casualties, one of whom Worrall carried in on his back. Later in the night an enemy patrol wiped out a Royal Montreal listening post where two men were stationed. This did not make an auspicious beginning, but Worrall was not discouraged, his patrols thereafter proceeding nightly into No Man's Land and gradually establishing overwhelming superiority. When the 14th Battalion was out of the line, patrols of the 13th Battalion carried on, the two battalions eventually coming to regard No Man's Land as their's from dark till dawn. The enemy finally accepted this state of affairs and sent out patrols at increasingly infrequent intervals.

On December 24th a sergeant of No. 4 Coy., apparently demented, walked over to the German line in broad daylight and was taken prisoner. That night the 14th Battalion was relieved by the 13th Highlanders, Canon Scott taking up a position to wish the incoming and outgoing men a " Merry Christmas "! Unfortunately, the spot chosen by the good padre was beside a slippery plank bridge, off which, in the pitch darkness, many of the troops tumbled into a foot or more of icy mud and water. Cursing and sputtering, the men crawled out of the ditch, the padre seizing them by the hand and wishing them the merriest of merry Christmases. It is not to be supposed that the humour of this situation was lost on the Canon, the men maintaining that his eye gleamed with laughter even in the dark. Certainly his cheery greeting under such circumstances appealed to the men who proceeded forward, or back, chuckling amusedly.

Reaching Kortepyp Huts late on the night of December 24th, the men of the 14th turned in for a few hours' sleep and then gave themselves over to celebration of the Christmas holiday. Routine training was resumed on the morning of the 26th and on the night of the 29th the unit moved into the front line once more. Some days later Trenches 139-141 were heavily shelled, Sergeants Neilson and Cowan and ten men being wounded and two men killed. That same night Sergt. W. C. Blackett of the recently formed Scout Section was accidentally killed while on patrol. A further loss to the Battalion at this time was caused by departure of Capt. F. A. C. Scrimger, V.C., to join the staff of No. 1 Canadian General Hospital. Capt. Scrimger's work as M.O. of the Regiment had been of the finest character and all ranks, appreciating what he had accomplished, joined in wishing him well.

II

January 1st, 1916, found the 14th Battalion, Royal Montreal Regiment, holding Trenches 136-141, with Headquarters at Fisher's Place. Four day tours in the line and in reserve continued throughout the month, each tour resembling closely the one which preceded it and the one which followed, and each adding a few names to the ever growing list of killed, wounded, or missing. On January 4th Lieut. J. F. Adams left the Regiment to take up an appointment in England, Lieut. J. H. Richardson following on the 12th of the month to take over duty in Canada. On January 31st the Regiment paraded at Kortepyp Huts, marching thence at 11 a.m. and reaching a point near Meteren at 4 o'clock in the afternoon. Here the men took over billets, the Battalion acting as Corps Reserve until the afternoon of February 20th.

On February 10th the 3rd Canadian Infantry Brigade was reviewed by Earl Kitchener. Some idea of the further activities of the Battalion while in Corps Reserve may be gained from the Battalion Diary. Amongst other items, this document mentions, physical drills, hut inspections, company drills, lectures to N.C.O's., platoon drills, bathing parades, baseball and football games, church parades, squad drills, musketry, signalling practice, grenade attack practice, smoke helmet drill, repairing and improving trench practice, lecture on " bombs in trenches ", lecture on " buzzer signalling ", lecture on " catapults and spring guns ", practice of battalion in attack, typhoid inoculations, and bomb throwing contests. While these varied events were taking place, the Battalion, technically speaking, was " resting ".

On February 20th the rest period came to an end, the Battalion marching to Red Lodge in the afternoon and relieving the 5th Canadian Mounted Rifles, of the 3rd Division, in Brigade Reserve. From Red Lodge the Royal Montrealers moved forward on the following afternoon, taking over Trenches 136-141 from the 4th Canadian Mounted Rifles. Relief was completed at 8 p.m. and the 14th Battalion carried out a six-day tour in the line, handing over to the 13th Battalion at 8.05 p.m. on February 27th. During the tour in the line, the Battalion Scouts, under Lieut. Dick Worrall, set about re-establishing Canadian domination of No Man's Land. Faced by experienced Prussian troops, the men of the newly arrived 3rd Canadian Division had been unable to maintain the measure of superiority which veterans of the 1st Division regarded as essential. A strong enemy patrol was encountered by Worrall's party soon after darkness had fallen on the night of February 21st. This German patrol was driven back, the men of the 14th pressing a vicious bombing attack which gave the enemy no rest until he retired behind the shelter of his own wire. Thereafter the Royal Montrealers maintained their supremacy. On several occasions the enemy made a fight of it, but before the tour ended he bowed to the inevitable and patrols of the Canadians waited for him in vain in the very shadow of his own wire.

Following relief by the 13th Battalion, the Royal Montreal Regiment spent February 28th and 29th at Red Lodge, whence working parties, 465 strong, were furnished to construct defences under supervision of the Engineers. From the 1st to the 25th of March the Battalion continued to move in and out of the trenches on the Messines front, furnishing large working parties to the Engineers at frequent intervals and, when in the line, instructing platoons from the 58th Canadian Battalion and the 1st Canadian Pioneer Battalion. On March 18th Lieut.-Col. F. W. Fisher left the Battalion to take over duties in England. Lieut.-Col. Fisher had commanded the Regiment for nearly five months, a period when no battle honours were gained, but during which the Battalion accomplished work calling for courage, endurance, and marked determination. No man of the 14th Battalion who went through the winter of 1915-16 on the Messines front will forget Trenches 135-141, the misery of life when the Douve overflowed its banks, the cruel monotony of sodden clothes, the exhausting toil of carrying heavy material through thigh-deep mud, the tragedies when sudden shelling blasted the flooded trenches, or the Colonel who shared in all the hardships and gave his best in the interests of those under his command.

CHAPTER VII

BACK TO THE SALIENT

Saint George he was a fighting man, as all the tales do tell;
He fought a battle long ago, and fought it wondrous well.
With his helmet, and his hauberk, and his good cross-hilted sword,
Oh, he rode a-slaying dragons to the glory of the Lord.

Saint George he was a fighting man, he's here and fighting still
While any wrong is yet to right or Dragon yet to kill,
And faith! he's finding work this day to suit his war-worn sword,
For he's strafing Huns in Flanders to the glory of the Lord.
—C. Fox Smith.

I

WHEN Lieut.-Col. F. W. Fisher returned to England on March 18, 1916, command of the 14th Battalion, Royal Montreal Regiment, was assumed by Major R. P. Clark, M.C., who shortly afterwards was promoted to the rank of lieutenant-colonel. Major Clark had crossed from Canada with the 1st Canadian Contingent, proceeded to France on the Staff of the 2nd Canadian Infantry Brigade, and subsequently served as Staff Captain at Canadian Corps Headquarters. There his work had won the Military Cross, and his personality, ability, and devotion to duty had marked him for promotion to command of a battalion. Accordingly, he accepted command of the Royal Montreal Regiment, just when that unit was completing its long period of service on the front opposite Messines and preparing to move northward into the Ypres Salient. On March 17th the first units of the Canadian Corps moved out, others following daily and marching to replace units of the British V. Corps, holding the Salient's southern curve. On April 4th Lieut.-Gen. E. A. H. Alderson, Canadian Corps Commander, took over the new area, the last Canadian unit moving into place four days later.

Before the move of the Corps was completed, the 2nd Canadian Division became involved in bitter fighting, of the type which sooner or later fell to the lot of any unit working in the bloody arc surrounding Ypres. For a month the battle swayed in and out of a series of mine craters near St. Eloi, testing the courage, fibre, and endurance of the 2nd Division, as the 1st Division had been tested, on ground a few miles away, in April of the previous year. And the test showed that the metal was the same, for the 2nd Division, though forced out of the craters which were the focus of the battle, fought until these positions were smashed beyond all recognition.

While the 2nd Division was fighting at St. Eloi, the 1st Division was moving northward from Messines. On March 25th the 14th Battalion marched from Red Lodge to Rest Area No. 2, near Bailleul, proceeding thence at 9.30 a.m. on March 28th and reaching Canada Huts, near Ouderdom, five hours later. On the occasion of this march the 3rd Brigade was under the command of Brig.-Gen. G. S. Tuxford, C.M.G., formerly Commanding Officer of the 5th Canadian Battalion, who had succeeded Brig.-Gen. R. G. E. Leckie, C.M.G., when the latter was wounded on February 17th. During the march the Brigade passed some Northumberland Fusiliers, coming out of the line after a successful local attack at the Bluff-International Trench position on the Ypres-Comines Canal. The Northumberlands, young lads for the most part, were in high spirits and seemed to feel that the coming "season" in the Salient would witness many satisfactory changes.

At 9.15 o'clock on the night of March 29th, the 14th Battalion relieved the 7th Battalion, Northumberland Fusiliers, in Brigade Reserve positions at Swan Chateau, Woodcote House, Sunken Road, Blauwe Poort Farm, Café Belge, and Canal Dugouts. These locations, familiar to all troops visiting the southern curve of the Salient, are famous in song and story, but Swan Chateau is probably the most famous of all. The inhabitants of the Chateau had been driven away by the approach of war, and the house had suffered appreciably from German shells; but in its battered moat there still floated a white swan, sole survivor of a flock whose dignified movements had delighted visitors in the far-off days "avant la guerre". This bird had suffered from the war and one eye had been torn out by shrapnel. Like the Chateau, however, the bird awaited with apparent fortitude the day when the Hun should tread the soil of France no more, accepting in the meantime such courtesy and attention as the khaki-clad allies of France cared to offer. At first the bird presented difficulties to the kind-hearted British Army, but long before the 14th Battalion arrived on the scene some genial adjutant had solved the problem by listing the swan as "trench stores". Each incoming unit signed a receipt for the "trench stores" in question and drew rations for the swan until relieved. Probably this swan is the only one which has appeared on the ration strength of the British Army.

Five days were spent by the Battalion in Brigade Reserve, several working parties being furnished to the Engineers and the whole time marked by that artillery and aerial activity conspicuously absent at Messines. This activity, coupled with the fact that the Divisional front extended from the Ypres-Comines Canal on the right to Mount

Sorrel on the left and included such famous positions as The Bluff, International Trench, and Hill 60, indicated to the men that mud, though objectionable, was no longer their principal foe. Accordingly, they prepared for whatever hard knocks the Salient might have in store.

On April 3rd the 14th Battalion moved forward at night to relieve the 13th Battalion in front line trenches opposite Hill 60. Battalion H. Q. was established behind a pile of earth, known officially as "Hill 59", but more familiar under its trench designation of "The Dump". Two other ranks were wounded during the relief which was completed at 10.20 p.m.

In the front line the Battalion spent five days, which were by no means uneventful. German aeroplanes dominated the Salient at this time and the enemy infantry commanded a view of the whole Canadian line, these circumstances assisting the enemy artillery and encouraging his snipers in the never-ending fight for local supremacy. Shelling of Battalion Headquarters occurred on April 4th, and on the 5th the enemy pounded the whole front with rifle grenades. Heavy shelling also took place, 4 men of the Battalion being killed and 9 wounded. Sharp reply to these demonstrations was made by the Royal Montreal Rifle Grenade Section on April 6th, the Trench Mortar Battery assisting by shelling heavily. Enemy snipers became active during the day and Lieut. F. R. Heuston, an original officer of the Battalion, was shot through the head and killed. Capt. T. R. MacKenzie, who had joined the unit in the previous November, was also shot through the head, being saved from death by his steel helmet. These had been issued a few days previously, experience having shown that thin steel would deflect shrapnel and was, consequently, more suitable than a cloth cap for trench headgear.

Two days after the death of Lieut. Heuston and the wounding of Capt. MacKenzie, Battalion Headquarters and the dugout sheltering the Officers' Mess, together with all the Battalion's records and documents, were destroyed by shell fire. One shell hit the telephone in the Orderly Room less than a minute after the Acting Adjutant, Capt. C. B. Price, D.C.M., had moved away. Shelling of the whole area continued into the night and relief by the 10th Canadian Battalion, which was to have taken place at 8 p.m., was delayed until 3 o'clock on the morning of April 9th. On relief, the 14th Battalion, which had suffered casualties totalling 7 killed and 43 wounded, withdrew to Canada Huts in Divisional Reserve.

At Canada Huts, and later, following a move to Dickebusch Huts on April 15th, the Battalion carried out a syllabus of training. A general impression of what such training involved can be gained from the programme of a day selected at random. On a certain day, then, No. 1 Coy. held the usual daily rifle and ammunition inspection, and practised musketry, and the N.C.O's. attended a lecture on the "Details of Discipline"; No. 2 Coy. held rifle, ammunition, and gas helmet inspections, practised musketry, and carried out squad and platoon drills; No. 3 Coy. held the usual inspections, practised "shell alarm", and paraded to Poperinghe for baths; No. 4 Coy., in addition to routine inspections and physical drill, practised on the rifle ranges; and the Machine Gun Battery, the Snipers, the Scouts, the Bombers, and the Signallers all practised their respective specialties. Officers took part in all training during the period and carried out the following special syllabus of their own:

April 10.—Lecture by Brigade Grenade Officer.
April 16.—Machine Gun demonstration, every officer firing several rounds.
April 17.—Revolver practice. Lecture by Battalion Machine Gun Officer.
April 18.—Course in throwing live grenades and firing rifle grenades.
April 21.—Lecture by A.D.M.S. on sanitation and prevention of disease.
April 22.—Lecture by Battalion Medical Officer on First Aid.

From April 17th to 22nd the Battalion furnished daily working parties, approximately 275 strong, diversion, following the day's work, being provided by passes to Poperinghe, where a soldiers' concert party, known as "The Follies", offered a brilliant programme of fun and laughter. On April 19th Lieuts. C. L. O'Brien, R. A. Pelletier, and C. G. Power moved into the line to assist the 13th Battalion, which had suffered severely at The Bluff and required experienced officers to replace casualties, pending the arrival of reinforcements.

On the night of Easter Sunday, April 23rd, the 14th Battalion relieved the 13th Battalion in The Bluff position to the left of the Ypres-Comines Canal. The Bluff itself, with a mine crater at its nose, was a long mound of earth thrown up on the north side of the Canal, which formed the Battalion's right flank. From the Canal bank a small front line trench (New Year's) ran up onto The Bluff. To the left were "The Loop", "International Trench", "The Pollock", and

"The Bean", in which many brave men had died and which, in places, were almost obliterated by frequent bombardment. In these trenches the 13th Battalion had suffered 173 casualties in eight days. Truly the Salient differed from Messines.

On April 24th, the first day in The Bluff positions, the 14th Battalion experienced comparative quiet, but on the 25th enemy snipers became active and Lieut. J. Howe and 2 other ranks were killed. On the following day an enemy mine was exploded some distance to the left, this starting a sharp duel between the opposing artilleries. April 27th, according to the Battalion Diary, was a "quiet" day, but even a quiet day in the Salient saw some names added to the list of casualties. On this occasion 1 man was killed and 12 wounded, and on the following day, which was "very quiet", 6 men were wounded. Six more were wounded on April 29th and on the 30th Lieut. G. K. Ross was killed by a rifle grenade. Altogether the casualties of the Battalion during the tour totalled 9 killed and 37 wounded.

Handing over the line to the 7th Canadian Battalion on the night of May 1st, the Royal Montreal Regiment moved for eight days into Divisional Reserve, two days being spent at the Hop Factory, south of Poperinghe Station, and six in the Rue de Boeschepe. Muster and bathing parades were held on the 4th of the month and on the same date a party of 6 officers and 500 other ranks moved forward to work with the Engineers. Major-Gen. A. W. Currie inspected the unit on the following day and a Battalion church parade was held on May 8th, this being followed by Battalion sports, which were witnessed by Lieut.-Gen. Sir E. A. H. Alderson, K.C.B., the Corps Commander. On the same date a draft of 80 reinforcements was received and Capt. F. W. Utton, previously with the 15th Battalion, became 14th Battalion Adjutant, succeeding Capt. E. A. Whitehead, who became Signalling Officer.

A feature of the time in Divisional Reserve occurred at evening in Poperinghe when the massed fife and drum bands of the resting brigade, Guards Division, beat "Retreat" in the town square. The medieval buildings of the square provided a romantic setting for this ceremony, which called to the minds of many present those British Armies of bygone days which had won undying fame on the historic fields of Flanders. Those men were born and bred within the confines of the British Isles. Now British fighting men from all corners of the earth stood in the old square and stiffened to salute as bands played that air which has become the anthem of an Empire.

"God save our gracious King,
Long live our noble King,
God save the King".

At night on May 9th the Royal Montreal Regiment left Divisional Reserve and moved forward to spend eight days in Brigade Support, with Battalion Headquarters at Swan Chateau. Each day a working party of approximately 5 officers and 400 other ranks was furnished to the Engineers, these parties suffering losses of 3 killed and several wounded. On the 14th of the month a draft of 89 other ranks was received; and on the 17th the Battalion relieved the 13th Battalion in Trenches 46-51, situated on the left of the 1st Divisional front on Mount Sorrel.

In Trenches 46-51 the Battalion spent eight days, uneventful for the most part, but marked by those spasms of rifle, machine gun, trench mortar, and artillery fire which always featured a tour in the Salient. Working parties of several hundred men were furnished each night during the tour; and casualties totalled 36, 6 other ranks being killed and 30 wounded. On May 23rd a small reinforcing draft was taken on strength; and on the night of the 25th the Battalion was relieved by the 7th Canadian Battalion. On the afternoon preceding relief Battalion Headquarters was shelled with 5.9-inch high explosive, the Medical Officer's dugout and dressing station being blown in and some supplies destroyed. Fortunately, there were no casualties. On relief the Battalion moved to Divisional Reserve in Dominion Lines, Lieut. C. G. Power, the Battalion Scout Officer, and a small squad of men being left behind to assist the 7th Battalion in a raid against some new German trenches. This raid was duly attempted, but the night selected was not dark, too many men, perhaps, were employed, and the Germans opened such heavy fire that success was out of the question. Accordingly, the raiders were recalled to the shelter of their own line. The new German trenches which the raid failed to penetrate were built, as is now clear, in preparation for the enemy attack launched some three weeks later. During the tour of the 14th Battalion in the front line they had been inspected by several Regimental patrols, Patrol Sergeant T. Hodgson on one occasion bringing back to the Canadian line a specimen of new type bath-mat flooring which a perspiring Hun had just placed in position. A mental picture of the German's indignation when he staggered forward with a second section of bath-mat and missed the first caused no little delight in the Royal Montrealers' trenches.

Meanwhile, at Dominion Lines, the 14th Battalion trained and furnished the working parties always expected from a unit in Divisional Reserve, the officers, when off duty, playing badminton, a game to which they were introduced through the enterprise of the Paymaster, Capt. F. B. D. Larken. Enterprise on the part of the Battalion Machine Gun Officer resulted in a kite, towed by a farmer's cart, being used to train the machine gunners in anti-aircraft fire. Just as this practice was proving a success and as the inventor visualized his probable reward, " cease fire " was sounded on order of the Brigade Commander, who objected to bullets from the practice raining down in his garden.

On the 28th of the month it was announced that Lieut.-Gen. Sir E. A. H. Alderson, K.C.B., had handed over command of the Canadian Corps to Lieut.-Gen. the Hon. Sir Julian Byng, K.C.B., M.V.O., a British officer of the 10th Royal Hussars, who had won distinction and promotion in the Sudan and South Africa and had added to an already enviable reputation while commanding the 3rd Cavalry Division of the " Old Contemptibles ". Subsequently Sir Julian Byng had served in Gallipoli, his experience and success warranting his promotion to command an Army Corps and assuring the men of the Corps selected that they would be led by a trained, energetic, and capable soldier. Five days after Sir Julian assumed command of the Canadian Corps its capabilities were tested to the utmost, the result being written on a splendid page of Canadian military history. The part taken by the 14th Battalion in writing that page is set down in the chapter which follows.

CHAPTER VIII

JUNE, 1916

> Before our eyes a boundless wall of red
>   Shot through by sudden streaks of jagged pain!
> Then a slow-gathering darkness overhead
>   And rest came on us like a quiet rain.
>
> —John McCrae.

I

WHEN the Canadian Corps moved northward in the spring of 1916, the 2nd Division, as has been mentioned, engaged almost at once in severe fighting near St. Eloi, and the 1st Division, following on the 2nd Division's heels, also endured sharp bombardments and attacks soon after reaching the Salient. Violent as some of the bombardments in the spring were, they fade to insignificance when compared with the tornado of high explosive which at 8 o'clock on the morning of June 2nd struck the lines of the 3rd Division, running from Bellewaarde Beek through Sanctuary Wood to Hill 62, Hill 61, Armagh Wood, and Mount Sorrel. Under a concentration of shell fire such as no British troops had previously seen, the front line of the 3rd Division was blown out of existence, Major-Gen. Mercer, commanding the Division, being killed and Brig.-Gen. Victor Williams, of the 8th Brigade, wounded and taken prisoner. The 4th Canadian Mounted Rifles, who held the line in front of Armagh Wood, suffered 626 casualties, and were practically annihilated; to the left the 1st Canadian Mounted Rifles lost their Commanding Officer, Lieut.-Col. A. E. Shaw, and suffered a casualty list of 367; still further to the left the Princess Patricia's Canadian Light Infantry lost 17 officers out of 22, Lieut.-Col. C. H. Buller being among the killed. Lieut.-Col. G. H. Baker, a member of the Canadian Parliament and Commanding Officer of the 5th Canadian Mounted Rifles, was also killed, and the 42nd Battalion, Royal Highlanders of Canada, the 49th Battalion, Edmonton, the 2nd Canadian Mounted Rifles, the Royal Canadian Regiment (Permanent Force), and numerous other units lost heavily in the opening bombardment or in the fighting which took place soon thereafter.

For five hours and forty-five minutes the Germans poured high explosives on the Canadian front line and support. Then, at 1.45 p.m., their infantry advanced to the assault, meeting little opposition

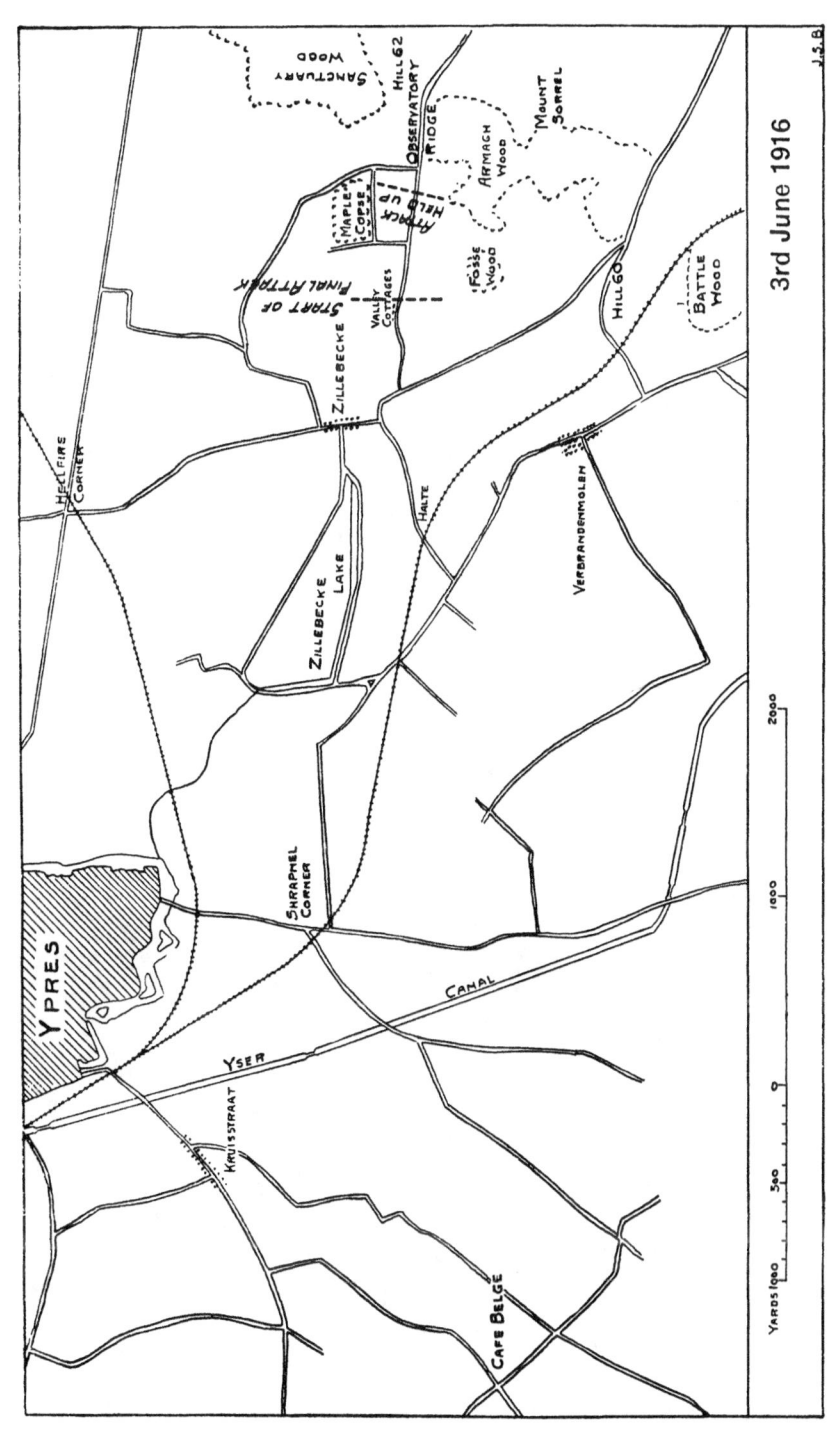

in the ruined and devastated front line, but suffering a sharp check on penetrating to the support line in Sanctuary Wood, Armagh Wood, and Mount Sorrel. In the support line the fighting was bitter. Encouraged by the ease with which they had overcome the dazed and shell-shocked remnants of the front line companies, the Germans pressed eagerly forward, sweeping small Canadian parties out of their way and hurling their strength against the secondary defences, determined at all costs to clear the road to Ypres. But, as in 1915, the troops standing before Ypres had no intention of permitting a Teutonic triumph. Outnumbered, dazed by shell fire, and at a disadvantage in every way, the supporting companies and battalions fought desperately and devotedly to prevent the enemy from penetrating the reserve system and turning the flanks. That they alone stood between the Germans and Ypres inspired the broken units with courage beyond that of despair. In the hand to hand fighting officers used rifles, bayonets, or bombs and set a splendid example to the small groups of ever-willing men. Conversely, when officers fell, the men fought on under an N.C.O., or even a private, regardless of the fact that death, wounds, or capture seemed their only possible reward.

Late in the afternoon, when Major-General Mercer's death was established, Major-General Hoare-Nairn, G.O.C.R.A. the Lahore Division, whose guns were covering the broken front, assumed command of the 3rd Canadian Division. At this time the situation, though somewhat improved by stubborn resistance in the support lines and by local counter-attacks, was critical in the extreme. Another German attack, it seemed, could not fail to smash through the weakened defences, barring the way to Ypres. To prevent such a happening, which would have involved Imperial divisions on the flanks in disaster, a counter-attack was essential, and time was a factor of importance. Accordingly, peremptory orders were issued summoning from reserve such troops as could be rushed to the point of danger.

II

When the German attack smashed through the lines of the 3rd Canadian Division early on the afternoon of June 2nd, 1916, the 14th Battalion, Royal Montreal Regiment, lay in rest at Dominion Lines, near Poperinghe, under Major Gault McCombe, who was commanding during the temporary absence of Lieut.-Col. R. P. Clark. Early in the day news of the intense bombardment was received, and several officers walked to high ground whence, far away in the Salient, a great cloud of dust and smoke indicated the scene of action. Soon after this party returned, the Battalion was ordered to " stand to ". Later orders to move forward were received and at 7.30 p.m. the march began.

Under command of Lieut. C. G. Power, Battalion Scouts and Intelligence men guided the companies and details to a rendezvous not far from Café Belge Corner. Speed was essential and the men marched steadily throughout the night, omitting the customary halts, but losing time none the less owing to congestion of traffic on the roads. Not far from the appointed rendezvous the Battalion was met by Staff Captain H. M. Urquhart, of the 3rd Brigade, and ordered to take up a position in battle formation with its left flank resting on Zillebeke Lake and the right flank on a point near Zillebeke Halte. Major McCombe was instructed to report to Brigade Headquarters in Railway Dugouts for further orders.

In obedience to instructions, the companies and details of the 14th Battalion moved independently across country to the locations assigned them. Different routes were chosen to avoid congestion and shell fire, No. 1 Coy., under Capt. R. W. Frost, reaching its destination about 1 o'clock on the morning of June 3rd and Nos. 2, 3, and 4 Companies, commanded respectively by Lieut. Dick Worrall, Capt. C. B. Price, D.C.M., and Lieut. W. E. Beaton, arriving in position not long after. Meanwhile the Machine Gun Section, commanded by Lieut. J. K. Nesbitt, had come forward from Café Belge independently. At Zillebeke Halte, Lieut. Nesbitt left two of his gun crews, under Corp. Fletcher, proceeding with Sergeant Lennan and the remaining four guns past Blauwe Poort Farm, where the dead of two batteries were strewn about, and on to a point where Major McCombe had established temporary Headquarters. From this point Lieut. Nesbitt led his men through Zillebeke Village and on up Observatory Ridge Road, skirting to the right when near Valley Cottages to take advantage of an area which afforded protection from enemy shell fire. Returning to the Road, Nesbitt's section encountered a party of the enemy who retired and touched off an S.O.S. rocket, which brought a withering blast of gun fire. Sergt. Lennan, Corp. Sullivan, and four men were wounded by this fire and all the party badly shaken. Shortly afterwards the 15th and 14th Battalions moved into position on Nesbitt's right, and formed the first line to defend the gap opened by the enemy's success at Mount Sorrel.

Meanwhile, plans for an extensive counter-attack along the whole Canadian front were maturing. On the right the 7th Battalion, with

SCENE OF ROYAL MONTREAL REGIMENT COUNTER ATTACK—3RD JUNE, 1916

Canadian Official Copyright

the 10th in close support, was ordered to retake the ground from Mount Sorrel to Observatory Ridge. In the centre the 15th and 14th Battalions, supported respectively by the 16th and 13th, were instructed to drive a counter-attack against Hill 62. On the left, and not in immediate touch with these attacks, the 49th and 60th Battalions, with the 52nd in close support, were ordered to restore the front from Hill 62 to a point where the Royal Canadian Regiment still held original front line trenches near Hooge.

When these counter-attacks were planned, 2 o'clock on the morning of June 3rd was named as "zero", but this allowed too short a time for the fresh battalions to come from reserve and deploy for action. Had it been possible to clear all roads and had the terrain for deployment been dry, the feat might have been accomplished. As it was, roads were congested with traffic, communication trenches in places were barely passable, and some units had to seek their jumping-off locations across marshy ground waist deep. Accordingly, "zero" was postponed once and again and confusion resulted, the 7th Battalion attacking at 7.37 a.m., the 14th at 8.17 a.m., the 15th at 8.35 a.m., and the 49th and 60th on the left at 7 a.m. By arrangement, the Staff of the 3rd Canadian Division was to fire six green rockets as a signal for the attack to begin. This sign would have been effective at 2 a.m.; at 7.10 a.m., when it was fired, day had broken and the green lights were almost invisible. Even when seen, the signal was recognized with difficulty, as rain had spoiled some rockets, and fourteen were ignited before six could be made to rise into the air. Six rockets at regular intervals constitute a signal; six rising irregularly leave just that element of doubt which in an attack is often the genesis of failure.

When Major McCombe returned from Brigade Headquarters in Railway Dugouts, he brought instructions for the Battalion to advance to a position in front of Zillebeke Village, the right flank of the Battalion to rest upon Observatory Ridge Road and the left flank on Maple Copse. In obedience to these orders the companies of the 14th moved independently forward through Zillebeke Village, with the Battalion Bombers, under Lieut. F. Owen, marching on the left.

Almost at once the advance of the Battalion encountered shell fire. Men began to drop in Zillebeke Village and casualties mounted as this point was passed. In front of the village Capt. R. W. Frost was blown into the air by shell fire, command of No. 1 Coy. passing temporarily to Lieut. W. R. B. Lugar, who showed judgment in reconnoitring his front and spreading his troops to fill a gap which had opened on his flank. Later Capt. Frost, who had resumed command of the company, was again hurled to the ground and partially buried by the burst of a shell, but for the second time he regained his feet and insisted that he was fit to " carry on ". At about 6 a.m. the Battalion reached the position whence it was to " jump off " for the final assault on Hill 62. Shell fire continued while the men dug in, Capt. C. B. Price, D.C.M., suffering his second severe wound of the war and Lieut. W. R. B. Lugar losing a leg through the same shell. Lieut. V. G. Rexford, who had served in the ranks and been granted a commission after recovering from injuries received in the Second Battle of Ypres, was also wounded at this time, as were a number of other ranks.

At 8.17 a.m. orders were received to advance and at once, under immediate command of Major A. T. Powell, the whole Battalion swept forward. Speaking of the advance, an officer of the 3rd Brigade Staff says, " It was one of the finest things I have ever seen. One hears occasionally of troops advancing ' as if on parade '. There was no question of this being a parade. Under the leadership of Major Powell, the old 14th advanced coolly, steadily, and splendidly. The lines were torn and bent by shell, rifle, and machine gun fire, but there was no faltering. When the front line was staggered and withered by fire, there always seemed someone to step into the gaps ".

Truly the gaps were filled; but sooner or later under fire such as the Germans concentrated on the advancing lines an attack must vanish into thin air, or dig in. Reluctantly, having lost two-thirds of his strength, Major Powell realized that such a moment had come. His men had marched all night, had deployed over unfavourable ground, had advanced under shell fire severe enough to shake the strongest morale, had dug in unshaken, and had then advanced for three hundred yards in broad daylight, under fire which had torn their lines to ribbons. Those who remained were undaunted; but the Battalion's strength had gone. Accordingly, orders were issued for the line to dig in. When this was accomplished the Regiment, under severe fire of all descriptions, held the front until relieved on the following morning, the firing line being manned by approximately 80 men, who, with the details and small parties operating on the flanks, represented what was left of the Battalion. No one can claim that the attack was an entire success, as it failed to attain its topographical objectives. Inasmuch, however, as it closed a dangerous gap in the secondary system of the Ypres defences and provided jumping-off positions for the great counter-attack of June 13th, it cannot be regarded as a failure.

Elsewhere on the front the result was the same, the assigned objectives proving beyond the power of flesh and blood to attain, but discipline and marked courage carrying the attacking battalions well forward.

For some time during the progress of the attack and while the men were digging in, Major McCombe, who at first established Headquarters in a cellar at Valley Cottages, was unable to keep in touch with his forward companies, but later, when this condition had been corrected, his grasp of the situation proved his ability to command under exceedingly difficult circumstances. A tribute to his work exists in a letter from an officer of the Battalion to a brother officer in hospital. The tribute is short, but complete: " Gault McCombe handled the situation splendidly ".

After the line advanced Capt. Utton and Capt. E. A. Whitehead carried out a reconnaissance and, following their report, Headquarters was moved to a dugout under the crest of Observatory Ridge. Between this dugout and the front line the Signallers, under Sergt. A. Close, established and maintained communication, their work being of the finest character. It is a principle of military operations that routine must continue under the most difficult circumstances, this probably accounting for the fact that on June 3rd a runner, who had made his way through the enemy barrage, arrived grimy and exhausted at 14th Battalion Headquarters with a message from London asking how many members of the Battalion had subscribed for War Loan.

III

The story of the advance and check of the 14th Battalion, Royal Montreal Regiment, has been outlined in the preceding pages, but no account of the unit's work on June 3rd would be complete without mention of the gallantry and splendid behaviour of certain details and isolated parties. On the extreme left of the attack Lieut. W. E. Beaton, commanding No. 4 Company, advanced with 35 men, encountering the enemy far in advance of the front line at a point near Hedge Street. At about 9 a.m. Lieut. Beaton, finding himself cut off from the main body of the Battalion and coming under enfilade fire from a machine gun, halted the eager advance of his little company, faced his men left to meet a threatened flank attack, posted sentries to guard against surprise, and sent out patrols to maintain touch with the enemy. All day, though wounded in the shoulder by a splinter of shell, he remained at duty, encouraging his men and setting a splendid example of levelheadedness and courage. At night the enemy concentrated gun and trench mortar fire on the position, rendering it quite untenable, whereupon Lieut. Beaton, taking advantage of the darkness, disengaged his contact patrols and successfully led the living remnant of his party back to safety in the Battalion lines. During the whole of this little feat of arms, Beaton received much assistance from Sergt. H. Hunt, of No. 2 Coy., who, when all officers of the company had fallen, had led the remaining men forward. Sergt. Hunt, throughout the day, showed great courage in leaving shelter to recover disabled men, or dress their wounds. Unfortunately, before nightfall, he was killed by an enemy trench mortar.

Equally gallant, but less fortunate than Lieut. Beaton, was Lieut. A. F. Major, who with a small party penetrated even further into the German lines. The full story of this little party can never be told, though it is established that its members fell fighting at some point far back of the German front. At another point on the left flank Sergeant B. Topham, of No. 3 Coy., led a party of 14 men and established contact with the enemy at a point near Durham Lane. When his advance was checked, Topham took up a position and for the whole day defied the enemy's efforts to eject him. Casualties he could not avoid; and gradually his little party dwindled. At night, together with some two or three survivors, he retired on the main body of the Battalion.

When the advance from in front of Zillebeke Village began, the Battalion Bombers, under Lieut. F. Owen, moved forward on the left flank. Proceeding up Durham Lane until they encountered a block, the Bombers moved out into the open, crawled from shell hole to shell hole, kept pace with the Battalion, and dug in on the same line. During the advance the detail lost Lieut. Owen, who was wounded by shell fire.

Covering the advance from positions previously taken up, teams of the Machine Gun Section, under Lieut. J. K. Nesbitt, accomplished excellent work. When their covering fire was no longer of value, they advanced with the Battalion, suffering heavy losses. One team, though reduced from 6 men to 2, kept its gun in action until relieved that night. At another spot Private Imray retrieved a gun which had been blown up, carried it forward, found ammunition to feed it, set it up unaided, and kept it in action throughout the day. At the height of the engagement Sergt. Bagnall returned from leave and brought forward the two guns which had been left at Zillebeke Halte the night before. He established a position in Maple Copse and reported to

Lieut. Nesbitt for further orders. While conferring with his officer Bagnall was seriously wounded by the burst of a shell, Lieut. Nesbitt escaping severe injury but being knocked over and dazed by concussion. Recovering, Nesbitt reported to Battalion Headquarters and guided stretcher bearers to Bagnall's assistance. It is worthy of note that these bearers, though in view of the enemy for some time, were quite unmolested.

Amongst the companies and Battalion details every officer who took part in the attack was killed, wounded, or blown up by shell fire. Capt. E. A. Whitehead, who had been wounded at the Second Battle of Ypres and, after rejoining, had for months served as Adjutant, acted as Signalling Officer during the early morning hours and then asked to be sent to the main body of the Battalion. Major McCombe was reluctant; but realizing how valuable Whitehead's presence might prove, he finally gave assent. A few minutes later news reached him that Whitehead had been killed while hurrying forward. Lieut. M. M. Grondin was also killed and Lieut. A. F. Major died after penetrating the German lines, as previously mentioned. Major Powell, though wounded, remained at duty until the new line was established, and then handed over the forward area to Lieut. R. A. Pelletier, who, though twice blown up and once rendered unconscious for a time, commanded until the Battalion was relieved. Lieut. J. E. McKenna was wounded in the hand, but did not leave his post; other casualties not previously mentioned including Lieuts. Dick Worrall, T. A. Evans, R. D. Torrance, R. C. MacKenzie, R. H. Walker, R. G. Marion, and C. L. O'Brien, the first, and the last two, original members of the Regiment who had been commissioned from the ranks.

Amongst the other ranks losses were severe. Company Sergeant-Major R. W. Rankin, of No. 1 Coy., was killed while trying to penetrate the German wire; Coy. Sergt.-Major G. Armstrong, of No. 3 Coy., was also killed during the attack, as was Coy. Sergt.-Major L. Duhamel, of No. 4 Coy. Many other valuable N.C.O's. were killed or wounded before the Battalion was relieved, the day's work costing the Regiment a total of 379 all ranks, killed, wounded and missing.

All during the attack the Battalion Medical Officer, Capt. W. J. McAlister, and the stretcher bearers under his command worked tirelessly to collect and evacuate the stream of wounded, much assistance being rendered by the Battalion Scouts and Intelligence men, under Lieut. C. G. Power, who, having guided the Regiment into the line, were ordered to Valley Farm. There they constructed a Regimental Aid Post. Later they advanced behind the Battalion, gathering valuable information and rescuing numerous wounded. When the aid post at Valley Cottages was rendered untenable by shell fire, they assisted Capt. McAlister in moving to a new post in Railway Dugouts. Throughout the whole engagement Lieut. Power set an example of high courage and displayed initiative in carrying out the varied duties falling to his lot.

IV

Early on the morning of June 4th the Royal Montreal Regiment was relieved from the front line by the 2nd Canadian Battalion and withdrew to Dominion Lines, moving to Patricia Lines on the afternoon of June 5th. While retiring through Zillebeke Village Capt. R. W. Frost, for the third time in 24 hours, was blown to the ground by a shell. Too dazed to walk, he was carried to Railway Dugouts, where he recovered and whence, on the following morning, he hastened to duty with the Battalion. He reported and expected to take over his company without delay, but, in view of the severe battering he had received, the Commanding Officer of the 14th ordered him temporarily to the Canadian rest station at Mont des Cats.

While marching back on the morning of June 4th the Royal Montreal Regiment, on the Ypres-Vlamertinghe Road, reached the transport lines of an Imperial artillery unit, the men of which had just prepared breakfast. With that quick sympathy for those who have been " in it ", the Imperials called to the Royal Montrealers to come and help themselves, thus earning the gratitude of a Canadian Regiment. In the haste incidental to times of war no formal acknowledgment of the courtesy was given, or expected. Eleven years have passed, but the kindness has not been forgotten. Such incidents provide cement with which are bound the enduring walls of Empire.

On arrival at Dominion Lines Capt. F. W. Utton, without delaying for food or sleep, began preparation of those lists which it is the duty of the Adjutant to produce following a great battle. To assist in obtaining accurate information on which to base these, Lieut.-Col. Clark, who had returned from leave, called for volunteers to proceed to the scene of the attack on June 3rd and search the torn ground for wounded. Lieut. Beaton, Lieut. Nesbitt, and 50 other ranks responded to this appeal and moved off after the briefest possible rest. Pushing into all sorts of dangerous corners, this party rescued a number of wounded and buried many dead, among the latter being Corp. Scott, to whom a Military Medal had been awarded on the day of the attack.

Throughout the search for wounded and the recovery of the bodies of the dead, Pioneer Sergt. Brayton accomplished valuable work which won recognition by award of the D.C.M. Unfortunately, 3 other ranks of the party were killed before the search came to an end.

On June 6th Private H. A. Davin was granted a commission and 20 other ranks were taken on strength from England, 150 other ranks following on June 7th, 15 on June 10th, and 308 on June 11th. On the 9th of the month Major-General A. W. Currie, C.B., commanding the 1st Canadian Division, visited the Battalion and addressed the men, a similar visit being paid on June 10th by Brig.-Gen. G. S. Tuxford, C.M.G., commanding the 3rd Brigade. Between the 6th and 12th of the month the Battalion equipped and reorganized and absorbed the men of the new drafts. At 5 p.m. on the 12th the unit moved from Dominion Lines to "D" Camp on the Vlamertinghe-Ouderdom Road, a party, under Capt. F. B. D. Larken, Battalion Paymaster, meeting the Regiment near its destination and directing the companies and details to billets. Hot tea, served on arrival, helped the men to forget the unpleasantness of a march in heavy rain.

At 1.30 a.m. on June 13th, Sir Julian Byng launched the 1st Canadian Division, under Major-General A. W. Currie, against the positions taken up by the Germans after the operations of June 2nd and 3rd. For the occasion the brigades of the Division were reconstructed, Brig.-Gen. Lipsett, on the right, commanding a brigade composed of the 1st, 3rd, 7th, and 8th Battalions, and Brig.-Gen. Tuxford's brigade on the left, being made up of the 2nd, 4th, 13th, and 16th Battalions. In reserve lay Brig.-Gen. Hughes, with a force composed of the 5th, 10th, 14th, and 15th Battalions. The actual assault was delivered by three battalions, the 3rd Battalion on the left, the 16th Battalion, Canadian Scottish, in the centre, and the 13th Battalion, Royal Highlanders of Canada, on the right. Roughly, these battalions had as their respective objectives Mount Sorrel, Hill 62, and the position to the north of Hill 62. Guns of all calibres were concentrated to support the attack, and on the flanks demonstrations and feint attacks were employed to mask the actual location of the assault.

The 14th Battalion was "in reserve" during the successful counter-attack on June 13th, but it must not be inferred that the men lay idle. On the contrary, parties moved forward at intervals after June 7th, and worked in every conceivable manner to assist the troops chosen for the assault. Previous to, and during, the attack the 14th Battalion furnished the following parties:—

Party "A"—2 officers and 158 other ranks. This party carried material and worked in the captured front line, digging trenches to link up the flanks of the 13th and 16th Battalions. Lieut. H. A. Davin, who had been commissioned a few days previously, was in command and was killed, together with 15 of his men. Lieut. W. A. Bonshor, who had won the D.C.M. while serving as Regimental Sergeant-Major, was wounded, as were 13 other ranks. Twenty-one other ranks were blown up by shell fire, or picked off by enemy sharpshooters, the names of these men, pending definite information as to their fate, being added to the Battalion's roll of missing, presumed killed.

Party "B"—1 officer and 38 other ranks. This party, under command of Lieut. H. E. Banks, carried small arm ammunition to the front line and supports. In passing through the enemy barrage one man was killed and one wounded. Three others failed to report and were, presumably, killed by shell fire.

Party "C"—54 other ranks. This party carried bombs from Brigade Reserve to the front line and supports. It suffered 7 casualties, 2 men being killed, 2 wounded, and 3 listed as missing.

Party "D"—42 other ranks. This party advanced with the attacking waves, attending to casualties and carrying stretcher cases to the dressing station. One man of the party was killed and another lost in the barrage.

Party "E"—2 officers and 108 other ranks. This party carried ammunition and bombs. It also carried rations to the 13th and 16th Battalions. One man was wounded.

Party "F"—17 other ranks. This party, though employed on dangerous work, i.e. wiring, under the supervision of the Engineers, was fortunate in coming through without losses.

Party "G"—21 other ranks, who served as Battle Stops at specified points. No casualties.

Party "H"—2 officers and 108 other ranks. This party carried wire and entrenching material. One of its members was missing when the roll was called, and 2 were reported wounded.

To express appreciation of the work accomplished by the Royal Montreal stretcher bearers, Lieut.-Col. V. C. Buchanan, D.S.O., Com-

Railway Cutting—Approach to Hill 60 Trenches, June, 1916, showing Entrance to Tunnel Extending Under German Lines

Canadian Official Copyright

manding Officer of the 13th Battalion, Royal Highlanders of Canada, wrote to Lieut.-Col. Clark as follows:—

> Dear Clark:—
> I want to thank you most sincerely for allowing your Stretcher Bearers to come up with the 13th in the recent show.
> The men did their work splendidly and were the means of saving many of our men's lives.
> They certainly did well and showed great heroism in the way they tended the wounded although exposed to heavy fire.
> You will please express to these men the deep appreciation of the 13th for the excellent work they did.
> I regret the casualties you have suffered and the lives lost.
> Yours sincerely,
> VICTOR C. BUCHANAN.

Lieut.-Col. J. E. Leckie, Commanding Officer of the 16th Battalion, Canadian Scottish, wrote in similar terms, and Major-General R. E. W. Turner, V.C., C.B., D.S.O., sent a note from Headquarters of the 2nd Canadian Division to congratulate the 14th on "the splendid work lately carried out".

At 7 p.m. on June 14th the Royal Montreal Regiment moved forward from Brigade Reserve into Brigade Support, Headquarters being established at Swan Chateau and the companies located three in the grounds of Chateau Seagard and one at Moated Farm. Here the Battalion remained for five days, providing working parties and training the recently joined drafts in the details of trench routine. Following the period in Brigade Support, the Battalion moved by bus to Kenora Camp, there to spend four days in Divisional Reserve.

On the night of June 24th the Battalion advanced to relieve the 4th Canadian Battalion in the front line, guides meeting the men at Zillebeke Halte and leading them into Trenches 45-52. Simultaneously, the 13th Battalion relieved the 7th Battalion in Trenches 53-58 on the left flank. When relief of the 4th Battalion was complete, No. 1 Coy. of the 14th occupied front line trenches on the right, No. 2 Coy. held the left front, No. 3 Coy. held trenches near Square Wood, and No. 4 Coy. was held in support near Battalion Headquarters at Battersea Farm.

The whole area taken over on this occasion bore evidences of the fierce fighting which had swept over it earlier in the month. The front line was in fairly good condition, but all communication trenches were badly damaged and, in some cases, obliterated. Approach to the line, therefore, had to be made across the open and precaution taken to avoid losses. In the operation order covering the relief officers were warned against careless conversation over the trench system of telephones, as the enemy was thought to possess efficient "listening sets." Accordingly, the Adjutant ordered that all important messages be delivered by runner and, to deceive listeners when less important matters were discussed, officers were instructed to address Battalion Headquarters as "Jack".

Before taking over the front, the 14th Battalion received a draft of officers from England. Amongst those receiving commissions just previously were Frank Higginson, A. L. McLean, D.C.M., J. W. Green, R. H. Hood, C. H. Sullivan, and W. Sharp. During the tour which began on June 24th the Battalion was commanded as follows:—

> Headquarters:—Lieut.-Col. R. P. Clark, M.C., Major Gault McCombe, Capt. J. W. McAlister (Medical Officer), Capt. F. W. Utton (Adjutant), and Lieut. A. Plow (Assistant Adjutant).
>
> Details:—Lieuts. J. K. Nesbitt, S. S. Jones, and A. L. McLean.
>
> No. 1 Coy.:—Capt. J. C. K. Carson, Lieut. J. E. McKenna, Lieut. W. W. Pickup, and Lieut. G. B. Murray.
>
> No. 2 Coy.:—Capt. G. E. Leighton, Capt. J. F. Adams, Lieut. D. J. Evans, and Lieut. C. H. Sullivan.
>
> No. 3 Coy.:—Lieut. C. G. Power, Lieut. R. H. Hood, Lieut. C. H. Sclater, and Lieut. J. Mills.
>
> No. 4 Coy.:—Lieut. W. E. Beaton, Lieut. R. A. Pelletier, Lieut. O. J. Larzen, and Lieut. E. M. Hyman.

The tour in Trenches 45-52 lasted five days and was by no means uneventful. British aircraft were active on June 25th and artillery on both sides fired at intervals. A gas warning was sounded on the morning of the 26th, the Battalion remaining on the alert until evening, when a change in the wind rendered the danger of gas remote. Twelve casualties occurred during the day, 3 men being killed, 5 severely shocked by bursting shells, and 4 wounded.

At 4 o'clock on the morning of June 27th the enemy opened a heavy "shoot" along the Canadian front, using artillery, trench mortars, rifle grenades, machine guns, and bombs. To the left several enemy attacks moved forward against the 13th Battalion, one of these being seen by Lieut. J. K. Nesbitt, of the 14th Battalion Machine Gun Section, who brought a gun into action against it and helped the Royal Highlanders to administer a sharp check. Further assistance was rendered by a platoon of No. 2 Coy., 14th Battalion, which co-operated with the 13th in holding the front until reinforcements arrived.

None of the attacks succeeded in penetrating the Highlanders' front, though one reached a 13th Battalion post in a trench sap. Strong forces of the enemy stood ready to move forward if the attacks of the battle patrols proved successful, but withdrew when the patrols failed to effect a lodgement in the Canadian lines. During the action the work of Signalling Sergt. A. Close, of the Royal Montreal Regiment, was most efficient. Working under heavy fire, he maintained communication between Battalion Headquarters and the front line, his courage and marked determination being recognized at a later date by award of the D.C.M.

At 5.15 a.m. the German bombardment ceased and the Royal Montrealers examined their damaged position. Several trenches had been destroyed, but more serious was a casualty list which totalled 29, Lieut. J. Mills and 16 other ranks having been killed, and 12 other ranks wounded. Additional casualties occurred on the following day, as a result of continued shell fire. No concentrated tornado of shelling swept out of the sky on this date, but high explosive burst in the lines at intervals, 4 men being killed and Capt. R. W. Frost severely injured by concussion.

Artillery activity again prevailed on June 29th, both sides hammering away hour after hour in one of the numberless duels familiar to those who knew life in the Salient. The trenches of the 14th, however, came in for little attention and the Battalion, accordingly, was in good condition when relieved at night by the 8th Canadian Battalion. Following relief, the 14th moved back to Brigade Reserve in Dominion Lines. So ended June, 1916, during which the Battalion suffered over 500 casualties, including a large proportion of officers and N.C.O's. In spite of these losses a confident Battalion faced the fighting which inevitably lay ahead, the reinforcing drafts acquiring rapidly the pride of Regiment which had so noticeably animated the fallen.

CHAPTER IX

FROM THE SALIENT TO THE SOMME

> All night the tall trees overhead
>   Are whispering to the stars;
> Their roots are wrapped about the dead
>   And hide the hideous scars.
>
> The tide of war goes rolling by,
>   The legions sweep along;
> And daily in the summer sky
>   The birds will sing their song.
>   —FREDERICK GEORGE SCOTT.

I

FOLLOWING the series of trench tours in the Ypres Salient in June, 1916, the 14th Battalion spent ten days in Brigade and Divisional Reserve, five days at Dominion Lines and an equal time at Patricia Lines. Then followed another series of tours in the Salient, these being completed on August 9th and the Regiment thereafter marching to a special area to train for participation in the Battles of the Somme.

All unconscious of what lay before them, the Royal Montrealers trained at Dominion Lines and Patricia Lines during the early days of July. Recognizing that a smart appearance helps to maintain morale, particularly after a month such as the Battalion had just experienced, Capt. Utton ordered company commanders and officers commanding details to pay strict attention to the neatness of their men. As a result of these orders and of the co-operation which the men extended, the Battalion, when it marched from Dominion to Patricia Lines, presented an appearance leaving little to be desired. At Patricia Lines the Regiment was visited by Major-Gen. A. W. Currie, C.B., G.O.C. the 1st Canadian Division; and was reinforced by several officers from England. Among the reinforcements were Lieuts. M. C. W. Copeland, J. F. Fitzpatrick, and G. L. Stairs, the last an original officer of the Battalion who had served for eight months in France during the previous year. Lieut. Fitzpatrick had also seen service in France, having been commissioned from the ranks of the 3rd Canadian Battalion.

At 8 p.m. on July 9th the Royal Montreal Regiment paraded at Patricia Lines and marched to Poperinghe Railway Station, entraining there for railhead, whence guides of the 28th Canadian Battalion led the companies and details into Trenches 33 to 38, between the Bluff and the Railway Cutting. In these positions, with Battalion Headquarters at Grand Fleet Street, the unit remained for five days. On July 10th some shelling and rifle fire resulted in the wounding of Capt. D. J. Evans and 9 other ranks, and on the following night rifle grenadiers, snipers, and machine gunners all took part in a stirring duel. On this date the 14th Battalion sent one man to Paris to represent the Regiment at a review of Allied troops on the French national holiday, July 14th.

Rifle grenade activity continued on July 12th, also on the morning of the 13th, when trench mortars on both sides joined in. This activity died down during the afternoon and was succeeded by desultory shell fire. As a result of the various bombardments, the Battalion suffered 12 casualties, Lieut. E. A. Adams, Lieut. W. W. Pickup, and 7 other ranks being wounded, and 3 other ranks killed. On July 14th the Battalion furnished working parties, totalling 3 officers and 323 other ranks, and at night handed over the front to the 13th Battalion.

On relief by the Royal Highlanders the 14th Battalion moved back to spend five days in Brigade Support, with Headquarters at Railway Dugouts and the companies billeted respectively at Canal Dugouts, Battersea Farm, Woodcote House, and Sunken Road. From these positions working parties nearly 500 strong were supplied each day, fine weather rendering these a shade less unpopular than usual. From Brigade Support the Battalion moved back on July 19th to occupy Dickebusch Huts in Brigade Reserve. Working parties continued in demand, but were smaller than those furnished from Brigade Support. On July 21st the Divisional Gas Officer visited the Battalion and inspected all gas equipment, following which Lieut. Betts, of the Headquarters Gymnastic Staff, lectured to officers and men on "Use of the Bayonet". On July 22nd Major Mills, of the Royal Flying Corps, lectured at Connaught Lines on "Aeroplane Observation", a group of officers and other ranks from the 14th Battalion attending, and on the 24th Lieut.-Col. R. H. Kearsley, D.S.O., addressed the commissioned ranks of the Battalion on "Responsibilities and Duties of Officers".

On July 23rd all ranks of the Battalion heard with pleasure that, for splendid work on June 3rd, Lieut. W. E. Beaton had been awarded the Military Cross. For his devotion to duty in caring for the wounded, a similar honour had been awarded to the Battalion Medical Officer, Capt. W. J. McAlister. This award came just as Capt. McAlister's tour of duty with the Battalion ended. On July 24th his position was taken over by Capt. C. E. Anderson.

Two days after Capt. McAlister's departure the 14th Battalion played the 10th Canadian Field Ambulance at football, the game being followed on July 27th by a sports day with the bands of the 2nd Brigade and the 15th Battalion in attendance. On July 28th bathing parades were held, and on the 29th the Battalion paraded in full marching order for inspection by Lieut.-Col. R. H. Kearsley, D.S.O. Divine Service was held on the morning of July 30th, the remainder of the day being given to the men to rest and prepare for another tour in the line. On the night of July 31st the Battalion moved forward to relieve the 3rd Canadian Battalion in Trenches 33 to 38, the same trenches in the Verbrandenmolen Sector as had been occupied earlier in the month.

At 2.45 a.m. on August 1st the 14th Battalion completed relief of the 3rd Battalion, Headquarters, as during the previous tour, being at Grand Fleet Street. Working parties, under Lieut. Jull, effected general repairs to the front, support, and reserve lines during the tour that followed. A new battalion headquarters was constructed, dugouts were built in the reserve line, and wire was laid to protect Verbrandenmolen Trench. On four days 410 men were assigned to these tasks, 395 being furnished on August 5th, and 243 on August 6th. On the whole the Germans were inactive. Trench mortar and artillery shelling took place on August 2nd, and on the 5th the left front was sharply bombarded with minenwerfers and whizz-bangs, but for the most part the days were marked only by that amount of shelling, bombing, and machine gun fire, which, in the Salient, was regarded as "normal".

An idea of the work accomplished during a "normal" Salient tour can be gained from the reports of Lieut. A. L. McLean, Battalion Intelligence Officer, on the period now under review. Working parties have been mentioned and a few words given to the attitude of the enemy, but little has been said of the details of routine. On August 1st the weather was foggy until 9.30 a.m. and so warm thereafter that heat waves prevented accurate observation, nevertheless snipers smashed five enemy periscopes, and the movements of an enemy balloon were carefully noted. A Stokes gun in the Battalion trenches threw 8 shells across No Man's Land, where at night a patrol found all quiet.

Observation was simpler on the following day, when 44 of the enemy in service uniform and wearing service cap, and one man with no cap, were seen passing a certain point. Forty-two rifle grenades were fired by men of the 14th during the 24 hours and a machine gun, located in Grand Fleet Street, fired at frequent intervals. Other machine guns treated the enemy parapets to occasional bursts of fire, and the Battalion snipers, in the absence of more attractive targets, smashed a number of enemy periscopes. At night a patrol of the 14th explored an old crater in No Man's Land; and a fixed battery of 6 rifles was trained on the spot where the 44 Germans had passed during the day. This battery was fired at intervals in the hope of causing losses.

On August 3rd the machine gun in Grand Fleet Street continued to annoy the enemy, other machine guns at night dispersing a German working party opposite Trench 36. Ninety rifle grenades were fired during the day; a small trench mortar fired 12 rounds, and the Stokes guns fired 53. Snipers smashed their usual quota of periscopes, and at night a patrol covered the ground in front of Trench 33 to within 15 yards of the German wire. In front of Trench 35 enemy wire was also examined, a subsequent report stating that it was in excellent condition and of the type known as " concertina barbed ".

" Nervous ", is the word applied to the attitude of the enemy on August 4th. Perhaps the anniversary stirred the Empire forces to unwonted activity and chilled the German heart with forebodings of inevitable doom. Be that as it may, the men of the 14th fired 190 rifle grenades to celebrate the occasion; the Stokes guns banged off 275 vindictive rounds; the 2-inch Trench Mortar loosed 99 shells filled with high explosive; and the snipers smashed 19 enemy periscopes. To finish the day, a 14th Battalion sergeant led a patrol of 3 men to a shell hole in front of Trench 33, whence an underground sap ran into the German line. Apparently the curiosity of this small party irritated the Hun, for suddenly a flare was thrown and simultaneously several of the enemy attacked with the bayonet. Three of the attackers were promptly shot, the sergeant and one of his party thereupon advancing and emptying their revolvers into a party of Germans crowding the sap. Groans followed, but all the garrison were not injured, for several emerged from the sap and threw bombs. No harm resulted, for by this time the Royal Montreal patrol had retired towards safety in the Canadian lines. With praiseworthy calmness. the sergeant and his three men had, during the whole encounter, expended just 18 rounds of ammunition.

British artillery pounded the enemy on August 5th, the 14th Battalion assisting in the good work by firing 104 rifle grenades and 41 rounds from Stokes guns. In addition, the machine gun in Grand Fleet Street so annoyed the Hun that he sought to silence it with a dozen rounds of shell fire. Other machine guns fired where enemy parties were thought to be located; and the Battalion snipers drove a working party to cover. On the following day a German sniper was killed, two small working parties were dispersed, and a patrol at night reported on the condition of the German wire. Observation was good during the day, and enemy trench repairs were noted; also the fact that at 3.20 p.m. a pigeon flew from back of the Canadian front to some point far behind the German line. At 8.25 p.m. a large party of Germans, their heads and rifles visible, passed a point well back of the line. A 14th Battalion fixed rifle battery opened fire, but results could not be established.

Though the tour from July 31st to August 6th was considered "quiet", the Battalion did not escape losses. Capt. J. F. Adams, an original officer, who some time previously had returned to Regimental duty after six months' absence, was wounded and Lieut. W. L. McCormack was evacuated suffering from concussion. Later in the tour Lieut. R. H. Hood was wounded, and amongst the other ranks casualties totalled 56, 7 men being killed and 49 wounded.

II

When the 7th Canadian Battalion took over the line on the night of August 6th, or rather at 3 a.m. on August 7th, the Royal Montreal Regiment moved back into familiar territory, Headquarters billeting at Swan Chateau, together with half of No. 1 Coy. and half of the Regimental Details. The remaining half of No. 1 Coy., plus Nos. 2 and 3 Companies, occupied the neighbourhood of Chateau Segard, and No. 4 Coy. was situated at Moated Farm. From these positions a working party of 6 officers and 370 other ranks moved forward on August 7th to bury cable under supervision of the Engineers, a similar party being supplied on August 8th. On this date the Battalion "stood to" during a bombardment and gas attack on troops to the Canadian left. No details of the attack were obtainable at the time and after a few hours the unit was ordered to "stand down". On the following day artillery on both sides was active, the enemy shelling British battery positions near Swan Chateau. At night the 4th Canadian Battalion took over the support positions and the 14th moved back to Victoria Lines.

August 10th was spent by the Battalion in preparing for the first stage of a march to the 2nd Army Training Area, west of St. Omer. Before this march began General Sir Julian Byng sent his B.G.G.S.

to call on Lieut.-Col. Clark and convey congratulations on the work which the Battalion had accomplished in the Salient. The envoy was further instructed to state that, after inspecting all battalions under his command, General Byng considered "that the 14th Battalion, Royal Montreal Regiment, was as efficient a unit as any in the Canadian Corps". Well pleased with this recognition and praise from the Corps Commander, the 14th Battalion marched from Victoria Lines at 6 a.m. on August 11th and reached billets in the Steenvoorde Area three hours and fifty minutes later. In this area the Battalion rested for the remainder of the day, réveillé sounding soon after midnight and the unit marching at 2 a.m. on the 12th to a Brigade rendezvous. Reaching this point at 2.45 a.m., the 14th Battalion picked up its place in the Brigade Column, which marched a quarter-hour later.

On this march Divisional Headquarters accompanied the Brigade, the whole column, over six miles long, being made up as follows:—

>Divisional H.Q., with Transport
>H.Q. Div'l. Engineers, with Transport
>Brigade H.Q., with Transport
>No. 4 Signal Section, with Transport
>15th Battalion, 48th Highlanders
>16th Battalion, Canadian Scottish
>14th Battalion, Royal Montreal Regiment
>13th Battalion, Royal Highlanders of Canada
>Transport of the 4 battalions brigaded
>Machine Gun Company, with Transport
>Trench Mortar Battery, with Transport
>1st and 3rd Field Companies, Canadian Engineers
>3rd Canadian Field Ambulance.

On reaching the Noordpeene Area at 9.55 a.m. the 14th Battalion moved into billets, Headquarters being set up in Point du Jour on the Watten-Cassel Road. From this spot the Battalion marched on the following morning, arriving at Eperlecques about 9.45 o'clock and billeting in a chateau and outbuildings about one-half mile from the town. No. 4 Coy. and the Intelligence Section billeted on the outskirts of the town.

For two weeks the Battalion remained at Eperlecques, carrying out a stiff programme of training, varied by baseball, football, and cricket matches against other units in the area. On August 14th the morning was devoted to practice of companies and battalion in attack; a muster parade and kit inspection taking place in the afternoon.

Battalion in attack was again practised on the following day, and on the morning of the 16th, manœuvres were carried out on the special Training Area, No. 4 Coy. defending a selected position against an attack by Nos. 1, 2, and 3 Companies. In the afternoon the 14th Battalion played the 16th at baseball, five runs in the second half of the ninth inning winning the game for the Royal Montrealers by a score of 8—7.

Company, platoon, section, and arm drills occupied the early morning of August 17th, these being followed by instruction to company bombers, bayonet fighting, and instruction to the Battalion Scouts. In the afternoon the men added to their sporting laurels by defeating a team from No. 3 Canadian Field Ambulance at football. On the following day the Battalion practised the advance, with special attention paid to flank and rear guards, also to the protection of a column at rest. Later in the day Capt. Betts lectured to the entire unit on "Use of the Bayonet".

A church parade was held on the morning of August 20th, this being followed by musketry practice on the rifle ranges, smoke helmet, company, platoon, and section drills. For their defeat at football the men of No. 3 Field Ambulance secured revenge by defeating the Royal Montrealers at cricket, rain later interrupting a football match between the 14th Battalion and the 1st Divisional Train.

Musketry practice on the ranges, with and without smoke helmets, featured the training on August 21st, the Divisional Gas Officer, on the same date, lecturing to 25% of the company and details personnel. Lectures on bombs and gas were also delivered on the afternoon of August 22nd; in the forenoon the Battalion had proceeded to the Training Area and once more practised attack. Clear indication of whither all this special training led was furnished on August 23rd when the Divisional Grenade Officer lectured on "The Use of Lewis Guns, Bombs, and Trench Mortars in the Battles of the Somme". Following this lecture a concert was held, men of the 13th, 15th, and 16th Battalions and of the 3rd Canadian Field Ambulance being invited to attend.

At 5.15 p.m. on August 27th the 14th Battalion, Royal Montreal Regiment, fell in at Eperlecques and marched to St. Omer Railway Station. Arriving at half-past eight, the Battalion entrained at 9.30 and at 10.03 the train of box cars got under way. It travelled all night and jolted into Conteville Station at 5.45 o'clock in the morning, the men detraining and marching to the outskirts of Coulonvillers, where billets were occupied at 8.55 a.m.

Continuing the move on August 29th, the Battalion left Coulonvillers at 7.30 a.m., marched steadily, and reached Pernois at 1.15 p.m. " Fall in " sounded at 7 o'clock on the morning of the 30th, when the Battalion joined other units of the 3rd Brigade in a march to la Vicogne. Some straggling had occurred on the previous day and attention of all ranks was called to the fact that this reflected on the discipline and training of the Regiment. Accordingly, when Lieut. W. Sharp, billeting officer, met the Battalion at la Vicogne at 12.05 p.m., no stragglers were reported. Having rested all afternoon on August 30th, the Battalion resumed the march at 7.30 o'clock on the morning of the 31st. In contrast to the previous days, which had been showery, August 31st was fine, sunny, and reasonably cool, the men enjoying the march which terminated at a camp in a wood north of Vadencourt at 12.45 p.m.

CHAPTER X

THE SOMME

> What place is this? What underworld of pain,
> All shadow-barred with glare of swinging fires?
> What writhing phantoms of the newly slain?
> What cries? What thirst consuming all desires?
> This is the field of battle.
> —Sir Henry Newbolt.

I

WHILE the units of the Canadian Corps were fighting in the Ypres Salient, Sir Douglas Haig, in conjunction with French armies on the right, struck the opening blows in that vast engagement now known as "The Battles of the Somme, 1916". The exact purpose behind this great series of battles was a mystery at the time, many students of the military situation viewing with uneasiness the tremendous waste of life and material and the slow daily progress of the Allied Armies towards undiscoverable objectives. Actually, the battles served many purposes. In the first place they relieved the French Army, which for months had been enduring almost unbearable pressure at Verdun; secondly, they prevented transfer of German troops to the Russian front; thirdly, they presented a serious threat to enemy communications along the line Cambrai-LeCateau-Maubeuge; and fourthly, they wore down the strength of Germany. Of all the purposes mentioned above, the last was the most important. By 1916 the war had entered on that phase which Sir Douglas Haig calls "the period of ceaseless attrition", that is to say, the period in which two great adversaries, putting forth all their strength, deliver those mighty blows beneath which one or other must eventually weaken. On July 6th, five days after the battle began, Col. Repington, Military Correspondent of the London "Times", visited British G.H.Q. by invitation. Maps, orders, and many confidential documents were shown to him, and one point emphasized over and again. "Remember", said General Charteris, of the Staff, "the purpose of this action is *to kill Germans;* all strategic objectives are secondary". Sir Douglas Haig, in his "Final Despatch" of the war, states his belief that in the German losses during the Battles of the Somme, 1916, and during the Flanders fighting, which culminated at Passchendaele in 1917, is to be found "the secret of our victory in 1918". That this whole "period of ceaseless attrition" was a vital factor in the ultimate collapse of the German Army, no one who reads Gen. Ludendorff's war memoirs can reasonably doubt.

General Ludendorff's admission that, following the Battles of the Somme, the German Army on the western front was "completely exhausted", has silenced many who at the time criticized Sir Douglas Haig severely. The public hoped for sensational victory, and was disappointed. The Government, too, was disappointed and querulous, though Mr. Asquith loyally supported the Commander-in-Chief. In France chagrin found expression in the humiliating dismissal of Marshal Joffre and General Foch. Joffre was succeeded by General Nivelle, who had achieved brilliant success in recapturing Forts Douaumont and Vaux at Verdun. Nivelle scorned the theory that attrition alone could bring Germany to her knees. He believed that seventy million people could be beaten by a coup. Despite grave warnings, he tested his belief in April, 1917. French graves along the Chemin des Dames, and a name since synonymous with failure, attest the measure of his success.

Following the sweep forward of the new British Armies on July 1st, Sir Douglas Haig moved division after division and corps after corps into action. In most places the first attack penetrated the front line with ease, but, as the assault bit deeper and deeper into the German lines, it lost the advantages of a first rush and encountered opposition which frequently brought it to a standstill. Never for long, however, was stalemate permitted to continue, exhausted troops, who could drive no further, and shattered battalions, which had lost all power to strike, being replaced in the line by fresh units, or at least by units rested and prepared to advance once more. And always there was the mud; and always the roar of guns. Some idea of the gunfire can be gained from the fact that during the five months of the battle the British alone fired 14 million 18-pounder shells and 5 million rounds from 4.5-inch howitzers. Seven hundred and thirty heavy guns backed the British armies in France on July 1st, many of these at the Somme, the total tonnage of the ammunition they expended being expressed in figures beyond anything the world had seen before. Small wonder that the battlefields of the Somme were torn and rent beyond all recognition.

II

After training for two weeks at the Special Area of the 2nd Army, near St. Omer, the Canadian Corps moved to take part in the Battles of the Somme. At 4.25 p.m. on September 1st the 14th Battalion,

Royal Montreal Regiment, completed a march from Vadencourt to the "Brickfields", north-west of Albert, where, in pouring rain, tarpaulins were propped up to provide "billets", which otherwise were conspicuously lacking. The Somme district at this time was divided into three areas, the fighting zone, the assembly zone, and the resting zone, with headquarters respectively in Albert, Rubempré, and Canaples. On arrival in Albert, therefore, troops were under no delusion as to what lay before them. Details might be unknown, but a tour in the line was certain. Accordingly, at the Brickfields, the men of the 14th, veterans of the Salient for the most part, prepared to face the unknown hazards of the Somme. A cheerful incident of the first day in the area was the posting of a list of promotions, Captains F. W. Utton, J. C. K. Carson, and J. F. Sumption becoming majors, or acting majors, and being succeeded as captains by Lieuts. J. K. Nesbitt, W. E. Beaton, M.C., and G. L. Stairs.

All day on September 2nd the 14th Battalion remained at the Brickfields employed in the multitudinous details of preparing for a tour in the line. At 7 p.m. the companies moved independently to billets in Albert, all ranks displaying interest as they passed the famous church crowned by the leaning statue of the Virgin, which hung precariously with outstretched arms, as if to protect and bless the troops beneath. Gradually a superstition had arisen that when this statue fell the end of the war would be at hand. Anxiously, therefore, men watched it from day to day, few being aware that French engineers had fastened it, lest it should fall at an inopportune time. In 1918, when Germany was about to sue for peace, the statue justified the superstitious by toppling heavily to the ground.

At 9.30 a.m. on September 3rd the 14th Battalion received a warning to be ready to move on two hours' notice. Somewhat later a party of 12 officers and 20 N.C.O's. moved forward to reconnoitre positions at Tara Hill and la Boisselle, the main body of the Battalion dividing into Protestant and Roman Catholic sections to attend Divine Service. On this occasion the Roman Catholic service was conducted by Major J. O'Gorman, who had been appointed Roman Catholic Chaplain of the Battalion some two months previously. Following the religious services, the Battalion, at 12.45 p.m., moved forward to Divisional Reserve positions at Tara Hill. From these trenches and bivouacs, the unit moved on the 5th to Brigade Reserve positions at the Chalk Pits.

From the Chalk Pits it was at one time suggested that the Battalion might move forward and attack Mouquet Farm, a position from which several Australian attacks had recoiled with heavy losses, but in the neighbourhood of which the 13th Battalion, in conjunction with the Australians, had secured a precarious footing. Moving forward into the line, Lieut.-Col. Clark joined Lieut.-Col. V. C. Buchanan, of the 13th Battalion, and carefully reconnoitred the front to see if an attack were possible. Judging from the experiences of the 13th and from the condition of the terrain surrounding Mouquet Farm that one battalion's strength would be dissipated without compensating gain, both officers agreed that a single battalion attack was inadvisable. Lieut.-Col. Clark reported accordingly to Brigade and the tentative plan was abandoned.

At night on September 6th the 14th Battalion was ordered to carry out a series of reliefs. In obedience to these orders No. 1 Coy. moved to Tom's Cut; No. 2 Coy. remained in the Chalk Pits; No. 3 Coy. relieved a company of the 16th Battalion in trenches at the most advanced point of the whole Somme Salient; and No. 4 Coy. relieved a company of the 13th Battalion in trenches and shell holes south and east of Mouquet Farm.

As the companies, following these reliefs, acted more or less independently, it will be necessary to follow them individually for some 48 hours. No. 4 Coy., commanded by Capt. W. E. Beaton, M.C., moved forward as instructed and completed relief of the 13th Battalion company at 2.30 a.m. Some casualties were suffered during the relief and shell fire continued throughout the night, but, in spite of this hindrance, the men set to work and improved the position by linking up scattered posts in shell holes and strengthening the front against the possibility of counter-attacks. Further defensive works were constructed on August 7th, the company being relieved at midnight by a company of the 8th Canadian Battalion and moving back to bivouacs at Tara Hill.

Meanwhile two platoons of No. 3 Coy. and one section of bombers, under Capt. G. L. Stairs, had moved forward to relieve the company of the 16th Battalion in the extreme tip of the Salient. Heavy shell fire met the advance and Capt. Stairs was instantly killed. As a result of the same fire Lieut. G. T. Bartlett was wounded. In addition to these serious losses, a party of bombers, under Sergt. J. W. Hoare, was buried by the upheaval of a great mass of mud and earth. Every effort was made by survivors to dig out the buried men, but five had perished before the rescue could be effected. Among these was Sergt. Hoare, a brave N.C.O. whom the Battalion could ill afford to lose.

Unfortunately, during the forward progress of the platoons of No. 3 Coy., the guides furnished by the 16th Battalion fell wounded. In a maze of unidentifiable trenches and water-filled shell holes this created a serious situation, as none of the Royal Montrealers knew the front, or had more than a hazy idea as to the location of the line. Day dawned as the remnant of the platoons struggled forward, but the courage of the men was high and permitted no thought of turning back. At last, at 10 a.m., one N.C.O. and thirty men, all that was left of the original two platoons, reported to the officer commanding the company of the 16th.

By this time news of the early casualties had arrived back at Battalion H.Q., and Capt. R. C. MacKenzie and Lieut. C. H. Sclater had been sent forward to replace the officers who had fallen. On arrival in the line, Capt. MacKenzie took command, his little force being strengthened during the morning by a platoon of No. 1 Coy., which with great daring managed to crawl to him over the open. Clinging to their section of front all day on September 7th, Capt. MacKenzie and his men prepared for what the night should bring. Shelling was severe throughout the hours of darkness. Accordingly, it was with relief that the weakened little force handed over the front at 6 a.m. on September 8th to a company of the 7th Canadian Battalion.

But the end was not yet; for just as relief was completed, two hundred men of the Prussian Guard, supported by artillery, attacked the front line. Eventually this attack was thrown back with severe losses, but before the Germans were defeated, Capt. MacKenzie and Lieut. Sclater were wounded, and a number of 14th Battalion bombers, who had taken a fine part in the fray, were killed, wounded, or captured. Among the killed was Private F. Purcell, who had accounted for not less than 20 of the enemy. When the Germans had been ejected from the Canadian front, the remnant of Capt. MacKenzie's command withdrew to Tara Hill.

Meanwhile, at 10 a.m. on September 7th, the situation on the front of the remaining companies of the 16th Battalion had become serious. At 10.30 a.m. the Royal Montreal Regiment received verbal orders to relieve the 16th completely, Lieut. G. B. Murray, Lieut. B. L. Cook, and 67 other ranks from No. 1 Coy. carrying out the order and completing the relief at 2.30 p.m. Seven casualties reduced Lieut. Murray's trench strength to 60 before the relief was complete, nevertheless he held his position all afternoon and night on September 7th and, following the wounding of Lieut. Cook and a number of men, organized counter-attacks when the enemy assaulted the front at 6.10 o'clock on the morning of September 8th. Having suffered approximately 50 casualties, Lieut. Murray, on relief by the 7th Battalion, withdrew about noon to the position which the Battalion had taken up at Tara Hill. Lieut. Murray's work during this engagement won for him a Military Cross.

While companies and detachments of the 14th Battalion were carrying out the operations described above, the main body of the Regiment held a position with the left flank resting on Mouquet Farm. Shell fire harassed the men during this time and a number were wounded. On the night of the 6th Hon. Major John O'Gorman, Roman Catholic Chaplain of the Battalion, was seriously wounded while devotedly ministering to casualties in No Man's Land. For the gallantry displayed on this occasion Major O'Gorman, priest, soldier, and gentleman, was awarded the Military Cross. In all, officer casualties for the engagement amounted to 1 killed and 5 wounded. Amongst the other ranks 44 men were killed outright, 116 were wounded, and 33 were reported missing. Many of these last, it was certain, had fallen unobserved in one or other of the countless shell holes, or mud-filled trenches, which formed so unforgettable a feature of the Somme.

II

At 9 o'clock on the morning of September 9th the 14th Battalion, Royal Montreal Regiment, marched from the bivouacs at Tara Hill to billets in the village of Warloy. "Fall in" sounded at 7 a.m. on the 10th, the Battalion marching to Herissart, moving thence at 1 p.m. on the following day, and arriving in Montrelet at 5.15. A muster parade and kit inspections occupied the time of the men on September 12th, and on the 13th, a cold and rainy day, the Battalion carried out squad, platoon, company, and arm drills at the Special Training Area. Similar drills and extended order movements were practised on the 14th, and on the 15th the Battalion started a march back towards the battlefields of the Somme, reaching la Vicogne at 9.15 o'clock in the morning and there resting over night.

As the Battalion approached the Somme, the British Army, for the first time in warfare, made use of tanks. About 50 of these monsters lurched to the attack on September 15th, amazing the 2nd and 3rd Canadian Divisions, whom they supported, and inspiring fear in the hearts of the enemy. Battle revealed defects in most of the tanks, but demonstration of their potential worth won a place for them as a recognized branch of the Service. German poison gas and the British tank represent the most important weapons conceived in the course of the Great War. Flame projectors and similar devices were occasionally effective on limited fronts; gas and the tank each involved adjustments affecting the whole realm of military tactics.

Continuing the march at 8 a.m. on September 16th, the Battalion reached Vadencourt four hours later and moved into camp in the wood north of the village. September 17th was spent in this location, kit inspection taking place in the morning and a Protestant Church Parade, Capt. Moffatt officiating, in the afternoon. On the afternoon of the 18th the Battalion marched to the Brickfields at Albert. Rain fell on the morning of the 19th, which was spent by the men in cleaning up and attending to repair of their clothing and kit. On the 20th the Regiment practised battalion in attack and on the 21st of the month a party of 4 officers and 225 other ranks was furnished to repair the Courcelette Road. Three men were wounded by shell fire on this occasion, a similar party on September 22nd proving more fortunate and escaping without losses.

An event of interest at this time was the issue to men of the Canadian Corps of coloured shoulder patches, which identified at a glance the unit to which any individual belonged. Each man was given an oblong patch, coloured red in the case of the 1st Division, and this was surmounted on the shoulder by a smaller patch, the colour and shape of which identified the brigade and battalion. This second patch, if blue, meant that the wearer belonged to the 3rd Brigade; if in the shape of a circle (i.e., a figure bounded by one continuous line), it meant that the man was a member of the first battalion in the Brigade, or, in other words, of the 13th Battalion, Royal Highlanders of Canada. If the blue patch consisted of a figure bounded by two lines, that is to say, a semi-circle, it marked the wearer as belonging to the second battalion in the Brigade, namely, the 14th Battalion, Royal Montreal Regiment. The third and fourth battalions of the Brigade, namely, the 15th Battalion, 48th Highlanders, and the 16th Battalion, Canadian Scottish, were similarly identifiable, the former by a three-sided (triangular) patch and the latter by a four-sided figure, cut square. Divisional and brigade patches, being sewn onto the sleeve of tunics at the shoulder, could be removed, or replaced, when a man left France, or was transferred.

On the afternoon of September 23rd the 14th Battalion moved from the Brickfields and relieved the 4th Canadian Battalion in Brigade Support positions. These positions were taken over by the 15th Battalion on the evening of the 24th, the Royal Montreal Regiment then proceeding to relieve the 10th Canadian Battalion in close support. Previous to this move of the main body, No. 1 Coy. had moved forward and taken over a section of Sugar Trench. No. 2 Coy. now advanced into Sugar Trench and connected up with No. 1 Coy., and Nos. 3 and 4 Companies proceeded to take over a position in Sunken Road.

In Operation Order No. 88, dated " In the Field ", September 25th, 1916, Lieut.-Col. R. P. Clark, M.C., notified officers and men of the Battalion of the task which lay immediately before them. Summarized, this document ordered that:—

(1) On September 26th the 14th Canadian Battalion will attack and take by assault:—
    (a) First Objective:—Sudbury Trench (between two points indicated).
    (b) Second Objective:—Kenora Trench (between flanking points similarly indicated).
    (c) Any other position held by the enemy south of Kenora Trench. (Provided that such position be within the boundaries indicated.)

(2) The following marks will be used to define the direction of objectives and the flanks of the advance:—
    (a) On the Left:—The crooked pole about 700 yards due north from left flank.
    (b) On the Right:—A bushy tree, due north from right flank.

(3) Assembly:—
    (a) No. 2 Coy. on the left.
    (b) No. 3 Coy. in centre.
    (c) No. 4 Coy. on the right.
    (d) No. 1 Coy. in support on Mouquet Road.

(4) Connecting Units:—
    (a) On the left:—15th Battalion.
    (b) On the right:—6th Can. Inf. Bde.

(5) Method of Assault:—
    The assault will be carried out on a three-company front, with one company in support. Each attacking company will have attached to it one platoon of the 16th Battalion for " mopping up " purposes.
    Each company will advance to the assault in five waves, on a frontage of one platoon. " Mopping up " party will accompany the second wave.

Great care must be taken to avoid bunching, or leaving gaps in the line.

(6) Prisoners:—

Prisoners will be sent to the Road Junction near present 14th Battalion Headquarters. They will then be handed over to a 16th Battalion escort, from whom a receipt for them will be obtained.

(7) Action on Taking Each Objective:—

(a) At zero hour, which will be named later, the intensive shrapnel barrage will begin, and the assaulting troops will advance up to it.

(b) On arrival at 1st Objective, the waves intended to reach the 2nd and final objectives will cross and reform beyond it, leaving in the 1st Objective only the parties detailed to "mop up" and consolidate.

(b) On arrival at the 2nd Objective, patrols will be pushed forward for reconnaissance. During the pause on the 2nd Objective, the line will be consolidated and arrangements made for the final assault.

(d) As soon as the Final Objective is reached, patrols will be pushed out as far as the barrage permits; Lewis gun posts will be established, and the new line consolidated.

(e) As each objective is reached, and the trenches behind vacated, the troops in support and reserve will close up to the vacated trenches.

(8) Artillery Arrangements:—

(a) The bombardment is now in progress and will continue until zero.

(b) At zero the heavy artillery will barrage in succession, Hessian, Kenora, Courcelette, North and South Practice, and Regina Trenches, also communication trenches leading from the flanks of Regina Trench. From these points the barrage will be lifted onto the Sunken Roads and Ravines leading south from the Valley of the Ancre, and onto Grandcourt Trench.

(c) At zero an intense shrapnel barrage will be put on 100 yards short of the German front line trench on the whole front of the attack. At zero plus 1 minute this barrage will lift to the German front

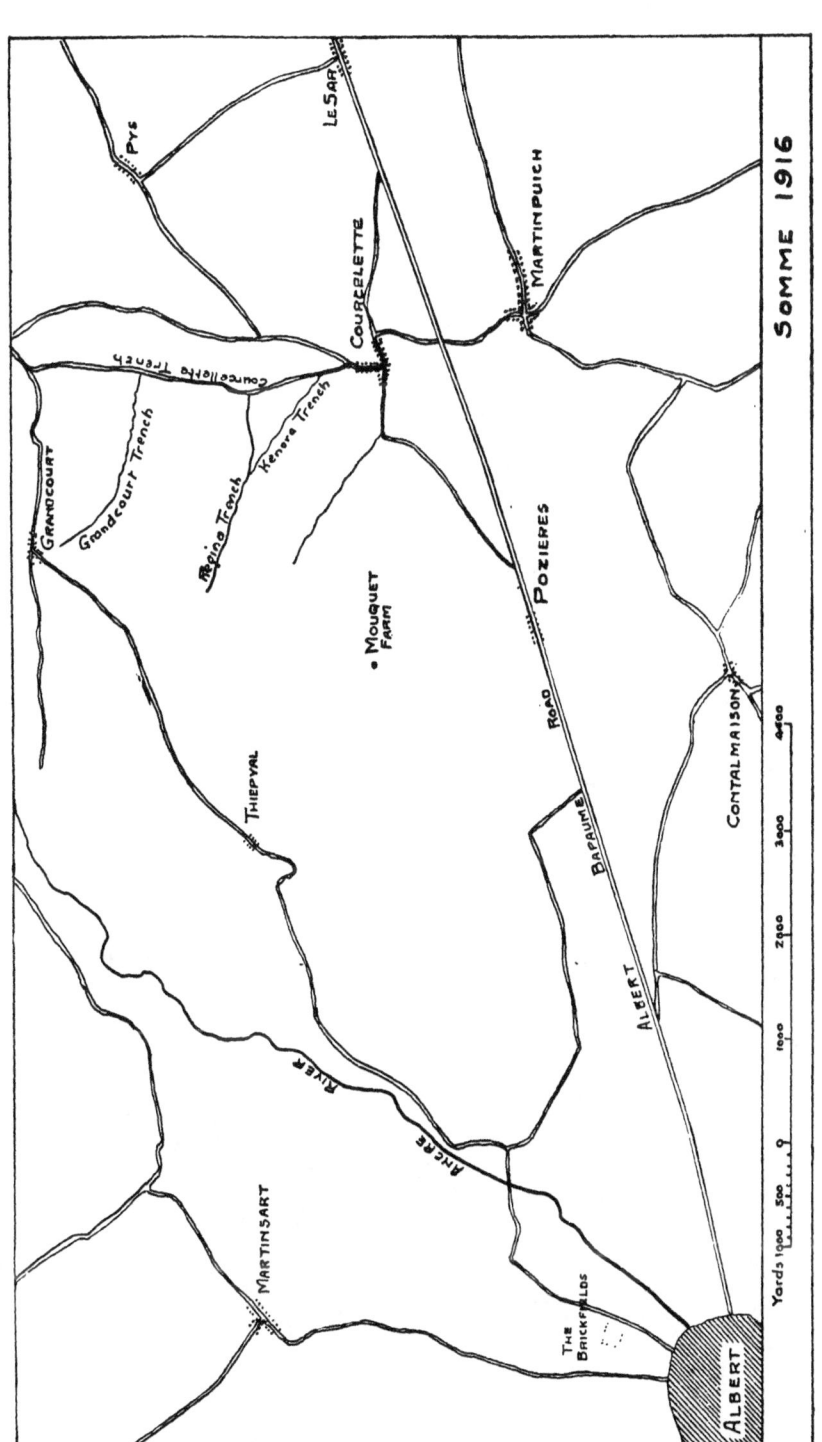

line trench (1st Objective) for 7 minutes. Barrage will then be lifted back 150 yards beyond the 1st Objective. Between objectives the rate of advance is calculated at 100 yards to 2 minutes.

(9) Assembly:—

All units will be ready in assembly positions THREE hours before zero, and before daylight, WITHOUT FAIL.

(10) Liaison:—

Major Gault McCombe will act as Liaison Officer at 3rd Brigade Headquarters. Lieut. J. F. Fitzpatrick will carry out similar duties at Headquarters of the battalion on the right flank.

(11) Contact Patrol:—

No. 7 Squadron, Royal Flying Corps, details patrols to fly at zero; at zero plus 1 hour and 45 minutes; and again at zero plus 2 hours and 15 minutes.

Flares, at these hours, will be lighted by the most advanced line of infantry when the contact machines sound a klaxon horn, or fire a Very light. Contact patrol machines are marked with a black band under the right lower plane and a blue streamer on the inside stay of the right wing. Flares can best be seen when the machine is approaching and not when directly overhead. If the sun is shining reflecting mirrors as well as flares will be used. Flares should be lit in groups of 3, and none should be used except by the advanced troops. A reserve should be kept for use after the line is consolidated.

(12) Flag Marks:—

Coloured flags will be used for marking the right flank during the advance. These are not to be placed in the ground, but will move forward with the advance.

(13) Synchronization of Watches:—

At Battalion Headquarters at 6 p.m.; at 12 midnight; and again at 4 a.m. preceding zero.

(14) Equipment:—

Troops must carry light marching order, 48 hours' rations, water bottles filled, 4 grenades, 120 rounds small arm ammunition, 6 sandbags, shovels, and picks. Troops will advance with fixed bayonets.

(15) Medical:—

Regimental Aid Post will be situated as at present.

Advanced Dressing Station will be at the Cemetery, Pozières. Field Ambulance is responsible for evacuation from Regimental Aid Post to Advanced Dressing Station. Walking cases will proceed to the Quarry on Pozières-Albert Road, between Tramway X and la Boisselle.

Any man sent to the rear, sick or wounded, must be tagged by the Medical Officer, or carry authority signed by an officer. Any man not in possession of either of these will be stopped by battle posts.

Captain Luton, M.O., will command 120 other ranks of the 16th Battalion detailed as stretcher-bearers.

During the attack no one is to remain behind with wounded officers or other ranks. The stretcher-bearers only must attend to this duty. It will be considered a grave breach of discipline if this rule is not strictly adhered to.

(16) Note:—

Should the assault on the Final Objective be considered impracticable, steps will be taken to drive the enemy from any high ground from which he can observe our approaches.

Further details as to barrages, the making of reports, the establishment of strong points, and the function of the Battalion machine guns were set forth in Operation Order No. 88. A few hours later Lieut. A. Plow, Regimental Adjutant, issued a Special Order supplementing the original. In brief this order stated that:—

(1) Zero will be at 12.35 p.m., September 26th.

(2) This time is to be communicated only to those whom it directly concerns. The telephone will not be used for this purpose.

(3) Watches will be carefully synchronized at 6 a.m. and 9 a.m., September 26th.

(4) The assaulting companies and all troops in the firing line will take the greatest care to conceal the assembly. They will not move into their jumping-off positions until the barrage opens.

(5) Bayonets will not be fixed until just before the zero hour.

III

In obedience to the instructions in Operation Order 88 and the Special Order issued as a supplement, the 14th Battalion, Royal Montreal Regiment, moved forward into front line trenches held by the 13th Battalion, and there awaited the hour of assault. The presence of so many troops crowded the trenches, but no hint of the congestion reached the enemy, and shelling was normal.

For the attack, No. 2 Coy. of the Battalion was under command of Major J. F. Sumption, who had with him Lieuts. E. B. Nelles, G. M. Sylvester, and S. S. Jones; No. 3 Coy. was commanded by Capt. C. G. Power, supported by Lieuts. W. Sharp and W. J. Holliday; No. 4 Coy. was led by Capt. W. E. Beaton, M.C., who had with him as platoon commanders, Lieuts. R. A. Pelletier, E. M. Hyman, and O. J. Larzen; and No. 1 Coy., in reserve, was under command of Major J. C. K. Carson, whose subalterns were Lieuts. H. E. Banks and E. H. Raymond.

During the long hours of the morning the men of the attacking companies lay in the front line trenches, smoking and chatting with the Highlanders. As noon approached final preparations were made and at 12.30 p.m. the lines obeyed the command, "Fix bayonets!" Then, at 12.34 p.m., the machine gun barrage opened and one minute later the first wave climbed the parapet. Seventy yards behind moved the second wave, accompanied by the "mopping up" party of the 16th Battalion, and followed a few moments later by the third and fourth waves.

It seems that the machine gun barrage gave warning to the enemy of what to expect. Certainly the attack was not an entire surprise, for when the second wave climbed the parapet the enemy had lined his trenches and was firing heavily. In spite of this lashing rifle and machine gun fire, the attack swept into the German line, proof that the Battalion had established contact with the enemy being furnished five minutes after zero when 45 prisoners were bundled back to the Canadian trenches. Little desire to fight was shown by the enemy at this stage, the number of dead bodies strewn about indicating that the preliminary bombardment had inflicted heavy losses.

At 1.03 p.m. observation showed that the men of the 14th were in full possession of their first objective. Accordingly, a party, under Coy. Sergt.-Major G. A. McLellan, was sent forward to establish a post which would defend the position against counter-attack. A counter-attack advanced at about this time, but, lacking strength, it broke down and failed to check the assaulting companies, which at

1.10 p.m. had driven over the crest of a small ridge on their immediate front.

Two minutes after the assault had reached the crest of the little ridge, No. 1 Coy. was ordered forward to consolidate the first objective. Meanwhile, under increasing shell, rifle, and machine gun fire, the attacking waves were moving forward, men falling in formidable numbers, but the remainder advancing steadily and dealing with such enemy parties as they encountered. At 2.40 p.m. Lieut. W. J. Holliday, who had succeeded to the command of No. 3 Coy. when Capt. C. G. Power fell wounded, reported that the final objective had been attained. This satisfactory report was confirmed by Lieut. R. A. Pelletier, of No. 4 Coy., who returned to Battalion Headquarters wounded. After having his wounds dressed, Lieut. Pelletier insisted on rejoining his company in the line. It would be agreeable to report that this brave officer survived, but such was not the case. He fell before the day was ended.

Meanwhile, in Kenora Trench, the men of the Royal Montreal Regiment were experiencing a severe test of their courage and endurance. Both flanks remained in the hands of the enemy, as the 31st Battalion on the right had been checked short of its final objective, as had the 15th Battalion on the left. Three German counter-attacks were launched during the afternoon, but these were beaten off and left a number of prisoners in Canadian hands. At intervals the German artillery barraged Kenora Trench and enemy bombers launched vicious attacks from the two flanks, and all the time enemy machine guns held the position under enfilade. At night barrage fire continued, the Royal Montrealers crouching behind such parapets as existed, but rising when necessity called to fling back enemy bombers who tried to rush the flanks.

By 3 o'clock on the morning of September 27th two-thirds of the garrison of Kenora Trench had fallen and Lieut. Holliday, the sole officer alive and unwounded, realized that his position was serious. To avoid possible capture, or the complete destruction of his command by shell fire, he decided to retire from Kenora into a reserve trench, which had been prepared some distance to the rear. He first saw to the evacuation of his wounded and then issued the order to withdraw. Showing every evidence of discipline and training, the survivors of the attack on Kenora Trench carried out this movement without further losses.

Having supervised the withdrawal to the reserve line immediately in rear, Lieut. Holliday reported to Battalion Headquarters and was informed that two platoons of the 16th Battalion had gone forward to reinforce him. With this added strength it was thought that Kenora Trench could be held. Accordingly, Holliday was ordered to attack and reoccupy the position without delay. Proceeding to the front, Holliday collected 17 men and with this small force advanced against his assigned objective. Amongst his men he distributed 7 tins of water, a shortage of which had caused much inconvenience on the previous day. What the Germans in Kenora Trench thought when the spectacle of an attack by 17 men presented itself, no one will ever know. Perhaps they imagined that the water tins contained Canadian " frightfulness ". Be that as it may, the majority fled, some half-dozen surrendering with little more than a show of resistance.

With Kenora Trench in his hands, Lieut. Holliday asked Lieut. Tupper, commanding the reinforcing platoons of the 16th Battalion, to move forward and assist in consolidation. Lieut. Tupper at once complied, his men working splendidly, aiding the men of the 14th in every way possible, and suffering with the latter when the enemy laid a barrage along the whole front.

At about 6 p.m. the Germans launched a bombing attack along Kenora Trench from the left, at the same time massing approximately 200 men on the right, with the obvious intention of cutting off the Canadians and forcing a surrender. As the enfilade fire of enemy machine guns rendered defence exceedingly difficult and as the strength of the German party on the right threatened irreparable disaster, Lieuts. Holliday and Tupper agreed that an immediate retirement to the reserve line was advisable. Accordingly, orders were issued and the withdrawal successfully carried out.

By the time that news of this second withdrawal from Kenora Trench had reached Brigade Headquarters, plans for further attacks on the flanks had been prepared. Lieut. Holliday, therefore, was ordered to hold his reserve position throughout the remainder of the night and, for the third time, to assault Kenora Trench at 2 o'clock on the morning of September 28th. Lieut. Tupper's party of the 16th Battalion was ordered to join in the attack. At the same hour, Holliday was informed, the 15th Battalion would attack on the left, and further to the left the assault would be pushed by units of the 2nd Canadian Infantry Brigade. On the right, it was stated, the 31st Canadian Battalion had already taken the final objectives. Had this information been correct, Lieut. Holliday's attack would have been protected from enfilade. Unfortunately, such was not the case.

Weary and exhausted from nearly forty hours of continuous fighting, but quite unsubdued in spirit, the men of the 14th and 16th Battalions prepared for the coming operation, Lieut. J. F. Fitzpatrick, the 14th Battalion Machine Gun Officer, and Lieut. A. L. McLean, of the Intelligence Section, moving forward to assist Holliday in leading the assault. Together, the subalterns collected a force of about 75 men and at 2 a.m. the attack started.

Pushing forward resolutely, the Royal Montrealers approached Kenora Trench, the vicinity of which was brilliantly lit by flares. Movement without discovery was impossible under such circumstances, and the enemy, perceiving the advance, promptly laid a field artillery and machine gun barrage between the Canadians and their objective. This barrage, powerful and well-directed, caused sharp losses amongst the men of the 14th, who were further harassed, as in the previous attacks, by vicious fire from both flanks. Realizing at 2.30 a.m. that the attacks on his flanks had not come forward as arranged, or that they had been checked short of their objectives, and finding that penetration of the enemy barrage would leave his party too weak to deal with resistance in Kenora Trench, Lieut. Holliday relinquished the attempt and withdrew the survivors of his force to the reserve trench whence they had "jumped off". In this position the detachment was relieved at 7 a.m. by the 25th Canadian Battalion, which previously had relieved the main body of the 14th Battalion.

In reporting to Brigade Headquarters on the operations of September 26th-28th, Lieut.-Col. Clark mentions the Battalion's heavy losses:—

> "I deeply regret to report the death in action of Lieut. E. M. Hyman; also that Lieut. R. A. Pelletier and Lieut. Wylie Sharp died of wounds, and that Lieut. G. M. Sylvester is missing.
>
> "The following officers were wounded:—Major J. F. Sumption, Capt. W. E. Beaton, M.C., Lieut. H. E. Banks, Lieut. E. H. Raymond, Lieut. E. B. Nelles, Capt. C. G. Power, Lieut. C. H. Sullivan, Lieut. G. B. Murray, Lieut. O. J. Larzen (shell shock), and Lieut. W. J. Holliday (remained at duty)".

Amongst the officers mentioned in the above list Lieut. R. A. Pelletier had previously distinguished himself during the advance of the Royal Montreal Regiment on the morning of June 3rd, 1916, and in the engagement now under review his courage and behaviour had commanded the respect of all. His death, therefore, was a matter of deep regret to the 14th Battalion. In Lieut. W. Sharp, too, the unit lost an officer who had proved courageous and efficient and had risen from the ranks after continuous service since 1914. Lieut. Sylvester had been with the Battalion for a shorter time, but during the period of his service had won the regard both of his superiors and those under his command. Major J. F. Sumption, O.C. No. 2 Coy., had served continuously with the Royal Montreal Regiment since May, 1915. After a period as a company officer he had taken over the duties of Battalion Quartermaster, but eventually, at his own request, he had returned to a company. Wounded early in the engagement on September 26th Major Sumption was evacuated to hospital, whence all ranks of the Battalion hoped that he would soon return. This was not to be, however, for his wounds proved severe and caused his death on the 22nd of October.

After referring to the losses amongst his officers, Lieut.-Col. Clark's report mentions the heavy casualties amongst the non-commissioned officers and men, 360 of whom were killed, wounded, or missing. Added to the losses in the previous tour, these brought the Somme casualties amongst other ranks of the Battalion to a total of 553. A less tragic aspect of the report is embodied in those paragraphs in which the Commanding Officer brings to the attention of Brigade the outstanding services of Lieut. W. J. Holliday, who led the three assaults on Kenora Trench; of Major J. C. K. Carson, who displayed courage and resource in command of No. 1 Coy.; of Lieut. E. B. Nelles, who was wounded while leading No. 2 Coy.; and of Lieut. Arthur Plow, who carried out the arduous duties of Battalion Adjutant. In addition, Lieut.-Col. Clark calls to Brig.-Gen. Tuxford's notice the excellent work of Capt. H. M. Urquhart, of the Brigade Staff, who, under heavy shell fire, supervised the delivery of material and untiringly assisted the Regiment in every conceivable manner.

The individual work of officers is mentioned in Lieut.-Col. Clark's report to the Brigadier. In addition the Commanding Officer and the Battalion have retained a lively appreciation of the devotion to duty and the courage displayed by those in the ranks. Amongst the N.C.O's. a splendid example was set by Sergeants A. Jobel, D. Woodward, J. J. Rousseau, T. T. Wilson, and E. Lépine, who behaved with great gallantry under circumstances trying to the last degree. Unfortunately, Sergts. Lépine and Rousseau were killed before the engagement ended. In dealing with enemy parties and in holding the line under overpowering shell fire, Privates R. H. Jones and J. Labelle also behaved in a manner that was outstanding even on an occasion when brave deeds were the order of the day.

IV

When the 14th Battalion was relieved by the 25th Canadian Battalion early on the morning of September 28th, the wearied men of the Regiment moved back to billets in Albert, resting there until 4 p.m. and then marching to spend the night in Warloy. Rain fell heavily on September 29th and the Battalion rested, a contrast being provided on the following day when in brilliant sunshine Major-Gen. A. W. Currie, G.O.C. the 1st Canadian Division, inspected the unit and expressed appreciation of the work just accomplished.

Strong working parties were furnished by the Battalion each day between October 1st and 5th, the latter date being marked by a move from Warloy to Albert, where Headquarters were established at 32 Rue des Illieux. On October 6th the Battalion paraded at 7.50 a.m. and moved forward into Brigade Support, passing the following day in the same positions and moving into close support on October 8th. Early on the morning of the 8th, the 13th Battalion, Royal Highlanders of Canada, and the 16th Battalion, Canadian Scottish, in conjunction with troops on the flanks, assaulted Regina Trench. Had this attack proved successful, the 14th Battalion would probably have become engaged. As it was, the Royal Highlanders encountered uncut wire, where, despite gallantry and able leadership, the companies suffered severe losses, a remnant of the attack returning to the jumping-off trenches and there standing fast. On the right front the Canadian Scottish drove into Regina Trench, killing and wounding many of the garrison. Failure on the flanks, however, forced a withdrawal.

Meanwhile, the 14th Battalion had taken over supporting positions in Sugar and Cable Trenches, with Headquarters in Gun Pit Road. Three officers and 80 other ranks were sent from these positions to carry material to the troops in the front line, and Major J. C. K. Carson and Lieut. W. J. Holliday, commander and second-in-command of the Battalion's forward details, reported to the C.O. 15th Battalion, which was in immediate support to the 13th and 16th.

All day on October 9th the Battalion lay in trenches in close support, awaiting any call that might come from the front line. No emergency arose, but on October 10th the unit was ordered to take over the Brigade frontage, these orders being cancelled when the depleted strength of the companies was realized. Some shelling occurred on the 10th, and by night, when the 7th Canadian Battalion

MEMORIAL TO MEMBERS OF THE BATTALION—SOMME, 1916

Canadian Official Copyright

relieved, six names had been added to the casualty roll, two of these being placed on the list of killed and four on the list of wounded.

Moving back from the support positions to the Brickfields, the 14th spent three days in bivouacs, the companies marching independently at 12.45 p.m. on October 13th to a point in Pozières, whence guides of the 5th Canadian Battalion led them to positions in Brigade Reserve. After two uneventful days attached to the 2nd Brigade, the Battalion was relieved by the 7th Canadian Battalion and withdrew once more to the Brickfields, where it was announced that the Regiment's part in the Somme battles had ended. Bitterness was the lot of every battalion at the Somme, and the 14th had tasted its share. In a little over a month 600 men had fallen with the result that, on parade, the Battalion presented the appearance of a depleted company rather than of that unit which for over two years had proudly borne the name, Royal Montreal Regiment.

CHAPTER XI

MONTREAL CRATER AND TRENCH RAIDS

*See you that stretch of shell torn mud spotted with pools of mire,
Crossed by a burst abandoned trench and tortured strands of wire,
Where splintered pickets reel and sag and leprous trench-rats play,
That scour the Devil's hunting-ground to seek their carrion prey?*
—JAMES H. KNIGHT-ADKIN.

I

AFTER six weeks of costly fighting at the Somme, the Canadian Corps was withdrawn and transferred to trenches on the Vimy front. Canada's participation in the Somme Battles of 1916, however, did not end when the Corps withdrew, as the 1st, 2nd, and 3rd Divisions on their way to Vimy passed the 4th Canadian Division, which, after gaining some weeks of experience in the Ypres Salient, was marching south. Coming into action at Regina Trench, the new Division maintained the Corps' reputation and earned a place alongside the veterans of Ypres, St. Eloi, and Mount Sorrel. Having gained distinction, the Division was welcomed into the Corps, when, at a later date, it followed the first three divisions to Vimy.

On October 16th, the 14th Battalion paraded at 10.30 a.m. and marched from the Brickfields at Albert to the outskirts of Bouzincourt, where a halt was made for lunch. No regret was felt by the men at leaving the Somme, except that evoked by the thought of the gallant officers and men who had fallen. To the memory of these the Battalion paid an impressive tribute by marching all morning in complete silence. Riding at the head of the Battalion, Lieut.-Col. Clark missed the usual singing and whistling and dropped back to see if the unwonted silence indicated reaction, or a sudden fall in morale, but such was not the case. Despite heavy losses at the Somme, the Regiment maintained its spirit and the silence was significant only as a spontaneous honour to the dead.

Singing and whistling once more, the Battalion resumed the march after lunch and reached billets in Warloy at 3.40 p.m. Proceeding on the following day, the Royal Montrealers halted for a night at a camp on the outskirts of Val-de-Maison, marching again on October 18th and billeting at 2.50 p.m. in Pernois. Rain fell heavily on October 19th and the Battalion rested, six other ranks being furnished to work at cleaning " muck and garbage from the streets and ditches of the village ".

" Fall in " sounded at 8.30 a.m. on October 20th, the Battalion marching shortly thereafter and reaching Prouville at half-past one, this move being followed on October 21st by a march to billets in Boffles and Fortel. Under command of Capt. F. B. D. Larken, a party moved next day to arrange billets for the Regiment at La Monte Joie Farm and Petit Houvin. Having passed the night in these, the Battalion proceeded to Ternas, leaving there at 10.30 o'clock on the morning of the 24th and reaching Magnicourt at 1.15 p.m. October 25th was wet and stormy, the men resting in billets all morning, but parading for inspection of gas helmets in the afternoon. In somewhat less than four hours on October 26th the Battalion marched from Magnicourt to Estrée Cauchie, proceeding thence on the following day and taking over Brigade Reserve positions in the Berthonval Area from the 7th Battalion, Hampshire Regiment, of the 73rd British Brigade.

In the dugouts and trenches of Brigade Reserve (Berthonval Area) the Battalion remained throughout the balance of October, parties averaging 100 all ranks being supplied each day to carry material, repair trenches, and work on the construction of deep dugouts in the support line. Before the end of the month it was announced that, for services during the Battles of the Somme, the Military Cross had been awarded to Major J. C. K. Carson and to Lieut. W. J. Holliday. The gallantry amongst other ranks was simultaneously recognized by the granting of Distinguished Conduct Medals to Acting Coy. Sergt.-Major A. Close, Pte. R. W. Jones, and Pte. J. Labelle; and Military Medals to Sergt. W. H. Miller, Sergt. W. Snideman, Sergt. W. Peat, Corp. E. S. Taylor, Pte. A. L. Bagshaw, and Pte. J. Bertram. Promotions from the ranks were also announced at this time, H. Armstrong, T. G. Beagley, G. A. McLellan, M.M., and E. Cowen receiving commissions won during the fighting earlier in the month. The depleted establishment of officers was further strengthened on October 30th when a draft, including a number of officers who had recovered from wounds received during the Salient fighting of the previous June, reported for duty from England. Major A. T. Powell commanded this draft, which included Capt. Dick Worrall, Lieut. F. Owen, and Lieut. W. W. Pickup, all recovered from wounds, also Lieuts. E. A. Adams, W. A. Kirkconnell, D. M. McRae, E. G. T. Penny, G. S. Ashby, C. F. Falkenberg, G. Hiam, J. P. O'Connor, L. R. Richards, J. E. Slessor, J. L. Stevenson, and D. W. Clarkson. At various dates during this period drafts of other ranks were taken on strength to replace, at least in part, the heavy losses which the unit had suffered at the Somme.

On November 3rd the Battalion advanced at 11.30 a.m. to relieve the 13th Canadian Battalion in front line and support trenches of the left sub-section, Berthonval Sector. Relief was completed at 2.20 p.m. and immediately parties, totalling 1 officer and 80 other ranks, began to build bombing and listening posts and to effect general trench repairs. Stronger parties carried on this work during the week the tour lasted, wiring and revetting also being necessary following a sharp bombardment by enemy trench mortars on November 4th. On this date Lieut.-Col. R. P. Clark, M.C., was wounded in the thigh, but was able to remain at duty. On November 5th several telephone S.O.S. tests were carried out, these demonstrating that the Battalion, in case of need, could count upon the field guns to open covering fire within 40 seconds of an alarm. On November 7th, a wet day, parapets collapsed in a number of places, as did the dugout Orderly Room and a sap leading to the Officers' Mess, 94 other ranks being required to restore these locations and protect them against further disintegration. Despite mud, Royal Montreal patrols were active in No Man's Land throughout the tour, much valuable information being gained and passed on to the 13th Battalion when that unit relieved at 12.45 p.m. on November 10th.

Following relief, the Battalion spent eight days at Estrée Cauchie in Divisional Reserve, in the course of which new box respirators were issued, working parties provided, and routine training carried out. Light snow fell on the night of November 17th, the Battalion marching in mist and rain on the following day to relieve the 5th Canadian Battalion in the right sub-section, Carency Sector. Relief was completed at 12.45 p.m. and the men settled down for another muddy tour in the front line.

Mud and working parties featured the next four days, a sharp trench mortar action at 2.30 p.m. on November 21st relieving the monotony, but resulting in 2 other ranks being killed. At noon on November 22nd the 13th Battalion relieved and the Royal Montreal Regiment withdrew to huts and farm buildings at Villers-au-Bois. Working parties of 5 officers and 184 other ranks moved from these billets on each of three following days to carry material to the line. Then, on November 26th, the Battalion relieved the 13th Battalion in the trenches occupied during the previous tour, and at once prepared for an operation in connection with the blowing of two mines.

These mines, when blown, opened a yawning cavity which, in honour of the troops who consolidated, was promptly named "Montreal Crater".

In a Special Operation Order and in a series of memoranda attached, Lieut.-Col. Clark deals with the plan for consolidating the crater. Summarized, his orders and comments were:—

(1) Operation:—On the 27th November, at an hour to be named later, the 176th Tunnelling Company will fire a mine.

(2) Consolidation:—The 14th Canadian Battalion will consolidate the near lip.

(3) Supports:—The 13th Canadian Battalion will place one company (approximately 150 all ranks) at the disposal of the O.C. 14th Battalion, as a battalion reserve.

(4) Officers:—

Officer in Command	Major A. T. Powell
Right Party	Lieut. E. Cowen
Centre Party	Lieut. D. W. Clarkson
Left Party	Lieut. D. M. McRae
Reserve Party (Right)	Lieut. G. A. McLellan
Reserve Party (Centre)	Lieut. J. P. O'Connor
Reserve Party (Left)	Lieut. C. F. Falkenberg
Adjutant to Major Powell	Lieut. J. L. Stevenson

(5) Personnel:—

Right Storming Party (Lieut. Cowen):—3 sappers, 2 N.C.O's. and 8 men; also 2 stretcher-bearers, 2 Lewis gunners, and 4 bombers.

Centre Storming Party (Lieut. Clarkson):—3 sappers, 1 N.C.O. and 10 men; also 2 stretcher-bearers.

Left Storming Party (Lieut. McRae):—3 sappers, 1 N.C.O. and 8 men; also 2 stretcher-bearers, 2 Lewis gunners, and 4 bombers.

Reserve Storming Parties:—Same strength as party supported.

(6) Action to Be Taken:—

On the mine being exploded, parties will advance as rapidly as possible to the objective and take up positions there.

(7) Relief of Personnel:—
   On completion of consolidation, the post garrisons will be relieved from the reserve parties.

(8) Equipment:—
   Each O.R. will carry light marching order (with 120 rounds of small arm ammunition), one extra bandolier (50 rounds S.A.A.), 4 Mills grenades, 12 sandbags, and 1 shovel.

(9) Flank Wiring Parties:—
   Two wiring parties, under Capt. D. Worrall, will advance on the flanks, simultaneously with the storming parties, and will proceed to wire the flanks.

(10) Advanced Battalion H.Q.:—
   Advanced Battalion H.Q. and Major A. T. Powell's H.Q. will be at junction of Tanchot and Heaton Trenches.

(11) Precautions:—
   On warning being given, all ranks must clear the area bounded by Uhlan - King - Gobron - Chalk Trenches to half-way between Tanchot and Uhlan, or continuation of same. Company commanders must personally see that this is done and advise Battalion Headquarters in writing.
   After debris from the explosion has fallen, positions will at once be reoccupied. All ranks must be warned to clear dugouts for explosion and to take shelter from falling debris immediately after.

(12) Action if Mine does not Explode:—
   If the mine does not explode, and after a consultation with the Tunnelling Officer, the original posts will be remanned, as at present.

(13) Emergency Party:—
   A party of 1 officer and 50 O.R. of the 13th Battalion will be detailed as a reserve to be ready, as a part or as a whole, to deal with any emergency.

(14) Runners:—
   Two runners with each of right, centre, and left parties. Four runners to remain with Major Powell. All runners to wear distinguishing marks and to have absolute "right of way" over all traffic.

(15) Trench Artillery Co-operation:—
   6 Stokes guns.
   4 Medium Trench Mortars.
   1 Heavy Trench Mortar.
   7 Rifle grenade stands.
   Rifle grenades to be used principally on flanks.
(16) Artillery Co-operation:—
   2 Batteries (12 guns) 18-pounders.
   1 Battery (4 guns) 4.5-inch.
   Artillery to engage enemy batteries and minenwerfer. Forward Observing Officer to be in suitable position (probably Ersatz Crater) with telephone and runners.
(17) Brigade Machine Guns:—
   To maintain a heavy barrage behind enemy lines, combined with general searching of enemy's territory. To open fire when the mine is blown and NOT BEFORE.
(18) Digging Parties:—
   Right, Centre, and Left:—Each 1 sapper, 1 N.C.O., and 10 men. Lieut. J. W. Maynard will be in charge of these parties. Communication trenches are to be dug zig-zag fashion to crater from our present front line.

Many further details were laid down in Lieut.-Col. Clark's Special Operation Order and Memoranda, the whole furnishing an example of care and attention to detail which, at a later date, was used to instruct the new battalions of the United States Army. Some time before the action the Battalion took on strength from England the complete brass band of the 106th Nova Scotia Battalion, under Sergt. P. F. Nass. Owing to the weakness of the companies, a number of the bandsmen took part in the Crater operation and several became casualties. The spirit displayed by the bandsmen on this occasion hastened their assimilation into the Regiment, which was pleased to possess the only brass band in the 3rd Brigade. In turn, the bandsmen were happy at the good fortune which had drafted them to a unit with a proud record of achievement in the field.

In preparation for the operations connected with the blowing of Montreal Crater, Major A. T. Powell withdrew the officers and men chosen for the attacking and consolidating parties to special billets not far from Villers-au-Bois. Here an area was taped out to represent the trenches in the vicinity of the operation, and the probable topography of the new crater was clearly indicated. Time was short, but each party rehearsed carefully the part it would be called on to play. Moving forward into the line, these parties took up their assigned positions and awaited the explosion. This came at 9.50 p.m., and within a few seconds the operation was under way. Contrary to expectations, little debris fell and no delay ensued from this cause, the consolidating parties moving forward without having suffered losses.

For a full minute after the explosion the enemy appeared dazed, then a minenwerfer came into action and white flares rose from behind the new crater, red distress flares following from the same locality and obviously calling for S.O.S. fire. Eight minutes elapsed; then a barrage fell on the crater area, preceded several seconds by a number of fish-tailed trench mortar torpedoes which burst in the Canadian front line.

Meanwhile, the consolidation parties of the Battalion had advanced to their respective objectives. Ten minutes after zero the parties on the left reached their assigned locations and found that the explosion had affected the positions scarcely at all. Accordingly, they set about improving the existing trenches and clearing them at the few points where parapets had fallen in. Simultaneously, the parties on the right reached their objectives and set to work to consolidate. Coming under the lash of the German barrage, all parties suffered losses, but after twenty minutes the shell fire slackened and after fifty minutes it died away.

As soon as enemy shelling subsided, the Royal Montrealers pushed a bombing post into the right of the old German front line, to act as a covering party while consolidation of the crater continued. Between 11 and 11.30 p.m. a party of one hundred Germans advanced across the open from their support line and dislodged the 14th Battalion bombers, who withdrew on their main body. Bombs and machine guns soon dispersed the enemy, who retreated in disorder, leaving a number of dead behind and yielding two wounded prisoners. On retreat of the enemy, 14th bombing posts, doubled in strength, were pushed forward, these dealing successfully with a group of about 9 Germans who attempted to interrupt the consolidation parties on the right.

Failing to achieve success with a small party, the enemy sent forward a stronger force at about 2 a.m. Retiring before this attack, the 14th bombers and a patrol took cover in the mine crater, while two machine guns opened fire and drove the enemy back. Shortly afterwards two lines of French wire were staked, pinned, and strung from the south lip of the crater outside the right T-head to Harting Street, and simultaneously the enemy began to consolidate his lip of the great hole in the ground. By 5 a.m. on November 28th working parties of the 14th had completed their task of making all front line and communication trenches passable by day and at 6 a.m. the consolidating parties were relieved by garrisons under command of Lieut. J. W. Maynard. So ended the highly successful minor operation at Montreal Crater, in which the 14th inflicted casualties on the enemy estimated at 75, exclusive of the troops killed by the explosion, and suffered total losses of 11 killed and 28 wounded.

In reporting on the operation to Lieut.-Col. Clark, Major Powell called to the latter's attention the support afforded by the company of the 13th Battalion, under command of Capt. J. Jeffery. Major Powell requested the C.O. of the 14th to thank this detachment and reported with pleasure that the Royal Highlanders' casualties consisted only of 1 man slightly wounded. He requested also that the thanks of the Royal Montreal Regiment be conveyed to the Officer Commanding the 1st Field Company, Canadian Engineers, whose men, first under command of Lieut. J. M. Jemmett and when the latter was wounded under Lieut. Harryet, co-operated splendidly in all phases of the undertaking. Continuing, Major Powell noted the gallant conduct of Lieut. E. Cowen, who consolidated the posts on the right and, entering the enemy lines, captured two prisoners and secured valuable identifications. The work of Privates G. R. Jones and E. F. Penford was also brought to the Commanding Officer's attention. These men, acting respectively as runners for Lieuts. Cowen and McRae, delivered messages to Major Powell's Headquarters after having been knocked down repeatedly by shell fire. Corp. J. A. Magneison is mentioned in the report for the able handling and disposition of his Lewis gun, which protected the consolidation parties on the right flank, and Pte. W. Allard is cited for his splendid bombing of enemy parties. Others whose work attracted notice and whose names have been set down in reports on the operation included Company Sergeant-Major J. Patterson, Sergt. W. Audette, Corp. W. Buckingham, Private J. A. Bertram, and Private A. J. Currie. Major Powell referred to the work of Sergt. Free, Canadian Engineers, who, at the Major's command, organized a party to replace one dispersed by shell fire, led it through the enemy barrage, reclaimed a portion of front line trench, and supervised all front line consolidation. In conclusion, Major Powell mentioned the " untiring support of Capt. D. Worrall, my principal assistant, and the dutiful conduct of all other officers associated in the enterprise ".

Following the operation at Montreal Crater, the 14th Battalion held the front line for two days, handing over to the 13th Battalion at 12.30 p.m. on November 30th and moving back to Hospital Corner in Brigade Support. Previous to relief troops occupying the posts in the crater made every effort to locate and rescue a number of Germans who, from tapping noises heard repeatedly, were buried somewhere, probably in an old dugout, under the tons of mud and debris which the explosion had cast up. Parties strove to place the sounds and had traced them to a certain small area when enemy fire forced all attempt at rescue to be abandoned. Gradually the tapping grew fainter and finally ceased. Doubtless the imprisoned Germans died of thirst, starvation, and want of air.

From November 30th until December 5th the Royal Montreal Regiment lay in Brigade Support, moving on the latter date to Divisional Reserve at Estrée Cauchie and proceeding thence on December 12th to relieve the 5th Canadian Battalion in the left sub-section, Berthonval Sector, of the front line. At this time the Battalion front line strength was made up of 26 officers, 430 bayonets, 70 machine gunners, 5 bombers, 24 signallers, 17 stretcher-bearers, and 18 Intelligence men, or 590 in all. This total was in turn divided amongst the companies as follows:—No. 1 Coy., 5 officers and 109 other ranks; No. 2 Coy., 5 officers and 110 other ranks; No. 3 Coy., 4 officers and 114 other ranks; No. 4 Coy., 4 officers and 151 other ranks; Headquarters, 8 officers and 80 other ranks.

Throughout the four-day tour that followed patrols and working parties of the Battalion were active. On December 14th the enemy bombarded heavily, approximately 104 large calibre shells falling in the front and support lines between the hours of 3 and 4 p.m. Retaliation for this fire was effected by Canadian Stokes guns and trench mortars, which damaged the enemy's parapets and wire. At 2.10 p.m. on December 16th the Royal Montrealers handed over the front to the 13th Royal Highlanders and withdrew to Brigade Reserve in Berthonval Wood, moving to Estrée Cauchie on December 21st and marching on the following day, in company with the other battalions of the 3rd Brigade, to rest billets in Bruay.

At Bruay, the Battalion passed Christmas and welcomed the New Year. The Officers' Mess and the Orderly Room were situated respectively at 69 and 71 Rue des Tombelles, and the men were comfortably billeted in the houses and buildings of the town. Routine training was carried out each day and on Christmas all who so desired were given an opportunity to partake of Holy Communion, or attend the celebration of Mass. No parades were held and the holiday was marked by a special dinner for the men, the bill of fare including a few unusual items such as port wine and cigars. In the evening the officers held a memorable dinner in the principal local hotel. Canon Scott, one-time Protestant Chaplain of the Regiment, was the guest of honour and the board was also graced by the presence of Hon. Capt. de la Taille, a member of the Jesuit Order and a gentleman of old France, who, though he had never set foot in Canada, had joined the Canadian forces and become attached as Chaplain to the Royal Montreal Regiment after the Battles of the Somme. For several months he remained with the Battalion, ministering unostentatiously, but conscientiously and generously, to the spiritual and temporal needs of the men, who regretted greatly when he was called to service with another unit. He and Canon Scott contributed much to the cheer and good-fellowship of the Christmas dinner, the latter concealing with a brave heart the deep sorrow recently caused by the death in action of a beloved son. An announcement which pleased everyone stated that, for conspicuous gallantry at the blowing of Montreal Crater on November 27th, Lieut. Edwin Cowen had been awarded the Military Cross, and that the Military Medal had been granted to Private W. Allard and Private J. A. Magneison.

II

For over a fortnight after New Year's Day, 1917, the Royal Montreal Regiment remained at Bruay, carrying out the customary training of a battalion in reserve and preparing for further tours in the line. On January 15th Lieut.-Col. R. P. Clark, M.C., relinquished command of the Battalion which was assumed by Major Gault McCombe, an original officer of the unit, who, during the period of Lieut.-Col. Clark's leadership, had served as Second-in-Command. On leaving the Royal Montreal Regiment, Lieut.-Col. Clark took command of the 2nd Canadian Battalion and, later, rose to command the 2nd Brigade of Canadian Infantry. For his services with the 14th Battalion he was awarded the D.S.O. and mentioned in despatches. Recognition of his later services was afforded when he was appointed a Companion of the Order of St. Michael and St. George, and mentioned in despatches four times. Through all the vicissitudes of his military career he maintained touch with the officers who had served under him during the Salient and Somme Battles of 1916 and never failed to express satisfaction when news reached him that the 14th was doing well. Conversely, officers and men of the R.M.R. rejoiced as honours and recognitions fell to his lot. Shortly after Lieut.-Col. Clark's departure Capt. J. K. Nesbitt, the Battalion Machine Gun Officer, left to take over duties, first in England and later with the North Russia Expeditionary Force. For services rendered against the Bolsheviks, Capt. Nesbitt was awarded the Military Cross.

Two days after Major Gault McCombe succeeded Lieut.-Col. R. P. Clark in command of the Royal Montreal Regiment, the unit marched from Bruay to Bully Grenay. At 8 o'clock on the following morning the Battalion commenced relief of the 18th Canadian Battalion, 2nd Canadian Division, in the left sub-section, Calonne Sector, No. 1 Coy. occupying trenches from the Double Crassier to Treize Alley; No. 2 Coy. taking over the front from Treize Alley to Edgware Road; No. 3 Coy. moving into close support; and No. 4 Coy. being held in reserve. Battalion Headquarters was situated at South Maroc. On the Double Crassier, which was the name given to two huge slag heaps, the opposing trenches were but 10 yards apart and conversation from the German line, or rather the murmur of voices, was frequently audible. The extreme left post of the 14th Battalion position, commanded at different times during the tour by Lieuts. H. Armstrong, G. A. McLellan, and J. E. Slessor, connected up with the extreme right post of the 2nd Battalion, The Prince of Wales's Leinster Regiment (Royal Canadians) whose officers and signallers shared a dugout with the Royal Montrealers. The Leinsters had participated in the training of the 14th Battalion in front of Armentières in 1915 and, alone of Imperial units, bore the title "Canadian", therefore they were interested to find themselves on the flank of a Dominion unit, and doubly so when they recognized a battalion they had trained.

For seven days the Battalion remained in the front line, the men enjoying the clear, cold weather, but on the alert, as the prevailing wind was favourable for the use of enemy gas. No gas attack took place, the only losses suffered being caused by shell fire, which killed one man and wounded two employed on a working party. At the conclusion of the tour the Battalion was relieved by the 13th Battalion and moved back to Brigade Support in the village of Calonne, where parties of 11 officers and 448 other ranks assembled each day for work on the Calonne and Maroc defences. On January 30th, following a light fall of snow, the 14th Battalion relieved the 13th Battalion in the front line.

Throughout February the Battalion carried out successive tours in the front line (Calonne Sector), in Brigade Reserve at Bully Grenay, and Brigade Support at Calonne. Working parties were ordered frequently, irrespective of whether the Battalion was in the line or reserve, these increasing in strength and frequency when, midway through the month, a period of frosty weather ended. Under the rays of a warm sun, followed by slashing rain, parapets softened, and trench bottoms, formerly hard as rock, melted into thigh-deep morasses of clinging mud. Only the labour of every available man for hours at a time preserved the trench system from disintegration.

In February the Battalion occupied the front line for a total of 16 days. All tours were "normal", the artillery on both sides firing frequently and trench mortars battering down parapets with annoying persistence. On the 1st of the month the Battalion suffered 11 casualties, no day's total surpassing this figure, but a nasty loss occurring on February 25th when the enemy raided No. 2 Coy. Under cover of darkness a party penetrated the Canadian wire by way of a gap cut by trench mortars. With skill the raiders evaded the 14th listening posts and surprised the front line, killing two men, wounding six, and vanishing with two wounded prisoners, Privates R. H. Green and C. J. Twamley, when attacked by a party organized and led by Lieut. D. Woodward. The enterprise and daring of the Germans on this occasion confirmed reports that the enemy had trained raid specialists. Certainly the operation reflected credit on those who planned it and on the party which carried it out. Private Green, whom the enemy captured, died as a prisoner of war and Private Twamley died, after repatriation, in December, 1918.

Having been raided, the 14th set to work to return the compliment. On February 27th Major A. T. Powell, commanding during the temporary absence of Lieut.-Col. McCombe, issued Special Operation Order No. 122, with instructions for the proposed retaliation. In brief, this order stated:—

> (1) General:—The 14th and 15th Battalions will raid the enemy trenches on the night of February 28th-March 1st. The object of the raid is to damage enemy trenches, inflict loss, and capture prisoners. The 14th Battalion party will consist of 3 officers, 77 other ranks, and 6 scouts.
>
> (2) Zero:—Zero hour will be 2 a.m. The limit allowed in enemy trenches is 15 minutes after zero.

(3) Code:— "Hussars"—Raid will take place.
"Dragoons"—Raid postponed 24 hours.

(4) Precautions:—Company commanders will take all necessary precautions to avoid casualties in the event of enemy retaliation. All killed or wounded *must* be brought in. Officers and other ranks are to be stripped entirely of identifications, particularly cap badges, numerals, sleeve patches, identity discs, pay books, buttons, letters, etc.

(5) Marking of Boundary:—The right company commander will detail a reliable N.C.O. to take up position inside our trench at our northernmost tape. This N.C.O. will be provided with a watch which will be synchronized at Advanced Headquarters at 1.45 a.m. At 2.15 a.m. this N.C.O. will fire a succession of Very lights towards our support line in a north-westerly direction. Major D. Worrall will personally show this N.C.O. the direction in which he is to fire. The object of this is plainly to mark our boundary.

(6) Recall:—The signal for the raiders to return will be the sounding of Strombos horns, the blowing of a bugle, and the burning of ground flares on enemy parapet.

(7) Signals for Brigade Machine Guns:—A small red light fired in a northerly direction from the Double Crassier will serve as a local Brigade Machine Gun signal to open fire. Later two red lights from the same position will signal the cease fire.

(8) Conclusion:—The officer on duty of No. 3 Coy. will assist in avoiding congestion in the front line after the raiders have returned.

(9) Co-operation:—The Canadian Corps Heavy Artillery, 4 batteries of 18-pounders, Stokes guns, and trench mortars will co-operate.

Following the appearance of the above order, Major Dick Worrall was placed in command of the raid and arranged the details, the code word "Dragoons" notifying all concerned that the raid had been postponed until the night of March 1st/2nd. Between the hours of 11 p.m. on March 1st and 1 a.m. on March 2nd, scouts of the 14th

Battalion reconnoitred in No Man's Land and reported all clear. Soon after their return the raid began.

In order to avoid confusion three parties of raiders will be followed individually. At 1.40 a.m. No. 1 party (Lieut. D. M. McRae and 25 other ranks) approached to within forty yards of the German line, the barrage being so perfectly placed that this move was accompanied by little danger. At 2 a.m. (zero) the barrage lifted to the enemy support line and No. 1 Party commenced operations, "A" Group, led by Sergt. Snow, bombing straight along the German parapet. Though wounded in the wrist, Sergt. Snow, an original member of the Battalion, continued to lead his men until their share in the operation had been completed. Meanwhile Corp. Price, leading "B" Group, jumped onto the enemy parapet and down into the trench where he was instantly killed by a shot from a German rifle. Seeing what had happened, Lieut. D. M. McRae leaped into the trench, grappled with the Hun who had fired, and took him prisoner. Moving along the trench "B" Group killed four Germans with bombs and drove the remainder of a small party back towards the support line. Continuing, "B" Group came to a dugout whence one German emerged and was taken prisoner. Other Germans paid no attention to shouted demands for surrender and were killed when the dugout was wrecked with explosive. Further along the trench another dugout was bombed with Mills grenades, and still another, containing a party of the enemy, was completely destroyed by a Stokes bomb on a four-second fuse. Following the destruction of these dugouts, Lieut. McRae, whose party had lost 1 killed and 5 wounded, withdrew his forces and awaited the signal to return to the Canadian line.

At zero No. 2 Party (Lieut. Pitcher and 24 other ranks) moved forward and entered the enemy line, "J" Group soon encountering a number of the enemy, two of whom were killed by bombs and two captured. Meanwhile, "H" and "G" Groups worked their way along the parapet, encountering opposition which caused delay at one point, but succeeding in killing one German and capturing two. Further along the trench this party destroyed a dugout with a number of the enemy inside. A few moments later two Germans were encountered, one of them wearing a large red cross on his sleeve. This individual pointed a revolver and cried "Hands up!" in English. He and his companion were thereupon killed by a bomb and rifle fire. Following this incident, the raiders reached another dugout and invited the occupants to surrender. Much shouting ensued, but, no Germans appearing, a mobile charge was exploded and the dugout destroyed. Lieut.

Pitcher, who led No. 2 Party successfully despite a wound in the left arm, now decided to withdraw along the trench, as time for the conclusion of the raid was rapidly approaching. During the withdrawal a German was found hiding on the bottom of a trench. This individual was added to the party's " bag " and conducted as a prisoner to the 14th lines.

When Nos. 1 and 2 Parties advanced to carry out the tasks assigned to them, No. 3 Party (Lieut. Beagley, 16 other ranks, plus two Lewis guns and crews) moved into position to block Okoweg Communication Trench and check any German reinforcements which might be sent to the garrison in the front line. This party met no resistance and suffered but one slight casualty. On the sounding of the Strombos horns, the party withdrew as ordered.

In compiling his report on the raid, Major Dick Worrall notes certain aspects which are of interest. The morale of the Germans he considered " good "; their trenches were " dry, bath-matted, and revetted ", but damaged by the Canadian artillery fire. The barrage for the raid was excellent, both as to timing and placement; but Major Worrall comments that the recall signals were lost amid the din and confusion of bombing and rifle fire, the bugle being heard but faintly and the Strombos horns, in many cases, not at all. To his report the commander of the raid attaches the following time-table of events as reported at Raid Headquarters:—

1.04 a.m.	Patrol reports wire cut.
1.40 a.m.	Raiding Party in position.
1.53 a.m.	Barrage starts.
1.56 a.m.	One green rocket from enemy line.
1.59 a.m.	One red rocket from enemy line.
2.04 a.m.	All going well.
2.06 a.m.	Bombing going on in enemy lines.
2.08 a.m.	One bright light from enemy line.
2.09 a.m.	One prisoner brought in.
2.18 a.m.	First enemy shell near our front line.
2.20 a.m.	Retaliation requested by O.C. Crassier.
2.21 a.m.	Five more prisoners.
2.23 a.m.	Lieut. Pitcher reports in slightly wounded.
2.24 a.m.	Nos. 1 and 2 Parties report in.
2.25 a.m.	Enemy retaliation on our front line.
2.28 a.m.	Lieut. Beagley and No. 3 Party report in.
2.36 a.m.	Enemy fire has ceased.

2.38 a.m. O.C. Crassier reports no casualties.
2.39 a.m. Right front line company reports all O.K.
2.40 a.m. Left front line company reports all O.K.
3.15 a.m. Advanced Headquarters closed.

Following the successful raid, the Batalion was relieved at 8.30 o'clock on the evening of March 4th by the 8th Battalion, Royal West Kent Regiment, Headquarters and the companies proceeding independently to billets in unoccupied houses in Bully Grenay. At 10 a.m. on March 5th the Battalion marched from Bully Grenay, passing through the towns of Hersin and Barlin and reaching Haillicourt at half-past twelve. Marching again three days later, the Royal Montreal Regiment swung through Houdain, Gauchin Légal, Estrée Cauchie, and Quatre Vents and billeted for the night in Cambligneul. On the 9th, at noon, the Regiment left Cambligneul, marched through Camblain l'Abbé, and at 4 o'clock reached its destination at huts in the Bois des Alleux.

Nine days were spent in this position and on the 18th of the month the Battalion relieved the 15th Canadian Battalion in Brigade Reserve at Maison Blanche, three of the companies occupying dugouts and one being billeted in a large cave. From Maison Blanche working parties of 5 officers and more than 500 men were supplied on each of the five days that followed, the personnel of these carrying material, cleaning trenches, and constructing dugouts. Several casualties were inflicted on these parties and one man was killed by the collapse of a dressing station in Elbe Trench. All ranks while at work were thrilled by the fight being waged for control of the air. As the infantry toiled at their unromantic tasks, far above their heads in the blue the winged legions of England and Germany dipped, swooped, and struck, British pilots fighting to guard the secrets of the Vimy Area and the Germans striving desperately to discover what the British sought to hide. On March 21st a red biplane defeated a British plane which fell at the junction of Claudot and Bentata Trenches, about 400 yards from 14th Headquarters. Other British losses occurred from time to time, but the defence was splendidly maintained. Knowing how secrecy would aid the attack which the British Army was mounting, officers and men of the 14th were cheered tremendously when attacking planes crashed to earth and were correspondingly depressed when crack German pilots, distinguished by their red planes, scored a victory.

At 6.30 p.m. on March 24th the Royal Montreal Regiment commenced relief of the 15th Canadian Battalion in the front line, Thélus

Sector, completing the operation at 10.15 p.m. without casualties. British artillery and trench mortars were active on the days that followed. The heavy guns shelled the German communications and ammunition dumps, and the field guns wrought havoc in the enemy's line and tore his defensive wire. This activity provoked retaliation, Douai, Elbe, and Sapper Trenches in the Royal Montrealers' area being subjected to several heavy bombardments and the whole front receiving more than a normal amount of shell fire. Special precaution against this fire was ordered with the result that casualties were negligible.

Early on the morning of March 29th a raiding party of the 14th Battalion, under Lieut. D. M. McRae, advanced against the enemy line, in conjunction with a special party of the 13th Battalion. Zero was at 3 o'clock and seven minutes before this hour the Canadian artillery, machine guns, and Stokes guns opened fire. At 3 o'clock an orange rain rocket rose from the German line, followed immediately by a green light which split into several balls of fire. These signals, and others set off in rapid succession, brought a barrage of 5.9-inch, 4.1-inch, and '77 mm. shells from the direction of Thélus, Bois Carré, and Farbus Wood. This barrage hampered the 14th Battalion party, which also encountered heavy wire. Lieuts. McRae and E. G. T. Penny, with a number of their men, penetrated the wire and entered the German line. No enemy was found, but Sergt Weir was killed before the raiders withdrew. The body they brought back with them to their own lines. At the point where the 13th Battalion attacked, entry into the German line was effected and a number of the enemy killed, the raiders escaping with a loss of but two men wounded. On the night following this operation the 14th Battalion was relieved by the 4th Canadian Battalion and proceeded to le Pendu Huts in Divisional Reserve.

CHAPTER XII

THE TAKING OF VIMY RIDGE

> The Germans laugh on Vimy Ridge
> Where once the children played,
> And on the slopes of Vimy Ridge,
> The bloody slopes of Vimy Ridge,
> The sons of France are laid.
>
> But soon, but soon, on Vimy Ridge
> Courage shall answer craft;
> Spring on the slopes of Vimy Ridge
> A sweeter sound shall waft.
> Children shall play on Vimy Ridge
> Where once the Germans laughed.
> —M. B. in the "Westminster Gazette".

I

"IN conjunction with the Third Army, the Canadian Corps will take the Vimy Ridge". Heading an operation order in April, 1917, this sentence informed the Canadian divisions of the task immediately before them. Momentarily, its audacity left its readers breathless, for in 1915 Germany had hurled back from the Ridge French troops of the old first line regiments, who had failed only because the task was beyond what flesh and blood could accomplish. Since that time the Ridge had been strengthened until the enemy boasted that its capture was beyond the power of any troops on earth. Months of study, however, led Sir Douglas Haig and Sir Julian Byng to believe that the Germans were wrong. Granted adequate artillery preparation, well-organized counter-battery fire at zero, and determined attacking troops, trained to the last notch of efficiency, they felt that the Ridge could be wrested from the enemy's grasp. This confidence was justified on April 9th, 1917, when the Canadian Corps took the Ridge in a single day's fighting.

Certain features of the capture of Vimy Ridge cause the engagement to rank amongst the important battles of 1917. In the first place it is probable that no operation had ever been more carefully rehearsed. Over a special area, prepared from aerial photographs and laid out to represent the German positions in every particular, the assaulting battalions carried out again and again the moves that would be demanded on the day of battle. So perfectly were the enemy positions reproduced that troops learned by heart the position of trenches, communication trenches, and supply dumps, and battalion commanders in many cases were able to select the exact dugout, far behind the German lines, which would serve as their battle headquarters. The photographs on which the taped reproduction of the German front was based were supplied by the Royal Flying Corps, which also photographed scores of German battery positions. Each of these was carefully located on the maps at Corps Headquarters and arrangements made to neutralize it by counter-battery fire at zero. This counter-battery organization proved effective and was a weighty factor in the Corps' success. Foresight in training Canadian crews to operate German field guns also met with appropriate reward, a number of captured German guns, formed into " Nos. 1, 2, and 3 Pan-Germanic Groups, Canadian Artillery ", coming into action at a critical moment and contributing materially to the British victory.

By coincidence, the date chosen for the assault on Vimy Ridge was the birthday of Erich von Ludendorff, Quartermaster-General of the German Army, and believed by many to have been the " brains " of the whole Teutonic military confederation. In his memoirs, Gen. Ludendorff admits that the British capture of Vimy " threw all his calculations to the winds ", and his diary reveals that on the night of the 9th he felt " deeply depressed ". His memoirs also admit that the Canadian attack on Vimy, and the simultaneous drive of British divisions to the south, puzzled him sorely. Vimy was valuable to the British throughout the remainder of 1917, and invaluable in 1918, nevertheless, he concluded from failure to continue the battle after initial success that some event beyond the broad reach of his intelligence had adversely affected the plan of action as originally conceived. This inference reveals the mind of a trained soldier. The capture of Vimy, and the British attack astride the Scarpe, represented all that had been retained of a comprehensive plan of action worked out by General Joffre and Field Marshal Sir Douglas Haig in the autumn of 1916. When General Nivelle took command of the French Armies, he rejected the plan which Joffre and Haig had agreed upon and substituted his project for a smashing, decisive blow on the Aisne. He even opposed the attack on Vimy Ridge, and officers of his staff when shown the plan of action at First Army Headquarters expressed fear that the Canadians would fail dismally. Fortunately, such was not the case. On the contrary, when Nivelle's offensive had been launched and shattered, the capture of Vimy shone as the one brilliant achievement in a dark period of disaster.

When the French attack failed, Sir Douglas Haig ceased operations on the Vimy front and concentrated his effort in Flanders.

Recognizing the tactical brilliancy of the Vimy success, but unaware, fortunately, of many circumstances attending the failure on the Aisne, Ludendorff is found wondering whether the British attack had any strategic purpose. It had; but the change from the Joffre-Haig to the Nivelle plan, and the collapse of the new plan when tested, rendered strategic objectives unattainable. Tactically, capture of the Ridge remained, and will always remain, one of the striking episodes of the war.

II

During the first four days of April, 1917, the 14th Battalion was stationed at le Pendu Huts in Divisional Reserve. From this location the Battalion on two occasions marched to Estrée Cauchie to rehearse with other battalions of the 3rd Brigade the coming attack on Vimy Ridge. The fact that the four divisions of the Canadian Corps were for the first time attacking side by side inspired confidence, which increased as the troops observed the vast stores of ammunition in the area, the success of British pilots in the air, and the painstaking attention being given to all preliminaries. At Estrée Cauchie the men entered into the enthusiastic spirit of the Brigade rehearsals, studied the area conscientiously, and strove mightily to perfect themselves in their respective parts. Care was taken lest troops, eager to practice their own tasks, should neglect what was taking place around them. In the assault casualties would force troops to assume duties originally assigned to others. Accordingly, parties were trained in their individual tasks, but the general plan was never lost to sight.

So far as the 1st Canadian Division was concerned, the plan of the operation called for an assault on that part of the Ridge lying S. and S.E. of Thélus. The 3rd Canadian Infantry Brigade was given two objectives, named respectively the Black Line, or Zwolfer Weg, and the Red Line, or Swischen Stellung. On the right flank was the 2nd Canadian Infantry Brigade and on the left the 4th Canadian Infantry Brigade. The assault of the 3rd Brigade was ordered with three battalions in line, the 15th Battalion, 48th Highlanders, under Lieut.-Col. C. E. Bent, on the right; the 14th Battalion, Royal Montreal Regiment, commanded by Lieut.-Col. Gault McCombe, in the centre; and the 16th Battalion, Canadian Scottish, led by Lieut.-Col. C. W. Peck, on the left. In close support was the 13th Battalion, Royal Highlanders of Canada, under Lieut.-Col. G. E. McCuaig.

On April 5th the 14th Battalion moved forward to Maison Blanche, completing occupation at midnight and moving forward again on the following day into front line trenches (Thélus Sector) with Headquarters in Bentata Tunnel. This vast cavern, electrically lighted and provided with side chambers and passages, was used to shelter troops during assembly for the Vimy attack. April 8th was the date chosen for the battle, but when the calendar showed that Easter fell on this day April 9th was substituted and the troops ordered to attack at 5.30 a.m.

Final instructions to the 14th Battalion were issued by Lieut. J. W. Maynard, Acting Adjutant, under date of April 3rd. In these orders details of the assembly, the advance to the Black Line, the reform after the capture of the Black Line, and the assault on the Red Line were enumerated. Following capture of the Red Line, other troops were to pass through and drive the attack forward. The 14th would then consolidate and withdraw to join the 13th as Divisional Reserve.

Special attention of all ranks of the Battalion was called to the fact that troops would attack exactly at zero and not wait for the barrage to lift from the German front line trenches at zero plus 3 minutes. More than three minutes would be consumed in crossing No Man's Land and it was desirable to give the enemy little time to come up from his dugouts and open fire. Similarly, following capture of the Black Line, troops of the 3rd attacking wave were ordered to work forward to within 60 yards of the barrage, which from zero plus 38 minutes to zero plus 75 minutes was to stand on a position 200 yards east of the Black Line. Officers were instructed to see to it, at this stage, that each wave moved forward in conformation with the corresponding wave of the 16th Battalion on the left flank. A slight bend in the position to be occupied by the Canadian Scottish made this co-ordination a matter for careful attention.

For the battle each man of the 14th Battalion was ordered to carry rifle, complete equipment less pack, 120 rounds of small arm ammunition, 2 Mills bombs, 5 sandbags, 48 hours' rations, unexpended portion of current ration, waterproof sheet, box respirator (worn at the alert), smoke helmet, goggles, 1 ground flare, and filled water bottle. In the case of bombers, rifle grenadiers, Lewis gunners, and runners, small arm ammunition was reduced to 50 rounds to permit the carrying of special equipment, or to aid rapid movement. Warrant officers and N.C.O's. were instructed to carry rifles with fixed bayonets, and officers were ordered to equip themselves with revolvers and Very signalling pistols. No maps of the British trenches and no papers of value to the enemy were to be carried by officers or men. All ranks were ordered to wear steel helmets, and each half of the Battalion was instructed to carry forward 33 picks and 67 shovels.

All night on April 8th the roads in the neighbourhood of Vimy Ridge echoed to the tramp of marching feet as the battalions of the Canadian divisions and the British divisions on the flank moved forward to the assembly. That the enemy knew an attack was contemplated is certain, for such vast scale preparations could not be entirely hid; that he suspected the day and hour is improbable, for, with minor exceptions, thousands of troops assembled without drawing appreciable shell fire. All was in readiness, therefore, when at 5.30 o'clock on the cold, blustery morning of April 9th, the guns opened fire and the infantry, in the half light of dawn, plodded forward behind the first British " creeping barrage " of the war, with a determination and relentlessness which carried them to decisive victory.

While the battalions in reserve were marching forward on the night of April 8th, the 14th Battalion moved into jumping-off trenches, completing occupation of these at 3.50 a.m. and notifying Brigade that the unit was ready for zero. Sharp at 5.30 a.m. the attacking waves of the Regiment stepped over the parapet and advanced towards the German front line, which at the moment was suffering the destroying wrath of a marvellously placed barrage. In the van of the Battalion's attack were Nos. 3 and 4 Companies, commanded respectively by Capt. W. W. Pickup and Major W. J. Holliday, M.C., the former on the right and No. 4 on the left. Both companies advanced in two waves, with Nos. 1 and 2 Companies supplying support and mopping up as German territory was captured.

Driving through the German front line, No. 3 Company brushed aside such opposition as the garrison afforded and advanced against a trench known as Eiserner Kreuz Weg. Here the defending Bavarian troops fought gallantly, holding back the Canadian advance until killed or wounded by bomb or bayonet. In the hand to hand fighting the Royal Montrealers soon established superiority, but the enemy, by clever use of his machine guns, forced payment for the ground torn from his grasp. Before the capture of Eiserner Kreuz Weg was accomplished Capt. W. W. Pickup and Lieut. H. B. Symonds had fallen, together with a number of N.C.O's. and men. In the deaths of Capt. Pickup and Lieut. Symonds No. 3 Coy. and the Battalion suffered a severe loss, for the former was an experienced officer who had recovered from wounds received in the summer of the previous year, and Lieut. Symonds, an original member of the Battalion, had won a commission after courageous service in the ranks.

Meanwhile No. 4 Coy. on the left had also suffered appreciably and Major W. J. Holliday, M.C., who had won distinction at Kenora Trench in September of the previous year, had fallen mortally wounded. Lieut. Francesco Gidony had also been severely wounded and could no longer lead his men in action. Major Holliday and Lieut. Gidony reached hospital and fought hard for life, but in each case the odds proved too high, the company commander dying on April 16th and his subaltern twenty-four hours later.

In spite of the setback caused by the casualties to officers and a high proportion of N.C.O's., the attack of Nos. 3 and 4 Companies drove forward, the men displaying a praiseworthy desire to let nothing interfere with the carrying-out of the pre-arranged schedule. On the right, where the attack of the Battalion joined with that of the 15th Battalion, German machine gun No. 10294 shot down many men of both units. Realizing how serious an obstacle this gun presented, Lieut. B. F. Davidson organized and led an attack against it. Game to the last, the gun crew met the Canadian assault with a shower of bombs, which dropped several of the Royal Montrealers in their tracks. Lieut. Davidson, however, penetrated the grenade barrage, shot the crew, and put the gun out of action.

On the left Company Sergeant-Major J. F. Hurley noticed a machine gun which, similarly, threatened to hold up the Royal Montreal advance. At the moment no assistance was available, so Hurley attacked the gun single-handed. Taking advantage of an instant when the attention of the crew was concentrated elsewhere, Hurley charged, bayoneted three Germans, and captured the gun. By this act he cleared the Regiment's path and saved many casualties.

Meanwhile stubborn fighting had carried Eisener Kreuz Weg, but not before machine guns firing from the Red Line had inflicted sharp losses, among the killed being Lieuts. L. B. Richards and J. L. Stevenson, who had displayed marked courage and devotion to duty. Capt. H. E. Banks, who had rejoined the Battalion after recovering from wounds received at the Somme, was wounded at this time, as was Lieut. N. McLeod, who had suffered wounds on two previous occasions and had been commissioned in recognition of service in the ranks. Lieut. E. G. T. Penny was also wounded, but was able to remain at duty.

Once the obstacle presented by Eisener Kreuz Weg had been surmounted, the attack of the Royal Montreal Regiment swept forward towards the 1st objective, the Black Line. Simultaneously, the 15th and 16th Battalions on the flanks overcame the difficulties on their

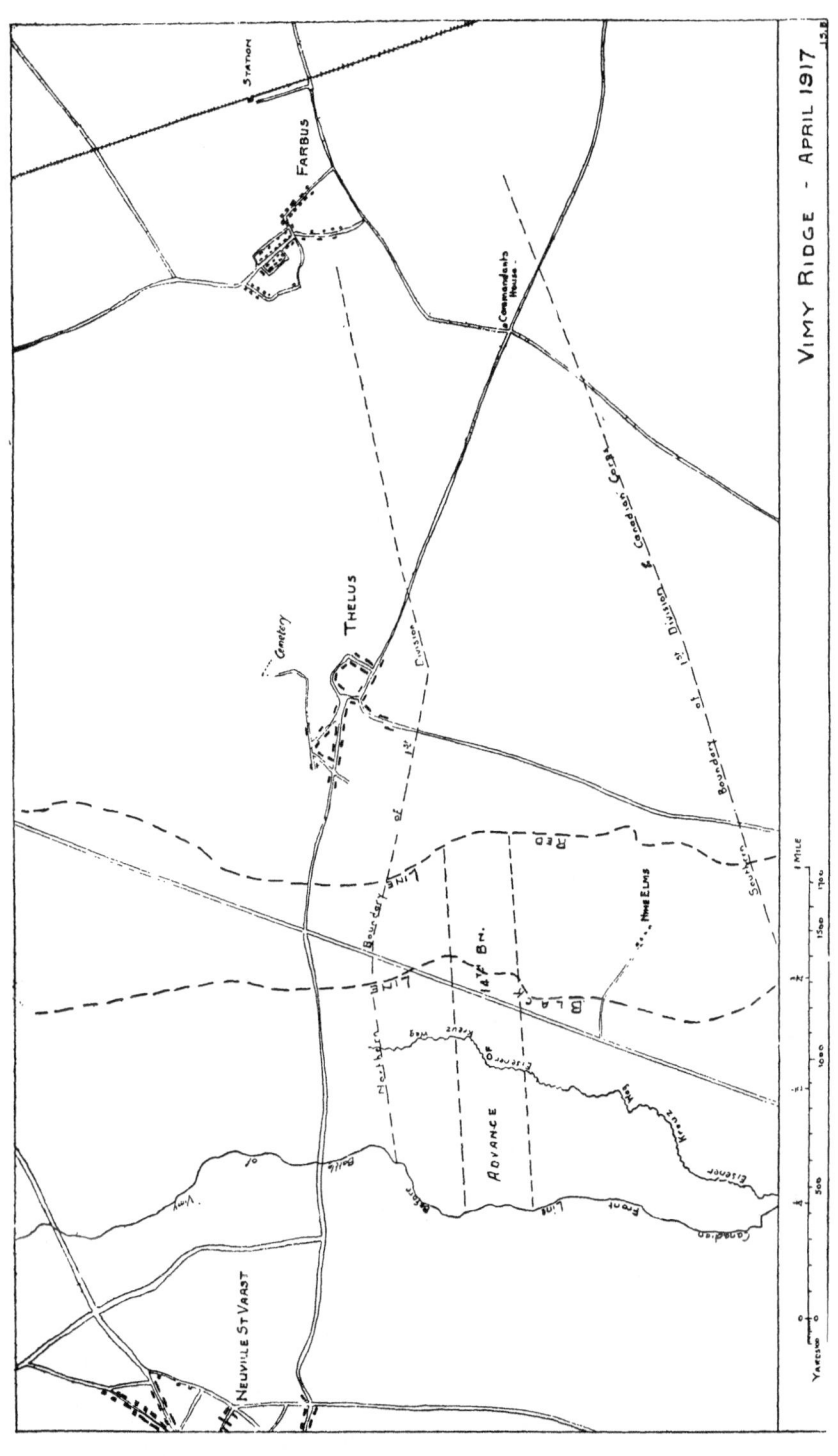

respective fronts and flung their attacking waves forward. Liaison between the three battalions was excellent, the 1st, 2nd, and 3rd waves conforming remarkably and maintaining a unity of action which added greatly to their strength. Opposition decreased at this stage of the engagement and the Black Line was captured without serious difficulty, though some bombing was required to subdue final resistance. In one dugout, afterwards used as Battalion Headquarters, Lieut. T. Hodgson and a party of Regimental Scouts captured 26 prisoners.

Halting in the Black Line in accordance with orders, the 14th Battalion reformed for the second stage of the battle, the 3rd wave passing through the first two waves and preparing to advance against the Red objective. Meanwhile, machine gun posts were pushed forward and the Black Line consolidated against counter-attack. For nearly half an hour the men of the 14th halted, while the British barrage stood steadily on a line 200 yards to the east. Redispositions having been effected, the 3rd wave, now become the 1st, advanced towards the barrage, which lifted at 6.55 a.m. and permitted an assault on the final objective.

The effect of the barrage in the area beyond the Black Line was marked, the ground being ripped and torn and the German trenches utterly demolished. Garrisons in many cases had been wiped out; elsewhere individuals remained alive, but too dazed to offer resistance. Attacking schedules were accordingly maintained, and the Red objective was captured at 7.10 a.m.

In the fighting at Eisener Kreuz Weg, at the Black Line, and during the final sweep forward to the Red Line, the bearing and behaviour of officers and men reflected credit on the Regiment's discipline and training. Able leadership was displayed by many of the junior officers, the work of Lieuts. T. Hodgson, E. G. T. Penny, D. Woodward, E. A. Adams, and N. M. Cowell being conspicuous. Company Sergeant-Major A. Close also showed capacity which marked him for early promotion, as did Sergts. J. R. McKinnon and R. J. Allan. Corp. J. H. Foley led his section with courage and ability, and Lance-Corporals W. Broughton, G. H. MacDonald, and J. Williams demonstrated soldierly qualities and quick appreciation of the situations that arose. In overcoming the resistance of enemy machine guns and in the hand to hand fighting at Eisener Kreuz Weg, Corp. J. A. Bertram and Privates J. Melvin, H. Hetu, R. Levis, F. Thompson, J. E. Muttart, G. E. Daughters, and P. G. Rumball displayed courage and gallantry of the highest order.

With the capture of the Red Line the active part of the 3rd Brigade in the Battle of Vimy Ridge was brought to a close. All four battalions of the Brigade had suffered losses, but in no case were these out of proportion when considered in relation with the striking nature of the Brigade's success. In the Royal Montreal Regiment 6 officers were killed, or fatally wounded, mostly by machine gun fire; and three officers were wounded. Amongst the other ranks casualties totalled 265, of whom 92 were killed and 173 wounded.

When the 3rd Brigade halted in the Red Line, troops of the 1st Canadian Infantry Brigade moved up and prepared to carry the assault forward. Snow and rain fell at intervals and a cold wind chilled the troops, but victory was in the air and the cold was disregarded. At 9.55 a.m. the battalions of the 1st Brigade stepped from the trenches of the Red Line and started across No Man's Land, which on the previous day had been territory far inside the German lines. By 11 a.m. the Brigade had captured the Blue Line and by 1 p.m. the Brown Line had also fallen. Down the eastern slope of the Ridge the 1st Brigade continued, halting while the artillery shelled Farbus Wood, then driving through the Wood, capturing several batteries of guns, and reaching the railway line beyond Farbus by 5.45 p.m.

Elsewhere on the front the result was much the same. The 2nd Canadian Division attacked with four brigades, each on a front of two battalions. The 4th and 5th Brigades captured the Black Line and the latter continued to the Red Line. The 13th Imperial Brigade then passed through, capturing Goulot Wood and many prisoners. By mid-afternoon the Division had captured all its assigned objectives and had pushed patrols through Farbus Village. The 3rd Canadian Division had not so far to go as the 1st and 2nd Divisions, but it cleared La Folie Wood, captured the Black Line soon after 6 a.m., and the Red Line three hours later. In the Red Line the Division halted, that position being its final assigned objective. On the front of the 4th Canadian Division on the left, the 87th and 102nd Battalions suffered severely, machine gun fire from a commanding position known as " The Pimple ", cutting the attacking waves to pieces. The 87th Battalion, Canadian Grenadier Guards, lost 60% of its personnel; in the 102nd Battalion all officers became casualties and command passed to a company sergeant-major. Other battalions of the Division suffered in proportion, but success in the end was not denied them, for by night they had reached their objectives and in the morning they drove the last German from Vimy Ridge. By this time a total of 3,342 prisoners had passed into Canadian hands.

Vimy Ridge, April, 1917

When the capture of the Red Line was reported to 14th Battalion Headquarters, Lieut.-Col. Gault McCombe and his staff advanced from Bentata Tunnel to a dugout in the Black Line. In common with many German dugouts in the Vimy Area, this hole in the ground was stocked with an enormous supply of bottled soda water, also with a quantity of sour and unpalatable bread. The soda water was refreshing, but the bread was altogether beyond what Canadians could stomach. As one officer remarked, " The smell of it is deplorable and the taste not even a German could appreciate ".

At 9.40 a.m. the Battalion withdrew from the Red Line to a position near Nine Elms, moving again before noon to an area between Eisener Kreuz Weg and the Sunken Road. Meantime stretcher-bearers worked untiringly to clear the field of wounded. In the Regimental area this task was quickly accomplished, the wounded being brought to a collection post not far from Battalion Headquarters. Unfortunately, difficulties of ambulance convoy in the rear area caused a delay at this point, a number of the 14th wounded being killed by shell fire while waiting to be carried further back. Apart from this purely local failure, the wounded were handled with the utmost efficiency. By noon many had reached hospitals back of the lines and by night few remained at the advanced dressing stations.

From noon on April 9th until dusk on the 10th, the 14th Battalion remained in the position between Eisener Trench and the Sunken Road, ready to move should the enemy counter-attack, or troops of the 1st Canadian Division require assistance. No appeal for help was forthcoming, however, and the Battalion moved back to take over Vase Trench from the 10th Canadian Battalion.

III

Four days were spent at Vase Trench, during which the men were fascinated by the activity around them. Thousands of troops were employed on the construction of roads and light railways; huts to shelter reserve units were springing up in all directions; guns were being manipulated and tractor-hauled forward; and in the air squadrons of planes manœuvred and fought as the opposing pilots sought to discover, or conceal, what was taking place beneath them.

At 5.30 o'clock on the morning of April 14th the Royal Montreal Regiment relieved the 3rd Canadian Battalion in a reserve position in Wittelsbacher Trench, moving forward again at dusk on April 15th and relieving the 5th Canadian Battalion in Bois de la Ville. Three days later the Royal Montrealers took over the left sub-section of the Brigade front (Arleux Sector) from the 13th Battalion, and Major A. T. Powell, who was commanding during the temporary absence of Lieut.-Col. McCombe, established his headquarters in a dugout in the railway embankment not far from Farbus Station.

For four days the Battalion occupied the front line, which ran along the Sunken Road near Willerval and consisted of shallow pits, providing a bare minimum of shelter. Cooking was well-nigh impossible, as the enemy batteries had the pits ranged to perfection and the slightest sign of life drew shell fire of barrage intensity. The enemy, smarting at the loss of Vimy Ridge, had no intention of permitting the Canadians to triumph unmolested. His exasperation and annoyance found a means of expression in expenditure of ammunition, individuals being sniped at by field guns and small parties provoking fire from batteries.

On several occasions during the tour in the front line the enemy laid a barrage along the line of the Farbus Railway. Perhaps he suspected that plans for a further attack were being completed, or possibly he hoped to inflict losses on some headquarters. Be that as it may, the shelling, though intense, was singularly unproductive, causing few casualties and no delay in the marking of assembly positions for the proposed new attack. Following relief by the 4th Canadian Battalion, which was completed at 12.40 a.m. on the morning of April 23rd, the 14th Battalion withdrew up Vimy Ridge and, crossing back over the summit, moved into reserve tents at Maison Blanche South Camp. Three days were spent in this position, the Battalion moving on April 26th to tents at Fond du Vase, on the 28th to Brigade Support positions in Bois Carré, and on the 29th to a position in support of the 13th Battalion (Arleux frontage).

May 1st, 1917, found the 3rd Canadian Infantry Brigade holding a line just east of Arleux-en-Gohelle, which had been captured four days previously by troops of the 2nd Brigade. In close support to the front line, the 14th Battalion, with a trench strength of 21 officers and 473 other ranks, lay in a series of small pits, each holding from 2 to 4 men. Shelling throughout the day threatened the unit, but for some reason the enemy gunners straddled the position and casualties were avoided. At night the Battalion was relieved by the 3rd Battalion.

When relief was completed at 1 o'clock on the morning of May 2nd, the Royal Montreal Regiment moved back to Island Traverse Trench and there spent the day in Brigade Reserve. Moving forward again at 11 o'clock that same night, No. 1 Coy. occupied dugouts in the railway embankment just north of Farbus Station, and Nos. 2, 3, and 4 Companies took over positions on the western edge of Bois de la Ville. At 9.30 a.m. on May 3rd, the Battalion was attached to the 1st Canadian Infantry Brigade to support operations in the neighbourhood of Fresnoy. Shell fire was heavy during the Fresnoy fighting and on May 3rd 12 other ranks of the Battalion were wounded. On the following day 3 were killed and 3 wounded. At night on May 4th the Battalion was relieved from close support and moved back to Brunehaut Farm, proceeding thence at 5.30 o'clock on the following morning and marching, via Mont St. Eloi and Camblain l'Abbé, to Corps Reserve billets in Estrée Cauchie.

So terminated the part played by the 14th Battalion in the spring fighting at Vimy Ridge. Following the assault on April 9th, the Battalion had spent three and a half weeks in the front line, or in reserve positions in the forward area, ever within range of German shells and never far from the zone of rifle and machine gun fire. Working parties during this period had taxed the strength of the unit severely and had permitted little rest or relaxation. All fighting and working demands had been met, despite which the Regiment, as it marched out to rest, showed few signs of exhaustion or fatigue. Legitimate pride was reflected in the bearing of the men, who realized that in days to come the fight they had waged at Vimy would add perpetual honour to the colours of the 14th Battalion.

CHAPTER XIII

HOLDING VIMY RIDGE

" We saw not clearly nor understood,
But, yielding ourselves to the master-hand,
Each in his part as best he could,
We played it through as the author planned."
—ALAN SEEGER.

I

AFTER the fighting on April 9th, 1917, and the exhausting tours in the front line at the foot of Vimy Ridge, the 3rd Canadian Infantry Brigade was withdrawn from active duty for a period of rest in Corps Reserve. All battalions of the Brigade had suffered at Vimy, the 16th Battalion having lost 21 officers, of whom 8 were killed; the 13th having lost all four company commanders and a number of experienced non-commissioned officers; and the 14th and 15th having been reduced to far below normal strength. All, therefore, welcomed the opportunity for reorganization and assimilation of reinforcements.

In the 14th Battalion reconstruction of the companies took place on May 6th, when changes amongst officers were effected and promotion given to men who had shown capacity during April. Further reorganizations were carried out on the following day when the Bombing, Lewis gun, and Intelligence Sections received attention. Bathing parades at Gouy Servins on May 8th refreshed and smartened the rebuilt unit for inspection by the Divisional Commander, Major-General A. W. Currie, C.B., at Chateau de la Haie on the afternoon of May 9th. On the following day the Battalion, strengthened to a total of 34 officers and 484 other ranks, marched again to Chateau de la Haie, where the 3rd Brigade was inspected by the Corps Commander, Lieut.-Gen. the Hon. Sir Julian Byng, K.C.B., K.C.M.G., M.V.O., who congratulated the battalions on the part they had taken in the capture of Vimy Ridge.

Three days after Sir Julian Byng's inspection the Protestant section of the Battalion, totalling 24 officers and 374 other ranks, marched to the Brigade Area to attend a service of thanksgiving for the victories granted to Canadian arms in April. All units of the Brigade were present; hymns were sung by the troops to music provided by the band of the 14th Battalion, and the service was conducted by the Chaplain General of the First Army, assisted by Chaplain Major A. H. Creegan and Chaplain Lieut.-Col. F. G. Scott. General Sir H. S. Horne, K.C.B., Commanding the First Army, was present, also Lieut.-Gen. Sir Julian Byng and Major-General A. W. Currie. Following the impressive and dignified religious ceremony, General Horne addressed to the troops a few words of congratulation on their work at Vimy and encouragement for the immediate future.

Routine training marked the following days, a break occurring on May 16th when the afternoon was devoted to Battalion sports, attended by Brig.-Gen. Tuxford, and another two days later when Brigade sports were held at Chateau de la Haie. Training of the companies and specialists was resumed on May 19th and continued without interruption until May 31st, when the Battalion paraded at 7.10 a.m. and marched to relieve the 27th Canadian Battalion in Divisional Reserve, near Berthonval Farm.

II

At 8 o'clock on the morning of June 1st, 1917, the 14th Battalion, Royal Montreal Regiment, vacated the lines taken over from the 27th Battalion and moved into the Paynesley Area to relieve the 22nd Canadian Battalion in Divisional Support. Relief was completed without casualties at 10.20 a.m., Headquarters being established in Paynesley Trench and the companies distributed partly in a large cave and partly in trenches and dugouts. Here the Battalion passed an uneventful day, under orders of the 2nd Canadian Division.

At 10.30 p.m. the companies of the 14th advanced to relieve the 19th Canadian Battalion in Brigade Reserve, a party under Major Dick Worrall, consisting of Lieut. P. Coombes, Lieut. D. W. Clarkson, Sergt. Harrison, Corp. F. M. Vandyne, and Corp. E. H. Hanley, proceeding to the 1st Canadian Divisional School, near Ferfay, to train 500 men who had arrived from England as a reinforcement. At 12.05 a.m. on June 2nd the main body of the Battalion, proceeding to relief of the 19th Battalion, encountered barrage fire at a point on the east slope of Vimy Ridge. By detouring, casualties were avoided, and fifty minutes later the relief was carried out.

On taking over from the 19th Battalion, Headquarters was established in the railway embankment about 300 yards south of Vimy Station and the companies located in positions not far away. A defence scheme, drawn up by Lieut.-Col. McCombe and issued by the Adjutant, Capt. Plow, notified officers and men that the Battalion must stand ready to assist the Brigade units in the front line. Red rockets in rapid succession would be the S.O.S. and, on sighting these, troops of the 14th Battalion would "stand to", pending the arrival of orders from Battalion Headquarters.

Between 7 and 11 o'clock on the morning of June 2nd, No. 3 Coy., grouped near the Old Mill, was subjected to shelling and 4 other ranks were killed. Later the fire shifted to the neighbourhood of Battalion Headquarters, the enemy gunners searching, so it seemed, for Canadian field batteries hidden not far away. At 9 o'clock in the evening three parties, each consisting of 1 officer and 100 other ranks, proceeded to the front line to work under orders of the 13th Battalion. June 3rd, the King's birthday and the first anniversary of the counter-attack at Maple Copse, was marked by an attack of the 4th Canadian Division at La Coulotte. The noise of the bombardment preceding this attack reverberated along the 1st Division's front, but no activity ensued. At night 6 officers and 300 other ranks of the Battalion worked on the construction of C.P.R. Trench, and one officer from each company, together with scouts, signallers, and runners, proceeded to familiarize themselves with the front held by the 13th Battalion.

On the night of June 4th German aeroplanes bombed near the Royal Montreal transport lines, and enemy guns shelled the Battalion trenches. Shelling continued on the morning of the 5th, particularly in the neighbourhood of Headquarters. At 11 a.m. one shell wounded Capt. Plow and killed the private to whom he was giving orders. A happier hour of the day brought news that the King had recognized the devotion to duty of Lieut.-Col. Gault McCombe by bestowal of the D.S.O. Announcement of this award was followed by news that the French Government desired to honour bravery displayed by Company Sergt.-Major J. F. Hurley on April 9th by award of the Médaille Militaire. Simultaneously, it was announced that the British Military Medal had been granted to Private G. Brewer.

At 10.30 p.m. the Battalion, with a trench strength of 500 all ranks, left Brigade Reserve to relieve the 13th Battalion in the front line; Nos. 1 and 2 Companies occupying the right and left sectors of Quebec Trench, with Nos. 3 and 4 Companies in support. Shelling immediately after the relief suggested attack, and defensive patrols with

Lewis guns were despatched into No Man's Land, but no attack developed. Gas shelling on June 6th forced the men to wear respirators for some hours, No. 3 Coy. being further inconvenienced at 8.45 a.m. when a German plane spattered the position with machine gun fire. In retaliation for these attentions and to deceive the enemy, British artillery laid down as a feint a 3-line barrage lasting ten minutes.

On June 7th an enemy plane again attacked the Battalion lines with machine gun fire. No success attended this effort, but later in the day gas shelling killed one man and caused four others intense suffering. The concentration of gas blew over the Canadian back areas and was undissipated when it reached Battalion Headquarters, 1,000 yards behind the firing line. Patrols moved freely in No Man's Land that night, but on the night of the 8th all parties were withdrawn, as the British I Corps, in conjunction with the 3rd and 4th Canadian Divisions, was carrying out a raid to the left. Heavy shelling preceded this venture and provoked retaliation, the vicinity of Royal Montreal Headquarters being bombarded for over three-quarters of an hour. Meanwhile, dense clouds drifted over the front line from a smoke barrage. Little information regarding the raid reached the 14th that night, but on the morrow all ranks heard with satisfaction that a German officer and 21 men had been captured.

June 9th and 10th were "quiet" days, according to the official Diary, which states that the Battalion endured desultory shell fire, rather brisk machine gun fire, and a measure of attention from enemy aircraft. At night on the 10th the 3rd Canadian Battalion marched forward to relieve and completed the operation at 1.05 o'clock on the morning of June 11th, the 14th Battalion thereupon withdrawing to Brigade Support at Thélus Cave. Two companies billeted in the cave, the remainder, plus two attached platoons from each of the 13th, 15th, and 16th Battalions, occupying the "funk hole" area immediately outside.

From dusk on June 11th until dawn on the 12th the entire 14th Battalion worked to wire reserve trenches a few hundred yards from Thélus Cave, continuing the work on the following night, and one company carrying it still further on the nights of June 14th and 15th. The 16th of the month was without incident, but at 10 p.m. on the 17th the Battalion marched to Winnipeg Huts, near Mont St. Eloy, and there entered Divisional Reserve. Eight days of routine training followed, in the course of which a draft of 1 officer and 40 other ranks was taken on strength.

At 7 o'clock on the evening of June 25th the Battalion paraded at Winnipeg Huts and marched to relieve the 3rd Canadian Battalion at Thélus Cave. When relief was complete, the Regiment, with a trench strength of 22 officers and 560 other ranks, garrisoned the "Ridge Line", the most westerly of six lines forming the 1st Division's defensive front. Battalion Headquarters, with Nos. 1 and 2 Companies, billeted in Thélus Cave, and Nos. 3 and 4 Companies occupied dug-outs close by. Three Lewis guns were mounted to protect the unit from enemy aircraft, which had formed the habit of attacking whenever opportunity offered. On June 26th a draft of 204 other ranks reported for duty to the Battalion, which lay under orders of the 1st Canadian Infantry Brigade in the Ridge Line. In the morning 1 officer and 20 other ranks worked under the 182nd Tunnelling Company at construction near Thélus Siding, returning after six hours to accompany the Battalion in a move forward.

At night the Brigade took over the line, the 15th, 13th, and 16th Battalions occupying front trenches and the 14th Battalion relieving the 5th Canadian Battalion in close Brigade Support. Relief was completed at 1.13 a.m. on this occasion and at 1.45 a.m. the G.O.C. 3rd Brigade assumed command of the area. A quiet day followed, the men avoiding movement, as the slightest activity brought shell fire. At 10.30 p.m. 2 officers and 210 other ranks were detailed to carry material to the front line. Near Engineers' Dump a section of this party was caught by gun fire, 3 other ranks being killed and 12 seriously wounded. Further casualties were prevented by Sergt. Henry Campbell, who scattered his men and personally directed them to positions of safety. Other parties, including one 168 strong which reported to the 182nd Tunnelling Company, were more fortunate and escaped losses.

At 7.10 p.m. on June 28th the 3rd Brigade mounted a "Chinese" attack, to divert attention from the north where the 3rd and 4th Canadian Divisions were undertaking more serious operations. The characteristics of a "Chinese" attack are smoke and noise, but on this occasion the 13th Battalion added dummy figures, controlled by strings and made to represent massed troops awaiting the signal to "go over". The dummies deceived the enemy who treated them to barrage fire without injuring the living troops in trenches to the rear.

For some days after the "Chinese" attack, the 14th Battalion continued to act as Brigade Support, supplying regular working parties to the 182nd Tunnelling Company and others, which deepened and widened Canada and Hudson Trenches. In order to mark Dominion Day, July 1st, all guns on the 1st Division's front fired simultaneously at 11 o'clock in the morning. The sudden crash of shells must have puzzled those Germans whose education regarding Canadian holidays had been neglected.

On the night of July 3rd No. 3 Coy. of the Royal Montreal Regiment relieved a company of the 8th Canadian Battalion in C.P.R. Trench, between Battalion Headquarters and the Mont Forêt-Lone Tree Road, and a section of No. 4 Coy. moved from north of New Brunswick Road to a position south of the road. On the following night the Battalion, 730 strong, relieved the 16th Canadian Scottish and two companies of the 13th Royal Highlanders of Canada in the Acheville Section of the Divisional front line (Acheville-Mericourt Sector), No. 4 Coy. holding Quebec Trench from its junction with the Acheville Road to Nova Scotia Trench, and a section beyond; No. 3 Coy. taking over Nova Scotia Trench to the point where it intersected the southern Corps boundary; No. 2 Coy. moving into left support, with three platoons in Montreal Trench and one platoon in New Brunswick Trench; and No. 1 Coy. providing right support, with three and a half platoons in Winnipeg Trench and one-half platoon in Brandon Trench.

In the front line the Battalion spent eight days. July 5th was quiet until 5 p.m., when a German heavy trench mortar, firing for the first time in the area, smashed parapets, buried a Lewis gun, and wounded six men. Retaliation by heavy artillery subdued this mortar, which remained silent throughout the night. From 11 p.m. until 2.30 a.m. a Royal Montreal patrol searched No Man's Land, but no enemy was found.

At 6.30 a.m. on July 6th the enemy bombarded with trench mortars, about 55 shells bursting in the Canadian wire, or close to the front line parapet. Simultaneously, the Germans registered with 4.9's and 5.1's, the wire-cutting and registration indicating to veterans of the Regiment that a raid was contemplated. On the chance that this obvious explanation of proceedings would prove correct, parties of the front line companies moved out to repair the torn wire as soon as darkness permitted. Casualties for the day totalled 1 killed and 3 wounded.

At 1.25 a.m. on July 7th, the enemy barraged the Royal Montreal front with trench mortars, 4.1-inch high explosive, and a varied supply of shrapnel. After ten minutes a section of the front was "boxed" by barrage fire and a party of 40 Germans advanced, presumably to raid. Cross fire from two Lewis guns soon struck this party, and the Canadian artillery, in response to a signal of two green lights, barraged the point where the enemy had cut the defending wire. Under machine gun and shell fire the Germans wavered and, despite efforts of a brave officer to rally them, finally fled. On retreat of the enemy, 2 N.C.O's. and 8 men advanced from the Royal Montreal trenches and remained in No Man's Land for some time, witnessing from a point of vantage retaliation for the raid which three batteries of Canadian artillery maintained until 2.45 a.m.

On July 8th the situation along the Battalion front was quiet, though a few shells were placed over the lines of the company on the right and two men were wounded. At night wiring parties completed repair of the gaps cut by the enemy previous to the attempted raid, and other parties deepened front line and support trenches, all being protected by a covering platoon from No. 1 Coy. Despite the exposed nature of the work allotted to the wiring and digging parties, all carried out their tasks without heavy losses. On the following day No. 1 Coy. was less fortunate, 2 men being killed and 4 wounded at 5 p.m. when the enemy shelled the vicinity of Winnipeg Road. At night patrols of the Battalion were withdrawn from No Man's Land when the enemy bombarded the front line. Later Capt. E. Cowen, M.C., D.C.M., commanding No. 4 Coy., was supervising a wiring squad when informed that Germans were approaching. To clear a field of fire for machine guns, Capt. Cowen withdrew his wiring party and was himself about to enter the Canadian front line when a bullet penetrated his lung. Badly wounded though he was, he stopped the stretcher-bearers who were taking him back to give instructions to Lieut. J. W. Maynard, who took command of the company pending the arrival of Lieut. T. G. Beagley. In wishing Capt. Cowen good luck and a speedy recovery, Lieut. Maynard voiced the sentiment of the men of No. 4 Coy., who were proud that Cowen had served in the ranks, earned distinction in many engagements, and displayed devotion to duty unsurpassed in the enviable records of the Battalion.

Working and wiring parties and patrols were again busy on the night of July 10th, and on the night of the 11th a special party covered the 13th Battalion front, where a trench was being dug in No Man's Land. Shortly before midnight on July 12th the Battalion, after an uneventful day, was relieved by the 12th and 13th Battalions,

York and Lancs. Regiment, the operation being completed at 2.20 a.m., without casualties. On relief the Battalion withdrew to the Paynesley Area, whence it marched at 3.30 p.m., by way of Neuville St. Vaast and La Targette Cross-Roads, to Divisional Reserve at Fraser Camp. Previous to the march, twelve officers proceeded to Barlin to attend the funeral of Capt. E. Cowen, M.C., D.C.M., who had died in No. 6 Canadian Casualty Clearing Station. As the body was buried these officers, standing at the salute, bore testimony to the affection and deep respect in which the late company commander was held by all ranks of his Battalion.

CHAPTER XIV

THE BATTLE OF HILL 70

What of the fight? With no vain boast
We meet the foeman on the field,
But each man's soul is as an host,
To fight, to die, but not to yield.

The glory of our splendid past
Shines on us as a quenchless sun,
That each and all may write at last
The simple tale of duty done.
—CLAUDE E. C. H. BURTON (" Touchstone ").

I

SOME time after the success at Vimy Ridge, Lieut.-Gen. the Hon. Sir Julian Byng was promoted to command the Third British Army, his place at the head of the Canadian Corps being taken by Major-General A. W. Currie, C.B., a Canadian-born citizen soldier, who had won distinction while commanding the 2nd Infantry Brigade at the Second Battle of Ypres, and, subsequently, had maintained his reputation for leadership while commanding the 1st Canadian Division. When Major-General Currie assumed command of the Corps, his place at the head of the 1st Division was taken by Brig.-General A. C. Macdonell, C.B., C.M.G., D.S.O., who had successfully commanded the 7th Infantry Brigade in some of the bitterest fighting of the war. Under these new commanders, the Corps was given the task of wrenching from German hands that rising ground east of Loos which on maps bore the unimaginative title " Hill 70 ".

Sir Julian Byng had demonstrated the value to an attack of painstaking preparation, and the Canadian Corps had learnt the lesson well. Accordingly, weeks before the Hill 70 operation, each unit's part was studied, rehearsed, and modified as rehearsal proved advisable. In general, the plan adopted called for attack by two divisions, the 1st Canadian Division on the left and the 2nd Canadian Division on the right. Each division was ordered to attack on a front of two brigades and, in the 1st Division, the 3rd and 2nd Brigades were chosen, the 3rd Brigade to be on the left. In turn, the 3rd Brigade was to attack on a front of three battalions, the 15th Battalion, 48th Highlanders, on the left; the 13th Battalion, Royal Highlanders of Canada, in the centre; and the 16th Battalion, Canadian Scottish, on the right. The 14th Battalion, Royal Montreal Regiment, was to act as Brigade Reserve.

BRIG.-GEN. F. S. MEIGHEN, C.M.G.
AUGUST, 1914—JUNE 19TH, 1915.

LT.-COL. F. W. FISHER,
OCT. 28TH, 1915—MARCH 18TH, 1916.

LT.-COL. GAULT McCOMBE, D.S.O.,
JAN. 15TH, 1917—APRIL 19TH, 1918

LT.-COL. W. W. BURLAND, D.S.O.
JUNE 19TH, 1915—OCT. 28TH, 1915.

BRIG.-GEN. R. P. CLARK, C.M.G., D.S.O., M.C,
MARCH 18TH, 1916—JAN. 15TH, 1917.

LT.-COL. D. WORRALL, D.S.O. (and bar), M.C.
APRIL 19TH, 1918—APRIL 20TH, 1919.

II

Unaware of what lay ahead, but anticipating action, the men of the 14th paraded at 6 p.m. on July 14th, in a field S.W. of the Camblain l'Abbé-Mont St. Eloy Road, with the details (No. 5 Company) under command of Lieut. E. A. Adams. Marching from this position, the Regiment followed the main road through Camblain l'Abbé and Estrée Cauchie to Gauchin Légal, where Lieut. B. T. Jackson and the Intelligence Section had arranged for billets.

At Gauchin Légal church parades were held on the morning of July 15th and kit inspection in the afternoon, deficiencies which the inspection revealed being made up by issues on the following day. On July 17th the Transport Officer was ordered to see that officers' chargers were at billets at 7.45 a.m., as the Battalion, including No. 5 Detail Company, was to march a quarter-hour later. Parading in column of route, Headquarters moved off at 8 o'clock, the companies following and maintaining inter-company distances of approximately 200 yards. From Gauchin Légal the Battalion marched to Fresnicourt, thence to Verdrel and on past Fosse 9 to Hersin, thence to billets in Braquemont. To smarten appearance of the unit on the march, the men were ordered to wear puttees in infantry fashion only, with no hose tops, stockings, or socks visible. Unmounted officers were instructed not to carry canes, sticks, or riding crops.

For five days at Braquemont the Battalion carried out routine training, special attention being devoted to bayonet fighting, gas helmet practice, bombing, and the formations used by platoons and companies in attack. At 3 o'clock on the afternoon of July 20th the Battalion, on orders from G.H.Q., paraded in full marching order before a professional camera man, who took moving pictures of the unit for War Office archives, and for exhibition in Canada. Following demobilization these pictures were shown in Montreal, where a number of ex-soldiers recognized themselves on the screen. Two days after the film was taken the Battalion marched from Braquemont, passed through Noeux-les-Mines and Barlin, and billeted in Ruitz shortly after noon.

On July 24th the companies proceeded independently to Houchin, where the men bathed in great vats of hot water and received clean underclothing and socks. Physical drill, rifle grenade practice, bombing, wiring instruction, and gas helmet drills occupied the time on July 25th, and on the following day a lecture informed all ranks of the tasks to be accomplished at Hill 70.

In Operation Order No. 151, issued at 10.40 p.m. on July 24th by Major Plow, Battalion Adjutant, Lieut.-Col. Gault McCombe, D.S.O., Commanding Officer of the 14th, deals with the duties of the companies, sections, and special parties in detail. Summarized, Lieut.-Col. McCombe's orders and explanations were:—

(1) General Plan:—In conjunction with other operations, the Canadian Corps will take the high ground north of Lens, on a date and at an hour to be named later.

(2) The Task of the 1st Division:—The 1st Canadian Division will attack with two brigades abreast, the 2nd Brigade on the right, the 3rd Brigade on the left, and the 1st Brigade in reserve.

(3) Brigade Flank:—The 138th British Brigade will be on the left of the 3rd Brigade attack. So far as is known at present, the 138th Brigade will take no direct part in the operation.

(4) Brigade Formation:—
  Right:—16th Battalion, Canadian Scottish.
  Centre:—13th Battalion, Royal Highlanders of Canada.
  Left:—15th Battalion, 48th Highlanders.
  Reserve:—14th Battalion, Royal Montreal Regiment.

(5) Brigade Objectives:—
  1st Objective:—The Blue Line. (About 1,000 yards east of Loos; running east of, and for the most part parallel to, the Lens-La Bassée Road, and passing through Bois Rasé and Bois Hugo.)
  2nd Objective:—The Green Line. (Between 250-400 yards in advance of the Blue Line.)

(6) Frontages:—Each of the three attacking battalions will attack on a two-company front, and each company will attack on a two-platoon front.

(7) Table of Frontages (approximate):—
  Brigade .... 1,400 Yards
  Battalion .... 466 "
  Company .... 233 "
  Platoon .... 116 "

(8) Procedure:—The three attacking battalions will go straight through to the Blue Line. This they will consolidate while the barrage stands in front for 41 minutes. They will reform during this time and continue the advance to the Green Line.

(9) Duties of 14th Battalion:—

(a) The 14th Battalion will not follow the attack. The primary duty of the Battalion is to hold itself in readiness to give immediate assistance to any battalion of the 3rd Brigade, and to render help should the enemy deliver a counter-attack.

(b) It must be borne in mind that there is a possibility of the enemy counter-attacking the left flank of the 3rd Brigade, as, once the attack has started, there will be no 3rd Brigade battalions remaining in the front line.

(c) Therefore, the 14th Battalion must be distributed so that it can hold the front line and guard the left flank, while at the same time it can be collected, in whole or in part, for immediate action.

(10) Assembly:—In view of the foregoing, the Battalion will assemble as follows:—

No. 2 Coy.—1 platoon in Meath Trench; 3 platoons in the reserve trench between Chalk Pit Alley and Railway Alley.

No. 1 Coy.—In the reserve trench between Railway Alley and English Alley.

No. 4 Coy.—In Tosh Alley, between English Alley and Chalk Pit Alley.

No. 3 Coy.—In Reserve Trench. The personnel of No. 3 Coy. will later be detailed for carrying parties. The Lewis gun and gun crews of the company will be attached to No. 2 Coy.

(11) Move following Zero:—After zero hour, when the hostile barrage dies down, as it will when the "fog of war" affects the enemy, the companies will move

forward to the front line and immediate support and will take up positions as follows:—

> No. 2 Coy.—1 platoon in Meath Trench (joining the platoon already there); 2 platoons between Chalk Pit Alley and Railway Alley.
>
> No. 1 Coy.—Between Railway Alley and English Alley.
>
> No. 4 Coy.—In Reserve Trench, between Chalk Pit Alley and Railway Alley.

(12) Command:—The 14th Battalion will not be used without orders from 3rd Brigade Headquarters to 14th Battalion Headquarters, unless all communication has been broken.

Any portion of the Battalion which reinforces one of the attacking battalions, will pass under the control of the O.C. the battalion reinforced.

(13) Headquarters:—14th and 13th Battalion H.Q's.—Meath Trench.

(14) Forward Report Centres:—Will be established by the attacking battalions as soon as possible and will be distinguished by the following flags:—

> 16th Battalion (right)—Red.
> 13th Battalion (centre)—Black.
> 15th Battalion (left)—Green.

(15) Contact Aeroplanes:—If the 14th Battalion is called upon to reinforce the attacking battalions, communication with the contact aeroplanes will be of the greatest importance. All ranks must be impressed with the fact that the smoke of the burning flares *Does Not* give our position away to the enemy artillery.

(16) Messages:—Messages and reports must be numbered, marked with the time and place, be as brief as possible, and be written on the back of specially-prepared sketch maps showing the German trenches. At the time of writing an officer will chalk his position on the sketch map. These maps will be issued as follows:—

> To Battalion Commanders 12
> To Company Commanders 12
> To Platoon Commanders 8

(17) Enemy Documents:—All papers, books, plans, etc., found in the enemy area must be carefully collected in sandbags and forwarded to Battalion H.Q. with as little delay as the situation permits.

(18) Carrying Platoons:—The attacking battalions will be reinforced by the following platoons for carrying purposes:—

    15th Battalion—2 platoons of No. 2 Coy.
    13th Battalion—1 platoon of No. 1 Coy.
    16th Battalion—1 platoon of No. 1 Coy.

These platoons will work under the Brigade Grenade Officer, Lieut. J. M. MacAdams, and will assemble in Reserve Trench.

(19) Dumps:—

    "A" Line—Battalion dumps.
    "B" Line—On Lens-La Bassée Road.

As soon as the situation permits, parties will commence to carry material from "A" Line to "B" Line.

    Main Divisional Dump — Lieut. McGovern (13th Battn.) in charge.
    Advanced Divisional Dump (Maroc) — Lieut. Lomas-Smith in charge.
    Divisional R.E. Park at Les Brebis.
    Divisional Salvage Dump at Bully Grenay.

(20) Medical:—

    Advanced Dressing Stations — Le Philosophe and Les Brebis.
    Collecting Posts—Fort Glatz and St. Patrick's.
    Regimental Aid Posts — Chalk Pit (off Tosh Alley); Tosh Keep; Craig Lockhart.

The Medical Officer of the 14th Battalion, Capt. John Graham, will be at Craig Lockhart. Stretcher cases will be cleared from the Chalk Pit and Tosh Keep posts by hand, via Loos Alley, English Alley, Don Walk, Dot Walk, and North Street, to Fort Glatz, thence by car to Le Philosophe and thence to Noeux-les-Mines.

Walking cases will proceed via communication trench as far as Village Line Trench, thence by cross-country track to the collecting point.

(21) Burials:—If the situation permits, the 14th Battalion will be detailed to clear the Brigade battlefield as far forward as the present enemy front line. If possible, the dead of the Brigade will be buried in Sains-en-Gohelle (Fosse 10) and Bully Grenay Cemeteries, all equipment being salvaged from the bodies and placed in dumps. If the situation will not permit burial of the fallen in the above cemeteries, a suitable spot on the battlefield will be selected, probably along the Lens-La Bassée Road.

(22) Signals:—The Canadian Corps S.O.S. signal is red, either rockets or Very lights, as many as possible fired in rapid succession. In addition, heavy rifle or machine gun fire breaking out any time after the Green Line is captured will be treated as an S.O.S. signal.

Bearing in mind the instructions quoted above, as well as many paragraphs of Operation Order No. 151, dealing with dress, equipment, supplies, and material, omitted here to conserve space, the 14th Battalion, 505 strong, paraded on July 27th and marched to Aix Noulette, there to carry out battle practice with the other battalions of the 3rd Canadian Infantry Brigade. For this practice an area representing Hill 70 had been prepared, with the German trenches taped out and every feature of the enemy lines marked as clearly as possible. Over this area the battalions rehearsed the assault, each company, platoon, and section, as during preparation for the attack on Vimy, carrying out, so far as was humanly possible, the duties that would fall to it in the actual hour of battle. To represent the barrage, a line of men with flags moved in advance of the assaulting battalions, halting and moving forward again in accordance with the arrangements for a standing barrage after the capture of the Blue Line. A curious feature of these manœuvres was that they were, in part, under direct observation from the distant enemy lines. Perhaps the slight haze screened them. In any event they were uninterrupted by aeroplanes, or shell fire, which was fortunate, as, owing to the importance of ripening crops, no other practice ground was available in the entire district.

On July 29th religious services were held in a tent owned by the Expeditionary Force Y.M.C.A. and in Ruitz Village church. Following these, the ribbon of the Military Medal was presented to No. 25933, Sergt. Henry Campbell, who had been awarded the decoration for bravery in charge of a carrying party near Vimy on June 27th. At noon on July 30th the Battalion Adjutant issued addenda to Lieut.-Col. McCombe's operation order dealing with the attack on Hill 70. Amongst other items announced were details regarding prisoners, barrages, etc., the more important of which are listed below:—

(1) Prisoners of War:—The Divisional Station for collection of prisoners will be at Maroc. Prisoners, on their way out, will be utilized as much as possible to carry stretcher cases.

(2) Stretcher-Bearers:—20 additional stretcher-bearers will be detailed—5 from each company—and will be assembled at Regimental Aid post before zero. They will wear a white bandage on the left arm as a distinguishing mark.

(3) Smoke Barrages:—Smoke barrages will be put on at zero by British troops on our left, to deceive the enemy as to the northern flank of the attack.

(4) Contact Patrol:—No. 16 Squadron, Royal Flying Corps, will fly at zero. The contact patrol will call for flares at zero plus 120 minutes. Flares will be lighted by the 13th, 15th, and 16th Battalions ONLY.

(5) Enemy Dugouts:—In the event of the 14th Battalion having to advance, all ranks must be aware of the fact that the 3rd Australian Tunnelling Company's "Investigation Party" goes forward at zero plus 24 minutes, to search enemy dugouts. This party will mark dugout entrances, "Dangerous", or "Considered Safe". German traps and mines are reported, and great caution must be employed in entering any dugout, unless the "Safe" sign has been placed thereon by the Tunnellers.

(6) Precaution:—Beyond doubt, in some recent operations, the enemy was informed as to the date and approximate hour of the attack. The most probable sources of such information are the improper use of the telephone and indiscreet talk of officers and men. Special attention is again directed to explicit instructions recently issued on this subject.

Heavy rain interfered somewhat with the training on August 1st, 2nd, and 3rd. In the morning on the 3rd Major-General A. C. Macdonell, C.B., C.M.G., D.S.O., the new leader of the 1st Canadian

Division, visited the Battalion at Ruitz and referred to the fine tradition which the unit had established. Later in the day the Battalion marched from Ruitz to Mazingarbe, there entering billets in Brigade Reserve.

After two days at Mazingarbe, the Battalion moved to relieve the 16th Battalion in the front line (Loos Sector). On reaching the village of Le Philosophe, the unit encountered severe shell fire, which killed 8 men and wounded 14, the casualties including the entire personnel of a Lewis gun section. Pushing through, or around, the danger zone, the companies completed relief of the 16th Battalion at 3.15 a.m. and established liaison with the 10th Canadian Battalion on the southern flank and the 6th Battalion, Suffolk Regiment, on the north. Fine weather prevailed during the relief, but the trenches were deep in mud as the result of previous rain.

August 7th was a busy day, as much material for the attack on Hill 70 was delivered at the Battalion dump. During the day some 200 enemy shells fell in the Regimental area without causing losses, or serious damage. At 9 a.m. the heavy artillery of the Corps bombarded the German front line, continuing the fire until 6 o'clock in the evening. On the left of the 14th front, "back lash" from this fire rendered evacuation of some trenches advisable. On August 9th the artillery again carried out a 9-hour "shoot", tearing the enemy wire and paving a way for the coming assault of the infantry. Retaliation for this fire was sharp and Lieut. L. M. Hooker was wounded. At night on the 9th the Battalion was relieved by the 3rd Battalion.

Following relief, the Royal Montreal Regiment marched to Noeux-les-Mines, proceeding on the following day to Fosse 7, Barlin, where, on August 12th, a Protestant church service was held in conjunction with the 13th Battalion, Royal Highlanders of Canada. Following this service routine training continued for one day, then, at 6.30 p.m. on August 13th, the Battalion marched to Mazingarbe, where the companies were reorganized for the Hill 70 operations, No. 3 Coy. being brought to a strength of 200, divided into 4 platoons, and Nos. 1, 2, and 4 Companies reduced to a two-platoon basis.

At 9.50 p.m. on August 14th, 1917, the Battalion left Mazingarbe Huts, the platoons donning box respirators as the forward area was reached and gas shells fell in large numbers. In spite of the obstacle which these shells presented, the Battalion, 589 strong (83 were on special duty), had reached assembly trenches and taken up position at 3.45 o'clock on the morning of August 15th. Forty minutes later the Canadian guns opened fire and the Battle of Hill 70 began.

At 5.30 a.m. 14th Battalion Headquarters was notified that the 13th and 15th Battalions had captured the Blue Line, and at 5.55 a.m. the 13th Battalion was reported to have captured its final objective, the Green Line. This report must have been premature, as it was 6.10 o'clock before the 13th and 16th Battalions stormed their way into the Green Line, both battalions having encountered stiff opposition and suffered severe losses. In both cases, however, the battalions had refused to check and had courageously maintained the pre-arranged schedule of progress.

At 7 a.m. the 14th Battalion sent four Lewis guns and eight posts of riflemen forward into the old Canadian front trenches, to guard against any counter-attack which might sweep through the decimated battalions in the new front line. Several counter-attacks were attempted, but the artillery smashed them, or they were dealt with by the reduced, but still effective, front line companies. From an advanced position on the left flank of the attack, Lieut. B. T. Jackson, Intelligence Officer of the 14th Battalion, who was attached to the 138th British Brigade for liaison, reported the assembly of counter-attacking forces near the Bois Dix-Huit. One counter-attack in strength, led by a German officer on a white horse, deployed under fire with a courage exciting the admiration of all observers. Courage alone, however, could not carry the attack forward and it wilted under the blast of concentrated shell fire which greeted it.

Lieut. Jackson was also witness to a stirring little action when Lieut.-Col. C. E. Bent, Commanding Officer of the 15th Battalion, was attacked by Germans who debouched from a dugout in his rear. Though taken by surprise, the gallant C.O. of the 15th showed fight and held off the enemy until his men rallied to his support and dispersed the attacking party. Lieut.-Col. G. E. McCuaig, of the 13th Battalion, had an equally narrow escape when prisoners near his headquarters were mistaken by a mopping-up patrol for active enemies and attacked with machine gun fire. McCuaig and the prisoners escaped injury, but one runner was killed and two signallers wounded.

Meanwhile, possibly as a result of the attack on Lieut.-Col. Bent, 14th Battalion received news that 15th Battalion Headquarters was in immediate danger. Lieut.-Col. McCombe thereupon issued orders for an attack on the left, with No. 2 Coy. leading the assault and No. 1 Coy. advancing in close support. Hardly had No. 2 Coy. started forward, when a message arrived stating that the situation had improved and no counter-attack would be required. On receipt of this message, No. 2 Coy. was ordered to reinforce the 15th Battalion on the left, No. 4 Coy. taking over the position which No. 2 vacated.

Throughout August 15th carrying parties of the 14th Battalion worked their way through enemy barrages, delivering much material at points where it was urgently needed. On the return trips many of these parties carried stretchers with wounded, all ranks displaying gallantry under fire and earning mention in the Commanding Officer's report to Brigade Headquarters. In one party, commanded by Lieut. J. M. Stephenson, two men, Privates Burke and Hall, refused to leave duty when wounded and worked faithfully until killed by a shell in Canteen Alley. Lieut. H. T. Rodger also remained at duty after suffering a painful wound.

At 1.30 o'clock on the morning of August 16th, No. 4 Coy. of the Royal Montreal Regiment reinforced the 15th Battalion, and Major Sheppard, of that unit, used 1 officer and 45 other ranks to strengthen the front line at the junction of the Blue and Green Lines, 1 officer and 20 other ranks to man the front line west of this junction, and 1 officer and 20 other ranks to garrison the Blue Line. No. 4 Company Commander was ordered to remain in the Blue Line and lead a counter-attack, should this prove necessary. One hundred other ranks were attached to him for the purpose.

Meanwhile, two companies of the 2nd Canadian Battalion reported for duty to 14th Battalion Headquarters and were ordered to take up a position in Gun Trench. At 2 a.m. Lieut.-Col. McCombe moved one platoon of No. 1 Coy. into the old front line and effected redisposition of several minor posts, all with a view to checking any enemy counter-attack on the left flank. At 3.45 a.m. he moved one company of the 2nd Canadian Battalion from Gun Trench to Reserve Line, on the right of Railway Alley.

All day on August 16th and all that night the companies of the 14th Battalion continued to carry out the tasks assigned to them. In the front line Nos. 2 and 4 Companies valiantly co-operated with the men of the 15th Battalion, sharing with the latter the hardships of maintaining and consolidating the newly-captured line and suffering proportionally from severe shell fire. At one point a platoon of No. 2 Coy., sadly reduced in strength, kept up an appearance of power by deputing one man to run up and down at night, firing Very lights over the parapet at frequent intervals. Lieut. René Bourgeois, who had won the Médaille Militaire and the Croix de Guerre while serving in the French Foreign Legion and who, throughout the present operation, had displayed courage and abundant good cheer, was killed, as was Lieut. J. G. Pope. Amongst other ranks, either in the actual front, or whilst employed on carrying parties, 17 were killed, 11 failed to answer at roll call and were listed as "missing, presumed killed", 80 were wounded, and 39 severely gassed. Lieuts. W. S. McCutcheon, Harry Edney, and Donald MacRitchie were also wounded.

At 5.10 a.m. on August 17th the 14th Battalion was relieved by two companies of the 3rd Canadian Battalion, No. 1 Coy. of the 14th proceeding to Gun Trench, No. 2 Coy. to the Village Line, No. 3 Coy. to Loos, and No. 4 Coy. to the Village Line. Battalion Headquarters remained in Meath Trench, Lieut.-Col. McCombe issuing orders to the company commanders regarding positions to be taken up in the event of emergency. Should all wires and communication be cut, company commanders were left to judge whether an emergency existed, or not.

On taking over their new positions, all men of the Battalion were re-equipped with bombs, small arm ammunition, and such articles as they had lost, or used up, in the course of the Hill 70 operations. Gas shelling caused much inconvenience at this time, consequently the men were not sorry when at 2.15 a.m. on August 20th the 5th Canadian Mounted Rifles carried out relief and the 14th withdrew to billets in Les Brebis. Here a poor welcome was provided, shell fire killing one man and wounding three. These casualties were attended by Capt. Graham, the Battalion Medical Officer, who, during the operations just concluded, had passed through his post over three hundred and seventy-five wounded, including many members of the 10th Battalion.

After resting for a few hours at Les Brebis, the Battalion marched, via Sains, to Fosse 7, Barlin, billeting there for the night, and marching on the 21st, via Ruitz and Haillicourt, to the reserve area at Marles-les-Mines. On arrival at Marles-les-Mines, the troops started to clean up and to repair clothing damaged in the operations just completed. On the afternoon of August 21st a reinforcing draft of 1 officer and 75 men reported for duty, and on the following day the Battalion received a visit from Major-Gen. A. C. Macdonell and Brig.-Gen. G. S. Tuxford, who congratulated the troops on the work carried out at Hill 70, but warned them that ceaseless effort would be required to maintain the reputation the Division had won.

CHAPTER XV

THE YPRES SALIENT AGAIN

> The ancient and the lovely land
> Is sown with death; across the plain
> Ungarnered now the orchards stand,
> The Maxim nestles in the grain,
> The shrapnel spreads a stinging flail
> Where pallid nuns the cloister trod,
> The airship spills her leaden hail;
> But—after all the battles—God.
> —ALAN SULLIVAN.

I

FOR ten days after the action at Hill 70 the 14th Battalion, Royal Montreal Regiment, remained in Corps Reserve at Marles-les-Mines, refitting, reorganizing, and carrying out training of a routine nature. On August 27th the Battalion paraded, 637 strong, for inspection by the Commanding Officer, Lieut.-Col. Gault McCombe, D.S.O., and subsequently marched to a field outside the village, where the 3rd Canadian Infantry Brigade was reviewed by Field Marshal Sir Douglas Haig, K.T., G.C.V.O., G.C.B., Commander-in-Chief of the British Armies in France. Sir Douglas, who was accompanied by Lieut.-Gen. A. W. Currie, Major-Gen. A. C. Macdonell, Brig.-Gen. G. S. Tuxford, and Sir George Perley, Canadian High Commissioner in London, inspected the battalions with care and congratulated the men on the quality of the work they had recently accomplished. Owing to heavy rain, the pipes of the Highland battalions developed a "throatiness" which rendered them unfit for action. The units of the Brigade, therefore, marched past the Commander-in-Chief to music provided by the brass band of the 14th.

Six days after Sir Douglas Haig's inspection, the Battalion paraded at 8.15 a.m. and marched, via Haillicourt, Barlin, and Hersin, to Divisional Reserve in Bouvigny Huts. Proceeding on the following night, September 3rd, the Battalion passed under command of the 9th Brigade and relieved the 58th Canadian Battalion in Cité St. Pierre, Headquarters and the companies billeting in cellars and dugouts within a radius of some 200 yards.

At 8 p.m. on September 4th the Royal Montreal Regiment advanced from reserve in Cité St. Pierre and, passing again under command of the 3rd Brigade, relieved the 116th Canadian Battalion in the right

THE BATTALION MARCHING TO REST BILLETS AFTER HILL 70—AUGUST, 1917

Canadian Official Copyright

sub-sector of the front line. On completion of the relief, Lieut.-Col. McCombe, together with Capt. Graham, the Medical Officer, and Lieut. D. E. Stewart, Acting Adjutant, established Headquarters under the ruins of Lens Hospital, while Nos. 1 and 3 Companies occupied the front line, with No. 2 Coy. in support and No. 4 in reserve. At this time the strength of the Battalion was divided as follows:—

Unit	Officers	O.R.	Lewis Gunners
Headquarters	5	13	..
Intelligence Section	1	25	..
Communication Section	1	36	..
Medical	1	5	..
No. 1 Coy.	4	118	4
No. 2 Coy.	6	116	3
No. 3 Coy.	4	144	4
No. 4 Coy.	4	140	4
	26	597	15

During the six-day tour that followed the enemy was active, shelling at not infrequent intervals and displaying interest in the advent of the new brigade by sending over a number of planes to reconnoitre. At 4.20 a.m. on September 5th a patrol of the Battalion reported an enemy working party, which was dispersed by shell fire. In retaliation, possibly, the enemy bombarded the 14th front on the night of the 5th, mixing gas shells with high explosive. As a result of the shelling 8 men were evacuated suffering from gas poisoning, one of them dying a few hours later. At 7.30 p.m. on September 7th, a shower of golden rockets rose from the German lines to the 14th Battalion left. Presumably these constituted an S.O.S., for soon afterwards the enemy laid down a barrage. After a few minutes he decided that his alarm was groundless and so notified his gunners by a rocket, which burst into gorgeous red flame.

During the tour in the front line, night patrols of the 14th Battalion checked the activities of the enemy and reported on the condition of his wire, while working parties deepened La Bassée and Conductor Trenches and carried quantities of material into the forward area. In addition to the casualties from gas, 1 man was killed and 15 wounded. Lieut. E. C. Morris was also wounded. An incident of the tour occurred one foggy morning on the front of No. 16 Platoon, when Lieut. D. MacRitchie noticed two individuals near a Battalion night outpost position. Corp. Aldridge reported that no Canadians were still " out ", so MacRitchie stood up on the parapet, covered the strangers with a rifle, and shouted. At the shout four hands shot into the air and two German machine gunners trotted to the Canadian lines to surrender. Questions disclosed that they were members of a German outpost squad who, seeking their own line, had become bewildered in the fog.

At night on September 10th the Battalion was relieved by the 16th Battalion and marched to Divisional Reserve at Marqueffles Farm, where on September 12th the horses of the Battalion were inspected by a veterinary officer of the Divisional Staff. On the following day two companies marched to the Gas School at Aix Noulette, where damaged respirators were exchanged and gas helmets thoroughly inspected. On the 16th of the month Roman Catholic and Protestant church parades were held, Major-General A. C. Macdonell joining in the latter, which was conducted in a field near the Battalion Orderly Room. Just previous to this the Battalion had bidden farewell to Capt. F. B. D. Larken, an original company officer, who, in 1915, had taken over the duties of Regimental Paymaster and since that time had served continuously, faithfully carrying out the difficult, and sometimes unappreciated tasks which fall to the Paymaster's lot. On leaving to take over duties in England, Capt. Larken bore with him the regard and good wishes of the whole Battalion. He was succeeded as Battalion Paymaster by Capt. S. G. Dixon.

Following the religious exercises on the morning of September 16th, the men of the Battalion rested until evening, and then marched to Cité St. Pierre to relieve the 13th Canadian Battalion in Brigade Reserve. Working parties of 7 officers and 350 men were supplied to the Engineers on several occasions during the tour that followed. Casualties were light until the early morning of September 21st, when the enemy bombarded with high explosive and gas. One gas shell burst within a few feet of the sentry at No. 4 Coy's. Headquarters and choked him before he could sound the alarm. Similar shells followed, their vapour flooding the H.Q. dugout and gassing a number of men within. High explosive then struck the billet of the Battalion Pioneers, tearing away the protective blanket and exposing the men to the full effects of gas shells which followed a moment later. The suffering of the men caught by the barrage of phosgene and mustard gas was severe. Temporary blindness followed in several cases, and over 60 men were evacuated with badly irritated throats and lungs. Officers also suffered from this shelling and several were badly gassed, amongst those evacuated being Lieuts. J. S. Brisbane, F. Browne, Daniel Woodward, and A. C. N. MacKay. Capt. J. R. Weaver, an

American citizen, who had crossed from Canada in the ranks of the Battalion and suffered wounds on three occasions, was gassed on September 22nd. He had received a commission in July of the previous year and had been promoted to a captaincy on September 16th. Following his recovery from the effects of the gas, he was granted discharge from the Canadian forces and received a commission in the United States Army. The concentration of gas on September 21st was not dissipated for many hours, the troops being forced to wear gas helmets throughout the day.

On the morning when the enemy shelled with gas, Brig.-General G. S. Tuxford sent for the Medical Officer of the 14th Battalion to attend an officer of his staff who was suffering from the effects of mustard gas. After a casualty return had been made out, the Brigadier accompanied the Medical Officer down the ruins of the village street, expressing rather exasperatedly his opinion of those who in a "gas dangerous" locality stirred from protected dugouts without a gas helmet available. Orders on the subject were strict, and the Brigadier was heatedly explaining the penalties which negligence would attract in future. "Any man", he exclaimed, "who leaves his gas helmet behind in this area should be———". At this moment the General halted, and abruptly bade the M.O. good-bye. Taken aback, Capt. Graham turned enquiringly to his French-Canadian orderly, who was convulsed with laughter. "W'en de General talk", explained the latter, "he forget dat he place hees own gas helmet on de chair in dat dugout. W'en we come hout jus' now, 'e's leave 'er be'ind".

At 11 p.m. on September 22nd the enemy once more bombarded Cité St. Pierre with phosgene and mustard gas, continuing to deluge the area until after 3 o'clock on the following morning. All working parties were accordingly cancelled and the men held as much as possible inside the protection of gas-proof dugouts. At night the Battalion was relieved by the 1st Battalion, Leicestershire Regiment, and marched back to Marqueffles Farm, reaching this position on the morning of September 23rd and proceeding at 5.30 p.m., via Bouvigny-Boyeffles and Petit Servins, to Grand Servins, and thence by cross-country trail to Corps Reserve in Estrée Cauchie.

Throughout the last week in September and for the first few days of October, the Battalion remained in Corps Reserve at Estrée Cauchie. Canon Scott, C.M.G., now become Senior Chaplain of the 1st Canadian Division, visited his old unit on October 3rd and lectured to the men on "Events of the Past Year", his interesting survey being followed by a visit from an officer of the Divisional Staff, who lectured to officers of the 3rd Brigade battalions on the vital subject "Gas". While the Battalion was at Estrée Cauchie it was announced that, for bravery and devoted service, the Military Cross had been awarded to Lieut. E. G. T. Penny and Lieut. A. L. McLean. Simultaneously, the courage and loyal co-operation of other ranks was acknowledged by the award of 23 Military Medals.

Following the training period at Estrée Cauchie, the Battalion paraded at 1 p.m. on October 4th and marched, by way of Maisnil Bouche, Grand Servins, and Petit Servins, to billets in Gouy Servins. Proceeding on October 5th, the unit entered Brigade Reserve in Zouave Valley, remained there for a few hours, and at night relieved elements of the 44th and 47th Canadian Battalions in the front line (Avion Sector).

With advanced Headquarters in Avion Trench under command of Major B. F. Davidson, M.C., the Battalion carried out a five-day tour in the front line. Enemy trench mortars were active on October 7th, but failed to interfere with Royal Montreal working parties which widened, deepened, and repaired Avion Trench and Cyril Communication Trench. On the 9th of the month the enemy shelled the reserve trench and scored a direct hit on a company dugout, wounding Lieut. A. E. Scott and Lieut. W. S. McCutcheon, both of whom had suffered wounds previously, the former at Festubert, in 1915, and the latter in the more recent fighting at Hill 70. At another point a shell completely demolished a Lewis gun, but, fortunately, the crew were sheltered at the moment and escaped injury. Later in the day two linesmen lost their way in No Man's Land and wandered into a German trench. Encountering a party of the enemy, the linesmen bolted for safety and one reached the Canadian lines uninjured, but the other failed to report. Search revealed nothing, and the name of the second linesman was accordingly added to the Battalion's roll of "missing".

At 3 p.m. on October 10th the 16th Canadian Battalion started relief of the 14th, completing the operation five and a half hours later. From the front line, Headquarters of the 14th, with Nos. 1, 2, and 4 Companies, withdrew to Brigade Reserve at Tottenham Huts, No. 3 Coy. passing under command of the 13th Battalion in Brigade Support. Following return of No. 3 Coy., the Battalion, on October 13th, marched via Carency, Souchez, Maisnil Bouche, and Estrée Cauchie, to the Reserve Area at Gauchin Légal. Here the Battalion remained for a week, parading at Verdrel on October 17th, when the Commander of the First British Army, General Sir H. S. Horne, inspected the 3rd Brigade, and again on the 19th, when Major Dick Worrall, M.C., commanding the Battalion during the temporary absence of Lieut.-Col. Gault McCombe, D.S.O., complimented all ranks on the smart appearance presented.

II

On October 19th, 1917, Lieut. D. E. Stewart, Acting Adjutant of the 14th Battalion, issued an operation order which notified the troops that the 1st Canadian Division would be transferred from the First British Army to the Second Army, the change over to take place on October 21st, 22nd, and 23rd. This order conveyed information that the Canadian Corps was once again to visit the Ypres Salient. Remembering the welcomes which the Salient had extended in 1915 and 1916, the veterans of the Royal Montreal Regiment received the announcement with a touch of grim humour, which confirmed officers in their opinion that the old unit was ready for whatever task might be assigned to it.

In preparation for a march to the new area, officers were instructed to reduce kit to a maximum of 50 pounds, and the Travelling Kitchens were given orders regarding the preparation of meals en route. Arrangements were also made to have an ambulance at the rear of the column, experience having shown that even the gamest soldier is sometimes compelled to fall out during a long march. Parading at Gauchin Légal on the morning of October 20th, the Battalion passed through the towns of Houdain, Rebreuve, and Ranchicourt, and reached Bruay five minutes before noon. Four men fell out during the march and six on the following day, when the Battalion marched through Marles-les-Mines, Lozinghem, Allouagne, Lillers, and Moultinville, to billets in Ham-en-Artois.

Proceeding on October 22nd, the Battalion passed through Isbergues and Berguette and reached Thiennes at 11.40 a.m. No straggling occurred on this occasion, but four men were declared medically unfit to march and given permission to ride in the accompanying ambulance, this privilege being granted again on the following day when the Battalion marched, via Wallon Cappelle, to farm buildings on the outskirts of Staple.

On arrival in Staple the Medical Officer, for the first time in his experience, was accorded a hostile reception by a woman of France. Billeting arrangements had placed the Battalion dressing station in an estaminet on the outskirts of the town, but the virago who owned the establishment refused the Canadian officer permission to enter, and the Town Major, unwilling to offend a not too friendly populace, yielded the point and bade the Medical Officer go elsewhere. Billets were scarce, but Capt. Graham was a man of resource. Denied admission by the lady of the house, he evicted a sow and eight offspring from an outhouse, cleaned up the sty, and established his station, ignoring the citizeness and the sow, both of whom loudly voiced their disapproval.

For a week the Battalion remained at Staple, carrying out training, supplemented on October 27th by a 30-minute night route march with gas helmets at the " alert ". On October 27th the 3rd Canadian Infantry Brigade was inspected by the Corps Commander, Lieut.-General Sir A. W. Currie, K.C.M.G., C.B., and on the 29th General Sir Hubert Plumer, G.C.M.G., G.C.V.O., K.C.B., A.D.C., Commander of the Second British Army, inspected the 14th Battalion, which was carrying out special training. General Plumer, who was accompanied by Major-General A. C. Macdonell and Brig.-General G. S. Tuxford, approved the training and expressed satisfaction at the knowledge of their work displayed by officers and men.

Meanwhile it had become clear that the Canadian Corps was to take part in the great Ypres battle which had begun at ten minutes to six on the morning of July 31st and was still in progress. At the time, the objectives against which Sir Douglas Haig launched his divisions were far from clear. It was realized that freeing of the Flanders coast would strike at the German submarine blockade, but long after hope of this had vanished, British brigades and divisions moved to the assault, gaining a few hundred yards of seemingly valueless territory at an appalling cost in life, limb, and material. As Field Marshal Sir William Robertson states, the battle for the most part was fought under atrocious conditions of weather, with well-nigh impassable mud and unfordable craters strengthening the German defence. Through this mud and past these craters the British, and several Australian divisions, had somehow driven their attack, battering against the concrete " pill box " defences until, to quote General Ludendorff, " the horror of the shell hole area at Verdun was surpassed. It was no longer life at all. It was mere unspeakable suffering ".

Realizing the suffering and being aware that the territory captured failed to pay for the cost, students of the situation wondered wherein lay the clue to Sir Douglas Haig's determination. Even the theory of a "period of ceaseless attrition" failed to explain what was taking place, for in such fighting the defence must suffer fewer losses than the attack. Only tremendous superiority in strength would justify "attrition" that favoured the enemy heavily; the students therefore sought a different explanation, which, after a long time, was forthcoming. To quote from the pages of "Sir Douglas Haig's Command", a trustworthy book: "The British Army struck and kept on striking to give the French Army, under Pétain, time to recover its morale after the collapse of Nivelle's offensive on the Aisne. This could not be stated in 1917, nor for a long time after". As is now known, General Nivelle's ghastly failure in the spring of 1917 reduced one division of the French Army to mutiny, and several others to a condition regarded as "unsafe". The British Army, therefore, was forced at any cost to engage the enemy and keep him from hurling his strength against that link of the Allied chain which had temporarily weakened.

As winter approached, Sir Douglas realized that he must carry the Passchendaele Ridge, or withdraw his forces from the blood-soaked ground captured during August, September, and October. To retire would have involved admission of defeat and confession of failure. In the circumstances, such action could not be considered. Passchendaele, then, *must* be taken, and without delay. In the spring the Canadian Corps had taken Vimy. In mid-summer it had taken Hill 70. Could it take Passchendaele? Sir Douglas decided that it could, or, at least, that it had a chance. Accordingly, he summoned it from Lens and placed the task before it, accepting the Corps Commander's plan of attack, which differed from that proposed by the G.H.Q. Staff.

Coming into action early on the morning of October 26th, 1917, the 3rd and 4th Canadian Divisions, in conjunction with a British and French offensive, ploughed their way through unbelievable mud, overcame bitter enemy resistance, and captured Bellevue Spur. Five days later the Canadian line was advanced 1,200 yards on a front of 3,000 yards, as a result of fighting bitter enough to defy description. Men perished by the score in battles waged for possession of a concrete "pill box"; many drowned in shell holes, filled with icy water; others are still "missing", no man having witnessed the victory over them of the all-engulfing mud. Something of the difficulty presented by mud can be gathered from the fact that evacuation of a single stretcher case, impossible after dark, demanded the united effort of six bearers for a period of as many hours.

Following the fighting on November 1st, the exhausted 3rd and 4th Canadian Divisions were withdrawn from the line and replaced by the 1st and 2nd Canadian Divisions, to whom was assigned the honour of completing what the 3rd and 4th Divisions had so splendidly begun. Leaving their jumping-off positions on November 6th, with full appreciation of the task before them, the 1st and 2nd Divisions stormed Passchendaele Ridge and swept down the slopes beyond. Sir Douglas Haig's judgment had proved correct, and the Canadian Corps had triumphed. But the Corps which withdrew from the Ypres Salient after Passchendaele was not the Corps which had answered the urgent call a month earlier. Three thousand men had laid down their lives in wresting the Ridge from German grasp; a thousand more had disappeared in the slimy mud of that evil district; and twelve thousand lay in hospital wounded. Sixteen thousand casualties in eleven days! No wonder that throughout Canada "Passchendaele" is a name evoking tragic memory.

Though the battalions of the 3rd Brigade were not used in the assaults on Passchendaele Ridge, their duties during the operations were arduous in the extreme, and called for sustained physical exertion. At 5 o'clock on the morning of October 31st the transport of the 14th Battalion marched from Staple, and established lines not far from Ypres at 4.30 in the afternoon. With a strength of 747 all ranks, the Battalion left Staple at 6.30 a.m., entraining at Ebblinghem an hour and a quarter later and reaching Ypres shortly before noon. From Ypres the Battalion marched through St. Jean to old trenches in the vicinity of Wieltje, the route recalling to the veterans of 1915 memories of gallant comrades now two-and-a-half years dead. Previous to reaching Camp "A" which had been selected for the overnight halt, Major Worrall, commanding the Battalion during the temporary absence of Lieut.-Col. McCombe, came under the orders of the 8th Canadian Infantry Brigade and was instructed to send two companies forward to Kansas Cross. Accordingly, Nos. 2 and 3 Companies, under command of Major B. F. Davidson, M.C., moved forward in full battle order. On reporting to the 8th Brigade, these companies, numbering respectively 4 officers and 130 men and 5 officers and 137 men, were disposed in support of the 5th Canadian Mounted Rifles.

THE YPRES SALIENT AGAIN

Meanwhile, at Camp "A" Headquarters, plus Nos. 1 and 4 Companies, had witnessed aerial activity on a scale which dwarfed anything in their previous experience. Day and night the Germans were taking advantage of temporary aerial superiority to bomb the Canadians' slender lines of communication. Over Camp "A" sailed one magnificent squadron of fighting planes, escorting heavily-laden Gotha bombers, which contemptuously flung down some fifteen bombs and then proceeded toward Ypres. All night aerial activity continued, the men of the 14th sleeping little as the ground shook to the concussion of the great air torpedoes. Fortunately, most of the bombing was nearer Ypres, the neighbourhood of the Battalion Transport Lines receiving attention, but the transport personnel escaping without losses.

At 4.30 p.m. on November 1st, Headquarters of the 14th Battalion, plus Nos. 1 and 4 Companies, moved forward from Camp "A", taking up Brigade Reserve positions at Capricorn Keep some four and a quarter hours later. On the morning of November 2nd Major Worrall, accompanied by Lieut. B. T. Jackson, Scout Officer, carried out a reconnaissance of the front line, and at night the Battalion, including Nos. 2 and 3 Companies, which had rejoined, moved in single file, via Infantry Track No. 6, to relief of the 1st Canadian Mounted Rifles. On taking over, Major Worrall established his Headquarters at Kronprinz Farm; Nos. 1 and 4 Companies moved into the actual front, and Nos. 2 and 3 Companies provided support. Command of the forward area was given to Major B. F. Davidson.

Following relief of the 1st Canadian Mounted Rifles, the Battalion was reinforced by a company of the 15th Battalion, these troops bringing the force under Major Worrall's command to a strength of 27 officers and 661 other ranks. At 1.40 a.m. on November 3rd about 60 Germans approached the left flank of the Royal Montreal position, but were driven back by fire from Lewis guns and shell fire from the supporting artillery. Three hours and five minutes later the Germans dropped an intense barrage between the front line and Battalion Headquarters, cutting communication and "boxing" the forward area completely. At 6.05 a.m. 3rd Brigade reported an attack on the 14th Battalion's right, adding that a break through was rumoured and instructing Major Worrall to govern his actions accordingly.

Acting on the assumption that a rupture of the right front had occurred, Major Worrall ordered the officers of the 15th Battalion to reconnoitre a defensive flank. Carrying out these instructions with skill and alacrity, the Toronto officers reported at 7 a.m. that they were ready to proceed. A few minutes previously, however, 3rd Brigade had telephoned stating that the rumour of a German intrusion on the right was unfounded. Accordingly, the idea of forming a defensive flank was abandoned. In a report dealing with the period of the enemy barrage Major Worrall records gratification and pride in the bravery of the Battalion runners. Undeterred by numerous casualties, these men penetrated the barrage over and again, carrying messages that enabled the companies in the front line and those in reserve to present a united front to the threatened danger on the right. Two runners, who had lost their way, dashed into the German line and were taken prisoner.

At 7.30 a.m. the enemy barrage suddenly died away, being replaced by sniping, intermittent gas shelling, and more or less constant machine gun fire. These caused a number of casualties, among the severely wounded being Major B. F. Davidson, M.C., Acting Second-in-Command of the Regiment and O.C. the front line. Throughout the engagement up to this time Major Davidson had shown the same courage and qualities of leadership as during the previous actions of the year. His loss, therefore, was regretted by all ranks of the Battalion, as was that caused by the wounding of two capable officers, Capt. J. H. Boutelle and Lieut. Gerald Hiam. On November 4th both sides shelled heavily, the 14th Battalion suffering appreciable losses, offset in some degree by the unusual number of Germans who fell to the Battalion snipers. Why the enemy were so careless is not clear, but at frequent intervals throughout the day the snipers were afforded easy targets. Possibly the Germans, seeking a wound, risked death to escape from that " area of unspeakable suffering " which was Passchendaele.

Late at night on November 4th the left half of the Royal Montreal Regiment's front line was taken over by the Hood Battalion, 63rd (Royal Naval) Division, the remainder of the Battalion, less No. 3 Coy., which remained in support, being relieved early on the following morning by the 3rd Canadian Battalion and withdrawing to Camp "A" at Wieltje. Here No. 3 Coy. rejoined the Battalion on November 5th, the entire unit suffering sharply at 5 o'clock on the morning of November 6th when Camp "A" was heavily bombarded.

At night on November 7th the Battalion filed up Infantry Track No. 5 to relieve the 3rd Canadian Battalion in a reserve position on Bellevue Spur. Shelling of the narrow, one-man track occurred during the relief and two other ranks were killed. Heavy shelling continued all day on November 8th, and again on November 9th, which was also marked by intense aerial activity. In the aerial fighting the Germans seemed to have attained a definite local superiority. Eighteen of their planes cruised over the Royal Montreal front at one time, several of the pilots sweeping low over the position and raking the trenches with machine gun fire. From this fire the 14th escaped without losses, but there was no avoiding the heavy fire of the German artillery and a number of Royal Montrealers were wounded, among these being Lieut. G. V. Whitehead, a brother of Capt. E. A. Whitehead, who had fallen in action while serving with the Battalion in June of the previous year.

Relieved by the 10th Canadian Battalion at 8.05 p.m. on November 9th, the Battalion moved back, by way of Infantry Track No. 6, to Capricorn Keep, where the men occupied the same area as on November 2nd. At Capricorn Keep the unit passed one night, being relieved by the 58th Canadian Battalion at 2.20 o'clock on the afternoon of November 10th and withdrawing to Camp "C", near Wieltje. From Camp "C", on the morning of November 11th, the Battalion proceeded in parties to a bath house established near Ypres on the bank of the Yser Canal. Here hot water and clean clothing rejoiced the hearts of the men, who were filthy, and correspondingly depressed, after the mud, blood, and fighting in the Salient.

Thus ended the part played by the 14th Battalion, Royal Montreal Regiment, in the Battle of Passchendaele. To other units had fallen the honour of carrying out the actual assaults and driving the enemy from Passchendaele Ridge, while the battalions of the 3rd Brigade had toiled at the unspectacular, but exhausting, tasks allotted to troops in support. Throughout the engagement the morale of the Battalion had left little to be desired. Under conditions which taxed strength and endurance to the utmost, the men maintained high spirits and at all times evinced willingness to accomplish whatever tasks fell to their lot. As mentioned previously, 4 officers had been wounded, not including Lieut. A. D. Brewer, who was evacuated on November 13th suffering from the effects of a wound and enemy gas. Lieut. Brewer had crossed from Canada in the ranks of the Battalion and had been commissioned in January, 1917, after recovering from wounds received at the Somme. Amongst other ranks, casualties at Passchendaele totalled 147, of whom 14 were killed, 7 presumed killed, 70 wounded, and 56 gassed.

And now the Corps was leaving the Ypres Salient behind. Thrice the Canadians had visited Ypres and thrice the Salient had given a bloody welcome. Thrice, however, they had torn victory from the jaws of defeat, saving the day in 1915, preventing disaster in 1916, and now, in 1917, wresting from German hands that Ridge which, uncaptured, would have annulled the gains of three months' fighting. Little of all this passed through the minds of the veterans as they left the Salient. They had been summoned from Lens to take Passchendaele, and the task had been accomplished. They had carried out a feat of arms which will endure in military history, and were glad that the job was over. The departure from Passchendaele was not a triumphal march. The Corps had triumphed, but the cost had been great. Without regret, the divisions bade the district adieu. Actually, they bade it a final good-bye. Other triumphs lay ahead, but Canada's work at Ypres had been completed.

CHAPTER XVI

WINTER ON THE LENS FRONT

> Now when we take the cobbled road
> We often took before,
> Our thoughts are with the hearty lads
> Who tread that way no more.
>
> And when we leave the trench at night
> And stagger 'neath our load,
> Grey silent ghosts as light as air
> Come with us down the road.
>
> —Patrick McGill.

I

ON completion of the operations at Passchendaele in November, 1917, the Canadian Corps moved back to take over the British front at Lens. Earlier in the season the Corps had held this front and had prepared an attack on Lens, but, Passchendaele intervening, the Lens project had been abandoned and was not now under consideration. The Corps had suffered in Flanders and was in no condition to undertake a large scale offensive, particularly as the season of favourable weather had definitely passed. In addition, developments in Russia and elsewhere had released large bodies of German troops, forcing the Allied armies to consider the defence of vital points rather than opportunities for attack.

On the whole western front no location offered Germany greater inducement to attack than the area commanded by Vimy Ridge, which protected the great coal mining district of France, as well as vital lines of communication. Realizing that Germany would attack somewhere in the spring and that a successful blow at Vimy might involve British disaster, Sir Douglas Haig ordered the Canadian Corps to strengthen the area's defences. Throughout the late autumn of 1917 and the winter and spring of 1918, therefore, huge working parties of Canadian infantry toiled, under supervision of the Engineers, to convert Vimy into a fortress of tremendous strength. Night after night, and in the day time where possible, thousands of men dug trenches, strung barbed wire, erected machine gun emplacements, burrowed into the earth to build shell-proof ammunition dumps, established water reservoirs, buried signal cables, and wrought in every way to fortify the area against the day when it might stand between Germany and military victory.

What was accomplished by the troops is best conveyed by a few examples. There was the "Army Line", 25,000 yards in length, consisting of front, support, and reserve trenches, with wire entanglements, machine gun emplacements, and bomb-proof command posts; the "Ecurie Switch", 12,000 yards long, and similar in construction to the "Army Line"; "July Line" consisting of front, support, and reserve trenches, extending for 9,000 yards; and "Paddock Switch" only 1,000 yards shorter. Twenty-two thousand yards of 2-line trenches were also dug and a vast system of lines with wire and machine gun emplacements was brought into being, chief amongst these being the "Reservoir Hill-Beaumont Line" of 25,000 yards, the "St. Pierre and La Plaine Switch" of 22,000 yards, the "Lens Road Switch" of 17,250 yards, and the "Thélus Ridge Line" of 15,000 yards. That the enemy observed the strength of the position and appreciated the significance of what had been accomplished seems obvious, for, when he struck with all the strength he could muster, he avoided Vimy, despite the fact that at no other point would a short advance have yielded commensurate return. To the working parties of the infantry, to the Tunnelling companies, to the Pioneer companies, and to the Engineer units, therefore, is due, at least in some measure, the fact that when Germany's vast effort had failed the British line on Vimy Ridge stood firm where it had stood in the autumn of the previous year.

II

On November 11, 1917, the 14th Battalion, Royal Montreal Regiment, began the move from Flanders back to Lens. Marching from the Wieltje area at noon, the Battalion proceeded to Ypres, entraining there at 4.10 p.m. and reaching Brandhoek some two hours later. After passing the night at Ridge Camp, Brandhoek, the Battalion paraded at 10.30 o'clock on the morning of November 12th and proceeded to a point where lorries were waiting. To eliminate delay the companies had been divided into "bus parties" of 25 men each and Lieut. D. MacRitchie detailed to supervise distribution. This plan worked well, and soon the busses were under way to the Merville Area, where the men billeted in farm houses not far from the town. Continuing the lorry journey on November 13th, the men were carried to Bethune, and on the following day to Fosse 10, near Sains-en-Gohelle. At Sains-en-Gohelle the Battalion remained for three days, at the end of which a squad, under Lieut. Patterson, cleaned up billets and joined the unit in a march, via Boyeffles and Bouvigny-Boyeffles, to Marqueffles Farm. Two days were spent in this location, the Battalion then marching to Brigade Reserve at Alberta Camp.

On November 22nd a party of officers and N.C.O's. from the Battalion reconnoitred the front line, Avion Sector, each officer making a sketch showing trenches, communication trenches, bombing posts, Engineers' dumps, and machine gun emplacements, and also reporting on defensive wire, gas defences, sanitation, opportunities for night patrols, and weak spots in the enemy wire. Three days later the Battalion took over from the 13th Battalion, Nos. 1 and 4 Companies moving into the front line, Nos. 2 and 3 Companies providing support, and all reporting completion of relief to Battalion Headquarters in Beaver Trench by use of the code word "Excelsior". At this time "Intelligence" reported movement in the German rear areas which might indicate an enemy withdrawal to the Drocourt-Quéant Line. Nothing in the character of the resistance offered to patrols of the Canadian battalions confirmed such a theory, but arrangements for an immediate advance were made should the retirement take place. In the meantime responsibility for detecting any such move rested with the units in the front line. In such circumstances patrols were necessarily frequent and aggressive.

On November 26th two men of the 14th Battalion were killed by enemy trench mortars, which were active in the morning and again at 9 o'clock at night. At 9.30 Battalion Headquarters asked the supporting artillery for retaliatory fire, this request being granted and the German front shelled for 40 minutes. In addition, a company of the Royal Engineers, using special apparatus, propelled 700 drums of gas into the enemy trenches, with satisfactory results. Later Lieut. B. T. Jackson led a patrol to the enemy wire to seek information regarding the rumoured retirement. When close to the German wire the Royal Montrealers sighted an enemy patrol, too strong to be attacked. "Freezing", the 14th patrol escaped detection and later returned in safety to the Canadian lines.

November 27th was a quiet day, but at 4 o'clock on the morning of the 28th the front woke to activity as the enemy pushed a raid against the left section of the Battalion, presumably to secure identifications. If such was indeed the purpose, the raid failed, for no 14th men were captured. In repelling the attack, however, 6 men were wounded, including Lieut. E. Evans, an original member of the Battalion, commissioned after recovering from wounds received in July, 1916. Two hours after repulse of the raid, the enemy attacked on the right front, driving into the Royal Montreal trench, but again failing to take prisoners. One man of the 14th was wounded in the action, but this casualty was more than offset when the Battalion's Lewis guns caught the raiding party and inflicted sharp losses.

Ill content with the result of his raids on November 28th, the enemy launched a more ambitious effort at 4.55 o'clock on the morning of November 29th, when, following a trench mortar bombardment, some 42 Germans advanced to the attack. Total failure dogged this party, which was routed with a loss of three prisoners, of whom one died whilst being carried to the 14th Battalion Aid Post.

At 4.45 o'clock on the morning of December 1st, the Canadian artillery, trench mortars, Stokes guns, and Brigade machine guns barraged the 14th Battalion front for five minutes, hoping to catch an enemy raid in No Man's Land. Undeterred by this exhibition of defensive power, the enemy pushed forward a raid at 6 o'clock in the afternoon, the effort coming under barrage fire and recoiling with sharp losses, but not before two men of the 14th had been killed and two wounded. Later a patrol of the Royal Montreal Regiment, under Lieut. B. T. Jackson, examined the ground over which the enemy had advanced. No dead were discovered, but, on reaching the spot where the dead from the previous raid were lying, the patrol noticed that one body concealed a bomb, arranged to detonate if the cadaver were lifted. The Germans, realizing that the Canadians would probably seek identifications, had used the body to bait a trap. Happily, this strategy went unrewarded.

At 12.50 a.m. on December 4th, following relief by the 1st Canadian Battalion, the Royal Montreal Regiment moved back to La Coulotte and there entrained, under supervision of Lieut. R. G. Savage, for Vancouver Camp at Chateau de la Haie. A week of training followed, devoid of unusual incident, except that supplied by voting for candidates in the Dominion election being held in Canada. Sections of the Battalion cast ballots on December 5th, and Nos. 2 and 3 Companies voted on December 8th. Secrecy of the ballot was preserved, consequently no statistics are available as to how the men viewed the chief issue of the campaign, namely, conscription.

On the morning of December 11th Lieut.-Col. Gault McCombe, D.S.O., inspected the Battalion, which was about to relieve the 8th Canadian Battalion in support in the Lens Sector. Marching at 3 p.m. to Summit Siding, opposite Chateau de la Haie, the men entrained in 20 cars (3 trains) and proceeded to Lens Junction, detraining at this spot and marching, via Angres, to Napoo Corner in Liévin, where guides of the 8th Battalion were awaiting them.

In support at Liévin the Battalion spent four days, on each of which parties, approximately 325 strong, carried material or repaired Adept and Approach Communication Trenches. Aerial activity was marked, and continued after December 15th, when the Royal Montrealers relieved the 13th Royal Highlanders of Canada in the right sub-section, Moulin Sector, of the front line.

In the front line the Battalion remained four days. On December 16th the enemy fired about 50 gas shells into the front trench, supplementing this bombardment by trench mortar shelling of the support and reserve lines. Neither the gas shells nor the trench mortar bombs troubled the Royal Montrealers appreciably, nor did enemy aeroplanes which attacked in the afternoon, but were driven off by British planes, assisted by anti-aircraft fire from machine guns.

At 7 p.m. on December 19th the Battalion was relieved by the 13th Battalion, Nos. 1 and 4 Companies moving to support positions in Liévin, and Headquarters, with Nos. 2 and 3 Companies, withdrawing to Brigade Reserve at Souchez Huts. On December 23rd the main section of the Battalion marched to St. Lawrence Camp and entered Divisional Reserve, Nos. 1 and 4 Companies withdrawing from Liévin and rejoining the unit that same night.

At St. Lawrence Camp the Royal Montreal Regiment passed its fourth Christmas away from Canada and its third on the soil of France. No parades were ordered, but in the morning Lieut.-Col. McCombe investigated the case of Private J. Adams, who had been arrested on Christmas Eve, charged with brawling and attacking men of a 4th Divisional battalion. The O.C. the battalion in question arrived to associate himself with Col. McCombe, and the enquiry at once began. One by one battered members of the 4th Division reluctantly testified that Adams was responsible for their deplorable condition. When nearly a dozen had given evidence, the 4th Division colonel called a halt. "Just a minute", said he; "am I to understand that the assortment of black eyes presented for our inspection this morning represent the work of one individual?" When assured that such was the case, the colonel turned to Lieut.-Col. McCombe. "As a favour to me", he said, "please dismiss Private Adams without punishment. Any man who can lick a dozen of my men commands my respect and admiration". In view of the fact that Adams had fought in self-defence, Lieut.-Col. McCombe complied with this request, dismissing the prisoner with a reprimand.

III

January 1st, 1918, found the 14th Battalion, Royal Montreal Regiment, still at St. Lawrence Camp in Divisional Reserve. Snow fell at intervals during the day, the white fields and the clean, open landscape reminding the men of New Year's Days in Canada when war was far from anyone's thoughts. War obtruded itself on this occasion, however, for in the morning an enemy plane approached the camp, but was driven off by machine guns.

For a week after New Year the Battalion remained at St. Lawrence Camp, occupied in routine training, varied on the evening of January 6th when 275 other ranks attended a revue by the 3rd Canadian Divisional Concert Party at Gouy Servins. On the morning following this entertainment the Battalion marched to the Reserve Area, Houdain, where routine training was resumed. At this point Lieut. T. Hodgson, M.C., M.M., who, following promotion from the ranks, had served as Battalion Scout Officer, left the unit on a secret mission. For months no news of him reached the 14th, but eventually it became known that he had joined the mission headed by Major-General L. C. Dunsterville, C.B., C.S.I., operating in Persia and the Near East.

A few days after Lieut. Hodgson's departure, No. 444193 Sergeant A. J. Mahar, who had enlisted in the 55th Battalion in May, 1915, and had been drafted to the 14th Battalion in August of the same year, also left to join General Dunsterville's secret expedition. The subsequent travels of this N.C.O. illustrate rather vividly the widespread nature of the Great War. His itinerary was as follows:—

Embarked Southampton, England	29– 1–18
Debarked Cherbourg, France	30– 1–18
Embarked Taranto, Italy	10– 2–18
Debarked Alexandria, Egypt	———
Embarked Suez, Egypt	17– 2–18
Debarked Koweit, Arabia	2– 3–18
Embarked Koweit, Arabia	2– 3–18
Debarked Basrah, Mesopotamia	———
Wounded Baku District, S.E. of Caucasus	31– 8–18
Hospital Kazian, Persia	2– 9–18

After recovering from his injury (a gunshot wound in the right shoulder), Sergt. Mahar saw the break-up of Dunsterforce and then volunteered for the British Military Mission to Siberia, under Major-General Sir A. W. F. Knox. He was accepted and:—

Embarked Basrah, Mesopotamia - - -	23–11–18
Touched at Bombay, India - - - -	
Touched at Hong Kong, China - - -	
Debarked Vladivostock, Siberia - - -	16– 1–19
Served in Siberia for nearly 10 months and sailed for home, Canada - - - -	1–11–19

On January 9th the Battalion's blankets were fumigated; on the 14th a number of men were given special practice in use of the tump line; and on the 18th Major-Gen. A. C. Macdonell visited the Battalion to inspect the training. Two nights later Major-Gen. Macdonell and Brig.-Gen. G. S. Tuxford honoured the Battalion by dining in the Officers' Mess.

On January 23rd réveillé sounded at 5.30 o'clock, breakfast was served at 6.30, sick parade was held at 6.45, and at 8.20 the unit marched, via Maisnil-les-Ruitz, Barlin, Hersin, Sains-en-Gohelle, and Fosse 10, to Bully Grenay. En route the Battalion marched past Lieut.-Gen. Sir A. W. Currie, Commander of the Canadian Corps, who took the salute and gave the unit careful scrutiny. At Bully Grenay training continued, the sole variation from the usual drills and practices being provided by a series of lectures on "The History of the Regiment", designed to give men of recent drafts a knowledge of what the Battalion had accomplished during its thirty-four months in France.

At night on January 31st, the 14th Battalion relieved the 5th Canadian Battalion in the Hill 70 Sector of the front line, No. 3 Coy. taking over the right front and No. 2 Coy. the left, with Nos. 4 and 1 Companies providing the respective supports. Soon after taking over the front, a patrol pushed forward to examine the enemy wire and was met with a shower of hand grenades and concentrated rifle fire, one man being killed and the remainder forced to retire. Unwilling that a body should fall into German hands and provide identification of the Regiment, the Scout Officer remained in No Man's Land until the bombing and rifle fire had died down. He then returned to the man who had been killed, lifted his body, and started back to the Canadian lines. At this juncture the Germans opened fire with rifles and a machine gun, despite which he persisted in his mission and reached his own front in safety.

Visibility was good on February 2nd, observers reporting much movement back of the enemy lines and calling attention of the artillery to several attractive targets. Considering that the movement during daylight indicated activity after dark, the Brigade machine guns and the Canadian field batteries carried out several " shoots " during the night, concentrating fire on the approaches to the German line and on those points where aeroplanes had fixed the location of enemy dumps.

Machine gunners on both sides were active on February 4th, and on the 5th Canadian 6-inch Stokes guns bombarded positions where machine gun emplacements were thought to exist. Previous to this, the Stokes guns had demolished two houses behind the German lines, where carrying parties indicated that some construction was in progress. Retaliation to the fire of the Stokes guns was undertaken by German trench mortars which wrecked the front of No. 2 Coy., killing two men and wounding two severely. Less successful was a bombardment on February 6th, when gas shells, mixed with high explosive, poured on the support line without causing serious damage, or inflicting casualties.

On the morning of February 7th enemy artillery shelled the Royal Montreal position and at noon retaliation was asked for. This was satisfactorily supplied by 18-pounders and heavy trench mortars, the German fire dying away in mid-afternoon and offering no hindrance to the 13th Battalion, which completed relief at 11 p.m. When the Highlanders took over the front, Headquarters and No. 1 Coy. of the 14th Battalion moved back to the Village Line, and Nos. 2, 3, and 4 Companies billeted in Loos.

For nine days the Battalion remained in the reserve positions taken over on the night of February 7th, supplying strong parties each night to dig communication trenches, construct defended localities, carry material, and string double-apron barbed wire. On several occasions these parties included every man who could be spared from other duties. At night on February 16th the Royal Montreal Regiment marched to Bully Grenay and there entered Divisional Reserve. No parades were ordered on the 17th, as the men were tired after the nightly working parties and badly in need of rest. The holiday also provided an opportunity for repair of clothing and equipment, which had suffered from the heavy nature of the work accomplished.

After eight days in Divisional Reserve the Battalion formed up at the iron gates on the main street of Bully Grenay and marched to relieve the 10th Canadian Battalion in the St. Emile Sector of the front line, Nos. 1 and 3 Companies taking over the actual front, with Nos. 2 and 4 Companies supplying the supports. In its new position the front of the Battalion extended between Nestor and Nabob Communication Trenches.

Indicating the changed situation on the western front at this time, as compared with that existing in February, 1917, a defence scheme drawn up by Major A. T. Powell, D.S.O., was issued to the 14th Battalion under date of February 28th. In this scheme Major Powell sketched the defensive possibilities of the area and issued instructions applicable to several eventualities. He pointed out that in the area were three defended localities, known respectively as "Thursday", "Friday", and "Saturday", and explained that work on the wiring of these would be required during the tour in the line. He illustrated how these localities could be used to check a German attack, but emphasized the importance of holding the front line and definitely ordered the men of the 14th to stand fast, come what might.

In further analysis of action to be taken should the enemy attack, Major Powell ordered all officers to consider five forms which the operation might assume, namely:—

(1) A Raid
(2) Trench Snatching
(3) A local attack, with limited objectives
(4) A great attack on a wide front
(5) A gas attack.

Officers were ordered to give thought to these possibilities and to acquaint subordinates with the action to be taken should any of the five occur. Special arrangements regarding S.O.S. signals were communicated in a supplement to the defence scheme. The Brigade S.O.S. was to be a succession of gold and silver rain rockets, repeated until the call for help was answered. In addition, officers were instructed to forward the S.O.S. by every means available, including, as circumstances might dictate, telephone, buzzer, or visual signalling. Battalions were instructed to arrange S.O.S. relay stations and to keep them manned continuously. In forwarding S.O.S. calls, officers were ordered to state whether the appeal was for defence against attacking infantry, attacking tanks, or against hostile gas which might cover an attack.

From February 25th until March 6th the Royal Montreal Regiment remained in the front line, working on the construction of defences, sending out defensive night patrols, and suffering appreciably from the activity of enemy artillery, trench mortars, aeroplanes, and machine guns, among the casualties being Lieut. B. M. Watson, who was killed in action on March 3rd. On the night of March 2nd the Germans sent a raid against the Battalion front without success, two parties being seen by Royal Montreal sentries and driven back before they could penetrate the Canadian wire.

It is impossible to enumerate the bombardments during this tour in the line, or give details of the frequent Regimental patrols. The tables which follow, however, illustrate in a measure how active the tour was. The first lists the patrols on the night of March 1st/2nd, and the second lists the fire of hostile artillery between 6 a.m. and 12 noon on March 3rd.

TABLE No. 1

Patrol No. 1—1 officer and 5 other ranks.
   Out 7.30 p.m. In 9.30 p.m.
Patrol No. 2—2 N.C.O's. and 6 men.
   Out 7.30 p.m. In 9.20 p.m.
Patrol No. 3—2 N.C.O's. and 6 men.
   Out 7.20 p.m. In 9.15 p.m.
Patrol No. 4—2 N.C.O's. and 6 men.
   Out. 3.30 a.m. In 5 a.m.

TABLE No. 2

Time	Rounds	Weapon
8.15 a.m.	2 rounds	Field Gun.
9.15 a.m.	8 rounds	Field Gun.
9.35 a.m.	12 rounds	Field Gun.
9.50 a.m.	7 rounds	Light Field Gun.
10.15 a.m.	8 rounds	Light Field Gun.
10.30 a.m.	10 rounds	Heavy Howitzer.
10.45 a.m.	7 rounds	Field Gun.
11.00 a.m.	15 rounds	Field Gun.
11.25 a.m.	12 rounds	Field Gun.
11.55 a.m.	8 rounds	Heavy Gun.
11.59 a.m.	7 rounds	Gas shells.

Following relief by the 13th Battalion on March 6th, the 14th Battalion took up Brigade Support positions in Cité St. Pierre, and there remained for one week, supplying frequent parties for work on reserve and communication trenches. At 7.35 a.m. on March 8th the enemy fired about 500 rounds of high explosive and gas shells into Cité St. Pierre, but failed to inflict casualties on the Battalion, which, five days later, marched to a camp in the Bois de Froissart, near Hersin, and there entered Corps Reserve.

Though the spring of 1918 brought the certainty of German attack, and all ranks of the Canadian Corps were trained in the defensive, the fact that the war would be won by offensive fighting was never lost to sight. Accordingly, on March 14th, 26 officers and 53 N.C.O's. of the 14th Battalion proceeded to Braquemont to attend a lecture on co-operation with tanks; and on March 18th the 13th and 14th Battalions combined in manœuvres with the VII Tank Battalion and contact planes of the Royal Air Force. In these manœuvres a company of tanks, under command of Major J. W. Winters, supported the infantry in a two-phase attack, involving capture of a Green Line, between the Bois de Noulette and the Bois de Bouvigny, and later of a Yellow Line some distance beyond. So spirited were the manœuvres and so eagerly did the troops carry out their part that the aspect of the engagement closely approximated actual warfare, service caps, worn in place of steel helmets, alone betraying that no casualties were expected.

CHAPTER XVII

GERMANY'S GREAT EFFORT

> The deep-blue heaven, curving from the green,
> Spans with its shimmering arch the flowery zone;
> In all God's earth there is no gentler scene,
> And yet I hear that awesome monotone;
>
> But still I gaze afar, and at the sight
> My whole soul softens to its heartfelt prayer:
> "Spirit of Justice, Thou for whom they fight,
> Ah, turn in mercy, to our lads out there!"
> —Sir Arthur Conan Doyle.

I

ON March 21st, 1918, Germany struck the first blow of a series planned to gain decisive military victory. When the United States of America joined the Allies in April, 1917, time became Germany's enemy. Given time, the United States could place in the field a force sufficiently strong to bring about Germany's downfall. The desperation of the German blows in the spring of 1918 is, therefore, understandable. They represented a last bid for victory. To quote Sir Douglas Haig: "The launching and destruction of Napoleon's last reserves at Waterloo was a matter of minutes. The corresponding German stage started on March 21, 1918, and lasted four months".

The decision of the German Higher Command to seek victory on the western front in the spring of 1918 was reached in the autumn of the previous year. After the bitter fighting in Flanders, which culminated with the operation of the Canadian Corps at Passchendaele, the German Staff prepared the Army for the spring offensive. To this end divisions were moved from the Russian front and from all points where they could be spared, with the result that 192 divisions were concentrated in France and Flanders, 46 divisions more than in November, 1917. Meanwhile the divisions of the British Army, with the exception of the divisions of the Australian and Canadian Corps, had been reduced from a 12-battalion to a 9-battalion basis, and the front had been extended to well over 125 miles. The French front was longer, but was menaced by no such concentrations as faced the British.

When the Germans attacked the Third and Fifth British Armies on March 21st, on a 50-mile front between Arras and La Fère, the

Fifth Army staggered under the blow and gave ground somewhat alarmingly. The retreat has been described as a rout, but such a phrase exaggerates the situation, though applicable to limited sections of the front. Actually, to use the simile Clausewitz made famous, the retreat was that of a wounded lion, battered and broken, but unsubdued, dangerous, and capable of rending any careless pursuer.

In following the German attack of March 21st to its halting place within reach of Amiens, the world at large missed the significance of events on March 28th, when the Seventeenth German Army attacked General Horne's First British Army on a 20-mile front from Puisieux to beyond Oppy, and was crushingly defeated. The failure of this attack, planned to smash the British front and roll up Vimy Ridge, settled the fate of the March 21st battle, which gradually came to a standstill, not, however, before 46 British divisions had been engaged, and 8 destroyed.

On March 29th, 1918, General Ferdinand Foch, of the French Army, was appointed to co-ordinate action of the British, French, and American Armies, his commission, however, when finally drawn up, specifically stating that, though he was to be Generalissimo, tactical direction was still the prerogative of the respective commanders-in-chief. Eleven days later the Germans, foiled in their effort to the south, shifted their attack to the Lys front and struck at a point held by the Portuguese Army Corps. So powerful was the blow that in three hours, with the exception of certain field batteries and individuals, the Portuguese Corps had disintegrated and withdrawn from active part in the Great War. Following initial success, the German attack swept forward on a wide front, driving back many British divisions and uncovering defences, until Ypres and the Channel ports were once more in danger. Having suffered casualties of 47,000 in the week ending on March 31st, 77,500 in the week ending on April 7th, and 48,000 in the week ending on April 14th, the British Army was seriously affected. On April 11th, however, Sir Douglas Haig issued an order showing that Germany had employed 106 divisions without separating the British from the French, capturing the Channel ports, or destroying the British Army. In concluding this famous order, Sir Douglas called on the troops under his command to stand fast: " Every position must be held to the last man. There must be no retirement. With our backs to the wall, and believing in the justice of our cause, each one of us must fight to the end ". The response to this appeal added one more page to the long and proud chapter of British military history.

Having failed in his effort to capture the Channel ports and destroy the British Army, the enemy, on May 27th, struck at the French between Soissons and Rheims. In the battle which followed the IX British Army Corps, composed of the 8th, 21st, 25th, and 50th Divisions, was cut to pieces, and later the 19th British Division also suffered severely. At the time no public mention of the presence of the IX Corps and the 19th Division was permitted, possibly in deference to the French, whose Intelligence Department refused to accept the British Corps Commander's warning that an attack on his front was being mounted. General Duchêne, Commanding the Sixth French Army, insisted that the front was quiet and a suitable place for the British Corps, exhausted after the March and April fighting, to rest. When the blow fell the British troops fought magnificently. They were overwhelmed, and the world heard nothing of their devotion, but General Maistre, Commanding the Army Group to which they were attached, has recorded his profound gratitude for the self-sacrificing service they rendered.

Two weeks after the attack in which the IX Corps suffered so severely, the enemy struck again at the French between Noyon and Montdidier, following this effort a week later by a great blow at Rheims. For a time the enemy drove the troops of our Ally before him, but by mid-July the French had stiffened their defence and, with the aid of American reinforcements, were more than holding their own. On July 18th Marshal Foch launched a successful counter-attack which marked the turning point in the 1918 campaign. Germany had shot her bolt; retribution was at hand.

II

While the battles of the spring were being fought to the north and south, the Canadian Corps was comparatively inactive. In March and April it held front line trenches, which were heavily bombarded on occasions, but were never the direct object of enemy attack. Then, on May 7th, the Corps, less the 2nd Canadian Division which was temporarily attached to the VI British Corps, was withdrawn to form part of a special striking force, known as "G.H.Q. Reserve", or "Army Special Reserve".

Long before this the Corps had recovered from the losses suffered in the autumn of 1917, and regained the condition which had carried Vimy, Hill 70, and Passchendaele. Its divisions had been maintained on a 12-battalion basis; its battalions had been kept at full strength; its four divisions were served by five divisional artilleries; its personnel possessed esprit-de-corps; its higher command included generals of ability and staff officers competent to a marked degree; and its auxiliary services were unrivalled on the western front. Realizing that these factors made the Corps the strongest individual striking weapon in Europe, and that, sooner or later, such a weapon would be required, Sir Douglas Haig and Lieut.-Gen. Sir A. W. Currie resisted all temptation to dissipate its strength in defensive fighting, and saved it against the inevitable hour of need.

When the German offensive opened on March 21st, the 14th Battalion was lying in Divisional Support at Bully Grenay. News of the battle was received on March 22nd, and on the 23rd the Battalion entered Army Reserve. On the 24th, following communication of a Special Order by Sir Douglas Haig, all ranks were kept close to billets, and preparations were made to move on short notice. At midnight on March 25th the Battalion "stood to" in expectation of orders for an immediate advance. Later the "stand to" was cancelled, but not before all officers and other ranks attached to the 3rd Australian Tunnelling Coy. and to the 1st Field Coy., Canadian Engineers, received orders to report back to the Battalion without delay.

At 6 a.m. on March 27th the Battalion fell in at Bully Grenay, marched thence to Boyeffles Chateau, and there joined the other battalions of the 3rd Brigade in a march to Canada Camp, Chateau de la Haie, where the Brigade continued to act as Army Reserve. Throughout the day the troops were interested in the coming and going of messengers and in the tension which obviously prevailed at Battalion Headquarters. Realizing the possible significance of such activity, a larger percentage of men than usual attended Protestant and Roman Catholic services, the former conducted by Canon Scott, one-time Chaplain of the Regiment, and the latter by Father Murdock, Catholic Chaplain of the 3rd Brigade.

At 11 p.m. Major Arthur Plow, the Adjutant, was called to Brigade Headquarters to receive orders. Returning on the run 25 minutes later, Major Plow summoned the officers and announced a move. No time to issue written instructions was allowed, the Battalion marching in 20 minutes to the football field, Chateau de la Haie, where the 3rd Brigade assembled. As anti-climax to the hurried departure from camp, the Brigade waited for busses until 3.20 a.m., but once these arrived delay ended, the troops being whirled to Marieux, where they were instructed to breakfast in the open fields. During the meal a German plane evinced curiosity, but no desire to attack. Shortly after noon the Battalion marched, via Thievres, to Famechon, where a halt was made to await more busses. At 4 p.m. these arrived, the men embussing and 75% of them reaching Calvary Camp, Agnez-lez-Duisans, in due course. The remainder, through error, debussed at Wanquetin and reached Calvary Camp late at night.

Tired and soaking after the long bus journey in pouring rain, the men of the 14th expected to sleep at Calvary Camp, but at 3.55 a.m. the unit marched to Brigade Support in Ronville Caves, under verbal orders from Brig.-Gen. G. S. Tuxford to counter-attack should the enemy break through at Telegraph Hill. In Ronville Caves, a vast cavern capable of accommodating more than a brigade of infantry, and extending under the heart of the city of Arras, the Battalion rested on March 29th and 30th. On the latter date "stand to" was practised at 5 a.m., the companies and all sections being ready to march in less than 20 minutes. At night 3 other ranks were killed and 7 wounded when, not far from an entrance to the Cave, a party was caught by shell fire. These brought the Battalion casualties for the month to a total of 11 killed and 25 wounded.

In March the authorized strength of infantry battalions of the Canadian Corps was increased by 100 other ranks, bringing the establishment to a total of 46 officers, including authorized attached, and 1,072 other ranks. On March 31st the effective strength of the Royal Montreal Regiment was 45 officers and 1,012 other ranks, though the fighting strength was but 37 officers and 792 other ranks. The discrepancy between the strengths was made up as follows:—

> On Leave:— 3 officers and 118 other ranks.
> Sick:— 1 officer.
> On Command:—4 officers and 102 other ranks.

March 31st, 1918, found the Battalion still in Ronville Caves, while the transport of the whole 3rd Brigade occupied lines in Agnez-lez-Duisans, about 8 kilometres away. From Ronville Caves the Battalion sent out a working party of 8 officers, 24 N.C.O's., and 240 men. This party, organized as a fighting unit, was commanded by Major R. C. MacKenzie, D.S.O., with Capt. D. W. Clarkson, M.C., as second-in-command, and Lieut. E. G. T. Penny, M.C., as adjutant. Shelling for a time interfered with the party, despite which 1,200 yards of double-apron wire were erected. On April 2nd another party installed over 1,000 yards of wire. This party was commanded by Major A. T. Powell, D.S.O., with Capt. J. H. Richardson, and Lieut. A. L. McLean, M.C., D.C.M., serving respectively as second-in-command and adjutant. As in the case of the April 1st party, shelling interfered with the wiring, but failed to inflict casualties.

At 8.20 p.m. on April 5th the Battalion left Ronville Caves and advanced to relieve the 4th Canadian Battalion in the Telegraph Hill Sector of the front line. Previous to this the rear details of the 3rd Brigade battalions had been formed into an emergency battalion, capable of counter-attacking should the enemy penetrate the front line. Command of this composite battalion was assumed by Lieut.-Col. C. W. Peck, D.S.O., Commanding Officer of the 16th Battalion, and No. 2 Coy. of the unit, formed from the rear details of the 14th Battalion, was placed under the orders of Major Arthur Plow, M.C., M.M.

On relieving the 4th Battalion, No. 1 Coy. of the Royal Montreal Regiment took over the left half of the front and No. 3 Coy. the right half, with Nos. 2 and 4 Companies supplying support. In these positions the companies passed two days, marked by shelling, but by no incident of outstanding interest. Early on the morning of April 8th the Battalion was relieved by the 1st London Regiment and marched to Agny, entraining there and reaching Berneville at 8 a.m. At 5.30 o'clock that afternoon the Battalion embussed and was carried to the Feuchy-Fampoux Sector, where it relieved the 2nd Battalion, Seaforth Highlanders, in support. On the following day Nos. 1 and 3 Companies moved back into reserve positions, previously occupied by the 16th Battalion. Simultaneously, the Battalion Transport and the 3rd Brigade "Special Battalion" moved from Agnez-lez-Duisans to Ecoivres. When near Acq, the "Special" column, at the moment under command of Major Plow, encountered shell fire directed by a German plane, which was avoided only by a detour of several miles. Compensation for inconvenience was later derived by the troops from news that the German plane had been driven down by a British machine and captured by Canadian soldiers billeted near Ecoivres.

After two days in support the 14th Battalion advanced on the night of April 11th and relieved the 8th Canadian Battalion in the front line (Feuchy-Fampoux Sector), where it remained until relieved by the 1st and 4th Canadian Battalions on the night of April 13th. Relief on this occasion was completed at 1.35 a.m., the Royal Montreal Regiment then moving back to Corps Reserve in Aubrey Camp.

At 4 o'clock on the morning of April 19th the 14th Battalion suffered a severe blow when a shell crashed into the Nissen hut occupied by Lieut.-Col. Gault McCombe and three officers of Battalion Headquarters. Lieut.-Col. McCombe, who had served the Battalion since its earliest days, had suffered wounds on two occasions, and, in addition to gaining the D.S.O., had been four times mentioned in despatches, was seriously injured. Major A. T. Powell, D.S.O., Second-in-Command of the Battalion, who had won distinction in the counter-attack at Mount Sorrel and in many engagements since that time, was wounded beyond hope of recovery, and died about 10 o'clock that same morning. Major Arthur Plow, M.C., M.M., Regimental Adjutant, was killed instantly. He enlisted in the Battalion in August, 1914, suffered wounds in 1916 and 1917, and at all times set an example of courage under adverse conditions. Testimony to the place he held in the esteem of his men and in that of officers of the 3rd Brigade was furnished that afternoon, when his body was committed to the grave in the presence of Brig.-Gen. G. S. Tuxford, representatives of the 13th, 15th, and 16th Battalions, and a full parade of officers and men of the Royal Montreal Regiment. The fourth victim of the explosion was Major R. C. MacKenzie, a fearless officer who had risen from the ranks to command of No. 1 Coy. Major MacKenzie had suffered wounds on two previous occasions, but each time had rejoined the Battalion with as little delay as possible. This time a badly injured hip, complicated later by gas gangrene, meant that his period of loyal service had ended.

On the wounding of Lieut.-Col. McCombe and the death of Major Powell, command of the 14th Battalion, Royal Montreal Regiment, passed to Major Dick Worrall, M.C., a soldier-adventurer whose career had been varied. Born in England, Major Worrall had wandered far and wide, the outbreak of war in August, 1914, finding him in the ranks of the American Army. Heeding the call of Britain, Worrall crossed the Canadian border and enlisted in the overseas unit being raised by the 1st Regiment, Canadian Grenadier Guards. His record with the 14th Battalion can be traced in the past pages of this book; his record as Commanding Officer will be set down in the pages which follow. Shortly after he assumed command, Capt. C. B. Price, D.C.M., was recalled to Regimental duty as Second-in-Command, and Lieut. D. MacRitchie became Adjutant. Battalion Headquarters, therefore, was officered by men who had previously served in the ranks.

III

At 8.20 p.m. on April 21st the Battalion advanced to relieve the 7th Canadian Battalion in the Gavrelle Sector of the front line, the rear details, under Capt. J. W. Maynard, joining other units of the

3rd Brigade and forming a "Special Battalion", similar to that brought into being at Telegraph Hill earlier in the month. On taking over the front, Lieut. B. T. Jackson, Lieut. G. B. McKean, Corp. Dixon, and other officers and men of the Battalion devoted time to reconnaissances for a raid in which the 14th and 16th Battalions were to co-operate on the early morning of April 27th.

In a Special Operation Order, dated April 25th, Lieut.-Col. Dick Worrall explains the raid plan. In effect, his orders were:—

>(1) Intention:—The 14th Battalion, Royal Montreal Regiment, in conjunction with the 16th Battalion, Canadian Scottish, will raid the enemy trenches on the night of April 26/27. [Note:—Later the date was changed to April 27/28.]
>(2) Organization and Command:—Lieut. J. Patterson, D.C.M., will command the raiding party, which will be divided into six groups, lettered A to F.
>>"A" Group (Lieut. B. A. Neville) will consist of 25 other ranks, including Lewis gun personnel.
>>"B" Group (Lieut. M. E. Beckett) will consist of 25 other ranks, including Lewis gun personnel.
>>"C" Group (Lieut. Gordon Beattie) will consist of 20 O.R.
>>"D" Group (Lieut. R. J. Allan) will consist of 10 O.R.
>>"E" Group (Lieut. G. B. McKean) will consist of 15 other ranks, including Lewis gun personnel.
>>"F" Group (Lieut. S. J. McEwen) will consist of 25 other ranks, including Lewis gun personnel.
>>In addition 1 scout and 1 stretcher-bearer will be attached to each group.
>(3) Assembly:—All groups must be in position 30 minutes before zero.
>>"A" Group:—Right flank to rest on Cable Avenue.
>>"B" Group:—Left flank to be in touch with Canadian Scottish.

"C" Group:—To be in two parties, supporting "A" and "B" Groups respectively. They will assemble 25 yards in the rear of "A" and "B" Groups.

"D" Group:—Will assemble in Cable Avenue.

"E" Group:—Will assemble in Hussar Trench.

"F" Group:—Will assemble in Cable Avenue in rear of "C" Group.

A party under Lieut. B. T. Jackson will cover the assembly of "A" and "B" Groups.

(4) Duties of Groups:—

"A" and "B" Groups will follow the barrage as closely as possible, will mop up listening posts (if any) in No Man's Land, and will enter the enemy front line immediately the barrage lifts.

"C" Group will support "A" and "B" Groups. "C" Group will remain on this side of the enemy parapet, ready to go to the assistance of any section that has difficulty in entering the enemy trenches.

"D" Group will push along Cable Avenue, mopping up the garrison of the block in this Avenue. "D" Group will post 3 bombers to prevent the enemy from retiring from his newly-built trench.

"E" Group will push along Hussar Trench, will mop up enemy blocks, will form a block of their own, and will post a Lewis gun so as to deal with a possible counter-attack from the south.

"F" Group will push along Cable Avenue, will work up in front of "D" Group, and will form a block. A section of "F" Group will mop up along Hoary Trench to the point where the tramway crosses the trench.

(5) Signal to Withdraw:—Six red ground flares will be lit along Trent Trench at zero plus 40 minutes.

(6) Method of Withdrawal:—"F" Group withdraws first. "A" and "B" withdraw next, followed by "C", which will cover their withdrawal. "D" Group withdraws next, followed by "E" Group, which returns via Hudson and Lemon Trenches.

(7) Artillery:—Heavy and Field Artillery will co-operate. A creeping and box barrage will be arranged as follows:—

　　Zero to zero plus 10 minutes—Plays on enemy front line.

　　Zero plus 10 minutes to zero plus 30 minutes—Plays on enemy second line.

　　Zero plus 30 minutes—Changes to box barrage, and stands awaiting further orders.

(8) Equipment:—Lewis gun sections to carry 12 magazines. Other ranks to carry rifle with bayonet fixed, 6 Mills bombs, 50 rounds small arm ammunition. Groups "D" and "E" will each carry 3 ammonal tubes. Each section of "A" and "B" Groups will carry a mobile charge. The two sections of "F" Group will each carry a mobile charge. Three men of each blocking party will carry shovels.

(9) Concealment:—Bayonets, hands, and faces will be blackened.

(10) Medical:—O.C. No. 4 Coy. will detail 12 stretcher-bearers. Advanced Regimental Aid Post will be in Northumberland Lane.

(11) Prisoners:—Too large escorts must not be provided. N.C.O's. in charge of sections must *not* bring prisoners back. No. 4 Coy. will take charge of prisoners once they reach our front line.

(12) Headquarters:—Lieut. Patterson will establish his H.Q. at our block in Cable Avenue.

(13) Captured Men:—All ranks must be warned that, if captured, they are not obliged to give any information except their name and number. Group commanders will warn their men, if captured, to guard against the German use of "stool pigeons".

(14) Identifications:—Everything that can be carried will be brought back to our lines. Enemy dead, if too far away to be brought in, must be stripped of papers and identifications. The Germans usually carry letters in the tail pockets of their tunics.

(15) Our Casualties:—Dead must be brought back to our lines. Wounded will be cared for by parties detailed for the purpose. Raiders must not stay

with wounded, or carry them back, while the raid is in progress.

(16) Synchronization:—Watches will be synchronized at 6 p.m., 8 p.m., and 10 p.m.

(17) Conclusion:—The purpose of the raid is to obtain identifications and kill Huns.

On April 26th Lieut.-Col. Worrall issued an order amplifying and amending the previous order. Chief among the amendments were those covering the barrage and those which moved "F" Group's retirement from first place on the list to last. The changed barrage was to strike as follows:—

> Zero to zero plus 20 minutes—Enemy front line.
> Zero plus 20 minutes—Lifts to 2nd line and there forms a standing box.

Shortly after midnight on April 27th the officers and men of the 14th who were to raid the enemy line moved silently to the assembly. Something in the secrecy of the occasion, in the tense quality of the silence, and in the diablerie of the black-faced figures who, with black bayonets fixed, moved in obedience to low-spoken commands, stirred the imagination of observers, who found themselves shivering with excitement, and with a strange sensation, nameless, yet akin to fear. Something ghastly was to happen; men alive at the moment would not see dawn; some would die in dugouts far below the ground; there would be shouts, cries, groans; the crack of rifles, the blinding flash of high explosive; the courage, the ferocity, the savagery, the fierce joy, the madness, of those hours when humans exterminate their kind.

At 1 a.m. the artillery opened fire and the raiders crossed No Man's Land. The barrage fell on the German front line and was so accurately placed that the raiders "leaned on it", stating afterwards that it was the most wonderful they had ever seen. The moment it lifted Lieut. B. A. Neville led "A" Group into the German trench, where opposition was immediately encountered, a German officer, with courage which roused admiration, charging at the head of a party of his men. During the "free-for-all" which followed the officer was shot through the head, whereupon resistance ceased. Proceeding along the trench "A" Group took three prisoners from one dugout and three from another. Other Germans in these dugouts refused to come up and were killed by mobile charges. Meanwhile the Lewis gun section attached to "A" Group sighted five Germans. Two of these were immediately killed and the other three driven into the British box barrage. Shortly after this, a party of the enemy counter-attacked, but was repulsed with bombs and the bayonet, all its members being killed, except two men, who surrendered.

The experience of "B" Group was similar to that of "A". On entering the enemy trench opposition was overcome by use of the bayonet, and later a German machine gun was put out of action by a rifle grenade and by a sudden attack, in which Lieut. M. E. Beckett shot down No. 1 of the gun's crew. Proceeding from the spot where this encounter took place, "B" Group bombed a number of dugouts, continuing operations until red flares burning along Trent Trench signalled the recall. In their work the men of "B" Group were assisted by "C" Group, who, finding that their support rôle was unnecessary, joined in the fighting under command of Lieut. G. Beattie, who personally shot down an enemy bomber.

Meanwhile "D" Group was courageously led by Lieut. R. J. Allan, who killed a German at a point where progress was blocked and ably directed rifle grenade fire against an enemy machine gun. Following the burst of a volley of rifle grenades, "D" Group rushed the machine gun, which was captured intact, together with several of its crew. Meanwhile, "F" Group had advanced to the attack and had been momentarily held up by an apron of concertina barbed wire. Pushing through this, Lieut. S. J. McEwen shot a German N.C.O. and led his group against a body of the enemy, two of whom were bayoneted and several captured. Later two more Germans were bayoneted, while defending a "pineapple" thrower, which the Canadians captured.

"E" Group, led by Lieut. G. B. McKean, M.M., had the hardest task of all. Hussar Trench was manned by a garrison which decided to fight to the end. Choosing a block in the trench as a suitable point for defence, the Germans held back the Canadians with bombs and rifle fire. Three times Lieut. McKean's party exhausted its supply of bombs and sent back to the Royal Montreal front line for more. And still the German block barred all progress. Realizing that time was slipping by, Lieut. McKean bade his men stand clear. Revolver in hand, he then ran, and dived head first over the obstruction. Crashing into a German, who seemed to be the enemy leader, Lieut. McKean bore him to earth, and killed him with a revolver shot. Simultaneously, the men of "E" Group swarmed over the barricade, swept aside opposition, and advanced against a second barricade further along the trench. Here the defending force fought for several minutes, retreating eventually to take refuge in a dugout. Approaching this dugout, Sergeant Jones called on the Germans to surrender and, receiving no reply, threw a mobile charge down the entrance. This charge destroyed the dugout and almost certainly killed those within. Unfortunately, a fragment from the explosion struck Jones, who was instantly killed.

So ended the highly-successful raid on the morning of April 28th. In a recapitulation of events submitted to Brig.-Gen. G. S. Tuxford, Lieut.-Col. Worrall gives the following information:—

14th Battalion Casualties:—
- Killed - - - - - - 2 other ranks.
- Seriously wounded - - - 1 other rank.
- Slightly wounded - - - 10 other ranks.

Enemy Casualties:—
- Prisoners (some slightly wounded) - 22
- Prisoners (seriously wounded) - 2
- Prisoners (died of wounds) - - 2
- Enemy killed (estimated) - - - 40

Material Captured:—
- 2 light machine guns.
- 1 box and belt for same.
- 1 pineapple thrower.
- 1 spool of telephone wire.
- 1 tripod, with registration instruments attached.
- 3 maps.
- 1 bagfull of sundry identifications.

When news of the striking success in the Gavrelle Raid spread, many units and individuals wired congratulations. Amongst the first to do so was Lieut.-Gen. Sir A. W. Currie, G.O.C. the Canadian Corps, whose message follows:—

"Please accept and convey to General Tuxford and to Random and to Rowdy"—Random and Rowdy being code words identifying the 14th and 16th Battalions—"my heartiest congratulations on their very successful raid last night. It was one of the most successful minor operations in the course of the war".

Major-General A. C. Macdonell, Commanding the 1st Canadian Division, wired the following message:—

"Please accept and convey to all ranks under your command who participated in the successful raid last night my heartiest congratulations".

Congratulatory messages, the generous tone of which officers and men of the 14th deeply appreciated, were also received from the 1st Canadian Infantry Brigade, the 2nd Canadian Infantry Brigade, the 1st Canadian Divisional Artillery, Brig.-Gen. G. S. Tuxford, Lieut.-Col. G. E. McCuaig, Commanding "Rufus" (the 13th Battalion), and from the 16th Battalion, Canadian Scottish.

At night on April 28th the 14th Battalion handed over the Gavrelle front to the 13th and withdrew to Brigade Reserve, Battalion Headquarters billeting on the Lens-Arras Road, at a spot about 2 kilometres from Arras, one company at Roclincourt, one at St. Catherine's Switch, and two at a point a little over a mile east of Battalion H.Q. Here the unit remained until May 6th, when it moved to Corps Reserve at "Y" Camp, Etrun. On May 19th, under orders from Brigade, the Battalion marched, via Habarcq, Le Hameau, and Izel lez Hameau, to Manin, where it entered Army Special Reserve.

CHAPTER XVIII

ARMY RESERVE AND TELEGRAPH HILL

> Rejoice, whatever anguish rend your heart,
> That God has given you, for a priceless dower,
> To live in these great times and have your part
> In Freedom's crowning hour;
>
> That you may tell your sons who see the light
> High in the heavens, their heritage to take;—
> "I saw the powers of darkness put to flight!
> I saw the morning break!"
> —Sir Owen Seaman.

I

THROUGHOUT the late spring and early summer of 1918 the Canadian Corps, in Special Army Reserve, trained diligently in anticipation of the day when Field Marshal Sir Douglas Haig would undertake offensive action against Germany. In the Corps all ranks understood the purpose of the long "rest" period, and sought to perfect themselves in the attack, marvelling meanwhile at the fortitude and self-sacrifice displayed by the divisions of the British Army which were bearing the burden of Germany's last effort to secure military victory. Splendid, too, were reports of courageous and sustained fighting by the troops of France, and news of the vast army which the United States of America was shipping across the Atlantic.

On entering Army Special Reserve on May 19th, the 14th Battalion, whose ration strength included 43 officers and 814 other ranks, prepared to take part with other battalions of the 3rd Brigade in manœuvres designed to furnish practice of brigade in attack. Following extensive operations on May 21st, the Battalion spent the night in a wood near Lignereuil, the veterans before "lights out" lying around camp fires and yarning to less experienced members of the Battalion regarding battles in those far-off days before steel helmets, gas masks, tanks, liquid fire, and creeping barrages had been thought of.

Resuming operations early on the following morning, the battalions conducted a series of interesting experiments in concealing machine gun nests by means of smoke-filled rifle grenades, in advancing against machine guns, and in establishing liaison with contact aeroplanes.

Much was learned from these experiments, the results providing a basis for special demonstrations during battalion manœuvres on May 23rd. Two days after the special manœuvres the Battalion marched from Manin to Ostreville, passing through the towns of Pénin, Averdoingt, and Marquay en route.

On May 27th the entire Battalion practised on the rifle ranges at Monchy Breton, and on the following day carried out training of battalion in attack. On May 29th the 3rd Brigade practised brigade in attack, the 13th, 14th, and 16th Battalions turning into "Germans" for the occasion and driving against the devoted 15th Battalion, which remained "British". Orders for the operations were issued to the "14th Brandenburg Battalion", by an individual signing himself "Ober Lieutenant F. Swartz", who instructed the Huns under his command to co-operate with the units led by "General von Quaig" and "Col. Hans der Pecksburg". The records of these officers cannot be traced in the archives of the German Army, but those who encountered them on May 29th, 1918, vouch for their resemblance to Lieut.-Cols. G. E. McCuaig, D.S.O., and C.W. Peck, D.S.O., the commanding officers of the 13th Royal Highlanders and the 16th Canadian Scottish.

Early in June all ranks of the 14th were pleased by announcement that Major R. C. MacKenzie had been awarded the D.S.O. At the time of the announcement Major MacKenzie was in hospital convalescing from the serious injuries received on the early morning of April 19th. News of his progress towards health, and similar reports regarding the condition of Lieut.-Col. Gault McCombe, D.S.O., wounded by the same shell, were received at about this time and warmly welcomed. Simultaneously with the posting of Major MacKenzie's D.S.O., it was announced that he, Capt. T. G. Beagley, Capt. B. T. Jackson, Lieut. E. C. Gough, and Regimental Quartermaster-Sergeant H. Reid had been mentioned in despatches; also that Sergts. W. A. Burrell and W. G. Stevens had been awarded the Meritorious Service Medal. As a fitting climax to these interesting announcements came news that, for valour during the raid at Gavrelle on the morning of April 28th, His Majesty the King had bestowed on Lieut. G. B. McKean, M.M., that most coveted of all British military distinctions— the Victoria Cross.

Following musketry practice at the Monchy Breton ranges on June 6th, a demonstration of message-carrying rockets on June 7th, and a long route march on June 8th, the 14th Battalion paraded on June 11th and marched to la Thieuloye, where a halt was made to test respirators by passing the men through the specially-constructed gas chamber. Tactical exercises and field training were carried out on June 12th and 14th, and on the 15th parties of 60 men followed one another all morning and during the early afternoon to the baths at Rocourt.

On June 16th the Battalion was to move from Ostreville to Ecoivres, but, owing to a sharp outbreak of influenza, the plan was abandoned. Several hundred men were sick, and suitable nourishment was hard to obtain, but the Paymaster, Capt. J. B. Patterson, scoured the country for eggs and, at his own expense, gave every patient an egg-nogg of stimulating blend. The fame of these smooth drinks spread, and to them many of the sick attribute rapid recovery, also an attempt by several other ranks to simulate influenza and reap the foaming reward. On June 18th Hebrew soldiers in the 14th were granted permission to attend a Jewish religious service held in the Y.M.C.A. tent at Monchy Breton, and, on the following day, ordinary training being disorganized by influenza, a number of men were given special instruction in the operation of Lewis guns. Special instruction in patrol work was given on several subsequent days by the Battalion Scout Officer, Lieut. G. B. McKean, V.C., M.M. On the 30th of the month the Battalion formed up at the main cross roads in Ostreville at 8.00 a.m. and marched, via Monchy Breton and Magnicourt, to billets in Frévillers.

Dominion Day, July 1st, was declared a holiday in the Canadian Corps, and given over to sport. At Tinques, between the Arras-St. Pol Road and the Railway, a vast arena had been laid out, with grandstands on one side for senior officers, nursing sisters, and distinguished guests, and a natural grandstand on the other, whence the troops could watch the sport, undisturbed by the presence of superiors. At 10 a.m. the sports began, continuing until late in the afternoon, by which time winners in track events, field events, baseball, football, lacrosse, and other contests had been decided. For the sports a squad of about 20 Royal Montrealers, under Capt. H. G. Brewer, had trained at Tinques for over a week. These men did well in their events and helped the 1st Division carry off the Corps championship.

Parading early on the morning of the 1st, the 14th Battalion marched to Tinques and there remained throughout the day, the men keenly interested in the sports and secondarily in the guests of the Corps, including H.R.H. the Duke of Connaught, Sir Robert Borden, Prime Minister of Canada, General John J. Pershing, Commander-in-Chief of the American forces, and many commanders of the French, American, and British armies. Such a gathering was unique and pre-

A Platoon of No. 2 Company, Frevillers, July, 1918—A Representative Platoon of the Battalion

cautions were taken against unfortunate incident, more particularly against aerial aggression, the likelihood of which was negatived by strong British defensive patrols.

In the evening, after witnessing the 1st Divisional Concert Party in a well-staged revue, entitled " Take a Chance ", the 14th Battalion returned to Frévillers, whence it marched on the following day to take part in a review of the 3rd Brigade at Béthonsart. On this occasion the Brigade was inspected by the Corps Commander, who was accompanied by the Right Hon. Sir Robert Borden, the latter addressing a few words to the troops and taking the salute of the battalions as they marched back to billets.

On July 6th the Battalion returned to the arena at Tinques to take part in a " Highland Gathering ", at which the battalions of the 3rd Canadian Infantry Brigade were hosts to all Highland and Scottish units in the neighbourhood, including the 15th (Scottish) and 51st (Highland) Divisions. Sports were again the chief feature of the day, the 14th showing excellently in the track events, but less conspicuously in contests of a more pronouncedly Highland nature, though Private Payeur, a French-Canadian member of the Regiment, was easily first in tossing the caber. Piping, wrestling, and tug-of-war contests were included in the programme, then towards evening the massed pipe bands of the Brigade and of the visiting battalions played " Retreat ", 284 pipers and 164 drummers marching and countermarching in parallel files, affording a sight memorable even in days when marching battalions were met at every cross-roads.

On the day following the Highland Gathering at Tinques, the 14th Battalion was paraded in the afternoon and a photograph taken for inclusion in the collection being made by the War Records Department of the Canadian Government. Shortly after this event, Lieut.-Col. Dick Worrall, M.C., Commanding Officer of the Battalion, was thrown from his horse while taking part in gymkhana practice and suffered a fracture of the collarbone. He was removed to hospital and, during his temporary absence, command passed to Major C. B. Price, D.C.M. Under him the Battalion, some days later, took part in Brigade manœuvres, outstanding by reason of the fact that, for the first time, field guns were detailed to accompany the attacking waves of infantry.

II

On July 13th, 1918, the 14th Battalion paraded in Frévillers at 1.30 p.m. and marched, via Béthonsart and Camblain l'Abbé, to Divisional Reserve billets in Anzin St. Aubin. Near this spot those sections of the Battalion not absent on working parties were reviewed at 2.30 p.m. on July 17th by Major-General the Hon. S. C. Mewburn, who some time previously had succeeded Major-General the Hon. Sir Sam Hughes as Canadian Minister of Militia and Defence. On the evening of the day following this review, the Battalion relieved the 18th Canadian Battalion in the front line at Telegraph Hill, 15 officers and 150 other ranks of the rear details marching simultaneously, under command of Capt. J. E. McKenna, to billets at Warlus, not far from the Battalion Transport lines at Berneville.

From July 18th until July 26th the Royal Montreal Regiment remained in the front line at Telegraph Hill, for the first few days under command of Major Price and then under Lieut.-Col. Worrall, who returned from hospital. On the whole, the tour was uneventful, though shelling was brisk on several occasions and aeroplanes, both Allied and German, passed overhead repeatedly. For the most part these machines ignored the front line and proceeded to the rear areas to bomb. Gas shelling of the rear areas was also a feature of this period, nor was the front line neglected, troops being compelled to don respirators on several occasions and British gas shells undoubtedly forcing the Germans to do likewise. In spite of shelling and the danger from gas, working parties and patrols of the 14th carried out their duties each night of the tour, which concluded early in the morning of July 27th, when the 13th Battalion relieved.

Withdrawing to Divisional Reserve near Achicourt, the Battalion rested until the afternoon of the 27th, when a party of 3 officers and 400 other ranks was supplied to dig trenches in the Brigade area. A similar party was furnished on the 28th, and another on July 29th. This last date was marked by an unfortunate occurrence when a faulty pipe failed to clear coke gas from a dugout occupied by other ranks at Battalion Headquarters. Four men were poisoned, of whom one died immediately and one in hospital a few hours later.

On July 31st the Battalion entrained at Achicourt Switch and proceeded to Fosseux. Simultaneously, the rear details marched from Warlus, and the Transport and Q.M. details from Berneville. Both sections joined the main body of the Battalion at Fosseux and brought the strength of the unit under Lieut.-Col. Worrall's direct command to a total of 40 officers and 869 other ranks. Soon after arrival at Fosseux it became clear that the Canadian Corps, following its long period of special training, was to undertake offensive operations. On July 31st the Battalion was in ignorance of where, or when, the blow would fall. That it would not be unduly delayed, however, was the opinion of those whose experience enabled them to explain that strange shiver of excitement which invariably affects a body of troops destined to attack in the near future. The secret of the attack was marvellously kept; none the less the Corps knew that action was imminent and knew also that, as in the past, the divisions would fail only if success were beyond the limits of endeavour.

CHAPTER XIX

GERMANY'S BLACK DAY

> I vow to thee, my country—all earthly things above—
> Entire and whole and perfect, the service of my love,
> The love that asks no questions: the love that stands the test,
> That lays upon the altar the dearest and the best:
> The love that never falters, the love that pays the price,
> The love that makes undaunted the final sacrifice.
> —Cecil Spring-Rice.

I

AUGUST 8th, 1918, will live in history, for on that date Field Marshal Sir Douglas Haig turned from the defensive and launched the first of a series of attacks, which halted only when the power of Germany had been shattered and Allied forces of occupation marched unopposed across the Rhine. Writing of the August 8th engagement, which has been named "The Battle of Amiens", General Ludendorff admits that, though the British possessed no great superiority, except in tanks, the German divisions between the Somme and the Luce were completely overwhelmed, their downfall causing consternation to the officers of the German Imperial Staff and forcing them to abandon hope of military victory. "August 8th", states the General, "was the black day of the German Army in the history of this war".

On July 13th General Sir Henry Rawlinson, Commander of the Fourth British Army, was instructed by Sir Douglas Haig to prepare a plan for the Amiens offensive. Four days later his draft, calling for an all-British attack, was approved, but subsequently, at the request of the French, it was altered to permit General Debeney's First French Army to co-operate. Difficulties arose in regard to employment of the French, but were amicably settled by the respective Commanders-in-Chief, with the result that when the battle ended the Paris-Amiens Railway had been disengaged, the threat directed at the junction of the British and French armies had been removed, the enemy had been thrown back approximately to his Roye-Chaulnes line of 1916, and the important Chaulnes railway junction had been brought under Allied gun-fire.

In structure, according to the military correspondent of the London "Times", the Battle of Amiens was chiefly a Canadian battle, the advance of the Canadian Corps on the Luce providing the crux of the entire operation. On the progress of the Corps depended the advance of the Australians to the left, and of the successive French divisions to the right, each of which was engaged only as the advance above it prospered. Explanation of why the French attack was held back is found in the desire of the French generals to bombard before launching their infantry. Sir Douglas Haig counted on the value of surprise, and could not permit preliminary shelling to reveal his plan. He compromised, therefore, and agreed that the French bombardment should begin at the moment when the Australian and Canadian waves plunged across No Man's Land. Three-quarters of an hour later the French infantry would follow.

On July 21st Sir Arthur Currie was informed of the coming operation and notified that, for the occasion, the Canadian Corps would be attached to the Fourth British Army. On July 29th the Canadian Divisional Commanders were told of the plan, but warned that the information was confidential and not to be discussed even with the most trusted subordinate. To deceive the enemy, they were instructed to continue preparations for an attack on Orange Hill, east of Arras. Meanwhile, rumours spread that the Corps was soon to engage in a great battle in Flanders, an appearance of confirmation attaching to these reports when the 27th Battalion, of the 2nd Canadian Division, the 4th Canadian Mounted Rifles, of the 3rd Canadian Division, two Canadian casualty clearing stations, and a buzzer section of the Canadian Signal Corps moved north, the battalions taking over trenches on the Kemmel front, where the quick-witted German Intelligence Department promptly identified them; the casualty clearing stations preparing for action at a spot where identification was not unlikely; and the buzzer sections sending messages in a code which trained German listeners could decipher.

Certain foreign observers attached to the Corps viewed the transfer of two battalions, two casualty clearing stations, and a buzzer section to the north as proof that before long the Corps would follow. Folding their tents, these gentlemen slipped north to secure good billets for themselves while such were still available. Procuring the billets, they settled down and awaited the Corps' arrival. Days passed; and then came news that the Corps, in a great surprise attack, had crashed through the German lines at Amiens. Reports of the foreign attachés on the Battle of Amiens are doubtless preserved in the archives of the nations concerned. The detailed account of the observers' personal experiences, and the deductions drawn therefrom, might well make interesting reading.

II

At 9 p.m. on August 3rd, 1918, the 14th Battalion, less No. 4 Coy., embussed at the cross-roads in Fosseux and proceeded to Frévent, where the men entrained. This operation was completed at about 1 o'clock on the morning of August 4th, the men making themselves as comfortable as possible in the famous "40 hommes 8 chevaux" box cars, and speculating with deep interest on where the trail they were following might lead. No one knew; but all realized that action was imminent. Lieut.-Col. Worrall carried sealed orders, which he was instructed not to open until the train had started.

Proceeding at 1.30 a.m., the box cars jolted along through the hours of darkness, continued their trundling progress as sunrise flushed the east, forged ahead throughout the morning of August 4th, and at 1 p.m. halted at Vieux-Rouen-sur-Bresle. Detraining, the men were given a hot meal, following which they marched 10 kilometres to Avesne, reaching this spot at 5.30 p.m. and billeting for the night. During the morning and afternoon of August 5th battle equipment was checked and deficiencies made good. At 7 p.m., in obedience to instructions issued at 4 p.m. by Capt. D. MacRitchie, Adjutant, the Battalion, in full marching order, formed up in Avesne and marched to a point on the Hornoy-Aumont Road, where, under supervision of Lieut. S. J. McEwen, M.C., the men embussed.

When all busses had their complement, the convoy got under way and travelled throughout the night, reaching a spot near Amiens at 5 o'clock on the following morning. Debussing, the men marched 12 kilometres to the town of Boves, which had been evacuated by its population, but was thronged with troops, massing for the Amiens offensive. After billeting in Boves all day, the Battalion formed up opposite the Town Church late that night and marched to a position just north of Gentelles. Shelling was encountered on the march and for a time it appeared that progress would be made only at the cost of heavy losses. A number of men were killed or wounded by a salvo of 5.9's, but eventually the zone of fire was passed and the Battalion distributed in reserve trenches.

All day on August 7th the Royal Montreal Regiment lay in the reserve trenches, the men keeping as quiet as possible and doing everything in their power to escape observation. On surprise hinged success of the Amiens battle. Accordingly, the field and heavy guns, though in position, dared not fire even registering shots; aeroplanes strove to keep observers back without betraying that there was any-

Hangard Wood where the 14th Battalion Attacked—8th August, 1918

thing special to conceal; and the infantry ate rations cold, lest the smoke of many fires should rouse the enemy to a sense of approaching danger.

At dusk on August 7th, the 14th Battalion took over positions for the attack from the 50th Australian Battalion, other units of the 3rd Brigade advancing simultaneously and preparing for action. When assembly was complete the formation of the Brigade was as follows:—

> On the Right— 16th Canadian Battalion.
> In the Centre— 13th Canadian Battalion.
> On the Left— 14th Canadian Battalion.
> In Centre Support—15th Canadian Battalion.
> In Right Support— 5th Canadian Battalion.

At 4.20 o'clock on the morning of August 8th, the attacking waves of the Canadian and Australian Divisions plunged forward to open the Battle of Amiens; and at the same instant the artillery of the French on the right roared in bombardment of the enemy line. From the moment when the Canadians left their trenches it was apparent that observation would prove difficult. A light ground mist prevailed, and soon this was thickened by the smoke of bursting shells, until sight was limited to a few dozen feet, or yards.

Undeterred by inability to see, Nos. 2 and 3 Companies of the 14th Battalion led the Royal Montreal attack, with Nos. 1 and 4 Companies moving steadily forward in support. On reaching the German front line, opposition was encountered, but this was feeble and was brushed aside by use of the bayonet. Continuing, the advance swept to a point in front of Morgemont Wood, where it was checked by a nest of eight light machine guns, which had escaped aerial observation. For a time these held back the Canadians, who were handicapped by a shortage of bombs, but, just as the situation became serious, tanks arrived and, lurching forward, crushed the nest out of existence.

Freed from intense fire, the Royal Montrealers pushed through Morgemont Wood and along its flanks, mopping up a number of enemy strong points, dislodging several carefully concealed snipers, and capturing numerous prisoners. On debouching from the wood, fire from a nest of heavy machine guns posted near Tittle Copse struck the leading waves of the attack and caused grievous losses. Summoning a party of his own men, as well as a group from the 3rd Canadian Battalion, Lieut. E. G. T. Penny, M.C., led a charge which drove into the German position, silenced the guns, and hammered the crews into submission. It would be gratifying to record that Lieut. Penny survived to enjoy the distinction which his leadership on this occasion would undoubtedly have brought him. Unfortunately, such was not the case. Together with a number of his men he fell ere the German opposition was finally overcome.

Following the miniature battle near Tittle Copse, the attack of the Battalion moved against the northern portion of Czech and Croates Trenches. Opposition was stiff at this stage of the operation and tanks were called on for assistance. Advancing against the German position, the tanks made one trip along the enemy trench, firing their machine guns and crushing the parapet in several places. Presuming that they had cleared a way for the infantry, the tanks made off, but the Germans had suffered less than the tank officers imagined and were able to offer strong resistance, the Royal Montrealers being compelled to substitute for frontal attacks a series of operations against the flanks.

Success eventually attended the outflanking moves, enfilade fire was opened on the German position, and soon a white flag indicated surrender. Forgetful of the known tactics of the Hun, a number of men advanced across the open to occupy the trench and accept the garrison's submission. These individuals paid the penalty of their trust and were killed by treacherous rifle fire. Angered by their death, the men of the Royal Montreal Regiment resumed the attack, grimly ignored two white flags which suddenly appeared, and shot without hesitation a number of the enemy who stepped onto the parapet with hands in the air. Whether this "surrender" was a further ruse, or whether the Germans, having exhausted the possibilities of treachery, expected to be treated as honourable prisoners of war, no one knows, as in the fighting which followed the garrison of the position was killed to a man.

When Czech and Croates Trenches had been captured, the attack advanced almost without opposition to its final objective, the Green Line, evidence of enemy demoralization being afforded by the sight, far ahead, of German soldiers, partly clad, evacuating dugouts and hastening to the rear. Rifle fire was opened on these fugitives, and numbers fell under the fire of Canadian field guns, which, even at this early stage of the battle, were moving forward and seeking targets in the open.

Thirty minutes after the action began, Lieut.-Col. Worrall decided to follow the attack as visual signalling was impossible, and telephone wires had been ripped up by tanks. This decision was hastened by the fact that, through runners losing their way in the fog, important messages were being delayed many minutes. Accordingly, the C.O. of the 14th moved up and established his Headquarters at a point not far from the Green Line, beyond which troops of the 2nd Brigade were exploiting the initial success.

When consolidation of the Green Line was completed, officers and men paused to consider the operation and count the spoils of victory. A large number of prisoners had been captured, but these had been bundled hastily to the rear and an exact count of them was difficult to obtain. Simpler was a reckoning of trophies, which included 9 field guns, 3 trench mortars, and 14 machine guns, all of which were marked with the Battalion stencil, their numbers taken, and a list of them forwarded to Brigade Headquarters. These trophies were captured by men of the 14th without assistance. In the capture of other field and machine guns, officers and other ranks of the Royal Montreal Regiment participated.

In offset to the number of Germans killed and to the list of prisoners and trophies, the Regiment suffered casualties totalling 159, this number being made up of 5 officers killed, 4 officers wounded, 13 other ranks killed, 103 other ranks wounded, and 34 other ranks missing. Later, a number of the missing were found to have passed through dressing stations other than the Battalion's own. In addition to Lieut. E. G. T. Penny, M.C., whose death has been mentioned, the Regiment lost four platoon commanders, Lieuts. A. S. Baird, F. K. Neilson, M.M., J. H. Davy, and W. A. Kirkconnell, all of whom had fallen while leading their troops against machine guns, or against those trenches where the Germans had offered stubborn resistance. Of the dead officers two, Lieuts. Neilson and Kirkconnell, had crossed from Canada with the Battalion in the autumn of 1914, the former in the ranks, and the latter on the commissioned establishment. Lieut. Neilson had served in France in the early days of the war and had been granted a commission after recovering from wounds received in December, 1915. Lieut. Kirkconnell, finding himself surplus to establishment when the Battalion crossed from Salisbury to France, served with the 23rd Reserve Battalion until the autumn of 1916, when he joined the 14th Battalion on the Vimy front. Returning to England, he again served with reserve units until April, 1918. From that time until his death he had commanded a Royal Montreal platoon.

On the list of wounded on August 8th were Lieuts. E. A. Adams, B. A. Neville, M.C., B. T. Jackson, and S. B. White, the last-named a captain of the 199th Battalion, who had reverted to see service in France. Lieut. B. T. Jackson had served in the ranks of the 14th Battalion and had been commissioned after recovering from wounds received in September, 1916, and July, 1917. Lieut. Neville, though wounded in the eye, was able to remain at duty.

When troops of the 2nd Brigade leap-frogged the 14th Battalion in the Green Line, the Royal Montrealers effected immediate reorganization in preparation for further action. The night of August 8th passed without incident, but at 6.50 o'clock on the morning of the 9th the Battalion received orders to advance in support of an attack being delivered by the 2nd Brigade, whose Headquarters had been established at a point near Cayeux. The 14th was the only 3rd Brigade battalion to become engaged on this date.

At 7 a.m. final instructions were received, and fifteen minutes later the Battalion moved off. Forcing the pace, in view of the urgent nature of his mission, Lieut.-Col. Worrall led the Battalion along roads congested with traffic to 2nd Brigade Headquarters, where he was ordered to take up positions in support of the 8th Canadian Battalion, which was preparing to attack. Ordering the 14th Battalion to follow, Lieut.-Col. Worrall advanced, reconnoitred the positions assigned to him, and, meeting the Battalion coming forward, directed the men to their places. A section of the assembly trenches originally chosen was commanded by higher ground, whence the enemy directed machine gun and artillery fire, the field guns including in their bombardment a high percentage of gas shells. Accordingly, Worrall changed the plan to meet the conditions and assembled his men in a less hazardous spot, the disposition being completed a few minutes before 11.30 a.m.

Shortly after the Royal Montrealers had taken up position it was announced that the 8th Battalion would attack at 1 p.m., and that the 14th would follow in close support. Warning of the attack seems to have reached the Germans, for between 11.30 o'clock and zero the assembly positions were heavily shelled, a number of men falling as a result of the fire and serious losses being avoided by the narrowest of margins.

Sharp at 1 o'clock the 8th Battalion attacked, and simultaneously the 14th swung into position to support, the move involving a flank advance through a small wood, which was being subjected to sustained fire. The value of manœuvres carried out during the period in Army Special Reserve was demonstrated at this time, the company, platoon, and section commanders displaying marked ability in leading their men through the wood to the desired point on the flank.

On debouching from the wood, the men of the Battalion suffered sharply from machine guns hidden in another small wood some distance forward. Grim evidence that the 8th Battalion had encountered similar fire was supplied by a number of dead, and a stranded tank gave warning that the infantry assault might lack mechanical assistance. Fortunately, the ground mist of the previous day was absent, and commanders could see what was taking place. In this instance skilful leadership solved the problem, the garrison of the opposing wood being held in play on the front of attack, while strong forces manœuvred for position on the flanks. Eventually the troops on the left gained a position, whence they launched an attack, supported by a tank which came back from a position far forward and attacked the wood on the right. Dismayed by this vicious onslaught, many Germans were killed and wounded, and over 50 taken prisoner.

At this stage of the action Major Saunders, of the 8th Battalion, requested support for his left flank, which had suffered severely. Realizing that the flank in question was important, as it connected with the right flank of another brigade, Lieut.-Col. Worrall sent forward No. 3 Coy. of the 14th with orders to support the 8th Battalion in every way possible. Shortly after this the Royal Montreal Regiment reached its assigned objective, and immediately started to consolidate. While consolidation was in progress Lieut.-Col. Worrall and Capt. MacRitchie advanced to appreciate the situation in the forward area.

After some time Worrall and MacRitchie reached a spot where some 60 to 80 officerless men of the 8th Battalion were used to prepare for a counter-attack, which could be seen massing in the direction of Fouquescourt. Simultaneously, a squadron of British cavalry trotted along the Meharicourt-Fouquescourt Road, obviously into a trap. Powerless to warn the horsemen, the Canadians watched them move to their fate. When they reached Fouquescourt Crucifix the enemy opened fire. Too late the squadron leader recognized his peril. Some of his men escaped; the majority sank to earth dead, dying, or severely wounded.

Finding that the point reached by the foremost men of the 8th Battalion was unsuitable for defence, Lieut.-Col. Worrall decided to consolidate a short distance to the rear. Spreading the personnel of his Headquarters along the line selected, he sent runners back and ordered the main body of the 14th Battalion to advance without delay. Meanwhile, after consultation with Major Saunders, he, as senior officer, took over tactical control of both battalions, and, as the troops on his left flank were not up, of some cavalry, which he used to fill the dangerous gap. While this was being accomplished Major Saunders returned to 2nd Brigade Headquarters to report on the situation and arrange for supplies of ammunition.

Meanwhile, to assist in maintaining touch with his flanking companies, Lieut.-Col. Worrall had commandeered two horses belonging to a major of whippet tanks. Mounted on one of these animals, Capt. J. H. Richardson set out towards the position on the left. To escape the fire of a small-calibre gun, the 14th officer spurred his horse and, without encountering the troops he sought, rode into the German lines. Realizing that he had overshot his mark, Richardson dismounted to reconnoitre a way back, but a bullet struck his foot, and the horse got away. Crawling on hands and knees, Richardson reached the Canadian lines and eventually reported to Battalion H.Q., where the owner of the lost horse was expressing vigorous resentment. Recognizing that the tank officer had a legitimate grievance, Lieut.-Col. Worrall expressed regret for what had happened, but explained that to obtain knowledge of the situation on the left was vital to the safety of his Battalion, and justified measures which in other circumstances might be thought high-handed.

By this time the enemy realized that his counter-attack was not to progress unopposed. Halting, therefore, he pushed forward machine gun posts, which inflicted losses on the men digging in. Whippet tanks advanced in an effort to subdue the machine gun fire, but the gunners were hard to find in the fields of nearly ripe grain. Two whippets were disabled before one machine gun nest had been destroyed, but other nests were silenced by the presence of the tanks, and consolidation was thereby assisted.

When consolidation had made some progress, Major Saunders, of the 8th Battalion, arrived back at the front from 2nd Brigade Headquarters, bearing written orders in obedience to which the 14th Battalion relinquished the front line and withdrew to a support position about 300 yards to the rear. During the night which followed the enemy attempted no further advance; instead he recalled his forward posts and retired, the 8th Battalion quickly recognizing his intention and pushing out patrols which established posts along the line of the Battalion's final objective.

In the fighting on August 9th officers and men of the 14th earned the commendation of their Commanding Officer for exemplary behaviour. Approximately 200 other ranks were casualties, of whom more than 30 were killed. Two officers were killed, and 10 wounded. Capt. T. G. Beagley, who had been promoted following service in the ranks, and had been wounded in July, 1916, was killed instantly, and Major D. W. Clarkson, M.C., who had served the Regiment for nearly two years, suffered wounds from which he died a few hours later. Capt.

J. H. Richardson was wounded as previously mentioned; Lieut. B. A. Neville, M.C., was wounded for the second time in 48 hours; and Lieuts. S. J. De la Haye, H. H. Robinson, M. E. Beckett, J. D. Patterson, G. Beattie, S. J. McEwen, R. M. Ievers, and J. Leno suffered wounds which necessitated their removal to hospital. Previous to joining the 14th, Lieut. McEwen had served in the ranks of the 60th Battalion, Victoria Rifles of Canada, and the 87th Battalion, Canadian Grenadier Guards; Lieut. Ievers had seen service with the 22nd French-Canadian Battalion; and Lieut. Leno had been commissioned from the ranks of the 3rd Toronto Battalion. The other wounded officers had served for varying periods with the Royal Montreal Regiment, and had at all times proved worthy. The loss of so many at one time was, therefore, a severe blow to the unit's establishment.

In addition to casualties, a battle necessarily involves vast expenditure of ammunition and supplies, and tremendous waste of material. Some idea of how material is flung hither and yon, usually by circumstances beyond the owner's, or carrier's, control, can be gained from a report forwarded to " Gogi "—the code word used at the time to indicate 14th Battalion Headquarters—by Capt. H. G. Brewer, O.C. No. 2 Coy. This report lists material salvaged by No. 2 Coy. on a day after the battle, and includes the following items:—German Material:—1 heavy machine gun, 7 medium machine guns, 7 machine gun barrels (spares), 48 loaded machine gun belts in carriers, 6 250-round machine gun belts, 1 medium trench mortar (complete with wheels and spare parts), 2 respirators, 5 mess tins, 5 steel helmets, 10 entrenching tools, 6 water bottles, 15 rifles, 6 bayonets, 20 packs, 10 scabbards, 2 machine gun water tanks, 8 shovels, and 4 picks. British material salvaged at the same time included:—20 Lee Enfield rifles, 6 entrenching tools, 8 bayonets and scabbards, 6 steel helmets, 2 sets of Webb equipment, 11 sets of Webb pouches, 6 3-inch Stokes gun shells, 30 Lewis gun magazines, 6 haversacks, 2 machine gun pouches, 8 water bottles, 3 shovels, 4 picks, 25 petrol tins, and 1 complete box of S.O.S. grenades.

On August 10th, 1918, the Royal Montreal Regiment lay in a support position not far from Warvillers. From this position the men, for the first time, witnessed a charge by a British regiment of cavalry. Riding up in fours on the left, the horsemen formed into lines of squadrons and swept magnificently to the attack. Unfortunately, they encountered a shattering barrage of black-smoked 5.9's, and then ran into barbed wire. In the wire the splendid unit was cut to pieces by machine gun fire. Though the mounted troops were not successful in this local action, their employment in the Battle of Amiens indicated that Sir Douglas Haig had not failed to appreciate what the absence of cavalry had cost Germany during the spring battles of the year. Few critics have covered this point, but many soldiers believe that when the enemy attacked the Third and Fifth Armies on March 21st, a few strong cavalry corps might have transformed a British defeat into irreparable disaster.

On the following day the Battalion, still weakened as a result of the fighting on the 8th and 9th, suffered a severe loss when Capt. J. C. K. Carson, M.C., and Lieut. R. J. Allan, M.C., M.M., were killed while reconnoitring an advanced position. Capt. Carson, before joining the Battalion in the autumn of 1915, had been a Staff Captain at Shorncliffe. He served with the Royal Montreal Regiment for 6 months in 1915-1916, for 10 months in 1916-1917, and finally for 3 months in 1918. Lieut. Allan, who was killed by the same shell, had served in the ranks of the Regiment, had been wounded on June 3rd, 1916, had returned to the ranks on recovery, had won the Military Medal, had been commissioned, and had won the Military Cross. In the death of these officers, therefore, the Battalion lost capable and experienced leaders.

III

On August 13th Sir Arthur Currie issued a "Special Order", dealing with the action of the Canadian Corps at Amiens. In it he says, "The first stage of this Battle of Amiens is over, and one of the most successful operations conducted by the Allied Armies since the war began is now a matter of history. The Canadian Corps has every right to feel more than proud of the part it played". On August 8th "the Canadian Corps—to which was attached the 3rd Cavalry Division, the 4th Tank Brigade, the 5th Squadron, R.A.F.—attacked on a front of 7,500 yards. After a penetration of 22,000 yards the line to-night rests on a 10,000-yard frontage. Sixteen German Divisions have been identified, of which four have been completely routed. Nearly 150 guns have been captured, while over one thousand machine guns have fallen into our hands. Ten thousand prisoners have passed through our cages and casualty clearing stations, a number greatly in excess of our total casualties. . . . From the depths of a very full heart I wish to thank all Staffs and Services for their splendid support and co-operation and to congratulate you all on the wonderful success achieved. Let us remember our gallant dead whose spirit shall ever be with us, inspiring us to nobler effort, and when the call again comes, be it soon or otherwise, I know the same measure of success will be yours ".

Previous to the appearance of Sir Arthur Currie's " Special Order ", Field Marshal Sir Douglas Haig had conferred regarding continuation of the operation with Marshal Foch. The French commander desired the British to drive forward in the area where success had already been achieved, but Sir Douglas was unwilling to waste the strength of his forces in ploughing across the shell-torn battlefields of the Somme, with no important strategic objectives in sight. Accordingly, he countered Marshal Foch's suggestion with a plan for smashing through the German line at a point where British success would involve Teutonic disaster. If co-operation on a vast scale by the French and American Armies could be arranged, the downfall of Germany, Sir Douglas pointed out, might be effected in the current calendar year. Reliable witnesses state that Marshal Foch hesitated, but at last agreed. The chance of concluding the war without another winter in the trenches, though admittedly slight, existed, and could not be allowed to slip by. Accordingly, the French leader endorsed the plan, and set about co-ordinating the Allied effort. The measure of his success is known to those who followed the forward sweep of the French, American, and British Armies in the " Hundred Days " before the Armistice brought hostilities to a close.

Unaware of what the future held in store, the 14th Battalion moved back on August 12th to the Beaufort Area, where the men occupied trenches about 300 yards in advance of the Beaufort Village Road. On August 15th Capt. D. MacRitchie, Adjutant, issued Operation Order No. 237, in obedience to which the Battalion moved forward at night to a position in the front line at Parvillers. Taking with them 193 new men, who had reported for duty from England, the companies relieved a battalion of the 7th Canadian Infantry Brigade without suffering casualties.

At noon on August 16th Brigade notified Battalion Headquarters that a German Alpine Division had moved into the line opposite and that minor operations might be expected. Later, in view of French successes near Goyencourt, all troops of the 1st Canadian Division were ordered to hold themselves in readiness for a sudden move. At 4 o'clock Brigade reported that French troops were driving the enemy from Goyencourt.

At 6 o'clock on the morning of August 17th Lieut.-Col. G. E. McCuaig, C.M.G., D.S.O., Commanding Officer of the 13th Battalion, notified 14th Headquarters that his troops had " pinched out " the village of La Chavatte, and were holding a position 200 yards beyond. On receipt of this information, No. 3 Coy. of the Royal Montreal Regiment, under Capt. J. Patterson, was ordered to advance at once to support the 13th against possible counter-attack. No. 2 Coy. was ordered to follow No. 3 after an interval of a few minutes. Both companies carried out the move without encountering opposition, and consequently without losses. Later in the day Brig.-Gen. G. S. Tuxford, C.B., C.M.G., met the Brigade Battalion Commanders at Royal Montreal Headquarters and discussed problems which the successful La Chavatte operation had created.

Early on the morning of August 18th shelling killed 2 men of the 14th Battalion and wounded 8, these casualties being more than replaced later in the day when a draft of 51 other ranks reported from a reinforcing camp. Gas shelling caused inconvenience on the night of the 18th, but helmets were donned and casualties avoided. At 7.10 p.m. on August 19th an S.O.S. signal rose from the Canadian front and within four seconds there came the reassuring crash of a protective barrage. If the enemy planned a raid, as was suspected, the weight of the barrage proved disheartening, for no Germans advanced, and at 9.50 p.m. all front line units reported that the situation was "normal".

Previous to the incident of the S.O.S. signal and the 4-second reply barrage, a party of French officers reconnoitred the 14th Battalion area, and at noon on the following day Brigade informed Royal Montreal Headquarters that control of the district had been turned over to a French Divisional Commander, and that French artillery would assume responsibility for support as from 10 o'clock on the morning of the 21st. These items indicated that the Corps' part in the Battle of Amiens had ended. Success had been granted, and successful troops were ever in demand. Something new was being planned, and the Corps was needed. That much was obvious; details rested in the trusted hands of the British Commander-in-Chief.

Even as the Canadian divisions withdrew from Amiens, troops of the Fourth and Third British Armies opened the Battle of Bapaume. After preliminary operations on August 21st, battle was joined on August 23rd on a 30-mile front from Lihons, south of the Somme, to the Mercatel Spur, south of Arras. Admirably led and courageously delivered, the attack struck down behind the old battlefield of the Somme from the north, forcing evacuation of this desolate area and permitting troops who had taken over the Amiens front to advance without costly frontal attacks. By this swift manœuvre Sir Douglas

Haig amply justified his refusal to press forward at Amiens, as General Foch had requested. More, he had prepared the way for further co-ordinated attacks based on sound, strategic principles. Amiens was a brilliant tactical coup; the fighting thereafter represented a combination of equally brilliant tactics and strategy.

CHAPTER XX

THE CORPS STRIKES AGAIN

For many a youthful shoulder now is gay with an epaulet,
And the hand that was deft with a cricket bat is defter with a sword,
And some of the lads will laugh today where the trench is red and wet,
And some will win on the bloody field the accolade of the Lord.
—Joyce Kilmer.

I

WHEN French divisions took over the front at Amiens, the Canadian Corps shifted secretly to Arras, there to act as the spear-head of an attack on the Hindenburg system of defence. There can be little doubt that the German troops in front of Arras were unpleasantly surprised when they found the Corps in action against them, in fact, one enemy officer is said to have shot five of his men to make the others fight at all. Complimentary to the Corps as such a tale is, it creates a false impression regarding the difficulties which the divisions were called on to surmount. Their's was no simple task. In places the enemy displayed poor morale, but elsewhere he fought courageously, aided by defences stronger than the Canadians, with all their varied experience, had up to this time encountered.

Something of the task which the Corps faced can be gathered from Sir Arthur Currie's report on the engagement, which refers to the plan of attack as follows:—

"The Canadian Corps on the right of the First Army, was to attack eastwards astride the Arras-Cambrai Road, and by forcing its way through the Drocourt-Quéant Line south of the Scarpe to break the hinge of the Hindenburg system and prevent the possibility of the enemy rallying behind this powerfully-organized defended area. . . .

"The four main systems of defence consisted of the following lines:—

    (1) The old German front line system east of Monchy-le-Preux.
    (2) The Fresnes-Rouvroy Line.
    (3) The Drocourt-Quéant Line.
    (4) The Canal du Nord Line.

" These, with their subsidiary switches and strong points, as well as the less-organized but by no means weak intermediate lines of trenches, made the series of positions to be attacked without doubt one of the strongest defensively on the Western Front ".

Months might well have gone into preparation for an attack such as that contemplated, but months were not available. Weeks even were denied the Corps Commander, who was ordered to attack four days after the general plan was revealed to him. Undaunted by such handicap, the Staff of the Corps set to work under Sir Arthur's direction, with the result that, at 3 a.m. on August 26th, the 2nd and 3rd Canadian Divisions plunged across No Man's Land in the opening engagement of the great battle. A difficult task faced these devoted troops, but by night, as a result of bitter fighting, Monchy-le-Preux, Guémappe, Wancourt Tower, and the crest of Héninel Ridge had been torn from German grasp. Renewing the assault at 4.55 o'clock on the morning of August 27th, the 2nd and 3rd Divisions overcame savage resistance, the one capturing Chérisy and crossing the Sensée River, while the other captured the Bois du Vert and the Bois du Sart, and drove its attack to the outskirts of Haucourt, Remy, Boiry Notre-Dame, and Pelves. It had been planned to withdraw the 2nd and 3rd Divisions on the night of August 27th, and to renew the attack on the 28th with the 1st Canadian and the 4th British Divisions, but this was found impossible and the wearied divisions in the line were ordered on. Responding magnificently, the 3rd Division smashed forward, capturing Boiry and Pelves, before being relieved at midnight by the 4th British Division. Attacking no less bravely, the 2nd Division encountered resistance so strong that little progress was possible. Some gains were made, but at night, when the 1st Division relieved, the line lay not far in advance of the position occupied in the morning. The men who fought on this section of the front smile grimly at reports of lowered German morale. With justice, they consider that on August 27th and 28th, 1918, the enemy was fighting as strongly as he had fought at any time during the war.

The battle fought during the last days of August and the first days of September produced immediate effect on the whole British front, the Germans abandoning their determined defence and withdrawing in some disorder to the Drocourt-Quéant and Canal du Nord Lines. Influenced both by the British attack and by French pressure on the Aisne, the enemy also began to withdraw from the line of the River

Vesle. On September 3rd the French armies to the British right reported that signs of this withdrawal were unmistakable.

II

Following relief by the 112th French Infantry Regiment on the night of August 21st, 1918, the 14th Battalion, Royal Montreal Regiment, moved back to the Warvillers-Beaufort area by a route which Lieut. G. B. McKean, V.C., M.M., and the Intelligence Section had previously reconnoitred. Here one day was spent, the unit parading that same night in obedience to orders issued by Lieut. A. H. Murphy, Acting Adjutant, and marching to Hangard Wood, a distance of approximately 15 kilometres. A few members of a recently-joined draft were inclined to make much of the hardship entailed by two weeks of fighting and a night march on sore feet so soon thereafter, but Lieut.-Col. Worrall pointed out that in the Royal Montreal Regiment hard work could be expected and complaints were out of order. The veterans vigorously endorsed these remarks and the new men, determined to prove themselves in no way unworthy of a place on the Battalion roll, accepted the rebuke without further comment.

Reaching Hangard Wood at 3.45 o'clock on the morning of August 23rd, the Battalion bivouacked until 9 p.m. on the 24th, when it marched to Boves, arriving at midnight and taking over billets in the houses of the town. In obedience to Operation Order No. 240, issued on August 25th by Capt. D. MacRitchie, Adjutant, the Battalion paraded in Boves at midnight and marched 9 miles over hilly roads to Saleux, halting once at a spot where the Y.M.C.A. supplied hot tea. At Saleux the Battalion breakfasted, after which the men boarded box cars and were carried to Aubigny. Detraining seven hours after leaving Saleux, the troops rested for a time, then embussed and proceeded to Dainville, whence they marched to billets in Arras.

Large calibre shelling of Arras caused uneasiness on August 27th, but no casualties resulted. At 5.30 p.m. orders were received for a move at 7 p.m. to near Tilloy Wood. Reaching this spot at 9 o'clock, after a wearisome march during which traffic frequently forced the men off the road into the ditches at the sides, the companies were distributed for the night in shelters and old trenches. At noon on August 28th the Regiment was informed that the 3rd Brigade would relieve the 5th Brigade, of the 2nd Canadian Division, that same night.

At 2 p.m. a party of the 14th Battalion advanced to establish touch with units of the 5th Brigade, but the mission failed, and it was

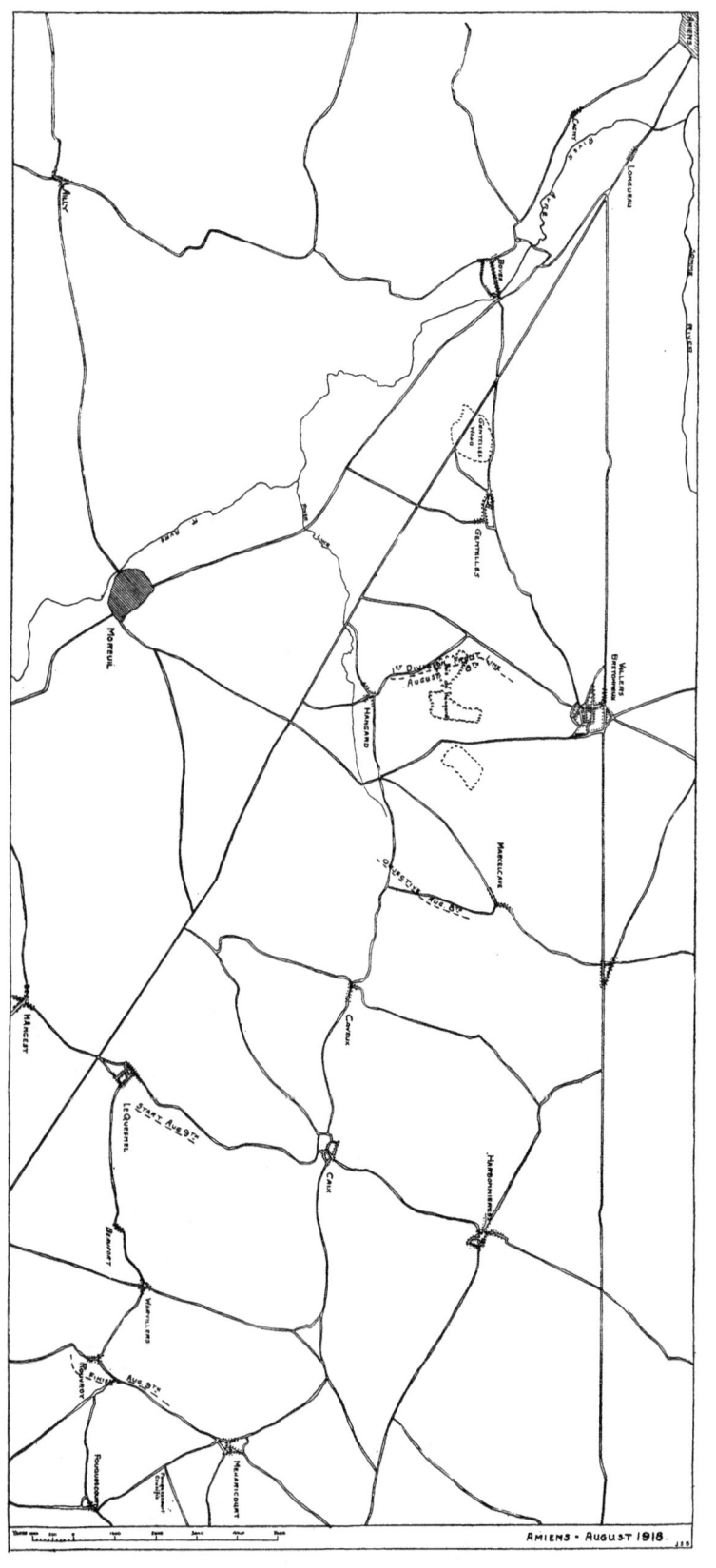

AMIENS · AUGUST 1918.

decided to rely for the carrying-out of relief on information to be obtained at 5th Brigade Headquarters. Marching at 9 p.m., the Battalion reported at 5th Brigade H.Q. and picked up guides for the move into the line. Traffic on the roads and difficulties incident to relief of units in contact with the enemy prevented a quick take-over, the last weary troops of the gallant 2nd Division not being released until dawn.

At 10.30 a.m. on August 29th the enemy shelled the 14th Battalion with gas, causing inconvenience and one or two casualties, which were more than offset by 143 other ranks who reported for duty from reserve. Including the members of this draft, the ration strength of the Battalion as August drew to a close totalled 31 officers and 921 other ranks. Before the end of the month, or at 4.45 a.m. on August 30th, to be exact, the 1st Canadian Infantry Brigade advanced through the lines of the 3rd Brigade and drove a sharp attack into the enemy lines. Bravely pushed, this assault met with success, despite heavy shell fire and a strong counter-attack launched by the enemy at 12.30 p.m. Following the counter-attack, observers reported that the Germans were retreating, this information confirming the success of the 1st Brigade and indicating to officers of the 3rd Brigade that action was imminent. The enemy could not be allowed to retreat unmolested and troops of the 3rd Brigade were in position to attack.

As expected, orders for an attack on September 1st were received by 14th Battalion Headquarters on August 31st. Zero was placed at 4.50 a.m. and the Battalion ordered to attack on a front of one company only, connecting on the right with the 15th Battalion and on the left with troops of the 2nd Canadian Infantry Brigade. Objectives were strictly limited and were chosen with a view to uncovering defences of the Drocourt-Quéant Line, against which operations on a major scale were pending.

In preparation for the attack Capt. D. MacRitchie, Battalion Adjutant, issued Operation Order No. 242, which may be summarized as follows:—

    (1) General Plan:—The Battalion will attack on a one-company frontage, from a position to be taken up to-night. (August 31st.)

    (2) Formation:—No. 4 Coy. will lead the attack, followed by Nos. 2, 1, and 3 Companies in the order named.

(3) Objectives:—Consolidation will take place at a point below the crest of the hill up which we attack, and in touch with the 15th Battalion on the right.

(4) Contact:—Every effort must be made to keep in touch with the 2nd Brigade on the left. No. 4 Coy's. advance will be regulated by the advance of the 15th Battalion on the right.

(5) Barrage:—The attack will advance behind a rolling barrage of approximately 100 yards every 4 minutes. Confirmation of this speed will follow.

(6) Signal:—No. 4 Coy., on reaching front objective, will fire a white Very light into the air.

(7) Consolidation:—Will be in depth. Positions will be determined by commanders on the spot.

(8) Opposition:—Little opposition is expected on our immediate front, but supporting companies must be prepared to form a defensive flank should the situation demand it.

(9) Possibility of Counter-Attack:—This must be considered as likely. Speed in consolidation is therefore essential.

In accordance with orders, the Royal Montreal Regiment moved forward on the night of August 31st, and relieved elements of the 1st Infantry Brigade on ground which the latter had captured during the day. Darkness complicated the move, which was difficult in any case owing to the confusion attendant on relief of troops whose map locations had not been established. Company officers of the 14th displayed fine leadership, however, and the Battalion was ready half an hour before zero, despite shelling, which wounded Lieut. R. L. Emmans and a number of other ranks. A few seconds before zero the enemy laid down a barrage which, had it been accurately placed, would have caused serious losses, but, possibly through defeated troops failing to report the amount of territory yielded, the German gunners fired on a line well to the 14th rear.

Hardly had the misplaced German barrage shattered the quiet of the early morning, when Canadian guns roared in answer and the waves of the attacking battalions flooded over No Man's Land. With the first wave of the Royal Montreal Regiment moved a battery of machine guns, under command of Captain Morris, which throughout the day aided the 14th and earned recognition in Lieut.-Col. Worrall's report to Brigade Headquarters. It had been intended that Stokes guns should also take part in the attack, but the gunners were unable to report until some hours after zero. When they arrived, the Commanding Officer of the 14th ordered them into action at Hans Trench, where they rendered valuable service.

Pushing forward immediately behind a rolling barrage, the waves of the 14th Battalion soon came in contact with the enemy, numbers of whom were routed out of shell holes and bundled to the rear. No. 4 Coy., under Capt. J. Patterson, which led the attack, included in its ranks many new men anxious to establish their fighting reputation, but at first little opportunity was afforded them, the enemy showing demoralization and surrendering eagerly. So complete was loss of morale in the German forward area that troops, who might easily have escaped, hurried joyfully to the Canadian rear.

As the 14th approached Hans Trench, resistance stiffened and the Germans, aided by 13 machine guns, prepared to stand fast. The new men of No. 4 Coy. now realized that their opportunity had come. Refusing to check, they leaped into the trench with the bayonet, killed more than 50 Germans, and quickly forced a surrender. The 13 machine guns defending the position they captured intact.

Shortly after the capture of Hans Trench, liaison was established with the 15th Battalion on the right and with the 5th Battalion on the left. Up to this time casualties in the 14th Battalion had been light, but once the enemy realized that the attack had reached its objective he began to exact payment for the territory so precipitously abandoned. As soon as the protective barrage died away, he launched a bombing attack down Hans Trench, covering the advance of his bombers with heavy machine gun fire. Defence of the captured section of Hans Trench, however, was in the experienced hands of Capt. H. G. Brewer, who quickly appreciated the situation and, at a block previously established, held the Germans at bay, strengthening his defence meanwhile by bringing into action a captured machine gun. Ill content with the result at this spot, the enemy bombed down Opal Trench, where the 5th Battalion was established. Fighting bravely against odds, the men of the 5th were pushed back until the flank of the 14th was uncovered. Simultaneously, a machine gun nest in Trigger Copse opened fire and harassed the Royal Montrealers severely.

When notified of the fire from Trigger Copse, a Canadian field battery came into action and silenced the nest without delay. More difficult to deal with was fire from the left flank, which hampered runners and caused sharp losses amongst the Battalion stretcher-bearers, who, as always, permitted nothing to stand between them and rescue of the wounded. Locating a machine gun nest at a spot where a road crossed Opal Trench, Lieut. F. J. Hurley, D.C.M., advanced to bomb. Twice he tried to get within range, but was driven back. Undeterred, Hurley advanced again, but fell shot through the head. Twice previously in the war he had been wounded; this time the bullet struck a vital spot, and death followed immediately.

Shortly after the death of Lieut. Hurley, the enemy drove a determined attack down Hans Trench, but again Capt. Brewer, Capt. G. V. Whitehead, and the garrison forced the Germans back with Boche "potato masher" grenades, collected from dead bodies in the area. Somewhat later the enemy surged down the trench behind a barrage of bombs, but once more he encountered resistance which he could not subdue. Exasperated by lack of success and, possibly, by realization that the Canadians were using his own pet "potato masher" grenades, the Hun gathered his forces and, for the third time, came roaring down on the block in Hans Trench. On this occasion he received an unpleasant surprise, for Stokes guns had been added to the defence and these shattered his attack completely.

Convinced that Hans Trench and the whole forward position had passed definitely out of his control, the enemy ceased bombing and increased machine gun fire and gas shelling, forcing the Royal Montrealers to keep well under cover and to wear respirators almost continuously. Miserable in the extreme were a large number of men of Nos. 1 and 3 Companies, under Capt. J. E. McKenna, who, though violently nauseated by the phosphorus in smoke shells, dared not remove their close-fitting helmets, owing to the deluge of enemy gas. These poor souls lay about in trenches and shell holes, too sick to care what was happening around them. Fortunately, the duration of violent nausea was brief.

Through a curious error, the planes of the Royal Air Force which were to have established contact during consolidation, missed their objectives and circled over an area some 3,000 yards to the rear. Faintly, the rearmost troops of the 14th Battalion could hear the klaxon horns calling confidently, then coaxingly, then despairingly, for assurance that all was well with the attack, and for flares outlining the area captured. Happily, communication to the rear by runner and telephone remained effective and the failure in aerial liaison produced no harmful results.

Meanwhile, in the captured position, officers and men of the 14th were enduring fire of all description. Capt. J. Patterson, an original member of the Battalion, who had been commissioned in 1917 and had suffered wounds in 1915, 1916, and 1917, was wounded for the second time in 24 hours, bringing to five his total of wounds in the service of the Regiment. Lieut. D. E. Stewart, who had worked loyally in the interest of the Battalion for sixteen months, was wounded and evacuated. Capt. J. E. McKenna, who had been wounded in June, 1916, was again wounded, but, as on the previous occasion, refused to leave his post. Capt. J. Pinault (attached) was wounded by a bullet which passed through both legs. The manner in which these officers bore their injuries so fired the imagination of the men that at least 40, suffering from flesh wounds, refused evacuation and declared themselves able and willing to take part in operations planned for the morrow.

III

While the companies of the 14th Battalion were fighting on September 1st, Headquarters was at work in preparation for a major operation to be undertaken on September 2nd. In essence, instructions for the attack were as follows:—

(1) Plan:—The general advance will continue on September 2nd, in conjunction with divisions on our right and left. The 13th Battalion, Royal Highlanders of Canada, and the 16th Battalion, Canadian Scottish, will pass through us to the attack, the 14th Battalion, Royal Montreal Regiment, thereupon becoming support to the 13th Battalion.

(2) Action Following Zero:—The 13th Battalion will attack and carry the Drocourt-Quéant Line. The 14th Battalion will be responsible for mopping up the Drocourt-Quéant and close support lines.

(3) Action Following Capture of Drocourt-Quéant Line:—A halt in the barrage will be made at a point east of the Drocourt-Quéant Support Line. During this halt the 14th Battalion will be reorganized. The 14th Battalion will then leap-frog the 13th and capture Cagnicourt, pushing on until Queer Street Trench is reached.

(4) Second Leap-Frog:—Following the capture of Queer Street, the 13th Battalion will come forward, leap-frog the 14th Battalion and proceed to capture of the final Brigade objective.

(5) First Phase:—During the first part of the operation the 14th Battalion will be in close support to the 13th Battalion and must be prepared to assist the latter if necessary.

(6) Formation:—The 14th Battalion will attack on a two-company front, No. 1 Coy. on the left and No. 3 Coy. on the right. No. 4 Coy. will follow No. 1 Coy. and No. 2 will follow No. 3. No movement from our present position should take place until the 13th Battalion has captured the Drocourt-Quéant Line. Then the 14th Battalion will move forward to mop up.

(7) Type of Fighting:—After the Battalion has captured Cagnicourt the fighting should merge into open warfare. The principles of such warfare will be observed, with scouts well out.

(8) Contact:—Every effort must be made throughout the operation to keep in touch with Battalion Headquarters by visual signalling.

On receipt of the above instructions, delivered late at night, company officers of the 14th reorganized under most difficult circumstances. Darkness and the scattered positions of platoons gave to the task an appearance of impossibility, but, as was so often the case, the seemingly impossible was accomplished, and all was ready before dawn. At 5 o'clock the artillery laid a rolling barrage along the Canadian front and in its wake the 2nd and 3rd Canadian Infantry Brigades, and troops of the 57th (West Lancs.) T. Division, on the right, assaulted the Drocourt-Quéant Line. Hard fighting followed, but success was not denied the attack, the 13th Battalion reporting at 7.10 a.m. that the Drocourt-Quéant Line and its immediate supports had been captured.

On receiving this information Lieut.-Col. Worrall ordered the 14th Battalion forward. The barrage had paused, according to arrangement, and guns which were to have fired on special targets had not opened up. The advance, therefore, began amid impressive silence. Men remarked on this and eyed the distant objectives uneasily. Silence, when one of the most formidable positions on the western front had just been stormed, seemed unwholesome, and the men wondred what evil the absence of noise might cloak.

Impressed by the silence, but thankful for the absence of shell fire, the Battalion pressed forward, mopped up a few minor points where enemy parties had been overlooked by the first waves of the attack, joined the 13th Battalion in the support line of the Drocourt-Quéant System, formed up to renew the assault, and impatiently awaited the signal to go over. By this time there was no lack of noise. Barrage fire had started again, machine guns were chattering viciously, bullets were snapping and cracking overhead, and from all sides came the confused roar which the men had learned to associate with the field of battle.

At 8 a.m. the barrage rolled forward and behind it the men of the 14th advanced to assault the village of Cagnicourt. Brushing aside such opposition as he encountered in the first few minutes of the advance, Lieut. A. L. McLean, M.C., D.C.M., led a party of No. 3 Coy. against a stubborn machine gun post. Outflanking this, McLean was bringing a 14th Battalion machine gun into action, when two Germans rose with their hands in the air. Though experienced, Lieut. McLean suspected no treachery. He rose and walked forward, but fell dead when the German machine gun again opened fire.

Enraged by the treachery resulting in the death of a fearless officer, who had crossed from Canada in the ranks and had served for over two years in France, the men of McLean's platoon charged the machine gun nest and bayoneted the gun crews, sparing none. Simultaneously, the men of the 14th sighted a body of Germans coming forward from Cagnicourt. Possibly these wished to surrender; certainly the cohesion of an attack was lacking. Taking no chances after what had just happened, the Royal Montrealers opened fire, killed a number of the enemy, wounded many more, and drove the remainder in confusion back to Cagnicourt.

Though suffering from a painful wound, Lieut. G. B. McKean, V.C., M.M., seized the opportunity presented by the retreat of the Germans to push his men around Cagnicourt, thereby nipping in the bud an attempt of the enemy to escape through the village to the rear. Driving the escaping Germans back into the village, Lieut. McKean and his scouts followed and joined forces with the main body of the Battalion, which stormed in from the north-west.

Immediately on entering Cagnicourt the troops of the Royal Montreal Regiment were met by the Medical Officer of a huge dressing station, who, in excellent English, requested the men from Canada to spare his life. Somewhat surprised, the Royal Montrealers explained that it was not their custom to kill medical officers, or wounded, and that neither the doctor nor his patients need fear ill-treatment. Satisfied, apparently, that he was dealing with troops who would observe the rules of civilized warfare, the doctor stopped a party which was about to bomb cellars and saps where enemy troops were concealed. "Wait!" he said, "I will get them up". True to his word, the doctor hurried from cellar to sap and shouted down the entrance of each, whereupon German soldiers by the score emerged into the light of day and surrendered. Well clothed, well nourished, so far as the men of the 14th could judge, and armed with scores of machine guns, these troops could have exacted bitter payment for every foot of ground yielded. Instead, apparently with the consent of a senior combatant officer, who was present, they surrendered without firing a shot. No count of them was taken, but Lieut.-Col. Worrall estimated that their number equalled the establishment of a full battalion.

Pausing but a few minutes in Cagnicourt, the waves of the 14th Battalion attack pressed forward against the Buissy Switch. Soon after leaving the village, Lieut. McKean inflicted heavy losses on a body of the enemy retiring towards the Bois de Loison, and almost at the same time Lieut.-Col. Worrall used a "sniping" 18-pounder, which was attached to his Headquarters, to cut down several parties with shrapnel. Meanwhile, troops under Lieut. A. T. Howell had reached a point where six 5.9-inch howitzers were dug in. No defence of these guns was attempted, the crews abandoning them as the attack approached. Together with a motor lorry captured in Cagnicourt village, they accordingly became Battalion trophies.

Soon after the capture of these guns, the advance of the Royal Montreal Regiment was checked by a battery of field artillery which the enemy, with courage and determination, brought into action in the open. Machine guns fired on this battery and gradually it was silenced, the attack of the 14th then sweeping forward into the Bois de Loison, where scores of Germans were captured and many, who sought shelter in deep saps, killed or wounded by grenades.

By this time the dashing attack of the 14th had out-distanced the assault on the right and left flanks. From the right came indications of heavy fighting, and it was obvious that troops on the left had encountered serious trouble in Villers lez Cagnicourt. Accordingly, under command of Capt. H. G. Brewer, the men of the 14th reorganized and awaited developments, suffering sharply meanwhile from machine guns located near the western outskirts of Villers lez Cagnicourt and in the Buissy Switch.

When reorganization had been effected, Capt. Brewer decided to advance to his final objective, the Buissy Switch. Dividing his forces, he placed Capt. G. V. Whitehead in control of the left section, and

Lieuts. R. H. Hood and A. T. Howell in charge of the right. The move which followed involved the ascent of a long, bare slope, overlooked by the enemy and exposed to fire. A more difficult approach would be hard to imagine, yet, by splitting into small parties and advancing by quick, short rushes, the Royal Montrealers overcame the difficulty and reached their objective without suffering disastrous loss.

No sooner had Brewer, Whitehead, Hood, and Howell disposed their men in the captured position than the enemy, realizing that the Royal Montrealers might be trapped, stopped his retreat and began to feed a battalion into the Buissy Switch. At the same time he stiffened resistance against battalions on the right, which had worked into Queer Street, and against troops of the 2nd Brigade, who were still fighting in Villers lez Cagnicourt. Realizing that opposition had stiffened and that a counter-attack was possible, Lieut.-Col. G. E. McCuaig, of the 13th Battalion, used one of his companies to form a defensive flank north of Cagnicourt.

All day on September 2nd Capt. Brewer and his men maintained their position in the Buissy Switch. Ammunition shortages threatened on several occasions, but were averted by small carrying parties of the Regiment, who, under heavy fire, dragged boxes of cartridges and bombs from points in the rear. In reporting on the events of the day, Capt. Brewer mentions the splendid support afforded by his officers, particularly by Capt. Whitehead. He also calls to the Commanding Officer's attention the bravery of Sergt L. Driscoll, Lance-Corp. W. P. Adams, Lance-Corp. F. S. Shorten, and Privates McAvity, F. West, A. Dube, F. R. Sparrow, H. P. Barker, D. A. North, A. J. Grosfils, J. G. Erskine, S. Medai, T. M. Kelly, J. Brand, J. Chase, and A. Fecteau.

At 8 p.m. an officer of the 10th Canadian Battalion worked through to Capt. Brewer with a party of about 15 reinforcements, all that remained of the two sections with which he had started some time earlier. At about the same time Lieut.-Col. Worrall, realizing that the garrison of Buissy Switch had suffered severely during the long hours of the morning and afternoon, ordered Nos. 3 and 4 Companies to reach the position if possible. Moving off in obedience to the Commanding Officer's instructions, Capt. H. A. Thompson led Nos. 3 and 4 Companies due east, and entered the Buissy Switch at a point within view of Buissy village. At this stage Capt. Thompson became aware of strong enemy forces moving in the Buissy Support Line, and realized that his chance of establishing contact with Capt. Brewer had vanished. Accordingly, he withdrew to a point some 500 yards west of the Switch and there remained until relieved by troops of the 1st Canadian Infantry Brigade early on the morning of September 3rd. Following his relief, the 1st Brigade moved forward and relieved Capt. Brewer's weary garrison in the front line.

Summing up the two days' work, Lieut.-Col. Worrall reports that at one time 30 German aeroplanes swept low along the Canadian front, and harassed the attack with machine guns. Counter-fire from the ground is often ineffective, but on this occasion Lance-Corp. West, of No. 2 Coy., hit one plane with a burst of fire and killed the pilot, whereupon the machine crashed. In reporting this incident Lieut.-Col. Worrall mentions that the Battalion Lewis gunners had brought down five planes in just over a month, creating a record seldom surpassed. Continuing his report to Brigade, the Commanding Officer of the 14th states:—" My casualties for the operation were 13 officers and 260 other ranks (324 other ranks since entering the area), including practically the whole of my Intelligence Section, along with the Scout Officer and Signalling Officer. During the past month I have lost 37 officers, 8 of whom were company commanders, 3 scout officers, 1 signalling officer, 4 C.S.M's., and practically the whole of my senior N.C.O's ". In offset to this serious list of losses, Lieut.-Col. Worrall records the killing and wounding of many Germans; the capture of a battalion of the enemy, 800 strong; the capture of a large dressing station, complete with officers and personnel; the seizure of six 5.9-inch howitzers, 16 field guns, 1 motor lorry, and an uncounted number of trench mortars, light machine guns, and heavy machine guns; also much valuable material.

Amongst the officers referred to in Lieut.-Col. Worrall's report were Capt. J. E. McKenna, commanding officer of No. 3 Coy., who, despite a wound received on the previous day, had led his men until knocked unconscious by the burst of a shell; Lieut. G. B. McKean, V.C., M.M., who, as previously mentioned, was wounded before the capture of Cagnicourt, but continued to lead his men until late in the afternoon; Lieut. J. G. Pullar, Signalling Officer, who lay on the field after his leg had been smashed by shell fire, noting the character of the opposition and forwarding reports to Battalion Headquarters; Lieut. W. S. Collins, commanding No. 1 Coy., who was wounded early in the attack, but remained at his post until wounded for the second time; Lieut. V. Quelch, commanding No. 4 Coy., who had served in the ranks and on the establishment of officers for a total of 33 months, and was badly wounded in the arm; Lieut. E. G. Campbell, who had

The Village of Beaurains near Arras—September, 1918

Copyright F. Wade Moses, Montreal

joined the Battalion in November, 1917; and Lieut. W. J. Cronk, who had been commissioned following service in the ranks. Both the last-named were wounded.

In clearance of wounded from the field of battle, the engagement on September 2nd illustrated vividly a point which Lieut.-Col. Worrall had emphasized frequently in reports, namely, the necessity of providing special stretcher parties from troops in reserve. The Battalion bearers, on September 2nd, toiled with the same admirable spirit which had marked their work throughout the war, but the area to be covered was too much for them and wounded would have lain unattended for hours, had it not been for Major E. E. Graham, M.C., Chaplain of the 13th Battalion, who took command of German prisoners and used them to carry casualties to the rear. Through the assistance rendered by this gallant officer and gentleman many wounded of the 14th Battalion were spared hours of suffering.

IV

Following relief by troops of the 1st Brigade, the 14th Battalion moved back into the Drocourt-Quéant Line, where the men were given a few hours' rest, interrupted by desultory shelling which wounded two men in No. 1 Coy. On the afternoon of September 3rd reorganizations were effected, as a result of which the Battalion, though much under strength and suffering from the loss of experienced officers and N.C.O's., was restored to something approaching its accustomed efficiency. At 5 p.m. on September 4th the unit vacated the Drocourt-Quéant Line and marched to Chérisy. Busses then conveyed the men to Warlus, whence they marched to billets in Berneville.

September 5th was devoted to checking casualty returns, to pay parades, and to a general process of cleaning up. This last operation continued on the following day when all other ranks bathed and received issues of clean clothing. Routine training commenced on September 7th and continued on the 8th, when Major C. B. Price, D.C.M., assumed temporary command, vice Lieut.-Col. Dick Worrall, M.C., who proceeded on leave. On September 9th the men welcomed back the Regimental Band, which had been absent at the Army School for some six weeks, and on the evening of the 10th all ranks enjoyed a vaudeville entertainment provided by the concert party of the 16th Battalion. Sports occupied the afternoon of September 11th, and on the morning of the 12th the Battalion paraded to receive Lieut.-Gen. Sir Arthur Currie, who spoke feelingly of what the Corps had accomplished and announced another big engagement in the near future. In the evening the men were well entertained by the 1st Divisional Concert Party.

At 1 p.m. on September 19th the Royal Montreal Regiment left Berneville, marched past Major-General A. C. Macdonell, the Divisional Commander, and proceeded to shelters and old trenches in the neighbourhood of Telegraph Hill, where five days were spent in organizing, equipping, and training for the great battle which Sir Arthur Currie had mentioned and which, unless all signs failed, was imminent.

Meanwhile, the whole Allied front was aflame. On September 12th the First American Army, with four French divisions attached, drove against the St. Mihiel Salient, capturing 16,000 prisoners and 450 guns, and freeing the Paris-Avricourt Railway. It is true that the American attack struck a position which the enemy had decided, even commenced, to evacuate, none the less the result was gratifying, marking as it did the first large-scale American operation in the war. A few days later, on September 18th, the Fourth and Third British Armies struck on a 17-mile front from Holnon to Gouzeaucourt. Though classed merely as a " preparatory " action, this engagement yielded 100 guns and 12,000 prisoners.

CHAPTER XXI

ACROSS THE CANAL DU NORD

> Hark! 'Tis the rush of the horses,
> The crash of the galloping gun!
> The stars are out of their courses;
> The hour of Doom has begun.
> —F. W. BOURDILLON.

I

EARLY in September, 1918, Marshal Foch and Field Marshal Sir Douglas Haig agreed on plans for continuation of the Allied offensive, to come into effect as soon as the First American Army, assisted by French divisions, had concluded operations against the St. Mihiel Salient. In his report on the plans adopted Sir Douglas states:—

> " Ultimately it was decided that . . . four convergent and simultaneous attacks should be launched by the Allies as follows:—
>
> " By the Americans west of Mézières.
>
> " By the French west of Argonne, in close co-operation with the American attack and with the same general objectives.
>
> " By the British on the St. Quentin-Cambrai front in the general direction of Maubeuge.
>
> " By the Belgian and Allied forces in Flanders in the direction of Ghent.
>
> " The results to be obtained from these different attacks depended in a peculiarly large degree upon the British attack in the centre. It was there that the enemy defences were most highly organized. If these were broken, the threat directed at his vital system of lateral communications would of necessity react upon his defences elsewhere ".

In the carrying-out of the comprehensive plan sketched above, a prominent part was assigned to the Canadian Corps. In early September, as told in the previous chapter of this book, the Corps broke through the hinge of the Hindenburg Line, opening the way for an assault on the Canal du Nord, which stood as a formidable barrier between the Allies and hope of early victory. "Upon the storming of this stupendous obstacle", states the author of "Sir Douglas Haig's Command", "depended the issue of the battle on the entire front southwards to St. Quentin". With full realization of the difficulties and of the serious consequences which would attend defeat, Sir Douglas confidently awarded control of the attack to Sir Arthur Currie and the actual assault to the men of the Canadian Corps. By crossing the Canal and capturing Bourlon Wood and the high ground northeast of the Wood, the Corps would protect the left flank of a huge operation to be carried out by the Third and Fourth British Armies. To assist the Corps in its dangerous mission, the 11th British Division and the 7th Tank Battalion were placed under the orders of Canadian Corps Headquarters.

A clear impression of the plan for the Corps' attack can be gained from Sir Arthur Currie's report. "This attack", states the Corps Commander, "was fraught with difficulties. On the Corps' battlefront of 6,400 yards the Canal du Nord was impassable on the northern 3,800 yards. The Corps had, therefore, to cross the Canal du Nord on a front of 2,600 yards and to expand later fanwise in a northeasterly direction to a front exceeding 15,000 yards. This intricate manœuvre called for most skilful leadership on the part of commanders, and the highest state of discipline on the part of the troops.

"The assembly of the attacking troops in an extremely congested area, known by the enemy to be the only one available, was very dangerous", but "careful arrangements were made by the counter-battery staff officer to bring to bear a specially heavy neutralizing fire on hostile batteries at any moment during the crucial period of preparation. These arrangements were to be put into effect, in any case, at zero hour, to neutralize the hostile defensive barrage on the front of attack.

"With the exception of the 2nd Canadian Division, which . . . would be in Corps Reserve at the time of the attack, every resource of the Canadian Corps was to be crowded in that narrow space".

As time progressed, details of the attack were discussed and settled, and the various units notified of the duties which would be theirs. Substantially, the order issued by the 3rd Brigade was as follows:—

> (1) On a date and at a time to be notified later, the 3rd Canadian Infantry Brigade will attack across the Canal du Nord, as part of an operation by the Canadian Corps.

(2) The Corps attack will be to form a defensive flank, facing northeast, to protect a major attack by the Third and Fourth Armies.

(3) The 3rd Brigade will attack on a one-battalion front.

(4) The 14th Battalion, Royal Montreal Regiment, will lead the attack.

(5) The 13th Battalion, Royal Highlanders of Canada, will follow the 14th across the Canal and "leap-frog" at a point on the far side, attacking north and east.

(6) The 15th Battalion, 48th Highlanders, and the 2nd Canadian Infantry Brigade will later "leap-frog" the 13th Battalion, attacking north and northeast respectively.

(7) The 16th Battalion, Canadian Scottish, will be in Brigade Reserve.

When notified of the part which the Brigade was to take in forcing the Canal du Nord, Major C. B. Price, D.C.M., commanding the 14th Battalion in the absence of Lieut.-Col. Dick Worrall, M.C., studied the situation from a battalion point of view and issued instructions which, in substance, were as follows:—

(1) Task of the 14th Battalion:—The 14th Battalion, R.M.R., will advance across the Canal on a two-company front of approximately 300 yards. Each company will be on a one-platoon frontage, unless conditions make it possible to increase same. No. 4 Coy. will be on the left, supported by No. 1 Coy. No. 2 Coy. will be on the right, supported by No. 3 Coy.

(2) Assembly:—The Battalion will assemble in the vicinity of Paviland Wood. The exact position will be notified later.

(3) Zero Hour:—Will be named later.

(4) Action after Crossing Canal:—Passing through the first belt of wire, No. 4 Coy. will swing to the left. No. 2 Coy. will pass through the second belt of wire and swing to the left, keeping touch with the 1st Canadian Infantry Brigade on the right. These companies will deal with the shell-hole system behind the first and second belts of wire.

(5) Consolidation:—Nos. 2 and 4 Companies on the Red Line, from the Canal Bank to junction with the 1st Brigade. No. 3 Coy. will become support to Nos. 2 and 4 Companies and will mop up the support position. No. 1 Coy. will mop up the village of Sains lez Marquion, after which it will consolidate behind Nos. 3 and 4 Companies and become Battalion Reserve.

(6) Barrage:—The barrage will advance at the rate of 100 yards in 4 minutes.

(7) Communications:—Visual Signalling Stations will be established at Battalion H.Q. and at the H.Q's. of Nos. 2, 3, and 4 Companies. Nos. 2 and 4 Companies will signal capture of objectives to contact planes by lighting red flares.

A few days later a sheet headed " Instructions No. 2 " was issued, with further details of the work to be accomplished. Amongst the more important, or interesting, paragraphs were the following:—

(1) Leap-Frog:—In addition to the Canadian troops already mentioned, troops of the 34th Brigade, 11th British Division, will pass through our position in the Red Line after the Blue Line has been captured.

(2) Barrage:—A special reverse protective barrage will be supplied during the mopping up of Sains lez Marquion. [Note:—Troops during this operation advanced towards their own guns, which dropped range as the operation progressed, instead of lifting as usual.]

(3) Signals:—Signals have been amended as follows:—
3 White Very Lights:—" We are here ".
3 Red Very Lights:—" We are held up here ".
3 Green Very Lights:—" All right, stop your fire ".

(4) Tanks:—If possible, four tanks of the 7th Tank Battalion will move forward at zero, cross the Canal, and assist in breaking the wire on the Brigade front.

Still further instructions were issued by Capt. A. H. Murphy, Acting Adjutant, on September 26th, and again the more interesting paragraphs are indicated:—

(1) Booby Traps:—A special party, Canadian Engineers, will accompany No. 1 Coy. into Sains lez Marquion to search for booby traps.

(2) Flares:—Gold and silver rain rockets rising from the Blue Line, just east of Bourlon Wood, will signify capture of that position by troops of the 4th Canadian Division.
(3) Signals:—
   (a) Flags Waved from Tanks to Infantry:—
       White and Green Flag:—" Come on ".
       Red and Yellow Flag:—" Am out of action ".
       Red-White-Blue Flag:— " Am withdrawing ".
   (b) Infantry to Tanks:—
       Helmet waved on rifle:—" Come to my help ".

II

At 6.30 p.m. on September 24th the 14th Battalion, Royal Montreal Regiment, marched from Telegraph Hill to Arras, where, after a delay of some four hours, the men entrained and proceeded to Bullecourt. Detraining at this spot at 6.15 a.m. on September 25th, the Battalion marched to the Hendecourt Area, whence, at night, the companies moved forward to relieve elements of the 18th Canadian Battalion in the Buissy Switch.

A few minutes before 3 o'clock on the following afternoon, Battalion Headquarters was notified by Brigade that zero hour for the Canal du Nord attack had been placed definitely at 5.20 a.m. on September 27th. At half-past eight o'clock on the evening of the 26th No. 4 Coy. of the Battalion moved off to seek its assembly position in Paviland Wood, Nos. 2, 3, and 1 Companies, and the Headquarters Coy., following at half-hour intervals. For the attack the companies were commanded respectively by Lieut. C. E. Tuttle, Major J. H. Richardson, Capt. R. H. Walker, and Lieut. D. Woodward.

During the concentration of the Corps for the attack on the Canal du Nord the enemy shelled, but not in volume sufficient to indicate that he was aware of what was taking place. A few gas shells fell in the area taken over by the Royal Montreal Regiment, but these caused no losses and interfered but little with the assembly, which was completed by 11.30 p.m., largely owing to assistance by elements of the 16th Battalion, who were holding this part of the front and were to act as Brigade Reserve. Curiously, a German machine gun nest, situated in the heart of the assembly position, was undiscovered until zero. At zero it was overwhelmed before it could open fire.

Before morning the right assaulting company of the 14th pushed forward a party to reconnoitre a wire and water-filled dyke, immediately to the front. This obstacle was to have been bridged, but circumstances had prevented, and the men assembled on the bank. Heavy rain, and the necessity of wearing gas helmets, rendered this movement difficult.

Sharp at 5.20 a.m., with a unanimity which demonstrated excellent watch synchronization, the Canadian guns opened fire, and the infantry, debouching from assembly positions, started forward against one of the most formidable lines of defence on the western front. Would the operation succeed, or was the task heavier than even the Corps, with all its proud record, could accomplish? On the morning of September 27th this question remained to be answered.

Advancing behind the rolling barrage, the men of the 14th crossed two water and wire-filled ditches, and moved steadily towards the banks of the Canal, sweeping aside several concealed machine gun posts and capturing a number of prisoners. On approaching the Canal, Lieut. H. Campbell, in obedience to orders, led his platoon against a point which enfiladed that part of the Canal where the Battalion was to cross. As foreseen, a nest of machine guns was found at this spot, and a stiff fight followed, but Campbell's men were not to be denied and before long the way was clear. Almost simultaneously, Lieut. A. T. Howell, of No. 4 Coy., advanced ahead of his platoon and killed the crew of a machine gun which was impeding his advance. A second gun thereupon surrendered.

At this stage of the operation machine gun fire from the far bank of the Canal threatened the waves of Nos. 2 and 4 Companies, which were preparing to slide down into the dry bed of the great Canal and scramble up the steep bank on the other side. Had the enemy maintained the line of the Canal with all the power of his massed machine guns, disastrous losses must have ensued; instead the Germans left the defence to a limited number of machine gun posts, which were silenced by field guns, Lewis guns, and rifle grenades.

Tumbling down into the great ditch at 5.45 a.m., the men of the 14th climbed the opposite bank and re-formed to continue the attack. Driving through thick belts of wire, the attacking companies swung to the left as ordered, and pushed towards their objectives in the Red Line. In the middle stages of the engagement Major C. B. Price, Officer Commanding the Battalion, was wounded, but, despite his injury, he directed the operation until 8 a.m., when Lieut.-Col. Dick Worrall arrived back from leave and took over. Half an hour before

ROYAL MONTREAL REGIMENT ASSEMBLY POSITION, CANAL DU NORD, 27TH SEPTEMBER, 1918

this, Major Price had the satisfaction of knowing that his forward companies had seized, and were holding, the Red objective. In the advance to this point Major J. H. Richardson and Capt. A. H. Murphy rendered services that were outstanding. After reaching the Line, Lieut. Howell and a sergeant of No. 4 Coy. captured 38 Germans in a large double-entrance dugout.

Meanwhile, No. 1 Coy. had wheeled to the left to mop up Sains-lez-Marquion. Assembling on the south-western outskirts of the village, the Royal Montrealers awaited the special reverse barrage, which was soon hammering the town severely, but despite which machine guns from the upper storeys of houses fired continuously. Rifle grenades were directed at the windows whence the machine guns were firing, and a number were silenced. Others were eventually put out of action by the barrage. Though wounded and badly bruised by shell fire, Lieut. Tuttle, commanding No. 1 Coy., climbed on a tank when the barrage rolled back and directed mopping up of the village. Opposition during this process was half-hearted. A number of machine gun nests fought to the last, but for the most part the enemy, unprepared to meet this attack from the rear, surrendered as soon as the Canadians reached close quarters. This accounts for the fact that in the village, which was cleared by 8.30 a.m., No. 1 Company captured between 300 and 350 unwounded prisoners.

Meanwhile, communication between the elements of the attack and Battalion Headquarters had been established and maintained in a manner that left little to be desired, largely due to the efforts of Lieut. A. Close, D.C.M., the Signalling Officer, who advanced with the attacking waves and established report centres as soon as objectives had been captured. Though casualties had seriously affected the Signalling Section in the engagements fought earlier in the month, the behaviour and efficient work of the Section on this occasion was held worthy of high commendation. Further evidence that the Battalion, despite losses, remained a fighting unit of marked efficiency was furnished by the smooth working of the chain of command. When officers fell wounded, juniors took control and carried on without loss of time, or decrease in the power of the attack; when junior officers fell, non-commissioned officers stepped into the breach. In several instances privates handled sections, and in one case a private capably led a full platoon.

As a result of the fighting up to the time when the 13th Battalion passed through the Red Line to continue the fanwise attack in the area beyond, the 14th Battalion had captured approximately 450 prisoners, more than three score machine guns, a number of trench mortars, an anti-tank gun, and much material, including a complete listening set of fine appearance and costly construction. In offset to these gains the Battalion had suffered a casualty list of over 200, including Capt. H. A. Thompson, an original officer, once previously wounded, who was fatally wounded at the head of his men. In addition, a number of officers were wounded. As already mentioned, Major C. B. Price, D.C.M., suffered his third wound of the war; and Capt. B. T. Jackson, Scout Officer, whose daring reconnaissances of the Canal had assisted the Battalion greatly, was wounded for the fourth time. Officers wounded for the second time included Lieut. A. T. Howell, M.C., Lieut. Daniel Woodward, M.C., Capt. R. H. Walker, and Lieut. J. G. A. Thatcher. Others on the list of wounded were Lieuts. E. G. Adams, Harry Andrews, C. P. R. Charlton, and Charles Craig.

Following the operations on September 27th, while the Battalion still held the Red Line, messages arrived from Sir Arthur Currie, Major-General A. C. Macdonell, and Brig.-Gen. G. S. Tuxford, expressing gratification at the manner in which the Canal had been stormed. On September 28th the Battalion remained in the Red Line in Divisional Reserve, equipping and reorganizing meanwhile in expectation of orders to participate in exploitation of the previous day's success, which was being pushed to the uttermost. As a whole, the day was uneventful, though marked by aerial bombing, which wounded two men, and by arrival of a reinforcing draft of 1 officer and 20 men.

When day dawned on September 29th, the Royal Montreal Regiment still lay in the Red Line of the Canal du Nord attack. Reorganization had been effected and the Battalion, though under strength, was prepared for whatever action might be demanded. This was well; for the higher command dare not allow the enemy to recover from the blow which loss of the Canal Line had inflicted. Events on all fronts were moving towards that climax which served as the supreme object of Allied effort, namely, victory without another winter of heartbreaking and soul-destroying trench warfare. With such an end in view, weary troops could be given little rest, lest the still wearier enemy prolong the campaign and procure a stale-mate peace during the winter.

That the Allied commanders had no intention of permitting such action was indicated by events along the front. On September 26th General Gouraud's Fourth French Army of 27 divisions, plus 4 divisions on the right, advanced in co-operation with 13 American divi-

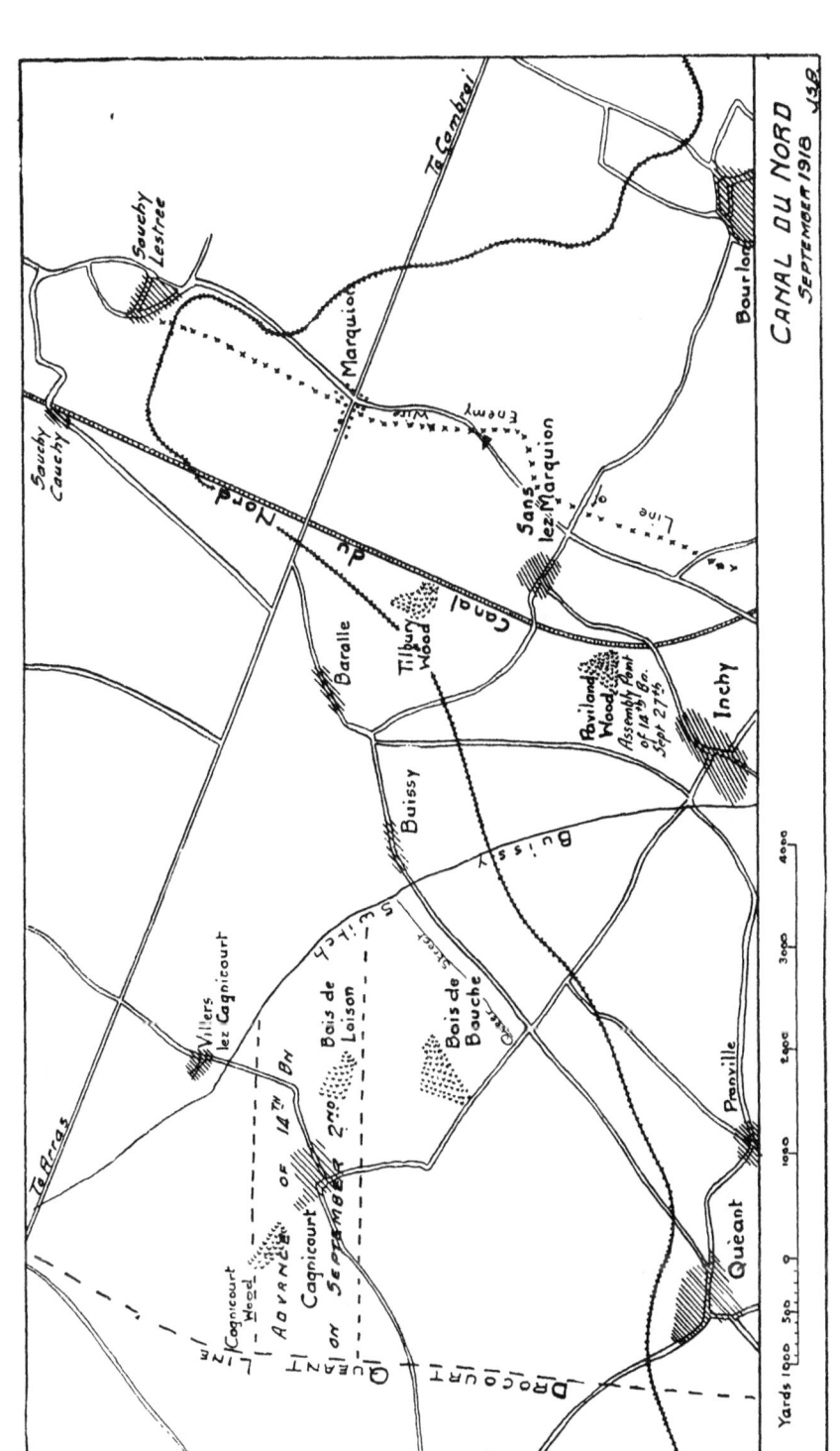

sions (equal in rifle strength to 30 French divisions) against German positions in the Argonne. Nineteen German divisions (six composed of first-class troops) faced this assault, and were driven back, together with an Austrian division attached. In places the Americans advanced too impetuously, with the result that their line on the night of September 27th was located from 1 to 2½ miles short of positions reported captured on the 26th. In spite of this situation, caused by inexperience similar to that displayed by the New British Armies in 1916, the Americans rallied, pushed their attack, and by October 12th had captured 17,600 prisoners. By the same date the French Army co-operating had captured 21,500.

Two days after the Argonne offensive began, 13 Belgian divisions and 6 British divisions, under command of the King of the Belgians, launched an assault on 12 German divisions in Flanders. In forty-eight hours this attack had reached the Menin-Roulers Road, 10 miles away, and had captured 300 guns and 10,800 prisoners. Of these, 200 guns and 6,000 prisoners were taken by the Belgians.

Explanation of German weakness on the Argonne and Flanders fronts (but 4 German assault divisions were in Flanders) is found chiefly by examination of the British centre. Here, on September 25th, 40 British divisions were opposed by 57 German divisions, including 18 recognized as divisions of assault. Despite this concentration, the British smashed the German front and compelled the enemy to yield the strongest organized line of defence west of the Rhine. In co-operation with her Allies, Britain, by this great battle, declared her definite intention of administering the coup-de-grace in 1918, and demonstrated her ability to do so. Hard fighting took place during October —fighting in some places bitter beyond imagination—yet recognizable as the desperate attempt of brave individuals, or battalions, or even divisions, to avert the inevitable. After the operations on September 27th and the days immediately following, including the British and Canadian assault on the Canal du Nord, the Allied armies drove forward, realizing that final victory lay within their grasp.

CHAPTER XXII

THE ARMISTICE

But yesterday the tourney, all the eager joy of life,
The waving of the banners, and the rattle of the spears,
The clash of sword and harness, and the madness of the strife;
To-night begin the silence and the peace of endless years.
—JOHN McCRAE.

I

WHEN the Canadian Corps drove across the Canal du Nord, captured Bourlon Wood, and with the assistance of the splendid 11th British Division secured the high ground overlooking the Sensée Valley and the city of Cambrai, the enemy realized that his hold on that important centre was seriously threatened. Cambrai was vital to his plan for a successful autumn military defensive and a winter political campaign for a drawn peace. Accordingly, as the Corps, in exploitation of the Canal success, uncovered point after point in Cambrai's defences, resistance stiffened till, in contrast to what had occurred at some places in September, Germany's troops were fighting with all the courage and determination which had marked their work of old. Referring to the actions which followed the crossing of the Canal, Sir Arthur Currie mentions that on September 29th, the 1st, 3rd, and 4th Canadian Divisions all made progress " in the face of severe opposition ". On September 30th further gains were made, but by this time the enemy was fighting with his back to the wall and with the courage born of despair. Accordingly, he flung reserves into the engagement and the Canadian divisions were forced to yield a portion of the ground captured. " The net gains for the day ", to quote the Corps Commander, " were the capture of Tilloy and some progress made on the right of the 3rd Canadian Division from Neuville St. Remy south ".

On orders from Headquarters of the 3rd Canadian Infantry Brigade, the 14th Battalion, Royal Montreal Regiment, marched from the Red Line of the Canal du Nord attack on September 30th, and relieved the 7th Canadian Battalion in a position north of Bourlon and near the Cambrai Road. From this spot Lieut.-Col. Worrall proceeded in the evening to attend a meeting of battalion commanders at Brig.-General Tuxford's H.Q. Returning at 7.30 p.m., Worrall summoned his company commanders and announced that the Battalion would attack early on the morrow. Plans were accordingly drawn up for an assault with No. 1 Coy. leading and Nos. 3, 4, and 2 Companies following in the order named.

At 11.45 p.m. Nos. 1 and 3 Companies moved off in pouring rain, Nos. 4 and 2 Companies following, but losing touch when heavy Brigade machine guns impeded progress. Darkness, mud, water-filled shell holes, barbed wire, and the fact that no reconnaissance of the area had been possible, rendered assembly difficult in the extreme, nevertheless the last man was in position, southwest of the Cambrai-Douai Road, facing the village of Sancourt, at 4.50 o'clock in the morning. Ten minutes later, with a total strength of 13 officers and 375 other ranks, the Battalion launched its attack.

At 5 o'clock on the morning of October 1st when the Royal Montreal Regiment advanced against the enemy, no barrage maps were available, the men knowing only that the curtain of fire would move back 100 yards every 4 minutes, with a halt east of the village of Blécourt and another on a line through the middle of the village of Bantigny. Pressing forward behind the barrage, the men penetrated a costly counter-barrage along the Arras-Cambrai Road and then passed through Blécourt without serious opposition, though machine gun fire struck the attack at intervals and inflicted a number of casualties.

Shortly after 6 a.m. the barrage lifted off Bantigny, and, under the leadership of the Commanding Officer, the waves of the Battalion moved to the assault. Soon, however, the barrage became "loose" and a number of guns dropped shells on territory into which the 14th had advanced, causing losses and a measure of disorganization. Communication with the artillery had not been established up to this time and visual signalling to the rear brought no results, accordingly Lieut.-Col. Worrall faced a problem. He solved it by ordering the men to take refuge in shell holes until the artillery definitely lifted.

About 7 o'clock a patrol of the Battalion pushed into Bantigny, defeated an enemy patrol which attempted to interfere, and returned with information that the cellars of the town were filled with Germans. Realizing that these troops, if given respite from shell fire, would man the machine gun defences of the village, and noticing that the barrage was lifting, Lieut.-Col. Worrall ordered his men to charge. Simultaneously, Major Bell-Irving, of the 16th Battalion, ordered his men forward on the right flank.

Success attended the assault of the 14th on Bantigny. One company pushed straight into the village by the main road, one by a road somewhat to the side, and a third by way of the village cemetery.

Taken by surprise, many of the garrison surrendered, approximately 100 being passed back to the units in support. Others fled, but a minority fought and died at their posts of duty. By 7.30 o'clock opposition in the village had been overcome and the forward companies of the 14th were advancing across the fields beyond, maintaining touch with the companies of the 16th Battalion on the right. All was going well at this stage and Lieut.-Col. Worrall ordered his reserve company to move through Bantigny, at the same time instructing his forward companies to push patrols to a sunken road some distance ahead.

Two batteries of enemy artillery, one in front and one to the left, came into action a little later, and machine guns firing from the left gave warning that the flank on that side had become exposed. Simultaneously, a German plane flew over the Canadian position, escaping from rifle fire and carrying back information as a result of which the enemy artillery and machine gun fire became more effective. Fortunately, the enemy ahead of the Royal Montrealers failed to appreciate the opportunity on the Battalion's exposed left flank. One enemy company attacked the Battalion front, was driven back, attacked again, and once more suffered a sharp check. Undeterred by two failures, the enemy again advanced in an effort to crush the Canadian front, but for the third time his attack broke down under fire from rifles and machine guns.

About 9 a.m. the enemy changed tactics and began to filter machine gunners along high ground north of Bantigny, the gun crews joining others already in position and opening heavy fire. At this time Lieut.-Col. Worrall sent Capt. A. H. Murphy, his Acting Adjutant, to complete disposition of the advanced companies and, if possible, to organize a rush against enemy field batteries, which were giving serious trouble. Communication had become difficult, as runners had been killed and several of the Signalling Section killed or wounded, including Lieut. A. Close, D.C.M., a gallant member of the original Battalion, who was killed early in the engagement by the enemy barrage on the Arras-Cambrai Road.

Disorganization of communications following the death of the Signalling Officer and a number of his section had created a serious situation. At 9.45 a.m. Lieut.-Col. Worrall determined to make his way back to Headquarters of the 13th Battalion, in support, and from there send a report to Brigade, his decision being hastened by news that additional field guns were coming into action against his front. Two runners whom Worrall sent back with this report were killed before they had gone fifty yards. At this time German artillery was firing heavily on Bantigny and Cuvillers, and smoke shells were screening troops working down a valley on the Battalion left. Additional artillery rendered the situation perilous. Leaving Capt. Murphy in command of the Battalion, Lieut.-Col. Worrall made his way back through the enemy barrage and, from 13th Battalion Headquarters, telephoned to Brig.-Gen. Tuxford, who ordered him to remain where he was, until Divisional Headquarters could obtain information as to conditions on the left flank.

Meanwhile, in the front line, the Canadian Scottish and the Royal Montrealers were suffering sharply from enfilading machine and field guns, and soon it became apparent that only by retirement could disaster be avoided. Accordingly, at a little before 10.30 a.m., the 16th Battalion moved back from Cuvillers, and simultaneously Lieut. H. Campbell, M.M., commanding the foremost company of the 14th, ordered his men back to conform. Covered by riflemen, the retirement was successfully carried out, Lieut. Campbell, though wounded, remaining until the last man was clear. He was then seen to start back himself, but he failed to reach the position where the retiring company stood fast. His name, therefore, was added to the roll of "wounded and missing". At a later date the Battalion heard with pleasure that the wounded officer had not perished, but was a prisoner in Germany.

Taking a stand not far from Bantigny, the companies of the 14th, under Capt. Murphy, faced a strong attack, supported by machine gun and artillery fire from the high ground to the left. Simultaneously, an equally powerful attack developed against the Cuvillers neighbourhood from the right. These threatened to cut off the Battalion, and Capt. Murphy realized that a further retirement must take place without delay. Accordingly, he directed a retreat towards a sunken road, which offered a line for continued resistance, though commanded by the enemy from three directions.

Manning the bank of the sunken road, the men of the 14th beat off a number of frontal attacks, supported by galling and costly enfilade. In one instance, without waiting for orders, seven men of the 14th and 16th stepped up and were killed in succession while operating a machine gun on the road's edge. During the morning the enemy worked into Blécourt and constantly reinforced his already strong establishment of machine guns. Shortly after noon, as casualties mounted and as rifle ammunition ran low, Capt. Murphy decided to withdraw along the sunken road in the direction of Chapel Corner. At this point the 14th connected up with troops already in position.

At 12.30 p.m. Lieut.-Col. C. W. Peck, D.S.O., of the 16th Battalion, and Lieut.-Col. Dick Worrall, M.C., of the 14th, advanced together in an effort to discover just how stood the situation in the forward area. Machine gun fire from the left flank was intense at the time and the two colonels could proceed only by short rushes. Convinced by this reconnaissance that any attempt to advance was inadvisable so long as the enemy controlled high ground on the flank, Lieut.-Col. Worrall withdrew all elements of the 14th Battalion into the sunken road, where they remained until relieved by troops of the 2nd Canadian Division late that same night. When relieved the trench strength of the Battalion totalled just 92 all ranks.

In reporting on the engagement of October 1st, Lieut.-Col. Worrall emphasized the bitter disappointment felt by his Battalion at having to yield a portion of the ground captured. The situation permitted no alternative, as to remain in the trenchless and shelterless area beyond Bantigny would have involved annihilation, or capture, following exhaustion of ammunition. Nevertheless, the men regretted the retreat and ignored the not inconsiderable ground which the attack had gained. To be forced back from their final objective was an experience which rankled.

Among the reasons for the partial failure was the breakdown of liaison between the attacking waves and the supporting artillery. As Lieut.-Col. Worrall mentioned in his report, German field batteries were served in full view of his men and could easily have been knocked out, had it been possible to inform the supporting artillery of their location. Against rifle and machine gun fire the gun crews were protected by armour-plated shields, but these would not have availed against shell fire. To prevent repetition of such a situation, Lieut.-Col. Worrall suggested that, as in the early September engagements before Arras, sniping field guns be attached to each assaulting battalion. Late in the afternoon on October 1st liaison with the artillery was definitely established, but by this time it was too late to carry the day's operations to a successful conclusion.

In continuing his report, Lieut.-Col. Worrall referred to the fact that the Royal Montreal Regiment went into action with but 13 officers and few experienced N.C.O's. He respectfully pointed out that, though on this occasion disaster had been avoided and all ranks had behaved in a manner to reflect credit on the Regiment, the policy of sending weakened units against positions of unknown strength was dangerous, and to be avoided if reinforcements could possibly be obtained. He added that, at the moment of writing, the 14th Battalion roll showed a strength of 8 officers only, with no regimental sergeant-major, no company sergeants-major, and a bare minimum of N.C.O's. If effective work was to be carried on, therefore, reinforcements were urgently needed.

The shortage of officers mentioned is explained by casualties suffered on October 1st. As mentioned previously, Lieut. A. Close, D.C.M., was killed and Lieut. H. Campbell, M.M., wounded and missing. In addition to these, Major J. H. Richardson was wounded for the second time, as were Lieuts. R. H. Filshill, R. A. Stewart, and C. E. Tuttle. Lieut. R. M. Lawton, an original member of the Battalion, was also wounded, and Regimental Sergeant-Major W. Farnell lost both his eyes. The loss of these officers, in conjunction with the grievous casualties sustained since the opening of the Battle of Amiens, left the fabric of the Battalion badly in need of repair.

II

When relieved by troops of the 2nd Canadian Division late on the night of October 1st, the 14th Battalion moved to a position near the Arras-Cambrai Road about half-way between Raillencourt and Marquion, where it remained, resting and refitting, until the morning of October 5th. Previous to leaving the area, the Battalion was strengthened by 171 other ranks, amongst whom were many French-Canadians. These men from the Province of Quebec reminded veterans of the time when No. 4 Coy. had been composed of French-speaking troops. No. 4 had never lost all its French personnel, but, after the 22nd Battalion arrived in France, officers and men of French descent had for the most part been posted to that unit, No. 4 Coy. of the 14th absorbing English-speaking troops as casualties and transfers removed French soldiers from the roll.

While the Battalion was in position between Raillencourt and Marquion, Sir Arthur Currie issued a Special Order dealing with the fighting of the previous five days. After referring to the completely satisfactory manner in which the Corps had carried out its task of protecting the flank of the Third and Fourth Armies, also to the viciousness of the enemy's machine gun defence, Sir Arthur states:—

"Every evidence confirms the fact that the enemy suffered enormous casualties. He fought stubbornly and well and for that reason your victory is more creditable.

You have taken in this battle over 7,000 prisoners and 200 field and heavy guns, bringing the total captures of the Canadian Corps since August 8th of this year to 28,000 prisoners, 500 guns, over 3,000 machine guns and a large amount of stores of all kinds.

"In the short period of two months the Canadian Corps—to which were attached the 32nd (British) Division for the Battle of Amiens, the 4th and 51st (British) Divisions for the Battle of Arras, and the 11th (British) Division for this Battle of Cambrai—has encountered and defeated decisively 47 German divisions; that is nearly a quarter of the total German forces on the Western Front. I am proud of your deeds and I want to record here my heartfelt thanks for your generous efforts and my unbounded confidence in your ability to fight victoriously and crush the enemy wherever and whenever you meet him".

Two days after this Special Order revealed the magnitude of the Corps' effort, the 14th Battalion marched from the Marquion district to the Vis-en-Artois area. At 5 p.m. on October 6th, the platoons of the 14th moved forward to the Monchy-le-Preux area to act as reserve for the 13th and 15th Battalions, which were occupying the front line, and the 16th Battalion, which was serving as Brigade Support. On the following day the rear details of the Battalion moved from the Vis-en-Artois area to a point about two kilometres west of St. Rohart Factory.

At this Factory all other ranks bathed on October 9th or 10th, the parades not interfering on the 9th when the Battalion, to maintain touch with the front, moved to a position some 2,000 yards forward. On the 11th of the month one officer from each company advanced to arrange relief of the 15th Battalion in the left Brigade section of the front line, but, as the enemy was in retreat with the Highlanders pressing on his heels, the operation was abandoned.

At 4 a.m. on October 12th the 14th Battalion advanced to a position not far from Sailly-en-Ostrevent, completing the movement in two hours and awaiting further orders. When these arrived the unit marched to a position in front of Sailly-en-Ostrevent, which had formed one of the strong points in the extension of the Drocourt-Quéant Line. Here troops of the 1st Canadian Infantry Brigade took over the front, and the 14th withdrew to an area south of Eterpigny and near the Arras-Cambrai Road.

While the 3rd Brigade had been employed in operations near Sailly-en-Ostrevent, Cambrai had fallen. Describing the culminating phase of the operations against the city, Sir Arthur Currie says:—

> "In spite of the darkness of a rainy night, the assembly was completed and the attack was successfully launched at 1.30 a.m. on October 9th. Rapid progress was made and at 2.25 a.m. the 2nd Canadian Division had captured Ramillies and established posts on the Canal there. . . .
>
> "By 3.35 a.m. our Infantry were well established on the eastern side of the Canal. The 3rd Canadian Division had cleared the railway, and their patrols were pushing into Cambrai, while the Engineers were commencing work on the bridges. By 8 a.m. the 2nd Canadian Division had captured Escaudœuvres and had established a line—to the north and east".

The advance was continued on the 10th by the 11th (British) Division and the 2nd Canadian Division, the 3rd Canadian Division having been withdrawn to the Inchy-Quéant area. Next day, with the 49th (British) Division on the right and the 2nd Canadian Division on the left, the Canadian Corps continued its drive forward. At 5 o'clock that same afternoon Sir Arthur Currie handed over command of the Corps front (less the 11th Divisional section) to the G.O.C. XXII Corps and at the same hour assumed command of the XXII Corps front, this exchange signifying that the Canadians' part in the great Cambrai battle was over.

Summing up the results achieved, Sir Arthur Currie reported:—

> "Since August 26th the Canadian Corps had advanced twenty-three miles, fighting for every foot of ground and overcoming the most bitter resistance.
>
> "In that period the Canadian Corps engaged and defeated decisively 31 German Divisions, reinforced by numerous Marksmen Machine Gun Companies. These divisions were met in strongly fortified positions and under conditions most favourable to the defence.
>
> "In this battle 18,585 prisoners were captured by us, together with 371 guns, 1,923 machine guns and many trench mortars. Over 116 square miles of French soil, containing 54 towns and villages, and including the city of Cambrai, were liberated".

All this, however, had been effected only at the cost of a grievous list of killed and wounded. Over 4,000 Canadians had been killed, 25,000 wounded, and 2,000 posted as "missing". The campaign to bring peace without another winter of warfare had cost Canada dear, and success alone could justify the price. Would success attend the efforts which still lay ahead?

III

On October 15th, 1918, Lieut.-Col. Dick Worrall and other officers of the 14th Battalion attended the funeral of Major-General L. J. Lipsett, G.O.C. the 4th British Division, who had fallen in action in the forward area. General Lipsett had served in the Canadian Corps and led its 3rd Division with marked ability, consequently it was with regret and profound respect that all present joined in the honours paid as the body of the dead officer was committed to earth. War provides contrasts, and the change from sorrow to rejoicing is often a matter of hours. This was exemplified on the day following General Lipsett's funeral, when Brig.-General G. S. Tuxford was host at a luncheon for H.R.H. the Prince of Wales. The commanding officers of the 3rd Brigade battalions assisted in welcoming the Prince, whose work as a soldier in France had commanded the respect and esteem of the whole Canadian Corps.

Following the luncheon, the men of the Battalion proceeded to Eterpigny, where gas helmets were tested in preparation for a tour in the front line. At 7 a.m. on October 18th, the Regiment marched, by way of Dury, Lécluse, Tortequenne, and Estrées, to a point where the Canal de la Sensée was crossed, and thence to Gœuelzin, which was reached about 11 a.m. Resting in billets until 4.30 p.m., the Battalion then proceeded about 3 kilometres to Erchin, arriving just at dusk. Shells were falling on the outskirts of the town, but good fortune attended the 14th and casualties were avoided.

At 6 o'clock on the morning of October 19th the Battalion leapfrogged the 8th Canadian Battalion and took up pursuit of the fast-retiring Hun. No opposition was encountered, and by 11 a.m. the advance had reached Somain. Rejoicing attended the progress of the Regiment, as the advance had now penetrated the "war zone" and was sweeping across country little devastated by shell fire. Capture of a village, therefore, did not mean occupation of a rubble heap, battered beyond all recognition; instead it implied liberation of a standing town, whose inhabitants for four years had endured virtual slavery. Unable to conceal their deep emotion, old men and old women—the youth of the towns had gone—rushed to embrace the soldiers, to offer little gifts, and to bedeck them with hastily-gathered flowers. Tears flowed, and even the eyes of the sympathetic troops were not altogether dry when someone produced a faded flag, symbolic to the people of all that made life worth living. The men of the 14th enjoyed the stirring scenes marking liberation of each little community, but orders that the fleeing enemy must be followed were not even momentarily forgotten. Accordingly, the Battalion pressed forward, leaving a grateful people behind. Not far beyond Somain, Lieut.-Col. Worrall and Lieut.-Col. C. W. Peck, V.C., of the 16th, sighted a patrol of Uhlans, whom they chased for a considerable distance. Both colonels tried to overtake the Germans, but the enemy horses were fast and easily left the Canadians behind.

At 1 p.m. the left flank of the Regiment swept past the village of Erre, and at 1.30 p.m. the advance reached Hornaing. Without delay, the Battalion pushed on to Helesmes, east of which a line was established for the night. While the companies manned the line, Battalion Headquarters occupied a billet in Helesmes, which had recently housed the German District Commandant. By every means in their power the people of the town tried to demonstrate how pleased they were to welcome British troops and bid the enemy over-lord good-bye.

On October 20th the 13th and the 15th Battalions continued the advance of the 3rd Brigade, with the 14th and 16th Battalions following closely in support. Opposition was encountered by the forward battalions, which suffered casualties, but eventually this was overcome, and at night a line was established somewhat to the east of Wallers. Interest was aroused during the advance on this day by vast plantations of cabbages and other vegetables. These had been laid out and tended by the Germans, who little thought that the product of their care would be gathered in by their enemies.

Advancing at 8.30 a.m. on October 21st, the 14th Battalion leapfrogged the 13th at a spot on the Grand Bray-Aremberg Road, and pushed pursuit of the enemy. By this time orders had been issued that troops were to be spared where possible and responsibility for avoiding casualties placed squarely on the shoulders of battalion and subordinate commanders. Accordingly, after several men had fallen, the 14th halted outside the village of Raismes until heavy machine gun fire and fire from field guns could be silenced. After some hours, during which Capt. MacRitchie prepared plans for an attack, this was effected, and the village occupied, the Battalion then holding the line of the St. Amand-Valenciennes Road for the night.

On October 22nd the Royal Montreal Regiment was relieved by the 52nd Canadian Battalion and marched back to billets in Fenain. Actually, this relief marked the end of the Battalion's fighting career, for while the 3rd Brigade was refitting, the armistice brought hostilities to a close. This could not be foreseen on October 22nd, and the men of the 14th withdrew to Fenain expecting to rest, equip, and re-engage with the least possible delay.

Three days after arrival at Fenain the Battalion paraded in honour of Sergt. A. J. Jacques, Sergt. J. C. McCowan, Pte. S. Medai, Pte. F. N. Jerome, Pte. F. Atkin and Pte. R. W. Baum, who were presented with the ribbon of the Military Medal and Bar; and in honour of 26 other ranks, who received the Military Medal. In October a number of honours lists were posted in which the services of officers and men received recognition. To the gratification of all ranks, Lieut.-Col. Dick Worrall, M.C., received the Distinguished Service Order, this award being followed by announcement that a Bar to the D.S.O. had also been granted. Similarly, Capt. H. G. Brewer was first informed that he had been awarded the Military Cross and soon thereafter that a Bar had been added. In addition to these popular awards, the Military Cross was granted to Capt. J. E. McKenna, to Capt. J. Patterson, D.C.M., and to Lieuts. V. Quelch, W. S. Collins, G. B. McKean, V.C., M.M., B. T. Jackson, J. G. Pullar, G. Beattie, H. H. Robinson, and E. C. Gough, all of whom had served with distinction and the majority of whom had become casualties in the fighting subsequent to August 8th. Recognition of the splendid work of N.C.O's. and men was afforded, not only by the Military Medals mentioned above, but by award of the Distinguished Conduct Medal to A/C.S.M. H. C. Byce, Sergt. W. J. Bucklee, Sergt. G. Fairbairn, Lance-Corp. C. A. Elliott, Lance-Corp. W. P. Adams, M.M., Pte. J. G. Erksine, M.M., and Pte. W. G. Hill.

November 1st, 1918, found the Battalion still in billets at Fenain. At 3 p.m. the 3rd Brigade paraded, together with transport, for inspection by Major-General A. C. Macdonell, G.O.C. the 1st Canadian Division, who expressed satisfaction at the rapidity with which the shattered battalions were being made ready for further service. On November 2nd the 14th took on strength a draft of 120 other ranks, 50 of whom had seen previous service, and on the 4th of the month Capt. E. A. Adams, Lieut. S. J. McEwen, M.C., and Lieut. R. M. Lawton, who had recovered from wounds, reported for duty, as did

Lieut. R. W. Collyer, who was assigned to the Intelligence Section. Several days later, Capt. J. Patterson, M.C., D.C.M., who had been wounded in the fighting at Arras, returned to the Battalion and assumed command of No. 4 Coy.

November 10th was marked by departure of a guard of honour, commanded by Capt. G. V. Whitehead, to assist in ceremonies attendant on the visit of the President of the French Republic to the city of Denain. This guard, which included Lieut. C. H. Sullivan, Lieut. A. D. C. Parnell, and 100 other ranks, carried out its duties satisfactorily and was complimented for its bearing and behaviour. Previous to its departure, a list of honours gained by other ranks of the Battalion in the fighting between September 27th and October 1st was posted. On this list appeared the name of Lance-Corp. F. N. Jerome, who was awarded a Second Bar to his Military Medal, and that of Acting Company Sergeant-Major H. C. Byce, D.C.M., who received from the French Government the Médaille Militaire. Bars to their Military Medals were awarded to Sergts. W. M. Miller, F. Gaudet, R. E. Carpenter, and F. H. Mundy, also to Corp. E. S. Record, Lance-Corporals H. Bureau and A. R. Smith, and to Privates L. Christie, C. A. Sherman, G. Munro, and M. D'Arcy. Simultaneously, 20 other ranks were awarded the Military Medal.

Meanwhile, in the front line, troops of the 2nd, 3rd, and 4th Canadian Divisions, in conjunction with British forces and in co-operation with great attacks by the French and American Armies, were driving the Germans from one position after another. As a result of heavy fighting at Mont Houy, Valenciennes was cleared of the enemy on November 2nd, but no pause in the attack ensued. Early on the morning of November 11th the 3rd Canadian Division captured Mons and there received orders to stand fast. German envoys had signed an armistice and the Great War was over. Curiously, so far as the British Army was concerned, it ended where it began, at Mons, in Belgium. In gun-pits from which it had fired at German cavalry scouts in 1914, a battery of British artillery fired just before hostilities ceased. Four years had intervened and a million British fighting men had died between the date when the battery opened fire against the German horsemen and the date when it fired for the last time against the enemy in grey. Something of this filled the hearts of Canadian troops who proudly marched past Sir Arthur Currie in Mons on that November day, for all realized that victory had been gained, not by the living alone, but equally by that gallant host which would answer no réveillé blown at the lips of man.

So far as the situation on the British front at the moment of the Armistice is concerned, it is clearly explained in Sir Douglas Haig's report of January, 1919.

" The military situation on the British front on the morning of November 11th ", writes the Commander-in-Chief, " can be stated very shortly. In the fighting since November 1st, our troops had broken the enemy resistance beyond possibility of recovery, and had forced on him a disorderly retreat along the whole front of the British armies. Thereafter, the enemy was capable neither of accepting nor refusing battle. The utter confusion of his troops, the state of his railways, congested with abandoned trains, the capture of huge quantities of rolling stock and material, all showed that our attack had been decisive ".

CHAPTER XXIII

OVER THE GERMAN BORDER

O England of our Fathers and England of our Sons,
Along the dark horizon line the day-dawn glory runs,
For golden Peace is drawing near, her paths are on the sea,
He grips the hearts of all mankind who stands for Liberty.
—FREDERICK GEORGE SCOTT.

I

SOON after the Armistice the British Army moved through Belgium to occupy German territory on the Rhine. Simultaneously, France, Belgium, and the United States sent armies to garrison bridgeheads, pending the negotiation of a treaty of peace. The sphere of occupation assigned to the British centred on Cologne, to reach which a long march was necessary. Troops, however, were anxious to join the Army of Occupation, and rivalry for a place in the Rhine Column was keen. So far as Canadians were concerned, the point was settled by announcement that the Corps, composed for the time being of the 1st and 2nd Divisions, would march, leaving the 3rd and 4th Divisions in billets in Belgium.

At 7.40 a.m. on November 11th, 3rd Brigade forwarded to the 14th Battalion, at Fenain, the formal announcement "Hostilities cease to-day at 11.00 hours". Hostilities ceased; but training continued, and on the 12th the Commanding Officer, appreciating that a sense of anti-climax might strike at efficiency, ordered rigid inspections.

Parading in full marching order at 7.30 a.m. on November 13th, the Regiment, with a ration strength of 805 all ranks, proceeded, by way of Erre, Hornaing, Helesmes, Wallers, Haveluy, and Herin, to join the Second Army at la Sentinelle. Nineteen kilometres were covered, and the march ended at 3.45 p.m. Major C. B. Price, D.C.M., rejoined on this date, assuming his former post of Second-in-Command, and Lieut. B. L. Butler reported from the 10th Reserve Battalion and was posted to No. 3 Coy. Lieut. R. A. Stewart and Lieut. L. M. Hooker reported on the 14th and 15th respectively, and were posted, the former to No. 1 Coy., and the latter to No. 2.

In obedience to Operation Order No. 308, issued by Capt. D. MacRitchie, Adjutant, the Battalion marched on the 14th of the month to Elouges in Belgium, a distance of 25 kilometres. Leaving la Sentinelle at 8 a.m., the column skirted Valenciennes to reach the Mons

Road, passed through St. Saulve, Onnaing, Quarouble, and Quiévrechain in France, crossed into Belgium at Quiévrain at 1.30 p.m., and reached Elouges at a quarter to five. Throughout the march the troops were greeted by many civilians, who were returning to the homes whence the Germans had driven them. The condition of many was pitiful; but all seemed full of hope and gratitude to the troops, whom they applauded as liberators of their soil and conquerors of their enemy. At one point the column encountered German officers, proceeding in a white-flagged motor to negotiate with British G.H.Q. The refugees spat on the ground at sight of this car and cursed to relieve their feelings, but made no attempt to delay its progress.

On November 15th the Royal Montreal Regiment marched 11 kilometres to Quaregnon, passing through the towns of Boussu, Hornu, and Wasmuel en route. The pace was slow, as the roads were congested, but the troops enjoyed the march, for the inhabitants along the way cheered enthusiastically. With emotion the good people thanked the troops for delivery from German oppression, abandoning restraint and weeping openly when, in the afternoon, the 14th Battalion brass band played Belgian patriotic airs, beloved of the people, but long "verboten". Many letters describing the rejoicings were mailed to Canada by the troops, these, for the first time in the campaign, not being subject to Army censorship.

In comfortable billets at Quaregnon the Battalion passed November 16th and 17th, the former date marked by the return to Regimental duty of Lieut. J. W. Green, M.C., D.C.M., who had been seconded to the 3rd Canadian Trench Mortar Battery, and the latter date by departure of 2 officers and 15 other ranks to represent the Regiment at a Thanksgiving Service in Mons. Lieut.-Col. Dick Worrall, D.S.O., M.C., Major C. B. Price, D.C.M., Capt. D. MacRitchie, and other officers of the unit attended a "Te Deum" Service in Quaregnon Parish Church.

Parading at 7.45 o'clock on the bright and frosty morning of November 18th, the Battalion marched north through Ghlin, Erbisoeul, and Jurbise to Lens, turning east at this point and marching to Montignies-lez-Lens, where it halted for lunch. Snow and rain fell during the afternoon, but the Battalion had now passed beyond the industrial section of Belgium and traffic on the roads had decreased, with the result that the day's march of 27 kilometres to Hubermont and Neufvilles was completed at 3.30 p.m. Along the entire route farmers and villagers extended a warm welcome, and several towns had erected "triumphal" arches. These tottered in some instances, but none fell, much to the relief of the troops who, having survived the war, were averse to becoming casualties of peace.

After two quiet days at Hubermont and Neufvilles, the Battalion, on November 21st, marched 8½ kilometres to Braine le Comte, passing through the town of Soignies en route. At Braine le Comte the unit spent November 22nd and 23rd, the former date marked by a visit to a local paper mill, where the men bathed; and the latter by a pleasant interview between officers and the town mayor, who was reluctant to sign billeting claims on the ground that Canadians had helped to free Belgium and were welcome to whatever hospitality true Belgians could offer. Though appreciating this friendly attitude, the officers stated that the Government could not allow the loyal population of Belgium to suffer financial loss from the presence of British troops. Still protesting, the mayor thereupon signed the warrants, amid assurances of mutual esteem.

Moonlight prevailed at 6 o'clock on the morning of November 24th when the Royal Montreal Regiment started a 25½-kilometre march. Passing through Ronquières, the unit proceeded to Nivelles, halting at this point for half an hour and then marching, by way of Thines, Vieux Genappe, and Genappe, to Ways, which was reached at 1.30 p.m. From Ways a number of officers visited the historic battlefields of Quatre Bras and Waterloo. Not far from these sites, forever famous, lay parks of surrendered German aeroplanes, motor lorries, and guns, demonstrating that the victorious spirit of the nineteenth century survived in the twentieth century British Army.

Continuing the march at 12.30 p.m. on November 25th, the Battalion passed through Mellery, Gentinnes, and St. Géry, and reached Cortil Noirmont at half-past four, averaging exactly 4 kilometres an hour. In billets at Cortil Noirmont the unit rested on November 26th, the day being uneventful, except for parades at which the men received pay sufficient to purchase Christmas gifts for home. Rain on the following day muddied the roads, despite which the Battalion marched 24 kilometres without any straggling. Starting at 8.45 a.m., the unit passed through Gembloux and Louzée, halted near St. Denis for lunch, then pushed on through Meux and Dhuy to Leuze, where billets were occupied for the night.

Throughout the march up to this time commissariat arrangements had been beyond criticism, and full rations had been served to the troops at every meal. On the 28th, however, owing to quite insuperable difficulties, the supply organization failed for the first time, with the result that the Royal Montrealers marched breakfastless from

Leuze, through Tillier and Hingeon, to Petit Warret, a distance of 14 kilometres. At Petit Warret, Lieuts. N. B. Cohen, J. G. Vallerand, F. MacKay, and L. Barrette, who had joined on November 25th, were posted for duty with the companies.

Orders were issued for continuation of the march on November 29th, but at 8 a.m. these were cancelled and the battalions of the 3rd Brigade instructed to stand fast, until ration supply could be assured. At 8.30 a.m. the 14th and 15th Battalions were inspected by Brig.-General G. S. Tuxford, who read aloud a message addressed to the Corps by Lieut.-General Sir Arthur Currie. In part, this memorable Special Order said:—" In a few days you will enter Germany and hold certain parts, in order to secure the fulfilment of the terms of the armistice ". . . . In Belgium " You will be received everywhere as liberators, but the kindness and generosity of the population must not cause any relaxation of your discipline or alertness. Your task is not completed, and you must remain what you are—a close-knitted army in grim, deadly earnest. German agents scattered throughout the country must not be able to report . . . any weakness or evidence of disintegration of your fighting power. It is essential that on the march and at the halt discipline must be of the highest standard. . . . All external signs of discipline must be insisted upon . . . clothing and equipment must be, if possible, spotless, well-kept and well put on. Badges and distinguishing marks must be complete, while the transport should be as clean as the circumstances will allow. In short, you must continue to be, and appear to be, that powerful hitting force which has won the fear and respect of your foes and the admiration of the world ". Concluding his message with instructions regarding conduct on German soil, General Currie said:—" You know that self-imposed, stern discipline has made you the hardest, most successful and cleanest fighters of this war. . . . I trust you, and the people at home trust you, while the memory of your dead comrades demands of you, to bring back that glorious record, pure and unsullied, to Canada ".

Facing a 20-kilometre march on November 30th, the 14th Battalion paraded at 8 a.m. and moved off, by way of Landenne and Tramaka, to Andenne, where the unit crossed the River Meuse. Before entering Andenne the 14th halted to permit troops in the town to move forward, but, owing to misunderstanding, this did not take place and the Royal Montreal Regiment was ordered to leap-frog instead. From Andenne the route led along the right bank of the Meuse to Gives, thence southeast through scattered hamlets to Belle Maison, where billets were occupied at 2.30 p.m. Owing to the hilly country traversed on this date, the men's packs were transported in lorries.

As a result of further difficulty with rations, the Battalion rested at Belle Maison on December 1st, many officers and men attending a service of thanksgiving in the local Roman Catholic Church. At 9.50 a.m. on December 2nd the unit left Belle Maison and marched up the wild gorge of a little river, known as Le Hoyoux. After lunching near Modave, the Royal Montrealers left the valley of Le Hoyoux and proceeded through rolling, wooded country to Bonsin, completing the day's march of 20½ kilometres at 4.20 o'clock in the afternoon.

On December 3rd, at Bonsin, announcement was made of honours gained by the 14th at the Canal du Nord. On this list appeared the names of Capt. B. T. Jackson, awarded a Bar to the Military Cross; and of Acting Captain A. T. Howell, Lieuts. C. E. Tuttle, A. Close, D.C.M., D. Woodward, and H. Campbell, M.M., who received the Military Cross. Greatly to the regret of the Regiment, Lieut. A. Close, after winning recommendation for award, had fallen in action during the fighting on October 1st. In addition to officers' decorations, the honours list contained recognition of splendid work by other ranks, Acting Coy. Sergt.-Major J. H. Foley being awarded a Bar to the D.C.M., and the Distinguished Conduct Medal being granted to Sergts. F. Burke, M.M., and J. Driscoll, M.M., to Lance-Corp. C. W. McCall, and to Privates C. Blakeman and C. V. Tuttle.

Following one day of rest at Bonsin, the Battalion paraded at 7 o'clock on the morning of December 4th and marched 42½ kilometres to Bra. The weather was bad, the roads ankle deep in mud, and the route of an up hill and down dale nature, but the men faced the long tramp as a test of their mettle, and reached Bra at 6.45 p.m. Between Bonsin and Bra the route led through the villages and small towns of Ocquier, Amas, Oneux, Tohogne, Bomal, Izier, Burnontige, Cherhal, Werboment, and Trou de Bra. At Izier, where the unit lunched, the men were given a ration of rum, which prevented chills and helped them to ignore the discomfort of soaking clothes. A similar issue when the unit reached Bra provided stimulation after the exhausting 12-hour march.

On December 5th the Regiment rested at Bra, but on the following day, in full marching order, it moved to Neuville, a distance of 19 kilometres, the Battalion Transport proceeding 2 kilometres further to Burtonville. The weather on this occasion was fair and the unit, marching at its best, presented a fine sight as it swung through Hierlot, Odrimont, Arbrefontaine, and Goronne. The German border now lay immediately ahead and all ranks were pleased at the thought of treading enemy soil. In preparation for this, the evening of December 6th was devoted to repair and polish of equipment, which had suffered on the march.

At 7.40 o'clock on the morning of December 7th, the 14th Battalion, Royal Montreal Regiment, paraded in Neuville and marched for the Border. Passing through Burtonville and Petit Thier, the unit reached Poteau at 10.25 a.m. and there marched from Belgium into Germany. Remembering those who had borne the heat and burden of the day, but had not lived to see Germany beaten, the men of the 14th, presenting evidence of that grim, hard-hitting efficiency which had been enhanced by the long march through Belgium, were played over the border by the Battalion brass band to the tune of "The Maple Leaf Forever".

Once across the border, the Battalion marched through marshy, wooded, and apparently not very prosperous country, to billets in the villages of Deidenberg, Montenau, Iveldingen, and Eibertingen. During the march children stared curiously, and shutters, opening and closing in the windows of many houses, indicated that the adult community, though absent from the streets, was deeply interested and concerned. No welcome was expected and none was hypocritically extended; on the other hand, no hostility was displayed and no unpleasant incidents occurred. Except for lack of flags and greetings, the first march of the Royal Montreal Regiment on German soil differed in no essential from those in France or Belgium.

Proceeding on December 8th, the Battalion marched 16 kilometres, via Amel, Mirfeld and Bullingen, to Murringen and Hunningen, where billets were occupied for the night. On the whole the country traversed was uninteresting, the roads being muddy, the few houses poor in appearance, and the district presenting an air of ill-kempt poverty. Sullenness marked the attitude of inhabitants in the villages where the 14th billeted, but, as on the previous day, little hostility was openly displayed, though difficulty was experienced at a few billets and several civilians had called to their attention a "hats off" order, which they seemed anxious to ignore.

Parading at 7 a.m. on December 9th, the Battalion marched through mountainous and wooded country to Sistig, a distance of 31½ kilometres. Leaving Murringen and Hunningen, the route led through Hollerath, Hellenthal, Kirschselffen, Blumenthal, and Reifferscheld, the first 15 kilometres through almost unbroken forest and the last lap over hills, with valleys and attractive scenery between. At

Sistig the inhabitants adopted a friendly attitude and professed dislike of the old German régime. Whether this attitude was sincere, or merely judged expedient, the Royal Montrealers had no time to ascertain.

Continuing the march at 8 a.m. on December 10th, the Battalion proceeded to Euenheim, covering the distance of 27½ kilometres, including stops, in exactly 8 hours. The route on this occasion led through settled country and included the towns of Sotenich, Kommern, and Wisskirchen. Many factories were passed and at Euenheim the men discovered a munition plant still turning out cases for shells. Another feature of the day's march was provided by passenger trains, running on regular schedules. After seeing the destruction wrought on the railways of Belgium, these trains in the country of the defeated enemy provided a subject for concentrated thought. In the week ending when the Battalion reached Euenheim, the unit marched on six days out of seven, and covered 158 kilometres of road. A little weary, but with spirits quite unsubdued, the men received the announcement that the unit would march again on the morrow.

Minus No. 7 Platoon, which was quarantined owing to a case of diphtheria, the Battalion, on December 11th, marched from Euenheim to Brühl, a distance of 25 kilometres. Rain fell, but roads were good, and the men were interested by approach to the valley of the Rhine. At Brühl the Battalion reached a point but 5 kilometres west of the River and approximately 10 kilometres from Cologne. Resting overnight at Brühl, the unit marched 12½ kilometres on the following morning to the outskirts of Cologne, where Battalion Headquarters and the companies were accommodated on the west bank of the Rhine in dwellings of no little magnificence. Here it was announced that the Battalion, on the morrow, would head the column which was to cross the Rhine at Cologne.

With every button shining and with equipment in faultless order, the 14th Battalion paraded at 8.05 a.m. on December 13th and marched around the western part of Cologne to its appointed place at the head of the 1st Canadian Division, which was about to cross the Rhine. Rain fell, but failed to detract from a military spectacle which will remain vivid to onlookers and participants so long as life shall endure. When the command to march was given, Major-General A. C. Macdonell, G.O.C. the Division, rode with a mounted escort through Cologne, followed by the 3rd Brigade, marching with fixed bayonets. Passing Cologne Cathedral, Lieut.-Col. Worrall, at 9.25 a.m., led the Royal Montreal Regiment onto the "New Bridge", across which the unit marched to the tune of "Rule, Britannia", played by the Battalion band. At the eastern side of the bridge, Major-General Macdonell took the Division's salute. By his side stood Brig.-General Tuxford, of the 3rd Brigade, and in the background hovered a few civilians. Bitter to the latter was sight of the proud Division when compared with shattered German units which had retreated across the Rhine not long before.

When the river had been crossed the Battalion unfixed bayonets and proceeded, by way of Ostheim and Heumar, to Rath, where it halted for lunch. Resuming the move in the early afternoon, the unit passed through Rosrath and reached Volberg at 3.45 o'clock, completing a march of 25 kilometres in all. Being the advanced unit of the Brigade Group, the 14th Battalion detached No. 4 Coy. for outpost duty, with instructions to connect up with the 29th (Imperial) Division on the left and the 2nd Canadian Infantry Brigade on the right. When this had been effected, the Battalion settled down for its first night in territory east of the Rhine. Not inappropriately, the occasion was marked by announcement that, for gallant leadership in the Canal du Nord operations, Major C. B. Price, D.C.M., Second-in-Command of the Regiment, had been awarded the D.S.O. A Bar to the D.C.M. was simultaneously granted to Sergt H. Weeks.

Accompanied by No. 7 Platoon, released from quarantine, the Battalion, on December 14th, marched 5½ kilometres from Volberg to Unter Eschbach, where the unit was ordered to stand fast. Taking it that the march into German territory had started at Fenain on November 13th, and had been completed when the Battalion billeted in Unter Eschbach, a survey of the whole operation is interesting. In 32 days the Regiment had covered 436 kilometres of road, or an average of just over 13½ kilometres a day. Eleven days, however, had been spent at rest, therefore the unit had marched on 21 days and had averaged just under 21 kilometres a march. For nine days previous to reaching Unter Eschbach the Regiment had halted over night only. The longest march was 42½ kilometres between Bonsin and Bra, and the shortest move was that just completed between Volberg and Unter Eschbach. With the exception of three days, when motor lorries had been available, the men had carried full equipment, including packs. All kit had stood the strain well, though boots were badly worn when the march was completed. With the exception of a case of diphtheria in No. 7 Platoon, the health of the men had left nothing to be desired. The ration strength of the unit, far from decreasing, had increased, through return of casualties, from 805 to

823. Considering these facts, Lieut.-Col. Worrall had reason to feel that in the march to the Rhine the 14th Battalion, Royal Montreal Regiment, had upheld the reputation gained on the field of battle. In obedience to the Colonel's orders, all officers of the Battalion, including those usually mounted, had accomplished the march on foot.

II

On December 16th, 1918, the Battalion was informed by 3rd Brigade that the area it occupied was to be considered as the main line of Canadian resistance and, accordingly, parties of officers and N.C.O's. were sent out to select positions for defence in the event of attack on the outpost line. Further reconnaissance took place on the 17th of the month and a plan of action was arranged. Little incident marked the next three days, but on December 21st the Commanding Officer's explanation of the Canadian Government's demobilization and dispersal scheme aroused intense interest. On the following day Protestant soldiers of the Battalion attended Divine Service in the church at Hoffnungsthal, and Roman Catholics attended a celebration of Mass at Altenbruck. In the church at Altenbruck, Mass was also celebrated at midnight on Christmas Eve.

Snow fell heavily during the night of December 24th, with the result that when réveillé wakened the Royal Montrealers on Christmas morn the scene bore all the earmarks of Canadian winter. Turkeys, promised for dinner, failed to arrive, but the Battalion cooks exercised the utmost skill and produced a meal which all declared excellent. Nos. 1 and 4 Companies dined together, as did the Headquarters Coy. and No. 2 Coy., but No. 3 Coy. held its dinner alone. Beer, rum punch, dates, apples, figs, and oranges were supplied to the men for dessert, and the tables were waited on by officers and senior N.C.O's. Lieut.-Col. Worrall visited each party and was everywhere received with cheers, the men being proud of the fact that he had left Canada in the ranks of the Battalion and risen through devoted service to command. At each dinner, in acknowledgment of the greeting, he expressed deep satisfaction in commanding such a Regiment.

At 6 p.m. the sergeants inaugurated their mess with a dinner which will live long in the memory of all privileged to attend, and at 8 o'clock the officers dined in a hall about a mile from billets. Preparation for this event had been placed in the hands of Capt. J. E. McKenna, M.C., who achieved a great success. During dinner the Battalion band played, and from a tree each guest received a gift bearing some relation to recent behaviour, or personal idiosyncrasy. The first toast was, of course, "The King", which all drank with traditional ceremony. Capt. McKenna then proposed "The Commanding Officer", which evoked prolonged cheers. The third and last toast of the evening, "Absent Comrades", was proposed by Major C. B. Price, and honoured in impressive silence.

In view of the splendid and joyous celebrations held on Christmas, the laconic entry of the Battalion Diary on December 26th, "No parades were held", provokes a smile. Training was resumed on the following day and continued until December 31st, varied for a number of men by permits for sightseeing bus rides to Bonn, and for others by a less romantic train trip to baths at Deutz. On December 31st No. 1 Coy. paraded to answer demobilization questions, this trifling incident, so far as the Battalion was concerned, marking the end of a momentous year in British history.

January 1st, 1919, was distinguished in the Royal Montreal Regiment by no departure from routine, though the men appreciated the action of Headquarters in arranging that the whole Battalion should be paid. On the following day Capt. A. H. Murphy, who had been appointed Battalion Educational Officer, arranged classes to help those men who in civilian life might be handicapped by defects in elementary education. Classes were also arranged for those whose pre-war occupations had proved unsatisfactory and who were anxious to qualify for more attractive posts. On January 3rd all men of the unit entrained at Unter Eschbach and proceeded to the Kaiser Wilhelm Baths at Deutz, this wholesale bathing being in preparation for presentation of colours to the Regiment on January 4th. These colours, brought from England by Capt. G. V. Whitehead and Capt. H. G. Brewer, M.C., were donated by Mrs. E. A. Whitehead, of Montreal, whose sons, Capts. E. A. Whitehead and G. V. Whitehead, had served in the Regiment, the former having laid down his life in the fighting on June 3rd, 1916.

In beautiful weather the Battalion paraded at Unter Eschbach at 1 p.m. on January 4th and, forming up on three sides of a square, awaited H.R.H. Prince Arthur of Connaught. The occasion was memorable, as, for the first time in the history of the British Army, a prince of the Royal House of Windsor was to present colours on the soil of a conquered enemy.

Arriving punctually at 2 p.m., Prince Arthur of Connaught, who was accompanied by Major-General Sir A. C. Macdonell and Brigadier-General G. S. Tuxford, received a royal salute, following which

Presentation of Colours by H.R.H. Prince Arthur of Connaught, 4th January, 1919, at Unter Eschbach, Germany

Canadian Official Copyright

Hon. Major A. H. Creegan consecrated the new colours. When the religious ceremony ended, Major C. B. Price handed the King's colour to Prince Arthur, who presented it to the Regiment, personified by Lieut. C. H. Sullivan on bended knee. The Regimental colour was then handed to the Prince by Capt. J. E. McKenna and presented by the former to Lieut. A. D. C. Parnell.

Closing ranks, the men of the Battalion then "stood easy" for the speech which, according to custom, Prince Arthur was to deliver. After mentioning that the occasion was unique in the history of the Army, His Royal Highness expressed on behalf of the Imperial troops warm friendship for the soldiers from overseas. He then spoke of his pride in presenting colours to a Regiment such as the 14th and assured the men that if they displayed in civilian life the same qualities as in the campaign, then Canada would not lack capable leadership. In conclusion, Prince Arthur demanded three cheers for His Majesty the King.

When the mighty shout for the King died away, Major-General Sir A. C. Macdonell called, "Three cheers for His Royal Highness Prince Arthur of Connaught", and once again German soil vibrated to a great roar of cheers. Following the cheers, the Battalion dressed back and gave the colours a "General Salute". The Colour Party wheeled and took position in the ranks, while the band played "God Save the King" in slow time. By happy coincidence, the wind freshened at this moment and the beautiful flags streamed out gloriously in the bright winter sunshine. Realizing the colours' significance and remembering the dead who had helped to win them, the men of the Royal Montreal Regiment saluted with deep feeling and then marched past the Prince with the colours in their midst. Appropriately, the impressive ceremony marked the conclusion of the Battalion's stay in Germany. The Rhine bridgeheads were taken over by Imperial troops and the Corps' garrison duty ended.

CHAPTER XXIV

HUY, BRAMSHOTT AND MONTREAL

> I said unto myself, "My way is barred;
> The cliff is high, and grim, and tempest-scarred."
> Yet step by step I mounted it, till, lo,
> I felt the free air on the summit blow.
> —ARTHUR CHAMBERLAIN.

I

PARADING in Unter Eschbach, Germany, at 2 o'clock on the afternoon of January 5th, 1919, the 14th Battalion, Royal Montreal Regiment, marched to Hoffnungsthal railway station and there entrained for Huy, in Belgium. Leaving Hoffnungsthal at 4.30 p.m., the train ran back over the Rhine and, while the men slept, over the Belgo-German border. At 10.30 a.m. it reached Huy, on the River Meuse, between Liége and Namur, where the men detrained. After breakfast at the station, the unit marched to a barracks which became its home for two months. Simultaneously, the officers found billets in the houses of the town.

Throughout the remainder of January time was devoted to routine training, sports, and educational classes, the last, through courtesy of local authorities, held in the buildings of Huy College. Soon after arrival Major H. A. R. Gagnon and Lieuts. J. G. Vallerand, N. B. Cohen, Francis MacKay, Maurice MacKay, and L. Barrette, all supernumeraries, were struck off strength and permitted to return to England. On January 17th Lieuts. D. Woodward, M.C., and H. H. Robinson, M.C., who had recovered from wounds, reported for duty and were assigned to their respective companies.

On January 19th the Battalion was inspected by the Commanding Officer, following which Protestants marched to Divine Service at the Kursaal Theatre and Roman Catholics to Mass in the Collegiate Church of Notre Dame. Pay parades were held on the 20th, and on the 21st all dismounted officers took part in a sharp walk between 7.30 and 8 a.m. This became daily routine, as the officers found exercise essential to offset the softening influence of life in billets. Mounted officers rode from 7.30 to 9 a.m. for the same purpose.

Following three hours of Battalion drill on January 21st, and bathing parades on the 22nd, the men, on the evening of the 23rd, marched to the Théâtre d'Union, where the 1st Divisional Concert Party provided entertainment. The concert parties had been good throughout the war; during the winter of 1919 they reached a height of efficiency seldom surpassed on the professional stage. By entertaining the troops in the evenings, they accomplished work worthy of wide recognition. The " show " on the night of January 23rd, in the opinion of the 14th Diarist, was " very good ", a judgment in which all ranks shared.

As January closed, interest was aroused by announcement that a composite company of 100 other ranks, under Major J. E. McKenna, M.C., would proceed to Liége in February to represent the Regiment in a review of the Division before Lieut.-Gen. Jacques, K.C.M.G., of the Belgian Army. On January 31st Brig.-General G. S. Tuxford inspected the Composite Company, which entrained for Liége at 8.30 a.m. on February 3rd. With colours flying, the company, on February 4th, headed the march past of a battalion made up from units of the 3rd Brigade. To the gratification of Major McKenna and his men, the company was singled out for commendation.

Having achieved distinction at Liége, Major McKenna was ordered to maintain his party and train for further ceremonial. On February 12th Lieut.-General Orth, K.C.M.G., Chief of the Belgian Mission at British G.H.Q., visited Huy and presented Belgian decorations to men of the Canadian Corps. On this occasion Major C. B. Price, D.S.O., D.C.M., commanded the battalion formed from the 3rd Brigade, including the company of the 14th. All units of the Corps were at their best and were complimented by General Orth on their soldierly bearing.

One week after the parade before General Orth, the 3rd Canadian Infantry Brigade was inspected by General Sir H. S. Rawlinson, Bt., G.C.V.O., K.C.B., K.C.M.G., Commanding the Fourth British Army. General Rawlinson expressed satisfaction with the work and appearance of the Brigade, adding that the bearing and swing of the Royal Montreal Regiment had particularly impressed him.

On February 22nd a first demobilization step was taken when some married men returned to England to accompany dependents back to Canada. Following departure of this draft, the Regiment welcomed Lieut. H. Campbell, M.C., M.M., who had been wounded and taken prisoner in the fighting on October 1st, 1918. Recovered from his wounds, and released from captivity by the armistice, Lieut. Campbell had expressed a desire to serve again with his old Battalion, and had been sent from England with orders to report at Huy. Lieut. J. H. Foley also reported at Huy and was assigned to duty.

On February 27th, Lieut.-Col. Dick Worrall, D.S.O., M.C., several officers of the Battalion, and a large number of other ranks attended the funeral of No. 140129, Lance-Corp. J. McDonald, of the Transport Section, who had died of influenza in No. 50 Casualty Clearing Station, and was buried in the Huy Military Cemetery. Regret was felt at the death of this non-commissioned officer, who had rendered faithful service and, together with all ranks of the unit, had anticipated return to Canada in a few weeks' time. Many other members of the Regiment were attacked by virulent influenza and pneumonia at this time, but all finally recovered.

With the advent of March, 1919, plans for demobilization of the Brigade assumed definite shape. On March 1st the four battalions paraded at Wanze for Brig.-General Tuxford's valedictory. After referring to the long period of his command and to the work which the Brigade had accomplished, also to the splendid soldiers whose graves marked the path of victory, Brig.-General Tuxford bade the Brigade farewell and its personnel good luck in the civilian life which lay ahead.

At one time or another during the next three days all men of the 14th Battalion bathed in preparation for a move to the base, and several small parties, who wished to be demobilized elsewhere than in Montreal, were transferred to special dispersal groups. Among the parties detached in this way were the following:—

> For Charlottetown, P.E.I. - 11 other ranks.
> For Quebec, P.Q. - - - 51 other ranks.
> For Halifax, N.S. - - - 7 other ranks.
> For St. John, N.B. - - - 9 other ranks.
> For Moncton, N.B. - - - 8 other ranks.

Lieut. L. B. Butler was transferred to command the party for Quebec.

II

At 7.30 o'clock on the morning of March 5th, 1919, the 14th Battalion, Royal Montreal Regiment, now attached to the "First Divisional Demobilization Group No. 8", marched to Huy railway station and there entrained in box cars for le Havre. A special Y.M.C.A. canteen car distinguished the train from the ordinary troop transfer, and provided the men with acceptable variations to the daily fare. During entrainment the Divisional Commander visited the station to wish all ranks a safe journey.

At 11 a.m. the train left Huy, passing through Namur at 1.50 in the afternoon and reaching Charleroi, where a halt was made for tea, at 5.15. Leaving at 8 p.m., the train proceeded to Mons, where it halted between 1.30 and 3.15 on the morning of March 6th, and then moved onwards to Douai, which was reached at 12.55 p.m. At all points en route the men were impressed by the extreme efficiency of all commissariat and supply arrangements. Between Douai and Arras the train passed through the devastated area of France, the scenes recalling to the Royal Montrealers many of their own adventures and experiences. The men found it strange to view the fields of battle from a train and, after the calm of the winter in Germany and Huy, the torn and shell-swept fighting zone aroused deep feeling.

Proceeding through Tinques, the scene of the Corps Sports on July 1st, 1918, the train reached Doullens and continued to Romescamps, whence it headed for le Havre. Detraining at le Havre at 2.45 p.m. on March 7th, the Royal Montreal Regiment marched to the Canadian Embarkation Camp and occupied billets until arrangements could be made for crossing to England. Accommodation at the Embarkation Camp was good, rations were excellent, and amusements varied. Conditions reflected credit on the camp personnel, nevertheless the troops, after a week of the camp life, were delighted by announcement that the Battalion would cross the Channel without further delay.

Parading at 1 p.m. on March 14th, the Regiment marched to the docks, and at 3 p.m. embarked on the *S.S. Queen Alexandra*, with a strength of 30 officers and 653 men. Sailing in fine weather at 4.20 p.m. (French time), the *Queen Alexandra* crossed the Channel without incident and dropped anchor off Weymouth at 11 p.m. (English time). In the morning the men were early astir and at 9 a.m. the Regiment, for the first time in over four years, set foot on the soil of England. Following a hot meal and distribution of bags containing a substantial cold meal, the Battalion entrained at 11 a.m. and proceeded to Liphook, arriving at 3 p.m. and marching immediately to " D " Wing, in the south section of Bramshott Camp. The Battalion Diary records that from the time of landing in Weymouth until the settling down in Bramshott, the Regiment was expeditiously handled, with every regard for the men's comfort, and in a manner to justify praise of those in control.

Between March 15th and 20th time of officers and men was spent in preparation of documents, or in medical and dental examinations, required previous to demobilization. On the 18th pay parades were held, each man receiving a minimum of £5, and soon thereafter leave to London, or elsewhere in the British Isles, began. On the 20th of the month 16 officers and 457 other ranks boarded a special train which left for London at 12.25 p.m.; on the 21st 2 officers and 75 other ranks followed; these being followed in turn by 2 officers and 63 other ranks on the 22nd, and 5 officers and 25 other ranks on the 24th. With the departure of the last group, " on duty " strength of the Battalion was reduced to 1 officer and 3 other ranks, though 18 other ranks, for personal reasons, refused leave and remained in camp. On the night of the 24th a few other ranks, who had spent their pay, reported and were placed on duty, the strength of the Battalion increasing each day thereafter until at the end of the month it was back to normal. In view of a warning order that the Battalion would sail on the *S.S. Belgic* on April 15th, all requests for extension of leave were refused after March 25th.

On March 27th His Majesty the King held an investiture at Buckingham Palace, and commanded attendance of a number of officers of the Royal Montreal Regiment, to receive honours won in the field. At this investiture Lieut.-Col. Dick Worrall, D.S.O., M.C., received a Bar to his Military Cross and the insignia of the Distinguished Service Order, with Bar; Major C. B. Price, D.S.O., D.C.M., received the Distinguished Service Order; Capt. H. G. Brewer, M.C., received the Military Cross and Bar, as did Lieut. J. W. Green, M.C., D.C.M.; Lieuts. H. H. Robinson, D. Woodward, and S. J. McEwen received the Military Cross. At a second investiture held by His Majesty in Buckingham Palace on March 29th, Major J. E. McKenna, Capt. A. T. Howell, and Lieut. B. A. Neville received the Military Cross.

On March 28th, 1st Canadian Division notified 14th Battalion that the unit would sail on the *S.S. Carmania* instead of on the *Belgic*, and that sailing had been postponed several days. The men were disappointed, but there was no help for it, and in any case time available for embarkation and demobilization documents was none too long. The last days of March and the early days of April were given to work on documents, with just sufficient training to keep the men fit.

On April 4th the Battalion was notified that sailing of the *Carmania* was scheduled for April 10th, and documentation was accordingly expedited. On the 5th of the month the Battalion bathed at the Area Baths and received clean underclothing. The 7th was marked by a visit on the part of Lieut.-General Sir Arthur Currie, G.C.M.G., K.C.B., and Major-General Sir A. C. Macdonell, K.C.B.,

C.M.G., D.S.O., who called at the Officers' Mess and afterwards chatted informally with a number of the men.

On April 9th orders for embarkation were received and at 11.30 o'clock that night the unit entrained for Liverpool. Breakfast was served at Crewe at 8.20 a.m. on April 10th and approximately two hours later the Battalion boarded the *Carmania,* which also carried the 5th, 7th, 10th, and 13th Battalions. At the dock to bid the troops farewell were Major-General Sir A. C. Macdonell, to whose famous "Red Patch" Division all the battalions belonged, and Brig.-General G. S. Tuxford, who for three years had commanded the 3rd Brigade. Both officers, realizing that neither the Division nor the Brigade would ever assemble again, bade the battalions good-bye with deep emotion.

Taken as a whole, the voyage was without incident. Sports occupied much time, and reading matter was distributed by the Y.M.C.A. A "Final Order" by the G.O.C. the 1st Division was distributed to the men, most of whom saved the pamphlet as a souvenir of stirring days and of the writer, who, by devotion to the interests of the men, had gained a high measure of affection and esteem. Throughout the voyage officers, non-commissioned officers, and clerks of the Battalion worked to complete documents, so that no tiresome delay in barracks in Montreal need ensue. Each man's account was audited and closed by calculation of the exact sum that would be due him on arrival, and medical inspections were carried out where necessary. When Canada was sighted, therefore, the 14th Battalion stood ready for immediate demobilization.

At 7 o'clock on the evening of April 18th, 1919, the *Carmania* docked at Halifax. The 13th Battalion disembarked first, the 14th following and entraining without delay. April 19th was spent en route and the morning of Easter Sunday, April 20th, was devoted to preparation for the march through the streets of Montreal.

At 1.45 p.m. a whistle on the Angus Shops of the Canadian Pacific Railway warned Montreal that the 13th and 14th Battalion trains were approaching Place Viger Station. Soon all three trains drew alongside the platforms and Montreal's original battalions had reached home. At the station the units were welcomed by a gathering of soldiers and civilians, including Major-General E. W. Wilson, G.O.C. the Montreal District, Brig.-Gen. W. O. H. Dodds, D.S.O., ex-Commander of the 5th Canadian Divisional Artillery, Brig.-Gen. J. B. White, and Brig.-Gen. C. W. Smart. To the delight of veterans of the 14th, two ex-Commanding Officers of the unit, Lieut.-Cols. F. W. Fisher and Gault McCombe, D.S.O., were also present.

After greetings and ceremonial in the station, the two overseas battalions formed up, with escorts and bands from the 1st Regiment, Canadian Grenadier Guards, the 3rd Regiment, Victoria Rifles of Canada, the 5th Regiment, Royal Highlanders of Canada, and the 65th Regiment, Carabiniers de Mont-Royal, for a march to the Peel Street Barracks. Leaving Place Viger Station, the units proceeded along Craig Street to the Champ de Mars, where Major-General Wilson took the salute, thence, by way of St. James Street, Beaver Hall Hill, and St. Catherine Street, to the destination. Marching with steel helmets, with bayonets fixed, and colours flying, the 14th Battalion at all points received an ovation, diminished no whit in volume by the fact that to the 13th Battalion, marching ahead, the citizens had paid enthusiastic tribute. Both battalions shared in a demonstration in honour of the deeds wrought on the fields of France. At the head of the 14th Battalion marched Lieut.-Col. Dick Worrall, D.S.O., M.C., and at the rear was Major C. B. Price, D.S.O., D.C.M., Second-in-Command. These officers, when the Battalion left for Valcartier in 1914, had marched in the ranks, the former in the detachment recruited by the Canadian Grenadier Guards and the latter in the section raised by the Victoria Rifles of Canada. Both, through efficiency, had risen step by step to the positions they now held. At the time of arrival in Montreal, No. 1 Coy. was under command of Major J. E. McKenna, M.C., No. 2 was commanded by Capt. G. V. Whitehead, No. 3 by Major H. G. Brewer, M.C., and No. 4 by Capt. A. H. Murphy. These officers had gained distinction in France and one, Major Brewer, had been promoted from the ranks of the original Battalion.

At Peel Street, after passing under a huge banner marking "The End of the Trail", the 13th Battalion, Royal Highlanders of Canada, entered the old High School Barracks to render a salute to the Regimental colours. The 14th Battalion, Royal Montreal Regiment, completed this impressive ceremony outside the barrack doors. The band played "O Canada", the Colour Party advanced, and, amid silence, the Battalion saluted the colours presented on the soil of Germany. Following this ceremony, the men entered the barracks, where, in a soldierly speech, impressive to a degree by reason of its deep feeling, Lieut.-Col. Worrall bade his command farewell. Then, at his "Dismiss!" the overseas unit broke ranks, never as such to reassemble.

So ended the career of the 14th Battalion, Canadian Expeditionary Force. Over 6,200 men passed through the ranks; 1,192 laid down their lives in action, or as the result of illness contracted on service;

Homecoming of the Battalion—Montreal, 20th April, 1919

and 3,277 were wounded. When informed that a history of the Regiment was to be compiled, Major-General Sir A. C. Macdonell, K.C.B., C.M.G., D.S.O., G.O.C. the 1st Canadian Division, paid a tribute than which the Battalion could ask no higher. "During the years of my command", he wrote, "they never failed me".

CHAPTER XXV

REORGANIZATION

Land of our birth, our faith, our pride,
For whose dear sake our fathers died;
O motherland, we pledge to thee
Head, heart, and hand through the years to be.
—RUDYARD KIPLING.

I

AFTER the cessation of hostilities, and more particularly as the time for demobilization approached, officers of the 14th Battalion, Royal Montreal Regiment, considered earnestly the future of the unit, and viewed with apprehension the possibility that no place for the Regiment might be found in the establishment of the Canadian Militia. In 1914 the Regiment had been recruited by the 1st Regiment, Canadian Grenadier Guards, the 3rd Regiment, Victoria Rifles of Canada, and the 65th Regiment, Carabiniers de Mont-Royal. Subsequently these regiments sent overseas service battalions bearing their own names, and commanding in a large degree their support and interest. The 14th Battalion, owing to these circumstances, found itself without a parent regiment to whom it could entrust its colours and the safeguarding of traditions established on the battlefields of France.

When demobilization took place, senior officers of the Battalion sought some means of preserving the Regiment from extinction. Through the good offices of Brig.-General F. S. Meighen, C.M.G., original Commanding Officer of the 14th, a meeting, to discuss the possibility of amalgamation, was arranged between Lieut.-Col. Dick Worrall on the one side, and Lieut.-Col. C. M. Strange, Commanding Officer of the Westmount Rifles, and John McKergow, Esquire, Honorary Colonel of that Regiment, on the other. Understanding the desire of the 14th to preserve the name under which it had served in France, the officers of the Westmount Rifles, following a series of conferences, generously agreed to amalgamation of the units, under the title "Royal Montreal Regiment". In appreciation of the sacrifice made by the Westmount Rifles in abandoning their honoured name, and in recognition of worth, officers of the 14th Battalion cordially accepted appointment of Lieut.-Col. Strange to command the newly-formed unit.

REORGANIZATION

While negotiations for amalgamation of the 14th and the Westmount Rifles were in progress, Lieut.-Col. Dick Worrall, following demobilization of the Canadian Expeditionary Force, received an appointment on the Staff of Major-General E. W. Wilson, G.O.C. the Montreal Military District. Here his soldierly qualities proved of the utmost value until, in March, 1920, he contracted pneumonia and died in the Royal Victoria Hospital after a brief illness. It is no exaggeration to state that Lieut.-Col. Worrall's sudden death shocked Montreal and brought grief to hundreds of military comrades. As mentioned in this book, his had been a notable career. Previous to the war he served in the Dorsetshire Regiment and, following honourable discharge, crossed to the United States, where eventually he enlisted in the American Army. When Britain declared war on Germany he was serving in an American unit, barracked on an island. The officer in command at this point joked at the turn of fate which prevented Worrall from serving his own country in her time of need. The Englishman, a trained soldier, knew better than to reply, but that night he and two British comrades slipped from the barracks and, evading sentries, swam ashore. Reaching land safely, Worrall and his companions " jumped " freight trains headed for Canada, the nearest spot where flew the flag under which they wished to serve. At a bridge crossing, Worrall's two companions were swept from the freight train and, presumably, killed, leaving the future Commanding Officer of the 14th Battalion, Royal Montreal Regiment, to continue his adventurous journey alone. Something of his subsequent career has been set down in this book, but only those who witnessed the scene when he was laid to rest in Mount Royal Cemetery can appreciate the place he had gained in the esteem of Montreal and in the affections of his fellow-soldiers. Snow fell gently as the gun carriage bearing his body, and the long procession of officers and men from all units in the district, marched slowly to a point on the eastern slopes of Mount Royal, where a party from the Royal Canadian Regiment fired three volleys, bugles sounded the " Last Post ", and mourners tendered their respectful farewell. From this point the body was conveyed to Mount Royal Cemetery and there quietly committed to earth.

Feeling that as a result of Lieut.-Col. Worrall's death the Regiment was more than ever bound to preserve traditions which he had helped to establish, the Royal Montreal officers worked to raise the new Militia unit to a satisfactory state of strength and efficiency. In this task none served with more unselfish devotion than Lieut.-Col.

F. W. Fisher, original Commanding Officer of the Westmount Rifles, who had left that unit to command the 23rd Battalion of the Canadian Expeditionary Force and, during the heart-breaking winter months of 1915 and 1916, had commanded the 14th Battalion at Messines. For the ultimate success attending efforts to establish the old 14th on a peace basis, the Regiment gratefully acknowledges Lieut.-Col. Fisher's large share of responsibility.

When the Canadian Militia was reorganized in 1920, the combined 14th Battalion and Westmount Rifles were given a place on the Militia List under the title "The Royal Montreal Regiment", with Headquarters at Westmount, P.Q. Two battalions were authorized, the first an "active" unit, and the second a "reserve" formation, with personnel to be called up only in the event of emergency, or national peril. Under this plan the Militia unit was composed as follows:—

The Royal Montreal Regiment

1st (Westmount) Battalion (14th Battalion, C.E.F.).
2nd (Reserve) Battalion (23rd Battalion, C.E.F.).

The General Order reorganizing the Militia stated that Commanding Officers of units must have had overseas experience. In view of this, Lieut.-Col. Strange resigned as Commanding Officer of the Royal Montreal Regiment to permit appointment of a successor with the required active service qualifications. Momentarily, the task of filling the position which Lieut.-Col. Strange had occupied so satisfactorily presented difficulties. Brig.-General F. S. Meighen, C.M.G., the first C.O. of the 14th Battalion, was not available, as he had assumed command of his original unit, the 1st Regiment, Canadian Grenadier Guards. Lieut.-Col. W. W. Burland, D.S.O., the second C.O. of the 14th, had similarly taken over the 3rd Regiment, Victoria Rifles of Canada. Other obligations prevented acceptance of the post by Lieut.-Col. F. W. Fisher, or Lieut.-Col. Gault McCombe, D.S.O. Owing to similar responsibilities, Lieut.-Col. R. W. Frost, one-time company commander in the 14th and subsequently Commanding Officer of the 87th Battalion, Canadian Grenadier Guards, could not take the position.

Though the inability of these senior officers to accept command of the Royal Montreal Regiment was regrettable, it left the position open to Major C. B. Price, D.S.O., D.C.M., who could rely on the support of many who had appreciated his loyal service in France and in the period following demobilization. Accepting the command, Major

Lt.-Col. C. M. Strange,
O/C 58th Westmount Rifles, 1915-1920.

Lt.-Col. C. B. Price, d.s.o., d.c.m.,
July 1st, 1920—July 1st, 1924.

Lt.-Col. J. E. McKenna, m.c.,
July 1st, 1924.

Price was gazetted lieutenant-colonel, and selected his officers. On July 2nd, 1920, when the General Order establishing the Regiment on a peace footing was promulgated, officers had been chosen, and on August 3rd Battalion Orders No. 1 announced the following establishment:—

Officer Commanding	Lieut.-Col. C. B. Price, D.S.O., D.C.M.
Second-in-Command	Major J. H. Richardson.
Adjutant	Capt. J. W. Green, M.C., D.C.M.
Quartermaster	Capt. W. B. Clark.
Assistant Adjutant	Lieut. A. D. Brewer.
Director of Music	Lieut. H. G. Jones.
Signalling Officer	Lieut. A. F. Shaw, M.C.
Musketry Officer	Capt. H. Armstrong.
	Lieut. (Bvt. Major) H. W. Tate.

No. 1 Coy.—Major J. E. McKenna, M.C., Capt. D. MacRitchie, Lieut. C. H. Sullivan, Lieut. J. S. Brander, Lieut. J. A. C. Thatcher, Lieut. R. B. Henry, Lieut. E. Walton.

No. 2 Coy.—Major G. V. Whitehead, Capt. N. M. Mowat, Lieut. J. E. Slessor, Lieut. B. R. Racey, M.M., Lieut. H. H. Whiteman, Lieut. M. E. Beckett, Lieut. C. P. R. Charlton, Lieut. G. D. C. Dobbin, Lieut. L. W. Taylor.

No. 3 Coy.—Major H. G. Brewer, M.C., Capt. A. T. Howell, M.C., Lieut. C. C. Edgell, Lieut. E. C. Renouf, Lieut. H. H. Campbell, M.C., M.M., Lieut. G. A. O. Brown.

No. 4 Coy.—Major R. H. Hood, Capt. T. A. Evans, Lieut. J. S. Brisbane, Lieut. P. K. Haldimand, Lieut. (Bvt. Capt.) C. L. O'Brien, Lieut. W. H. Harrison, Lieut. J. R. Norris.

Once the new Regiment was officially authorized, recruiting and training began, a number of old 14th Battalion and Westmount Rifles men forming a nucleus around which the unit was slowly but steadily formed. Headquarters took over the Mess of the Westmount Rifles above a chemist's shop at the corner of St. Catherine Street and Greene Avenue, and established an Officers' and Sergeants' Mess. Training quarters were secured by leasing an old church on Stanley Street, which, during the war, had been used as a drill hall by the Irish-Canadian Rangers. In spite of the difficulty presented by separation of H.Q. and training quarters, the spirit of the Regiment survived, with the result that when Major-General Sir Henry Burstall, Inspector-

General of the Forces, conducted a coast to coast inspection in 1922, he found the unit worthy of special commendation, an honour shared by not more than a dozen regiments throughout Canada.

Previous to this, Brig.-General W. O. H. Dodds, C.M.G., D.S.O., accepted an invitation to become Honorary Colonel of the Regiment. The choice of Brig.-General Dodds for this post of honour was happy, as he had been instrumental in organizing the Grenadier Guards company of the 14th for active service and had assisted the combined companies by every means in his power. He then proceeded overseas with the field artillery of the First Contingent and became eventually G.O.C. the 5th Canadian Divisional Artillery. Throughout the difficult period of reorganization he placed his services at the disposal of the Regiment and assisted in dealing with many vexed problems. Through his generosity, and that of other friends, the Regiment was able to celebrate the King's Birthday, 1922, in camp grounds at Carillon, loaned for the occasion by Brig.-General C. J. Armstrong, who had succeeded Major-General E. W. Wilson as G.O.C. the Montreal Military District. This expedition, repeated in the years following, fostered esprit de corps and recalled to veterans days spent in the rest camps or reserve areas of France.

When the Royal Montreal Regiment's place on the Canadian Militia List had been assured, officers considered the question of affiliation with a unit of the Imperial Army. To strengthen the ties which bind Canada in loyalty to the Throne, such association seemed desirable to officers, who felt that affiliation with The Prince of Wales's Own (West Yorkshire Regiment), the old 14th Foot of the British Army, would be singularly appropriate. Informal enquiry as to whether, or not, the West Yorkshire Regiment would welcome affiliation brought a cordial affirmative from the Commanding Officer. Accordingly, a formal request for affiliation was fyled and, with the approval of His Majesty, King George V, granted.

The Regiment with which the Royal Montreal Regiment thus became affiliated originated at the time of Monmouth's Rebellion in 1685. Its first Commanding Officer was Col. Sir. Edward Halls, who, it is interesting to note, received a stipend of 12/ a day, while his second-in-command and adjutant were rewarded for their services at a rate corresponding closely to that paid a Canadian private in 1914, namely, 5/ a day. Following the Rebellion, the Regiment, under the name, "14th Regiment of Foot", was established on a basis of 10 companies of 60 men each. It fought in Scotland in 1690-1, and in

Flanders, against the French, in 1692. In 1704 it saw service at Gibraltar, and in 1766 it was sent to Halifax, where, under command of General the Hon. William Keppel, it remained for some years, leaving headquarters to participate in the scenes which heralded the revolution of the American colonies, and to fight in the Battle of Bunker Hill. Later it took part in operations in the West Indies and, still later, returned from the Old Country to garrison the Citadel at Quebec. A battalion of the Regiment fought at Corunna, and at Waterloo the 3rd Battalion, with 38 officers, 33 sergeants, and 548 men, suffered a number of losses. The Regiment took part in the Crimean War and participated in the siege of Sevastopol. In 1881 the Regiment, which for some years had been known as "The 14th (Buckinghamshire) Prince of Wales's Own", changed its designation and became "The Prince of Wales's Own (West Yorkshire Regiment)". In common with all County Regiments of the British Army, the unit rose to the need of England in August, 1914, battalion after battalion being sent on active service. The affiliation, therefore, was that of an old and a young regiment, the one with traditions of long standing, in which the other had demonstrated worthiness to share. Since affiliation, officers of both units have endeavoured to promote friendly feeling between the Regiments and to make of the association something more than a name.

As time passed after 1920, it became clear that conditions under which the Royal Montreal Regiment was labouring would slowly kill esprit de corps, and that, to prevent disaster, better quarters were essential. Accordingly, under the leadership of the Honorary Colonel, Brig.-General W. O. H. Dodds, D.S.O., and of the Commanding Officer, Lieut.-Col. C. B. Price, D.S.O., D.C.M., a campaign to secure an armoury was begun. An "Armoury Association" was formed, with Brig.-Gen. Dodds as President, Lieut.-Col. Fisher as Vice-President, Lieut.-Col. Price as Secretary, and other friends of the Regiment making up the personnel. After prolonged negotiations, the City of Westmount leased to the Armoury Association for 99 years, at a rental of $1.00 a year, land on St. Catherine Street, not far from Westmount Park. Simultaneously, the Sun Life Assurance Co. of Canada loaned to the Association a sum of $143,000, the Government of the Dominion of Canada agreeing to pay to the Armoury Association each year, as rent for the completed building, a sum sufficient to pay interest on the Sun Life Company's loan, plus an amount for sinking fund purposes, sufficient to extinguish the principal of the loan in 20 years. The Armoury Association, meanwhile, agreed to raise $37,000, representing the difference between the total of the Sun Life loan and the estimated cost of the building.

On completion of agreements between the Armoury Association, the City of Westmount, the Dominion Government, and the Sun Life Assurance Co., a contract for erection of the new building was drawn up, and on June 1st, 1925, the first sod was turned. The work progressed favourably from that time, the completed building being turned over by the contractors in December. Meanwhile, Lieut.-Col. Price's term as Commanding Officer had been completed and leadership of the unit had passed to Major J. E. McKenna, M.C., who received promotion to the rank of lieutenant-colonel.

On December 28th, 1925, the new building, which commemorated those who had died in France, was formally opened by the Hon. E. M. MacDonald, Canadian Minister of National Defence. Amongst those participating in the ceremony, in addition to ex-officers and officers on the active list of the Regiment, were Major-General J. H. MacBrien, C.B., C.M.G., D.S.O., Chief of Staff; Major-General E. C. Ashton, C.M.G., Quartermaster-General of the Canadian Forces; and Brig.-Gen. C. J. Armstrong, C.M.G., G.O.C. the Montreal Military District, all of whom had provided generous assistance in planning and completing the armoury project. Other guests included Lieut.-General Sir R. E. W. Turner, V.C., who came from Quebec for the occasion; the Venerable Archdeacon F. G. Scott, who, as Canon Scott, had been the Regiment's first Protestant Chaplain; Col. D. R. McCuaig, Commanding the 5th Regiment, Royal Highlanders of Canada; Lieut.-Col. C. F. C. Porteous, M.C., who had served as a subaltern with the 14th and, since demobilization, had succeeded to command of the 3rd Regiment, Victoria Rifles of Canada; Lieut.-Col. G. S. Stairs, Commanding Officer of the 1st Regiment, Canadian Grenadier Guards; Lieut.-Col. A. V. Tardiff, of the 65th Regiment, Carabiniers de Mont-Royal; Mr. McLagan, Mayor of the City of Westmount; Mr. Paul Mercier, M.P., in whose parliamentary constituency the armoury was situated; and a large number of distinguished citizens and soldiers.

Previous to the reception of guests, the Regiment, under command of Lieut.-Col. J. E. McKenna, M.C., with Major H. G. Brewer, M.C., as Second-in-Command, and with the companies commanded respectively by Major R. H. Hood, Major G. V. Whitehead, Capt. A. T. Howell, M.C., and Major H. Armstrong, was drawn up on three sides of a square for salute to the colours, reception of the Minister of National Defence, and religious dedication of the new building. When

Lt.-Col. F. A. C. Scrimger, v.c.

Captain G. B. McKean, v.c., m.c., m.m.
Accidentally killed in 1926

the colours had been honoured, and the Minister accorded right of entry in the name of the King, Hon. Capt. H. Laws, Chaplain of the Regiment, offered the following prayer, dedicating the armoury and expressing in simple words the ideals which had prompted its erection:—

"Almighty and Eternal God, King of all Kings, Who hast put it into the hearts of Thy servants to erect this building for the training of men who are to serve their King and Country, and to the memory of the gallant dead of this and sister regiments, who laid down their lives in the Great War, we dedicate this building to Thy service, and to the service of our Empire. And we pray Thee that the men who now, and in time to come, train within these walls may be true to the high and noble ideals of those fallen comrades, who made the name of this Regiment glorious in service. And may Truth, Justice, and Right ever flourish here, to the glory of Thy Holy Name".

APPENDICES

APPENDIX A

The Royal Montreal Regiment

HONOUR ROLL

KILLED IN ACTION OR DIED OF WOUNDS

Adamchuk, Pte. Jack
Adams, Pte. David
Adams, Pte. Dunbar
Adams, Pte. William George
Adcock, Pte. Thomas F.
Addison, Pte. Joseph
Aitken, Sergt. Robert
Alcock, Pte. Charles
Alford, Pte. Robert A.
Alexander, Pte. William
Allaby, Pte. Hanford S.
Allan, Corp. Emmett F., M.M.
Allan, Corp. Leonard
Allan, Lieut. Robert James, M.C., M.M.
Allen, Pte. Edwin C.
Allen, Pte. Francis W.
Allison, A/Sergt. James
Amand, Pte. Philip
Anderson, Pte. Bernard B.
Anderson, Pte. Joseph
Anderson, Pte. Oscar
Anderson, Pte. Samuel
Anderson, Pte. Thomas R.
Anderson, Pte. William J.
Andre, Pte. Adrien
Andrew, Pte. Oswald A.
Angell, Pte. Albert
Ankers, Pte. Edward
Appleton, Pte. Arthur E.
Arbon, Pte. George
Argue, Pte. James R.
Armstrong, C.S.M. George
Armstrong, Corp. Noble H. J.
Arnold, Pte. Edward
Arsenault, Pte. Theodore F.
Arundell, Sergt. John D. H.
Ashley, Pte. Monson Frederick
Ashworth, Pte. James
Aubin, Sergt. Napoleon

Bagshaw, Pte. Walter
Bain, Pte. Frederick
Bain, Pte. Robert
Baird, Lieut. Andrew Stuart
Baisbrown, Pte. Noel
Baldwin, Pte. Horatio
Balleine, Pte. Allan Cyril
Barca-Carp, Pte. Vladimir
Bardsley, Pte. Colin G. C.
Barker, Pte. Hubert P., M.M.
Barnes, Pte. Thomas James
Barraclough, Pte. Joe
Barter, Lance-Corp. Harold
Bartholomew, Pte. Verne
Bartlett, Pte. George L.
Basque, Pte. Alexander
Batten, Pte. James
Batuk, Pte. Sam
Beagley, Capt. Thomas G.
Bears, Pte. James H.
Beaton, Capt. William Evan, M.C.
Beattie, Pte. William
Bedard, Pte. Rodolphe
Beeson, Corp. Edward J.
Beggs, Pte. Bernard
Belair, Pte. Fred.
Belanger, Pte. Leo
Belanger, Pte. Lucien
Bell, Pte. George
Bell, Pte. John Robert
Bell, Pte. Reginald, M.M.
Bellamy, C.S.M. John Henry
Bellew, Pte. Ronald
Belyea, Pte. William N.

HONOUR ROLL

Bennett, Pte. Frederick
Bennett, Pte. James
Bennett, Lance-Corp. Percy F.
Bent, Pte. John A.
Bermudez, Pte. Manuel
Berry, Pte. Mark
Berryman, Pte. George
Berthiaume, Pte. Armand
Bertram, Corp. John A., M.M.
Bertrand, Pte. Fred
Beswick, Sergt. Archie Neville
Betts, Pte. Magnus
Biggs, Pte. George Edward
Binet, Pte. Alfred
Bingham, Pte. Herbert N.
Binks, Pte. Joseph A. S.
Birrell, Pte. Robert
Bish, Pte. Henry G.
Bissonnette, Pte. Wilfred
Black, Pte. Bob
Black, Lance-Corp. Daniel, M.M.
Blackett, Sergt. William C.
Blaikie, Pte. Stanley
Blake, Pte. Frank
Blakeman, Pte. Claude, D.C.M.
Blandford, Sergt. Archie
Blaney, Pte. James
Blomlie, Pte. John Arnold
Blyth, Pte. Alfred
Boa, Pte. Frank T.
Boddie, Pte. Alexander T.
Boivin, Pte. Henri
Bolduc, Pte. Laurent
Bolton, Pte. Jacob
Bolton, Pte. Joseph
Bond, Pte. Arthur
Boniface, Pte. Charles
Booth, Pte. Harry
Bouchard, Pte. Celestin
Boudreau, Lance-Sergt. Antoine
Boudreau, Pte. Henri
Bourcier, Corp. Eugene
Bourgeois, Pte. Blair
Bourgeois, Lieut. Rene
Boute, Pte. John
Bowden, Pte. James H.
Bowen, Pte. Brinley T.
Bowron, Pte. William C. W.

Bowyer, Lance-Corp. J. Lorne
Boyce, Pte. Arthur
Boyce, Pte. William P.
Boylan, Pte. James H.
Bradbury, Pte. Alec
Bradley, Pte. Joseph
Brand, Pte. John
Brand, Pte. Robert G.
Bremner, Lance-Corp. Reginald O.
Brennan, Corp. William Henry
Brewis, Pte. Joseph
Briere, Pte. Armand
Briggs, Pte. Oscar W.
Brinkhurst, Corp. John
Brinn, Lance-Corp. Frank
Brissette, Pte. Georges
Broadworth, Pte. Ernest M.
Brock, Pte. Emanuel
Brodeur, Pte. Ernest
Brooks, Corp. Earl
Brooks, Lance-Corp. John
Brotherhood, Lieut. Wilfred Cashel
Broughton, Lance-Corp. William
Brouwer, Pte. Gerritt
Brown, Pte. Arthur
Brown, Pte. Harry C.
Brown, Pte. Hugh
Brown, Pte. John Henry
Brown, Lance-Corp. John W. H.
Brown, Pte. Lorne
Brown, Pte. Wilfred P.
Buchanan, Pte. Orville A.
Budgen, Pte. John
Bull, Pte. Frank
Burberry, Pte. Alfred
Burke, Pte. William
Burnet, Pte. Ernest
Burnett, Pte. George
Burnett, Pte. Harry C.
Burnie, Pte. James
Burritt, Pte. Alfred C.
Burroughs, Lance-Corp. Cecil A.
Burrows, Pte. George P.
Burt, Pte. John (correct name Matthew H. Todd)
Bush, Pte. William G.
Bussell, Pte. William
Butler, Lance-Sergt. Frederick P.
Buxton, Pte. John

Cadorette, Pte. Pierre
Caine, Pte. John
Caldwell, Pte. Gault Gaston
Cameron, Corp. Evan Stuart
Cameron, Pte. Laurence
Campbell, Pte. Colin
Campbell, Pte. John
Campbell, Sergt. John Douglas
Campbell, Pte. Samuel T.
Caravan, Pte. James
Card, Sergt. Charles A.
Carey, Pte. Alfred
Carey, Pte. Edward (correct name Edward Carey White)
Carkner, Sergt. R. M.
Carmell, Pte. John W.
Carnahan, Pte. John T.
Caron, A/Sergt. Joseph Isaie
Carpenter, Pte. John
Carriere, Pte. Joseph
Carriere, Pte. Leopold
Carson, Pte. James
Carson, Capt. John C. K., M.C.
Carter, Pte. Arthur J.
Carter, Pte. Sidney Charles
Cartwright, Pte. Joseph
Casey, Pte. John Joseph
Casey, Pte. Thomas G.
Castonguay, Pte. Felix
Castonguay, Pte. Napoleon P.
Cater, Pte. Thomas
Catherwood, Pte. Ewart
Chaisson, Pte. William
Chambers, Pte. Herbert C.
Chandler, Pte. Harold
Chanu, Sergt. Henry
Chapadeau, Pte. Joseph Edmund
Chappell, Pte. Sydney B.
Charbonneau, Pte. Magloire
Cherrier, Sergt. Raymond
Chessell, Pte. Frederick
Chew, Pte. Albert
Chicoine, Pte. Emile
Chinneck, Pte. Arthur B.
Chippendale, Pte. George
Chubb, Pte. Frederick
Chudleigh, Pte. Walter S.
Clark, Pte. Alexander
Clark, Pte. James
Clark, Pte. Thomas H. C.
Clarke, Pte. Andrew W.
Clarke, Lance-Corp. Elihu J.
Clarke, Pte. John H.
Clarkson, Major David William, M.C.
Clayton, Pte. Reuben
Cleary, Pte. William H.
Clement, Pte. Ensign
Clifford, Pte. Frank
Clifford, Pte. Thomas
Clinch, Lance-Sergt. Thomas J.
Close, Lieut. Arthur
Clune, Pte. William C.
Cobb, Pte. Chester
Cobley, Pte. Sidney
Coleman, Pte. David John
Coleman, Pte. Joseph
Collins, Pte. John J.
Collins, Pte. Maurice J.
Colton, Pte. George
Colwell, Pte. Ralph
Colwell, Pte. Walter J.
Connors, Pte. William P.
Conroy, Pte. Michael J.
Conway, Pte. Joseph
Cook, Pte. George W. M.
Cook, Pte. Walter B.
Cook, Pte. Walter C.
Cooke, Pte. Percy H.
Cooley, Pte. James
Coombes, Pte. Edward James
Cooper, Pte. James R.
Coote, Pte. Frederick D.
Corcoran, Pte. John B.
Corey, Pte. Walter C.
Corin, Pte. Charles W. A.
Cote, Pte. Aquilas
Cote, Corp. Ernest
Cote, Pte. George F.
Cotton, Pte. James
Coubrough, Pte. David
Coull, Pte. Leslie G.
Court, Pte. George
Cowen, Capt. Edwin
Cowen, A/Corp. John
Coznik, Pte. Nick
Crabb, Pte. George A.
Craik, Pte. William
Crane, Pte. William
Crawford, Pte. Fred.
Crawford, Pte. Joseph

HONOUR ROLL

Creighton, C.S.M. James A.
Crerar, Pte. John Stewart
Crockett, Sergt. Parker H., D.C.M.
Cronkwright, Pte. Wilbert John
Crook, Pte. Wilfred Ernest
Crowell, Pte. Gordon H.
Cumming, Pte. John
Cunning, Pte. John F.
Cunningham, Pte. Edward
Currin, Pte. Ernest
Curtis, Pte. William
Cusson, Pte. Arthur
Cuyler, Pte. Charles Henry

Dabate, Pte. David
Dailey, Pte. D.
Daly, Pte. John
Dalton, Pte. John P.
Damphouse, Pte. Joseph
Daniels, Corp. Nicholas, M.M.
Dastou, Pte. Amedee
Davidson, Pte. John L.
Davies, Pte. Edward
Davin, Lieut. Henry Arthur
Davis, Pte. Harvey H.
Davy, Lieut. John Harper
Dawson, Pte. Hector
Day, Pte. Henry
Denman, Pte. Clarence B.
Dennis, Pte. James (correct name Hugh McCabe)
Denny, Pte. William
Desilest, Pte. William
DesJardins, Pte. Wilfred
Desroche, Pte. Arthur
Devine, Pte. Frank
Devlin, Pte. Archie
Dewhurst, Pte. Thomas
Dick, Lance-Corp. Roy B.
Dickey, Pte. William
Dickson, Pte. David
Dimma, Pte. Charles S.
Dionne, Pte. Charles
Dixon, Pte. George
Doherty, Pte. James
Doiron, Pte. Charles W.
Donnelly, Pte. John Austin
Donogen, Pte. John
Dostert, Corp. Peter

Doucet, Pte. Meddie
Dower, Pte. Edward
Drummond, Pte. Archibald M. D.
Drysdale, Lance-Corp. Arthur
Duhamel, C.S.M. Ludovic
Duncan, Pte. Robert
Dunlop, Pte. Andrew F.
Dunn, Pte. George
Dunn, Pte. William James
Dupont, Pte. James Arthur
Dupuis, Pte. Francis
Dupuy, Pte. Harry L.
Durance, Pte. Ernest
Dyer, Pte. Charles E.

Easdale, Pte. William G.
East, Pte. Edward James
Eaton, Pte. Robert
Ede, Corp. William F., M.M.
Eden, Pte. Harry A.
Edwards, Pte. James
Egan, Pte. Michael J.
Eggleton, Pte. Clarence G.
Elderkin, Pte. Vernon
Ellison, Pte. Reginald F.
Elliott, Pte. Clarence Arnold, D.C.M.
Elliott, Pte. Cecil Arthur
Elliott, Pte. Robert (No. 26194)
Elliott, Pte. Robert (No. 464136)
England, Pte. Albert
England, Lance-Corp. Harold
English, Pte. Walter
Ensum, Pte. Edward Walter
Evans, Pte. Samuel R.
Evers, Pte. Lewis

Fagan, Pte. Edward
Fagan, Pte. Thomas
Fairbairn, A/C.S.M. Gilbert, D.C.M.
Farley, Pte. Howard H.
Faulkner, Pte. William
Faylor, Pte. Ralph T.
Fecteau, Pte. Alfred A.
Fegan, A/Sergt. William Patrick
Fenton, Pte. William R.
Ferguson, Pte. Ernest R. J.
Ferguson, A/Corp. Wilbert
Ferish, Pte. Charles

Few, Pte. James
Finder, Lance-Corp. Charles
Finlayson, Pte. John P.
Finley, Pte. Ernest J.
Fiset, Pte. Jean
Fisher, Pte. Charles A.
Fisher, Pte. Henry
Fisk, Pte. James W.
Fitzpatrick, Pte. Patrick
Flanagan, Pte. Frank
Fletcher, Pte. Arthur J.
Fletcher, Pte. Dudley
Flood, Corp. Arthur H.
Flynn, Pte. Daniel
Flynn, Pte. John
Forbes, Pte. Benjamin
Ford, Pte. Edwin
Forsythe, Pte. Ernest
Fortin, Lance-Corp. Albert
Fotheringham, Lance-Corp. James, M.M.
Fougere, Pte. Alexander
Fountain, Pte. Fenny
Fournier, Pte. Emile
Francey, Pte. George
Frazee, Pte. Frank E.
Freeman, Pte. Douglas
Freeman, Pte. Michael
French, Pte. Walter F.
Fry, Pte. William Frank
Fry, Lance-Corp. William Henry
Frye, Pte. Eraytus Howard
Fulton, Pte. James

Gaboury, Pte. James
Gadoury, Pte. Louis
Gagnon, Pte. Lucien
Galbraith, Pte. Neil
Gallant, Pte. Anthony Prosper
Gallant, Pte. Hector
Gallant, Pte. Jean Baptiste
Gallison, Pte. Frank
Gandy, Pte. Robert Bertie
Garbett, Sergt. Ernest G.
Garner, Pte. Herbert F.
Garon, Pte. Joseph E.
Gaudet, Sergt. Frank, M.M. (Bar.)
Gaudreau, Pte. Isidore
Gauthier, Pte. Frank

Geoffroy, Pte. Joel Aime
Gervais, Lieut. Joseph A.
Gibson, Pte. Thomas D.
Gidony, Lieut. Francesco
Gifford, Pte. Allan
Gilbert, Corp. Grantley
Gilbert, Pte. John Oliver
Gillespie, Pte. Archibald James
Gingras, Pte. Joseph O.
Gionais, Pte. Benjamin
Godsall, Pte. Alfred
Goedike, Pte. Louis
Golding, Pte. Lyman E.
Goodman, Pte. Bert
Goodman, Pte. Walter
Goodwin, Pte. Francis
Gorrell, Corp. Richard
Goss, Pte. William J. B.
Goudal, Pte. Peter J.
Goudreau, Pte. Alfred
Goudreau, Pte. Flavien
Gough, Pte. Howard
Gould, Sergt. Albert E.
Goulet, Pte. Joseph
Govang, Pte. John E.
Grace, Pte. William
Gracie, Pte. Robert L.
Grant, Pte. Robert W.
Grant, Corp. William
Gratton, Pte. Donat
Gratton, Pte. Joseph U. C.
Gravel, Pte. Edmond
Graves, Pte. James Henry (correct name John E. Devlin)
Gray, Pte. Austin
Gray, Pte. William
Green, Pte. Arthur J.
Green, Pte. Francis J.
Green, Pte. Robert Henry
Grey, Pte. Anthony
Greenfield, Pte. Thomas E.
Greenway, Lance-Corp. Samuel T.
Gregory, Lance-Corp. George H.
Grondin, Lieut. Maurice M.
Groves, Pte. William S.
Guertin, Pte. Joseph Antoine
Gutteridge, Pte. Leslie A.

Hackett, Pte. Michael J.

HONOUR ROLL

Hackney, Pte. Frederick
Hadfield, Pte. Arthur
Haldeman, Pte. Frederick
Hale, Pte. Corrie
Hall, Pte. Robert
Hall, Pte. Robert B.
Hallett, Pte. Arden Roy
Hamblet, Pte. Thomas
Hamilton, Pte. James H.
Hamm, Pte. William W.
Hammill, Pte. Thomas P.
Hammond, Pte. Frank J.
Hancock, Sergt. Matthew J.
Handrahan, Pte. Barney
Hann, Pte. William E.
Hanson, Lance-Corp. Walter L.
Harbus, Pte. Thomas
Harding, Pte. Thomas S.
Harper, Pte. McDonald F.
Havill, Pte. William
Hawkins, Pte. Samuel
Hawley, Pte. Herman E.
Hayhurst, Corp. Cornelius
Haylock, Pte. George Edward
Hazelgrove, Lance-Corp. Arthur W.
Hazlett, Pte. Francis
Heather, Pte. Fred William
Henders, Pte. Wilfred E.
Hetu, Pte. James
Heuston, Lieut. Francis Robert
Hewison, Pte. Ivan
Hicklin, Pte. Charles H.
Higginson, Corp. Harry S.
Hilberg, Pte. Harold O.
Hind, Pte. James
Hirshuk, Pte. H.
Hixon, Pte. James J.
Hoare, Lance-Sergt. John William
Hockley, Pte. Henry
Hodgen, Pte. William
Holliday, Major William J., M.C.
Hollis, Pte. Henry E.
Holman, Pte. A.
Hooper, Pte. Ellis
Hooppel, Pte. James H.
Hornett, Pte. Albert J.
Horton, Pte. Alfred
Houle, Pte. Henri
Howe, Lieut. John
Howgego, Pte. Arthur W.

Hughes, Pte. William
Huke, Lance-Corp. John William
Hulekowich, Pte. John
Humphreys, Pte. Albert Edward
Humphreys, Pte. Mark
Hunking, Pte. Haviland H. H.
Hunt, Pte. Charles E.
Hunt, Sergt. Henry
Hurley, Lieut. Francis Joseph, D.C.M.
Hyman, Lieut. Eugene N.

Iles, Pte. Harold Edward

Jagoe, Pte. Hugh A.
James, Pte. Samuel F.
Jarvis, Pte. John D.
Jennings, Pte. Frederick S.
Jennings, Pte. Thomas
Jensen, Pte. Jens P.
Jimmo, Pte. William, M.M.
Johnson, Pte. Lionel William
Johnson, Sergt. Michael, M.M.
Johnson, Pte. William H.
Johnston, Pte. George E.
Johnston, Pte. James
Jones, Pte. Arthur
Jones, Pte. Arthur Stanley
Jones, Sergt. David
Jones, Pte. George
Jones, Pte. James
Juckes, Pte. Richard S.
Judge, Pte. Raymond Harry
Juett, Lance-Corp. Daniel W.

Kalabza, Sergt. William
Kearney, Pte. John H.
Kearns, Pte. Melville C.
Kearns, A/Sergt. Raymond
Keefe, Pte. Michael J.
Keen, Pte. Percy
Keen, Pte. Reuben C.
Keenan, Pte. Harry
Kehoe, Pte. Thomas
Keiller, Pte. William A.
Kelly, Pte. William
Kemp, Pte. Cyril John
Kennan, Pte. William James

Kennedy, Pte. Harold M.
Kennedy, Pte. Frederick
Kenny, Pte. Francis
Kenyon, Pte. George
Kilch, Pte. Alexander
Kindred, Lance-Corp. Louis A.
King, Sergt. Ernest W.
King, Lance-Corp. John, M.M.
Kingsley, Lance-Corp. Charles E.
Kinlock, Pte. Frank
Kirkconnell, Lieut. Walter Allison
Kiss, Pte. Albert G.
Knight, Pte. William A.
Knott, Pte. Francis

Lacroix, Lance-Corp. Louis S.
Laframboise, Pte. Willie
Laird, Pte. William A.
Lambert, Pte. John
Lancaster, Lance-Corp. Thomas A. V.
Langevin, Pte. Ovila
Langlois, Pte. J. Raoul
LaPierre, Pte. Albert M.
Lapointe, Pte. Charles
Larisey, Pte. John
Lariviere, Lance-Corp. Louis J.
Larocque, Pte. Charles
Laurent, Pte. Georges
Laurie, Pte. James R.
Laurin, Pte. Horace
Lavigne, Pte. Robert
Lavis, Pte. Arthur
Lavoie, Pte. Alphonse J.
Lavoie, Pte. Paul E.
Lawler, Pte. Thomas
Lawton, Pte. Eustace
Leashuk, Pte. Karp
Leavitt, Pte. Henry J.
Lebrun, Pte. Wilfred
Leclair, Sergt. Joseph
LeClair, Pte. Lemuel
LeCornu, Pte. Philip F.
Lecrau, Pte. William
Leduc, Lance-Corp. Donat
Lee, Pte. John
Lefebvre, Pte. Lorenzo
Lefler, Pte. Marshall
Legault, Pte. Paul E.
Legge, Pte. Robert E.

Leggett, Pte. Albert
Lemay, Pte. Alfred
Lemay, Pte. Henry
Leonard, Pte. Frederick
Lepine, Sergt. Eugene
Lesage, Sergt. Paul
Leslie, Pte. Richard
Lessard, Pte. Joseph R.
Leveille, Pte. Albert
Levesque, Pte. Henri
Levesque, Pte. Walter
Lewis, Pte. Arthur J.
Lewis, Pte. David
Lewis, Pte. William T.
Leyland, Lance-Corp. George H.
Libby, Pte. Harry W.
Linelberg, Pte. Yaakim Gerhart
Lister, Pte. Robert Winfield
Little, Corp. Roy F.
Littlejohn, Pte. Arthur
Livingood, Pte. Warren
Lloyd, Pte. Leslie M.
Lockett, Lance-Corp. Levi
Lockwood, Pte. Hubert F.
Lomax, Pte. Cyril Charles
Long, Pte. Irven
Lord, Pte. Joseph
Loup, Corp. Alexander
Lovette, Pte. Derrek
Low, Pte. Walter Cecil
Lowe, Pte. Charles
Lowrie, Pte. Lester
Lucasevitch, Pte. Ivan
Lupien, Pte. Valaire
Lynds, Pte. Berry
Lyons, Lance-Corp. Charles
Lyttle, Pte. Robert

MacDonald, Pte. Donald A.
MacDonald, Pte. Robert Graham
MacDougall, Pte. James
MacIntyre, Pte. Gordon C.
MacLean, Pte. James
MacLeod, Pte. James Howard
MacRae, Pte. Samuel Finley
Madden, Pte. Fred.
Magnan, Pte. Adelard
Maher, Pte. Michael
Mahoney, Lance-Corp. Patrick

HONOUR ROLL

Major. Lieut. Albert Frederick
Makepeace, Pte. Lionel E.
Maltby, Pte. Arthur
Manks, Lance-Corp. George
Manley, Pte. Percy E.
Mann, Pte. Sifton
Manusar, Pte. Harry
March, Pte. Herbert
Marcotte, Pte. Aime
Markham, Sergt. Frederick A.
Marshall, Sergt. Charles
Marshall, A/Sergt. Clarence
Marshall, Pte. John R.
Martin, Corp. Alfred Henry
Martin, Pte. Edward
Martin, Pte. Fidele J.
Martin, Pte. Frederick C.
Martin, Pte. John
Martin, Pte. Joseph
Martin, Pte. Thomas J.
Massey, Pte. Francois X.
Matheson, Pte. Angus Samuel
Matheson, Pte. Frederick
Mathews, Pte. George Clarence
Matthews, Pte. Alonzo
Matthews, Pte. John
Mattocks, Pte. George
May, Sergt. Francis Lorne
May, Lance-Corp. William
May, Pte. William Henry
Mayes, Pte. Harold Elmer
Maynard, Pte. Frank Charles
McAlpine, Pte. Albert
McArthur, Pte. Harry
McArthur, Sergt. William C., M.M.
McAssey, Lance-Sergt. George H., M.M.
McAuley, Pte. Peter A., M.M. (No. 444189)
McAuley, Pte. Peter A. (No. 713048)
McAvoy, Pte. Michael
McBurney, Pte. Fred William
McCall, Pte. Arthur Earl
McCallum, Pte. James F.
McCann, Pte. Philip
McClentic, Pte. Cyrus William
McColl, Pte. Daniel Hose
McCormack, Sergt. John
McCormack, Pte. Michael John
McCormick, Pte. Daniel

McCormick, Pte. Hugh R.
McCombs, Pte. Frederick G.
McCurdie, Pte. William
McCusker, Pte. Pat
McDavitt, Lance-Corp. James
McDiarmaid, Pte. James
McDonald, Pte. Duncan
McDonald, Pte. Malcolm
McDonald, Pte. William H.
McDuff, Pte. Eusebe
McFarland, Pte. Walter
McFern, Pte. Thomas E.
McGarry, Pte. Jack
McGeachy, Lance-Corp. Duncan
McGillivray, Pte. James
McGowan, Pte. Thomas
McGuigan, Corp. Samuel
McGuire, Pte. James
McKay, Pte. David
McKean, Pte. William B.
McKeegan, Pte. James
McKell, Pte. Fred.
McKenna, Pte. Peter Joseph
McKenzie, Lance-Corp. George C., M.M.
McKinnon, Lance-Corp. Allan J.
McKinnon, Pte. Daniel N.
McKinnon, Sergt. John Rose, M.M.
McKnight, Pte. William J.
McLaren, Pte. William D.
McLean, Lieut. Archibald L., M.C., D.C.M.
McLean, Pte. Charles
McLennan, Pte. John A.
McLennan, Pte. William
McLeod, Pte. Angus A.
McLeod, Pte. Jack
McLeod, Pte. Kenneth A.
McMahon, Pte. Samuel
McMann, Pte. Leslie
McNaughton, Pte. George Andrew
McNaughton, Pte. Peter
McNulty, Pte. John Henry L.
McPhail, Pte. Neil
McQuarrie, Pte. James A.
McQuarrie, Pte. John
McRae, Pte. Alexander R.
McTurk, Pte. John G.
Melanson, Pte. Joseph
Mellson, Pte. William C.

Melnik, Pte. Ivan
Mercer, Corp. George Herbert
Messier, Pte. Hector
Metelka, Pte. Alexander
Metherell, Pte. Edward
Mildon, Pte. Bronson
Mildon, Pte. James R.
Miller, Pte. Herbert L.
Miller, Pte. James P.
Miller, Pte. Samuel John
Miller, Pte. William S.
Milloy, Pte. Mathew
Mills, Lieut. John
Mitchell, Pte. Charles A.
Mitchell, Pte. Henri
Mitchell, Pte. Patrick
Mitchell, Pte. Roy T. (correct name R. T. Berryhill)
Mitchell, Pte. Stanley
Mitchell, Sergt. Thomas
Moffatt, Pte. Morley Everd
Molt, Pte. Charles M.
Mondeau, Pte. Clinton
Monk, Pte. George H.
Moody, Pte. Richard
Moon, Pte. Percy D.
Mooney, Corp. James
Moore, Pte. Alexander W.
Moore, Sergt. Thomas
Moran, Pte. John
More, Pte. Harold
Morgan, Pte. Ernest A.
Morgan, Pte. George
Morin, Pte. Alfred
Morris, Pte. Reginald J.
Morrison, Pte. Edward Roy
Morrison, Pte. Frederick W.
Morrison, Pte. Harry
Morrison, Pte. John
Morrison, Pte. John H.
Morrison, Pte. Joseph
Morrow, Pte. Lorance Thomas
Morrow, Pte. William W.
Morvan, Pte. Herne
Moss, Pte. William
Movshuk, Pte. Demetre
Muir, Pte. Archie
Mulholland, Pte. Robert
Mundy, Pte. Thomas
Munn, Pte. Archibald

Munn, Pte. Percy J.
Murchison, Pte. John M.
Murphy, Pte. Arthur
Murphy, Pte. Frank
Murray, Pte. Alexander
Murray, Pte. Barnard
Murray, Pte. Clarence
Murray, Pte. Hector
Murray, Pte. John
Murray-Browne, Pte. Orde
Murtagh, Pte. Lawrence
Musgrove, Pte. Marshall T.
Mustchin, Pte. Harold
Muttart, Pte. Edward
Muttart, Pte. Ernest
Muttart, Corp. Jesse E., **M.M.**
Myles, Pte. Thomas J. E. B.

Nadin, Pte. Chris
Neil, Pte. James S.
Neilson, Lieut. Frank Kenny
Nelson, Pte. Linder
Nesbitt, Lance-Corp. George
Newby, Pte. John
Nicholls, Pte. Percy Henry
Newton, Pte. Bernard
Nicholson, Pte. Raymond
Nightingale, Pte. Wilfred J.
Nikitin, Pte. Feofilak
Nirenberg, Pte. Israel
Niven, Pte. Alexander
Noble, Pte. Nelson A.
Noonan, Pte. William
Norton, Lance-Corp. Cecil **H**.
Noyles, Pte. Walter George
Nuttall, Pte. Herbert
Nutting, Pte. John

O'Brien, Pte. Thomas P.
Officer, Pte. William
O'Grady, Lance-Corp. John J.
O'Kane, Pte. Daniel
Osgood, Pte. Wilfred J.
O'Sullivan, Pte. James
Ouellette, Pte. Dieudonné

Packer, Pte. John
Pake, Pte. John

HONOUR ROLL

Paquette, Pte. Leme
Paquin, Pte. Leopold
Paradis, Pte. Alfred
Paradis, Pte. E.
Paradis, Pte. Joseph
Parker, A/Corp. **Charles W.**
Parker, Pte. George
Parkinson, Pte. Charles
Parry, Pte. Bernard H.
Parsons, Pte. George
Patch, Pte. Charles N.
Pate, Pte. Sidney
Paul, Pte. George W.
Pavluchuk, Pte. Tony
Payment, Pte. John H.
Penford, Pte. Albert
Penny, Capt. Edward G. T., M.C.
Pepin, Lance-Corp. Donat
Perrins, C.S.M. John Walter
Peters, Pte. Frank
Petrie, Lance-Corp. Alexander, **M.M.**
Philip, Pte. Alexander E.
Piché, Pte. William Edward
Pickard, Pte. Albert D.
Pickup, Capt. Walter W.
Pierce, Pte. William W.
Pike, Pte. Edwin J.
Pimblett, Pte. Alfred
Place, Pte. Charles S.
Planche, Pte. Norman E.
Platt, Pte. Richard
Plow, Major Arthur, M.C., M.M.
Plumadore, Pte. Charles
Plumridge, Pte. Joseph
Pogson, Pte. Victor
Poirier, Pte. Auguste
Poitras, Pte. Anthime
Pope, Sergt. Alfred J.
Pope, Lieut. **Jerry Gordon**
Portelance, Pte. Joseph
Porter, Pte. Frank A., **M.M.**
Portsmouth, Corp. Eldon E.
Potterton, Pte. David
Potvin, Pte. Louis Victor
Poulton, Pte. Alfred J.
Povar, Pte. Simson
Powell, Major Alan Torrence, D.S.O.
Powney, Pte. Robert
Pratt, Lance-Corp. Bertie James
Pratt, Pte. Daniel Burns

Pratt, Pte. Mark A.
Presant, Pte. Bert
Preshong, Pte. Bert
Prevost, Pte. Frank
Prevost, Pte. Theophile
Price, Corp. **Henry James**
Price, Pte. Richard
Prince, Pte. Lawrence
Prockson, Pte. **Edwin Charles**
Procter, Pte. Herbert
Purcell, Pte. Francis

Quick, Pte. Harold Ewart

Raby, Pte. Arthur G.
Racette, Pte. Jean B. F.
Raggett, Pte. Sidney
Ramsay, Sergt. Alexander
Rankin, C.S.M. **Richard William**
Rattigan, Pte. John P.
Raverty, Pte. Joseph J.
Rawson, Pte. Arthur
Ray, Pte. Arnold
Ray, Pte. Charles N.
Reddall, Pte. Frank
Reddicliffe, Pte. Frederick
Reid, Pte. Walter
Reid, Pte. William
Richard, Lieut. **Lawrence Brown**
Richmond, Pte. Reginald **A. A.**
Riggall, Pte. Edward
Riopel, Pte. Josephat
Roberts, Pte. Frederick
Roberts, Pte. **John**
Robertson, Pte. Edmund
Robertson, Pte. Ian
Robertson, Pte. John C.
Robertson, Pte. Norman H.
Robey, Corp. Leonard
Robinson, Pte. Thomas
Rogers, Pte. Gerald A., **M.M.**
Rogers, Pte. Walter J. T.
Rolfe, Pte. Reginald N.
Rose, Pte. Gaston
Ross, Lieut. Gordon Knox
Ross, Pte. William
Rouleau, Pte. Benjamin
Rousseau, Sergt. Joseph, M.M.

Rowbotham, A/Corp. Walter
Rowland, Pte. Hubert L.
Roy, Pte. Arthur
Roy, Pte. Donat
Roy, Pte. John H.
Russell, Lance-Sergt. Fred
Russell, Lance-Corp. George F.
Russell, Pte. James
Ryan, Pte. Ernest
Ryan, Pte. Herman
Ryan, Pte. Patrick

Sadgrove, Pte. Edgar
Sage, Pte. Samuel C. (correct name Ernest G. F. Fielder)
St. Denis, Pte. Oliver
St. Laurent, Pte. Adelard
Sambell, Pte. Thomas George
Sanders, Pte. Thomas H.
Sanders, Pte. Richard I.
Sant, Pte. William
Saunders, Pte. Ernest W.
Schoumik, Pte. Serva
Schuler, Pte. Joseph
Schuler, Pte. Theodore
Scott, Pte. Cecil Edgar
Scott, Corp. Robert, M.M.
Scott, Pte. Robert L.
Seale, Pte. Wilbert Thomas
Seely, Pte. Wesley N.
Seguin, Pte. Antonio
Shanks, Pte. Alexander
Shannon, Pte. Howard Alex.
Sharp, Lieut. Wylie
Shaw, Major Allan Crawford
Shelding, Pte. Harvey
Shepard, Pte. Alvie Skinner
Sherar, Pte. William D.
Shergold, Pte. Frederick
Sheridan, Pte. Philip
Sheridan, Pte. William J.
Shirco, Pte. Fred
Short, Pte. George P.
Silke, Pte. Joseph H.
Sime, Pte. John
Simmons, Pte. Harmon J.
Simpson, Pte. Arnold
Sinfield, Pte. Alfred
Sirett, Pte. Bert K.

Skilton, Pte. George H.
Slater, Lance-Corp. Thomas
Slater, Pte. Richard
Smith, Sergt. Albert Ernest
Smith, Pte. Alexander
Smith, Pte. Bertram H.
Smith, Pte. Charles
Smith, Pte. James
Smith, Pte. John
Smith, Pte. Marshall
Smith, Pte. Melvin T.
Smith, Pte. Norman M.
Smith, Pte. Percy J.
Smith, Pte. Roy A. M.
Smith, Pte. Walter E.
Smith, Pte. William J.
Smith, Pte. William W.
Snow, Pte. John T.
Soady, Pte. George P.
Southorn, Pte. Norman
Sparrow, Pte. Francis R., M.M.
Sparrow, Pte. Robert
Speers, Pte. George
Spiers, A/Sergt. Robert
Spiggs, Pte. Albert E.
Spurr, Pte. Edwin Leon
Stairs, Capt. Gavin Lang
Stairs, Lieut. George William
Stanton, Pte. James R.
Staples, Pte. Edwin Alfred
Steacie, Capt. Richard
Steele, Pte. Eric Gauntlett
Steeves, Pte. Malcolm A.
Stephens, Pte. Richard E.
Stevenson, Lieut. James Lloyd
Stewart, Pte. George Alexander
Stewart, Pte. Leon Benson
Stigepcich, Pte. Arsen
Stuart, Pte. Ralph B.
Stumpf, Pte. Herbert
Suberville, Pte. Auguste
Sullivan, Pte. James
Sullivan, Sergt. John
Sullivan, Pte. William
Sumption, Major John F.
Sussens, Pte. Fred C.
Swann, Lance-Corp. Harold H.
Swift, Corp. Fred
Swift, Corp. George
Swindlehurst, Lance-Corp. Arthur

HONOUR ROLL

Swindley, Pte. Douglas
Syder, Pte. Sydney
Sylvester, Lieut. George M.
Symonds, Lieut. Herbert Boyd

Taillfer, Pte. Joseph
Tapp, Pte. Adolphis
Tardy, Pte. Robert W.
Taylor, Pte. Charles N.
Taylor, Pte. John G.
Taylor, Sergt. Wellesley S.
Teahen, Pte. Michael
Theriault, Pte. Nectaire
Therrien, Pte. Ismail Theophile
Thibault, Pte. Alcide
Thimot, Pte. Odelpha
Thomas, Sergt. Thomas
Thompson, Pte. Henri O.
Thompson, Capt. Henry Aubrey
Thompson, Pte. Robert William
Thompson, Pte. Samuel
Thompson, Pte. Thomas
Thomson, Pte. George
Thomson, Pte. Roland F.
Tipler, A/Corp. Harry
Toirier, Pte. Odelon
Tope, Pte. Whitney
Topping, Pte. Alexander
Torrance, Pte. John
Trapnell, Pte. Donald M.
Trott, Pte. William
Turley, Sergt. George
Turner, Pte. Edward
Turner, Pte. Walter
Turner, Sergt. William (No. 25774)
Turner, Lance-Corp. William (No. 25652)
Turner, Pte. William Charles
Turner, Pte. William H.
Twaddle, Pte. Alexander

Vaillant, Pte. Hector
Vaulson, Pte. Charles
Vigneault, Pte. Theophile
Von Berg, Pte. Leslie C.
Vosburgh, Pte. Ernest

Walker, Pte. John
Walker, Lance-Corp. William F.

Wallace, Pte. Walfred J.
Wallis, Pte. Albert
Wallis, Sergt. Alexander
Walsh, Pte. Harrison Henry
Warbrook, Pte. Thomas
Ward, Pte. Albert E.
Ward, Pte. John W.
Wareham, Pte. John
Warminton, Major John Nicol
Watson, Lieut. Basil M.
Weatherbie, Pte. Francis C.
Weir, Sergt. Joseph
Wells, Sergt. Arthur
Wells, A/Sergt. Harry W.
West, Pte. Arthur
West, Pte. Bill Jim
West, Pte. Lewis E.
Wharton, Pte. J. A.
Wheaton, Pte. Arnold H.
Whitby, Pte. Charles D. B.
Whitehead, Capt. Edward Ashworth
Whitehead, Pte. Frank E.
Whiting, Pte. Edward
Whitton, Pte. George
Wiffin, Pte. Frederick
Wilcox, Pte. Clement James
Wilcox, Pte. Harry (correct name Harry Smith)
Wilkinson, Corp. John F.
Williams, Pte. Frederick
Williamson, Capt. George Massey
Williamson, Pte. Hugh Stephen
Wilson, Pte. William
Wilson, Pte. William O.
Winter, Pte. Robert
Winton, Pte. David
Wiseman, Pte. Edouard
Wood, Pte. John Thomas
Woodforde, Pte. Walter
Woodrow, Pte. William
Woods, Pte. Ernest
Woods, Pte. John Henry
Woodwards, Pte. Robert J.
Wragg, Sergt. Herbert
Wright, Pte. William
Wyatt, Pte. Herbert V.

Young, Pte. Frank E.
Young, Pte. Lester B.

Young, Lance-Corp. Wendell H.
Young, Pte. William H.
Zachareviez, Pte. Sirge
Ziegler, Pte. Frederick

ACCIDENTALLY KILLED

Condey, Pte. John
Curry, Pte. Alexander
Duseigne, Pte. Armand
Hudson, Pte. Charles
Lapointe, Pte. Lucien
Martel, Pte. Maurice
McDonald, Pte. William
Myers, Pte. Roy
Peek, Pte. Richard A.
Robertson, Pte. Harry
Robitaille, Pte. Maurice
Trudel, Pte. Urbain

DIED OF ILLNESS WHILST PRISONER OF WAR

Coughlin, Pte. James M.
Denevers, Lance-Corp. Henry
Maughan, Pte. Edgar E.

DIED

Aitcheson, Pte. James
Anderson, Pte. Daniel H.
Anderson, Pte. James J.
Arel, Pte. Odilon
Ashe, Pte. Ralph
Beauchemin, Corp. Napoleon
Benson, Pte. Charles
Buchanan, Pte. John Alexander
Callaghan, Pte. John
Campbell, Pte. William G.
Chandler, Pte. John K.
Chittleburgh, Pte. George
Corkill, Pte. Cecil
Croteau, Pte. Albert
Dalton, Pte. Martin
Dorman, Pte. Wesley H.
Dupuis, Pte. Weller
Gray, Pte. Thomas
Haines, Pte. Harry Albert
Harding, Pte. Fred
Harrison, Pte. Robert B.
Hartley, Pte. William H.
Hartwick, Pte. Herbert
Hayes, Pte. Frank
Hinton, Pte. Albert
Ingalls, Pte. Ernest
Johnstone, Pte. George L.
Kirtland, Lance-Corp. Allan F.
Laforce, Pte. Paul
MacDonald, Pte. John
Malcolm, Pte. Alex.
Manderson, Pte. Gordon W.
McDonald, Pte. Ewen
McGrath, Pte. Edward
Morrison, Pte. Allan
Murray, Pte. Albert
O'Donohue, Pte. John M.
Patterson, Pte. Leo
Pichette, Pte. Stanislas
Quirk, Pte. Patrick J.
Randall, Corp. Arthur S.
Reid, Pte. Allan M.
Robertson, Pte. J. W. Russell
Ross, Sergt. Samuel S.
Sarrazin, Pte. Joseph
Shenfield, Pte. William
Smith, Pte. Albert
Thompson, Pte. Frank
Twamley, Pte. C. J.
Urwin, Pte. Alexander
Walker, C.S.M. Charles
Watters, Pte. James
Williams, Pte. Frank

APPENDIX B

The Royal Montreal Regiment

HONOURS AND AWARDS

14th Battalion, C.E.F.

THE VICTORIA CROSS

Lieut.-Col. F. A. C. Scrimger
(Medical Officer)

Capt. George Burdon McKean

THE DISTINGUISHED SERVICE ORDER AND BAR

Lieut.-Col. Dick Worrall

THE DISTINGUISHED SERVICE ORDER

Brig.-Gen. R. P. Clark, M.C.
Lieut.-Col. W. W. Burland
Lieut.-Col. Gault McCombe

Major Robert C. MacKenzie
Major Alan T. Powell
Major C. B. Price

THE MILITARY CROSS AND BAR

Lieut.-Col. Dick Worrall
Major H. G. Brewer

Capt. J. W. Green
Capt. B. T. Jackson

THE MILITARY CROSS

Lieut.-Col. William J. McAlister
  (Medical Officer)
Major David W. Clarkson
Major Bernard F. Davidson
Major W. J. Holliday
Major J. E. McKenna
Major Arthur Plow
Major C. G. Power
Capt. W. E. Beaton
Capt. J. C. K. Carson
Capt. W. S. Collins
Capt. Edwin Cowen
Capt. Thomas Hodgson
Capt. A. T. Howell
Capt. George B. McKean
Capt. John Patterson
Capt. E. G. T. Penny

Capt. Victor Quelch
Capt. C. E. Tuttle
Capt. Daniel Woodward
Lieut. R. J. Allan
Lieut. Gordon Beattie
Lieut. Henry Campbell
Lieut. Arthur Close
Lieut. E. C. Gough
Lieut. Sydney McEwen
Lieut. A. L. McLean
Lieut. D. M. McRae
Lieut. G. B. Murray
Lieut. B. A. Neville
Lieut. H. N. Pitcher
Lieut. J. G. Pullar
Lieut. H. H. Robinson
Lieut. R. A. Stewart

THE DISTINGUISHED CONDUCT MEDAL AND BAR

A/Coy. Sergt.-Major John Foley   Sergt. Harry Weeks

THE DISTINGUISHED CONDUCT MEDAL

Major C. B. Price
Capt. W. A. Bonshor
Capt. Edwin Cowen
Capt. J. W. Green
Capt. J. M. Stephenson
Lieut. W. J. Bucklee
Lieut. Arthur Close
Lieut. W. G. Hill
Lieut. F. J. Hurley
Lieut. Joseph Labelle
Lieut. C. R. Lennan
Lieut. A. L. McLean
Lieut. A. R. Snow
Reg. Sergt.-Major Wilfred Farnell
A/Reg. Sergt.-Major Arthur Handcock
Coy. Sergt-Major D. M. Robinson
A/Coy. Sergt.-Major H. C. Byce
A/Coy. Sergt.-Major Gilbert Fairbairn
A/Coy. Sergt.-Major Daniel Thompson
C.Q.M.S. Percy Little
C.Q.M.S. B. J. Topham
Sergt. Bertram Brayton
Sergt. Frank Burke
Sergt. A. E. Chatwin
Sergt. P. H. Crockett
Sergt. R. H. Drake
Sergt. John Driscoll
Sergt. W. R. Duncan
Sergt. G. W. Logan
Sergt. Joseph Williams
Corp. W. P. Adams
Corp. C. W. McCall
Lance-Corp. C. A. Elliott
Pte. Claude Blakeman
Pte. J. G. Erskine
Pte. R. H. Jones
Pte. J. A. MacDonald
Pte. J. R. Mallette
Pte. A. B. Smith
Pte. C. V. Tuttle

THE MERITORIOUS SERVICE MEDAL

Sergt. W. A. Burrell
Sergt. W. G. Stevens
Pte. James Hayward

THE MILITARY MEDAL AND TWO BARS

Corp. Frank N. Jerome

THE MILITARY MEDAL AND BAR

Capt. Thomas Hodgson
Lieut. Henry Campbell
Lieut. Joseph Labelle
Coy. Sergt.-Major W. M. Miller
A/Coy. Sergt.-Major A. J. Jacques
Sergt. Robert W. Baum
Sergt. R. E. Carpenter
Sergt. Frank Gaudet
Sergt. J. C. McCowan
Sergt. George Munro
Sergt. S. E. Record
Lance-Sergt. Michael D'Arcy
Corp. Hercule Bureau
Corp. Steven Medai
Corp. W. S. Whitehead
Lance-Corp. A. R. Smith
Lance-Corp. Fred West
Pte. H. F. Atkin
Pte. Laurence Christie
Pte. S. B. Clarke
Pte. George Lindsay
Pte. F. H. A. Mundy
Pte. C. A. Sherman

HONOURS AND AWARDS

THE MILITARY MEDAL

Major Arthur Plow
Capt. George B. McKean
Lieut. R. J. Allan
Lieut. W. A. Burrell
Lieut. G. H. MacDonald
Lieut. G. A. McLellan
A/Coy. Sergt.-Major Lawrence Driscoll
A/Coy. Sergt.-Major Thomas Duffin
A/Coy. Sergt.-Major John Foley
C.Q.M.S. R. A. Bagshaw
A/C.Q.M.S. H. F. Michel
A/C.Q.M.S. William Peat
Sergt. Herbert Arnold
Sergt. W. E. Barnaby
Sergt. George Berryman
Sergt. W. J. Bone
Sergt. Frank Burke
Sergt. A. E. Chatwin
Sergt. J. W. Chivers
Sergt. Robert Cowley
Sergt. A. E. Cowling
Sergt. William Craib.
Sergt. John Driscoll
Sergt. Antonio Dubé
Sergt. E. A. Endersby
Sergt. Harry Evans
Sergt. Richard Hill
Sergt. Michael Johnson
Sergt. H. T. Jordon
Sergt. G. J. Kelly
Sergt. Robert Lewis
Sergt. G. B. MacDonald
Sergt. J. A. Magneison
Sergt. W. C. McArthur
Sergt. Daniel Moreau
Sergt. J. R. McKinnon
Sergt. J. H. O'Brien
Sergt. Fred Pickup
Sergt. Herbert Readshaw
Sergt. Joseph Rousseau
Sergt. E. S. Taylor
Sergt. Henri Thibault
Sergt. F. J. Thibodeau
Lance-Sergt. Arthur Dobson
Lance-Sergt. G. H. McAssey
Lance-Sergt. Donald McDonald
A/Sergt. G. B. Barbour
A/Sergt. R. W. Grey

A/Sergt. William Williamson
Corp. W. P. Adams
Corp. E. F. Allan
Corp. J. D. Anderson
Corp. J. A. Bertram
Corp. G. C. Broadbent
Corp. C. E. Buchanan
Corp. Thomas Chenard
Corp. Nicholas Daniels
Corp. L. D. Dewar
Corp. W. F. Ede
Corp. J. A. Grant
Corp. Donald Hume
Corp. J. H. Hurst
Corp. T. M. Kelly
Corp. H. C. P. Leaman
Corp. N. W. Lord
Corp. Jesse E. Muttart
Corp. P. T. Scott
Corp. Robert Scott
Corp. F. T. Shorten
Corp. C. V. Sifton
Corp. T. P. Steele
Corp. A. G. Tilton
Corp. William Watt
Lance-Corp. Daniel Black
Lance-Corp. H. H. Brown
Lance-Corp. P. H. Casey
Lance-Corp. C. E. Conrad
Lance-Corp. James Fotheringham
Lance-Corp. J. W. Hunt
Lance-Corp. L. J. Jack
Lance-Corp. C. C. Jones
Lance-Corp. John King
Lance-Corp. John McIvor
Lance-Corp. G. C. McKenzie
Lance-Corp. Clifford Moore
Lance-Corp. Edwin Newton
Lance-Corp. Alfred Norton
Lance-Corp. Alexander Petrie
Lance-Corp. Donald Smith
Lance-Corp. Isidore Theriault
Lance-Corp. John Thompson
Lance-Corp. J. E. Williams
A/Corp. W. J. Francis
A/Corp. Melvin Wheeler
Pte. William Allard
Pte. W. E. Atkins

Pte. H. P. Barker
Pte. L. H. Barrett
Pte. Alphonse Belanger
Pte. Reginald Bell
Pte. J. W. Bews
Pte. J. A. Birds
Pte. I. H. Bowden
Pte. G. B. Brewer
Pte. J. T. Burkitt
Pte. J. T. Butler
Pte. A. Cameron
Pte. F. X. Cardinal
Pte. James Chase
Pte. Walter Clark
Pte. Bartholomeu Coady
Pte. M. H. Conolly
Pte. David Crombie
Pte. Leonard Darbyson
Pte. Christopher Davis
Pte. V. S. B. Dawkes
Pte. Raymond Duval
Pte. J. G. Erskine
Pte. J. N. Gill
Pte. S. H. Graham
Pte. F. B. Groat
Pte. A. J. Grosfils
Pte. Walter Halbert
Pte. Frank Hannon
Pte. G. A. Hardiman
Pte. W. F. Harley

Pte. Alexander Hunter
Pte. A. B. Imray
Pte. William Jimmo
Pte. G. T. Lapworth
Pte. F. S. Lawson
Pte. A. D. MacTavish
Pte. George Mathews
Pte. P. A. McAuley (No. 444189)
Pte. John Melvin
Pte. Arthur Mercier
Pte. James Moonan
Pte. H. J. Morgan
Pte. Walter Morton
Pte. John Neilan
Pte. Louis Plouffe
Pte. F. A. Porter
Pte. W. M. Potter
Pte. B. R. Racey
Pte. H. S. Record
Pte. Robert Renton
Pte. Robert Roberts
Pte. G. A. Rogers
Pte. P. G. Rumball
Pte. C. M. Sherritt
Pte. G. C. Smith
Pte. F. R. Sparrow
Pte. William Stokes
Pte. S. J. Tatton
Pte. E. A. Walsh
Pte. A. T. West

MENTIONED IN DESPATCHES FOUR TIMES
Lieut.-Col. Gault McCombe

MENTIONED IN DESPATCHES TWICE
Lieut.-Col. Dick Worrall
Major R. C. MacKenzie
Major A. T. Powell

MENTIONED IN DESPATCHES

Brig.-Gen. R. P. Clark, M.C.
Brig.-Gen. F. S. Meighen
Lieut.-Col. W. W. Burland
Major C. B. Price
Capt. W. A. Bonshor
Capt. Thomas G. Beagley
Capt. Edwin Cowen
Capt. Benn T. Jackson
Capt. J. M. MacAdams
Capt. J. M. Stephenson

Lieut. E. C. Gough
Lieut. J. G. Pullar
Lieut. H. B. Symonds
Lieut. T. T. Wilson
A/Reg. Sergt.-Major Arthur Handcock
R.Q.M.S. Harry Reid
A/Coy. Sergt.-Major A. E. Hawkins
Sergt. Henry Chanu
Sergt. T. P. Creagh
Sergt. J. W. Yates

HONOURS AND AWARDS

BROUGHT TO THE NOTICE OF THE SECRETARY OF STATE FOR WAR

Sergt. A. L. Moodie

FOREIGN DECORATIONS

MEDAILLE MILITAIRE (French)

Capt. J. M. Stephenson
Lieut. F. J. Hurley
A/Coy. Sergt.-Major H. C. Byce

CROIX DE GUERRE (French)

Capt. J. M. MacAdams

LEGION D'HONNEUR—CROIX DE CHEVALIER (French)

Lieut. Henri Quintal

CROIX DE GUERRE (Belgian)

A/Coy. Sergt.-Major John Foley
Sergt. Henry Chanu

Lance-Corp. Bruce Cooper
Pte. Arthur H. Corney

MEDAL OF ST. GEORGE—THIRD CLASS (Russian)

Pte. Armand Barrette

CROSS OF ST. GEORGE—FOURTH CLASS (Russian)

Lieut.-Col. Dick Worrall

Pte. John J. Montague

APPENDIX C

HONOURS AND AWARDS

(Granted to officers and men of the 14th Battalion, Royal Montreal Regiment, following promotion or transfer to other units):

COMPANION OF THE ORDER OF ST. MICHAEL AND ST. GEORGE

Brig.-Gen. R. P. Clark, D.S.O., M.C. Brig.-Gen. F. S. Meighen

OFFICER OF THE ORDER OF THE BRITISH EMPIRE

Lieut.-Col. P. R. Hanson Major R. S. Smith
Lieut.-Col. T. R. MacKenzie Major F. W. Utton

THE DISTINGUISHED SERVICE ORDER

Lieut.-Col. Henri DesRosiers Lieut.-Col. R. W. Frost
Major G. E. Leighton

THE DISTINGUISHED FLYING CROSS AND BAR

Capt. C. F. Falkenberg

THE MILITARY CROSS

Major W. D. Adams Major R. H. Thomas (C.A.M.C.)
Major V. E. Duclos Capt. R. G. Marion
Major W. M. Pearce Capt. J. K. Nesbitt
Major C. F. C. Porteous Lieut. A. F. Shaw

THE DISTINGUISHED CONDUCT MEDAL AND BAR

Sergt. George L. Butterfield

THE DISTINGUISHED CONDUCT MEDAL

Reg. Sergt.-Major William Wallis Sergt. Edward C. Moorby
Coy. Sergt.-Major John H. Patton Lance-Sergt. Alexander Fernie
Sergt. Leonard D. Johnson Corp. Thomas G. Clarke

THE MERITORIOUS SERVICE MEDAL

R.Q.M.S. R. L. Bagshaw, M.M. A/Sergt.-Major A. P. Thwaites
R.Q.M.S. T. J. Kirkwood C.Q.M.S. J. S. Tracey
R.Q.M.S. George Tod Sergt. J. H. Harrison

HONOURS AND AWARDS

THE MILITARY MEDAL

Lieut. William Bailey
Lieut. R. G. H. W. MacCarthy
Lieut. G. W. Morrison
Coy. Sergt.-Major Andrew Pringle
Sergt. Gustaf Anderson
Sergt. W. E. Baker
Sergt. Ernest Van Alstyne
A/Sergt. R. C. Bailey
Corp. C. J. Nicholls
Corp. James Post

A/Corp. Milton Hanlan
Gunner Lester Beck
Pte. J. M. Boucher
Pte. C. F. Kinghorn
Pte. J. H. Mason
Pte. Henry Moran
Driver John Morrison
Pte. Arnold Smith
Pte. Joseph Thiviérge

MENTIONED IN DESPATCHES FOUR TIMES

Brig.-Gen. R. P. Clark, C.M.G., D.S.O., M.C.

MENTIONED IN DESPATCHES TWICE

Lieut.-Col. W. W. Burland, D.S.O.
Major W. M. Pearce, M.C.

Major F. W. Utton, O.B.E.
Capt. Frank Higginson

MENTIONED IN DESPATCHES

Brig.-Gen. F. S. Meighen, C.M.G.
Lieut.-Col. A. S. English
Lieut.-Col. Henri DesRosiers, D.S.O.
Lieut.-Col. R. W. Frost
Major W. D. Adams, M.C.
Major G. E. Leighton, D.S.O.

Major R. S. Smith, O.B.E.
Capt. S. G. Dixon
Capt. R. C. Lalor
Capt. G. F. Mason
Sergt. H. J. Goskar

BROUGHT TO THE NOTICE OF THE SECRETARY OF STATE FOR WAR TWICE

Lieut.-Col. F. W. Fisher
Major Rudolphe DeSerres
Major R. H. Thomas, M.C. (C.A.M.C.)

BROUGHT TO THE NOTICE OF THE SECRETARY OF STATE FOR WAR

Brig.-Gen. R. P. Clark, C.M.G., D.S.O., M.C.
Brig.-Gen. F. S. Meighen, C.M.G.
Lieut.-Col. W. W. Burland, D.S.O.
Lieut.-Col. Henri DesRosiers, D.S.O.
Lieut.-Col. R. W. Frost, D.S.O.
Lieut.-Col. P. R. Hanson, O.B.E.
Lieut.-Col. T. R. MacKenzie, O.B.E.
Major J. F. Adams
Major W. P. Oram

Capt. F. W. Lock
Capt. I. G. Robertson
Capt. R. deV. Terroux
Lieut. H. S. Duncan
Lieut. E. C. Morris
Lieut. G. F. Skelton
A/R.S.M. R. J. Boyd
A/R.S.M. T. J. Wallis
A/Sergt.-Major A. P. Thwaites
A/Sergt. Pierre Klein

FOREIGN DECORATIONS

LEGION D'HONNEUR—CROIX DE CHEVALIER (French)

Major Hercule Barré

CROIX DE GUERRE—AVEC ETOILE EN BRONZE (French)

Sergt. John R. Skinner

CROIX DE GUERRE (French)

Pte. Fréjus St. Hilaire

CROIX DE GUERRE (Belgian)

Major G. E. Leighton, D.S.O. Capt. G. F. Mason
Major R. S. Smith, O.B.E. Pte. James Watson

CROIX DE GUERRE (Czecho-Slovakian Republic)

Major J. F. Adams

APPENDIX D

COMMISSIONS

The following officers of the 14th Battalion, Royal Montreal Regiment, were commissioned after service in the Battalion ranks.

Lieut.-Col. Dick Worrall, D.S.O., M.C.
Major Gordon Ernest Leighton, D.S.O.
Major Robert C. MacKenzie, D.S.O.
Major Charles Basil Price, D.S.O., D.C.M.
A/Major Hugh Graham Brewer, M.C.
A/Major Richard Henry Hood
A/Major Arthur Plow, M.C., M.M.
Capt. Thomas G. Beagley
Capt. William A. Bonshor, D.C.M.
Capt. John W. Green, M.C., D.C.M.
Capt. Alfred T. Howell, M.C.
Capt. George B. McKean, V.C., M.C., M.M.
Capt. John K. Nesbitt, M.C.
Capt. John Patterson, M.C.
Capt. Victor Quelch, M.C.
Capt. John Rex Weaver
A/Capt. Edwin Cowen, M.C., D.C.M.
A/Capt. Stanley Humphries
A/Capt. Benn T. Jackson, M.C.
A/Capt. Archibald L. McLean, M.C., D.C.M.
A/Capt. John Myhoe Stephenson, D.C.M.
A/Capt. Christopher H. Sullivan
A/Capt. Daniel Woodward, M.C.
Lieut. Edward George Adams
Lieut. Robert J. Allan, M.C., M.M.
Lieut. Harry Andrews
Lieut. Harold Armstrong
Lieut. Aubrey Durant Brewer
Lieut. Henry Campbell, M.C., M.M.
Lieut. Charles P. R. Charlton
Lieut. Philippe Chevalier
Lieut. Arthur Close, M.C., D.C.M.
Lieut. Roy Ward Collver
Lieut. Percy Coombes
Lieut. Walter J. Cronk
Lieut. Henry A. Davin
Lieut. Ellis Evans
Lieut. Rae H. Filshill
Lieut. Joseph A. Gervais
Lieut. Ernest C. Gough, M.C.
Lieut. Frank Higginson
Lieut. Thomas Hodgson, M.C., M.M.
Lieut. John Howe
Lieut. Francis J. Hurley, D.C.M.
Lieut. William Kennedy
Lieut. Richard M. Lawton
Lieut. René Gustave Marion, M.C.
Lieut. Hugh A. McInnes
Lieut. George A. McLellan, M.M.
Lieut. Norman McLeod
Lieut. Frank Kenny Neilson
Lieut. Charles L. O'Brien
Lieut. Francis Owen
Lieut. Alfred D. C. Parnell
Lieut. Hubert N. Pitcher, M.C.
Lieut. James G. Pullar, M.C.
Lieut. Volney G. Rexford
Lieut. Albert Edward Scott
Lieut. Wylie Sharp
Lieut. Ray A. Stewart, M.C.
Lieut. Herbert Boyd Symonds
Lieut. James G. A. Thatcher
Lieut. Donald Urquhart
Lieut. Harry H. Whiteman

The following non-commissioned officers and men of the 14th Battalion, Royal Montreal Regiment, were granted commissions in units of the Canadian Expeditionary Force.

Bacque, Lance-Corp. Frederick (213th Battalion)
Bailey, Corp. William, M.M. (Canadian Machine Gun Corps)

Bucklee, Sergt. William J., D.C.M.   (Quebec Regiment)
Burrell, Sergt. William A., M.M.   (Quebec Regiment)

Chevalier, Pte. Pierre   (23rd Reserve and 22nd Battalions)
Clarke, Pte. Melville R.   (130th Battalion)
Cleghorn, Pte. Andrew G.   (Canadian Army Service Corps)
Crosier, Pte. Charles   (139th Battalion)

Dextrase, Pte. Rosario   (Reserve Units)
Diver, Lance-Corp. John W.   (Quebec Regiment)
Duncan, R.Q.M.S. Hugh St. C.   (23rd Reserve Battalion)

Edgell, Corp. Geoffery Stephen   (Reserve Units)

Ferguson, Sergt. William M.   (Reserve Units)
Forneri, Pte. David A.   (23rd Reserve and 73rd Battalions)

Gauthier, Sergt. Origene   (23rd Reserve Battalion)
Giroux, Corp. Joseph A.   (10th Reserve Battalion)
Glanvill, Pte. Mark   (Reserve Units and 85th Battalion)

Henry, Pte. Reginald B.   (Quebec Regiment)
Hill, Lance-Corp. William G., D.C.M.   (Quebec Regiment)
Howe, Lance-Corp. James E.   (Reserve Units)

Jackson, Pte. William H.   (Hon. Lieut. Canadian Army Pay Corps)

Jeffery, Pte. Edward   (17th Reserve and 16th Battalions)

Labelle, Sergt. Joseph, D.C.M., M.M.   (Reserve Units)
Lang, C.S.M. Daniel G. G.   (13th Reserve Battalion)
Leigh, Pte. Alfred   (Quebec Regiment)
Lennan, Sergt. Colin R., D.C.M.   (Reserve Units and Khaki University)
Lalor, Pte. Robert C.   (G.H.Q. 3rd Echelon)
Lock, Corp. Frederick W.   (Reserve Units)

MacCarthy, Pte. R. G. H. W., M.M.   (Canadian Machine Gun Corps)
MacDonald, Sergt. George H., M.M.   (Quebec Regiment)
Mason, Pte. George Francis   (17th Res., 25th, and 16th Battalions)
McConnell, Pte. Russell W.   (Quebec Regiment)
McCulley, Pte. Clarence C.   (145th Battalion)
Mitchell, Pte. Ernest S.   (Reserve Units)
Morgan, Pte. Edward F.   (23rd Reserve Battalion)
Morrison, Corp. George W., M.M.   (Reserve Units)
Murray, Pte. Robert McL.   (Reserve Units)

Oram, Sergt. William P.   (Hon. Major Pay Office, London and Ottawa)

Owens, Pte. Owen N. H.   (Quebec Regiment)

HONOURS AND AWARDS

Pain, Lance-Sergt. Alexander   (Canadian Army Pay Corps)

Radcliffe, Sergt. George H.   (Reserve Units)
Roche, Pte. Thomas J.   (Quebec Regiment)
Rooke, C.S.M. James A.   (87th Battalion, Can. Gren. Guards)

Sanders, Pte. Lionel A.   (242nd Battalion)
Shaw, Pte. Arthur F.   (Canadian Engineers)
Snow, Sergt. Augustus R., D.C.M.   (23rd Reserve Battalion)
Southin, Sergt. John William   (143rd and 29th Battalions)
Stewart, Pte. Robert H.   (Reserve Units)

Vining, Corp. John G.   (Quebec Regiment)

Waite, Pte. Bertram E.   (Manitoba Regiment)
Whelan, Sergt. Joseph E.   (Quebec Regiment)
Wilson, Sergt. Thomas T.   (Reserve Units)

Young, Sergt. Ralph Stuart   (23rd Reserve Battalion)

The following non-commissioned officers and men of the 14th Battalion, Royal Montreal Regiment, were granted commissions in the Imperial Army.

Barltrop, Lance-Corp. Arthur H.
Bishop, Pte. Earl H.
Bullick, Pte. Andrew
Burns, Pte. William B.
Butcher, Sergt. Herbert Cecil
Cameron, Pte. Francis B.
Crowther, Pte. Ronald
Dashwood, Pte. Henry Godfrey
Davidson, Lance-Corp. Ronald H.
Dion, Pte. Julien
Grant, Pte. John W.
Grummitt, Pte. Joseph R.
Henry, Pte. Alfred S.
Hopkins, Pte. Arthur E.
Johnston, Pte. Alexander L.
Jones, Pte. Richard A.
Laing, Pte. Harold J. G. (Indian Army)
Lane, Pte. Charles F.
Malone, Pte. Archie D.
O'Dell, Pte. Oliver H. C.
Pickthall, Pte. William R.
Rait, Corp. James M.
Robertson, Pte. Robert Ward S.
Russell, Pte. John Joseph
Savage, Pte. Ivan Burke
Schultz, Pte. Charles F.
Sharkie, Pte. Frederick W.
Slubicki, Pte. John
Taylor, Pte. Eric E. H.
Townsend, Pte. Hugh Vere
Turner, Pte. Arthur R.
Van Someren, Pte. Eric Cecil
Wingard, Pte. Hume S.

APPENDIX E

THE ROYAL MONTREAL REGIMENT
(14th BATTALION, C.E.F.)

ITINERARY

1914

August 24—Left Montreal. (By train.)
25—Arrived Valcartier.

September 30—Sailed from Quebec (on *S.S. Alaunia* and *S.S. Andania*).

October 3—Sailed from Gaspé Basin.
14—Arrived Devonport, England.
15—*Alaunia* Section disembarked (6.30 p.m.). Marched to Plymouth Station.
16—*Alaunia* Section entrained (12.45 a.m.). Reached Patney Station (dawn). Marched to Camp at West Down South.
18—*Andania* Section disembarked and entrained at Plymouth Station.
19—*Andania* Section arrived Patney Station. Marched to Camp at West Down South.

December 21—Moved to huts at Lark Hill.

1915

February 10—Left Lark Hill (9 p.m.). Entrained at Amesbury.
11—Arrived Avonmouth. Embarked Transport *Australind*.
12—Sailed from Avonmouth.
15—Arrived St. Nazaire, France.

ITINERARY

February 16—Left St. Nazaire by train (7 a.m.).
18—Arrived Hazebrouck (6 a.m.). Marched to Flêtre.
23—Left Flêtre (8 a.m.). Marched to Armentières.
24/28—Armentières. Platoons and H.Q. into Front Line.

March 2—Marched to Bac St. Maur.
3—Into Front Line. (Fleurbaix.)
6—Relieved. To Rue du Quesne. (Brig. Res.)
9—Into Front Line. Rue Petillon. (Fleurbaix.)
13—Relieved. To Rue du Quesne.
17—Into Front Line. Rue Petillon. (Fleurbaix.)
20—Relieved. To Rue du Quesne.
24—Into Front Line. Rue Petillon. (Fleurbaix.)
26—Relieved. To Estaires. (Rest Billets.)

April 7—Marched to Cassel.
15—To Steenvoorde.
16—Bus to Poperinghe. Into Front Line. (St. Julien.)
21—Relieved. To St. Julien and St. Jean.

THE BATTLES OF YPRES, 1915. (22 April-3 May.) (See text.)

May 1—In trenches on Yser Canal.
3—Relieved. To Transport Lines near Vlamertinghe (dawn).
4—Marched to near Bailleul. (Arriving at dawn, May 5.)
14—Marched to near Robecq. (Arriving 6.30 a.m., May 15.)
17—Marched to trenches at Le Touret. Later back to Essars.
18—Forward to trenches at Le Touret. Later forward to Indian Village.

BATTLE OF FESTUBERT. (19-22 May.) (See text.)

22—Relieved. To le Hamel.
26—Into the trenches. Festubert.
29—Relieved. To Rue de l'Epinette. (Reserve.)
31—To Oblinghem. (Rest Billets.)

THE ROYAL MONTREAL REGIMENT

June
: 6—Into the Line. (Givenchy.)
10—Relieved. To Bethune.
19—To Reserve Billets. (Beuvry.)
22—Into the Line. (Givenchy B3.)
24—Relieved. To Reserve Billets. (Beuvry.)
26—To Neuf Berquin. (Arriving 4 a.m., June 27.)
27—To Outersteene.
29—To Nouveau Monde.
30—To la Crêche.

July
: 5—Into the Line. (Ploegsteert.)
9—Relieved. To the Piggeries.
14—Into the line. (Ploegsteert.)
18—Relieved. One-half Battalion to Defended Locality N. of Strand, one-half Battalion to billets. (La Grande Munque Farm.)
21—To Kortepyp Huts (near Neuve Eglise). (Div. Res.)
29—Into the Line. (Ploegsteert.)

August
: 2—Relieved. To the Piggeries.
6—Forward to Res. Line for Trenches 135-138.
10—Relieved. To billets. (Div. Res.)
19—Into the Line. (Trenches 135-137.)
23—Relieved. To Courte Dreve Farm.
29—Into the Line. (Trenches 135-137.)

September
: 4—Relieved. To Kortepyp Huts. (Div. Res.)
8—Into the Line. (Trenches 135-137.)
13—Relieved. To Courte Dreve Farm. (Brig. Res.)
17—To Kortepyp Huts and Westhof Farm.
21—To Locre.
24—Into the Line. (Lindenhoek.)
25—Relieved. To Kortepyp Huts and Westhof Farm. (Arriving 5 a.m., September 26th.)
26—Into the Line. (Trenches 113-120.)

October
: 3—Relieved. To Aldershot Camp (near Neuve Eglise).
4—To Courte Dreve Farm. (Brig. Res.)
8—Into the Line. (Trenches 135-137.)

ITINERARY

October   14—Relieved. To Kortepyp Huts. (Div. Res.)
          20—Into the Line. (Trenches 135-138.)
          25—Relieved. To Courte Dreve Farm. (Brig. Res.)
          30—Into the Line. (Trenches 135-138.)

November 4—Relieved. To Kortepyp Huts. (Div. Res.)
          9—Into the Line. (Trenches 135-138.)
          14—Relieved. To Courte Dreve Farm. (Brig. Res.)
          15—To Red Lodge. (Ploegsteert Wood.)
          18—Into the Line. (Trenches 135-138.)
          22—Relieved. To Kortepyp Huts. (Div. Res.)
          26—Into the Line. (Trenches 136-141.)
          30—Relieved. To Red Lodge. (Brig. Res.)

December 4—Into the Line. (Trenches 136-141.)
          8—Relieved. To Kortepyp Huts. (Div. Res.)
          12—Into the Line. (Trenches 136-141.)
          16—Relieved. To Red Lodge. (Brig. Res.)
          20—Into the Line. (Trenches 136-141.)
          24—Relieved. To Kortepyp Huts. (Div. Res.)
          29—Into the Line. (Trenches 136-141.)

1916

January   3—Relieved. To Red Lodge. (Brig. Res.)
          7—Into the Line. (Trenches 136-141.)
          11—Relieved. To Kortepyp Huts. (Div. Res.)
          15—Into the Line. (Trenches 136-141.)
          19—Relieved. To Red Lodge. (Brig. Res.)
          23—Into the Line. (Trenches 136-141.)
          27—Relieved. To Kortepyp Huts. (Div. Res.)
          31—To Meteren. (Corps Res.)

February 20—To Red Lodge. (Brig. Res.)
          21—Into the Line. (Trenches 136-141.)
          27—Relieved. To Red Lodge. (Brig. Res.)

March   4—Into the Line. (Trenches 136-141.)
          10—Relieved. To Kortepyp Huts. (Div. Res.)

THE ROYAL MONTREAL REGIMENT

March
17—Into the Line. (Trenches 136-141.)
24—Relieved. To Red Lodge. (Brig. Res.)
25—To Rest Area No. 2. (Bailleul.)
28—To Canada Huts. (Near Ouderdom.)
29—To Swan Chateau (south of Kruisstraat). (Brig. Res.)

April
3—Into the Line. (H.Q. at " The Dump ".)
8—Relieved. To Canada Huts. (Div. Res.)
15—To Dickebusch Huts. (Brig. Res.)
23—Into the Line. (The Bluff.)

May
1—Relieved. To Hop Factory, Poperinghe. (Div. Res.)
3—Moved to Rue de Boeschepe.
9—To Swan Chateau. (Brig. Sup.)
17—Into the Line. Mount Sorrel.
25—Relieved. To Dominion Lines (near Ouderdom). (Div. Res.)

June
1—Dominion Lines. (Brig. Res.)
BATTLE OF MOUNT SORREL. (2-3 June.) (See text.)
4—To Dominion Lines. (Brig. Res.)
5—To Patricia Lines (north of Wippenhoek). (Div. Res.)
12—To " D " Camp (S.W. of Vlamertinghe). (Brig. Res.)
14—To Swan Chateau. (Brig. Sup.)
19—Bus to Kenora Camp (north of Reninghelst). (Div. Res.)
24—Into the Line. Battersea Farm (S.E. of Zillebeke).
29—Relieved. To Dominion Lines. (Brig. Res.)

July
4—To Patricia Lines. (Div. Res.)
9—Into the Line. Bluff and Railway Cutting.
14—Relieved. To Railway Dugouts, etc. (Ypres). (Brig. Sup.)
19—To Dickebusch Huts. (Brig. Res.)
21—To Patricia Lines. (Div. Res.)
31—Into the Line. Verbrandenmolen Sector.

ITINERARY

August
6—Relieved. To Swan Chateau. (Brig. Sup.)
9—To Victoria Lines (S.W. of Reninghelst).
11—Marched to Steenvoorde Area.
12—Marched to Noordpeene Area.
13—Marched to 2nd Army Training Area (N.W. of St. Omer).
27—Marched to St. Omer Station. Entrained (9.30 p.m.).
28—Arrived Conteville (5.45 a.m.). Marched to Coulonvillers.
29—Marched to Pernois.
30—Marched to la Vicogne.
31—Marched to Vadencourt.

THE BATTLES OF THE SOMME, 1916.

Battle of Thiepval Ridge (26/28 September).

September
1—Marched to Brickfields, Albert.
2—Marched to Albert. (Rue Hurtu.)
3—To Tara Hill. (Div. Res.)
5—To Chalk Pits. (Brig. Res.)

6/8—**Operations at Mouquet Farm.** (See text.)
9—To Warloy.
10—Marched to Herrissart.
11—Marched to Montrelet.
13/14—Battalion in manœuvres.
15—Marched to la Vicogne.
16—Marched to Vadencourt.
18—Marched to Brickfields, Albert.
23—Forward into Brigade Support.

24/28—**Battalion in Attack, Kenora Trench.** (See text.)
28—To billets in Albert. (Arriving at dawn.)
28—Marched to Warloy. (4 p.m.)

Battle of the Ancre Heights (6/10 and 14/15 October).

October
5—Marched to Albert.
6—Forward into Brigade Support.
8—Forward to Sugar and Cable Trenches. (Close Support.)
10—Relieved. To Brickfields, Albert.
13—To Brigade Reserve.

October 15—To Brickfields, Albert.
16—Marched to Warloy.
17—Marched to Val de Maison.
18—Marched to Pernois.
20—Marched to Prouville.
21—Marched to Boffles and Fortel.
22—Marched to Petit Houvin and La Mont Joie Farm.
23—Marched to Ternas.
24—Marched to Magnicourt.
26—Marched to Estrée Cauchie.
27—Marched to Berthonval Area. (Brig. Res.)

November 3—Into the Line. Berthonval Sector. (Left Sub-Section.)
10—Relieved. To Estrée Cauchie. (Div. Res.)
18—Into the Line. Carency Sector. (Right Sub-Section.)
22—Relieved. To Villers-au-Bois. (Brig. Res.)
26—Into the Line. Carency Sector. (Right Sub-Section.)
30—Relieved. To Hospital Corner. (Brig. Sup.)

December 5—To Estrée Cauchie. (Div. Res.)
12—Into the Line. Berthonval Sector. (Left Sub-Section.)
16—Relieved. To Berthonval Wood. (Brig. Res.)
21—To Estrée Cauchie. (Div. Res.)
22—To Bruay. (Rest Billets.)

1917

January 17—To Bully Grenay.
18—Into the Line. Calonne Sector. (Left Sub-Section.)
25—Relieved. To Calonne Village. (Brig. Sup.)
30—Into the Line. Calonne Sector. (Left Sub-Section.)

February 5—Relieved. To Bully Grenay. (Brig. Res.)
11—Into the Line. Calonne Sector. (Left Sub-Section.)
17—Relieved. To Calonne Village. (Brig. Sup.)
22—Into the Line. Calonne Sector. (Left Sub-Section.)

ITINERARY

March
5—Relieved. To Haillicourt. (Brig. Res.)
8—Marched to Cambligneul.
9—Marched to Bois des Alleux. (Div. Res.)
18—To Maison Blanche. (Brig. Res.)
24—Into the Line. Thélus Sector.
29—Relieved. To le Pendu Huts. (Div. Res.)

April
5—To Maison Blanche. (Div. Res.)
6—Into the Line. Thélus Sector.
BATTLE OF VIMY RIDGE (9/14 April). (See text.)
10—To Vase Trench. (Reserve.)
14—Moved to Wittelsbacher Trench.
15—To Bois de la Ville.
18—Into the Front Line. Arleux Sector. (Left Sub-Section.)
22—Relieved. To Maison Blanche South Camp. (Tents.)
26—To Fond du Vase. (Tents.)
BATTLE OF ARLEUX (28/29 April).
28—Forward into Brigade Support. (Bois Carré.)
29—Move to Support Position to left of Brigade Support. (Arleux Sector.)

May
1—Relieved. To Island Traverse Trench. (Brig. Res.)
2—Forward into Brigade Support.
THIRD BATTLE OF THE SCARPE, 1917. (Capture of Fresnoy, 3/4 May.)
4—To Brunehaut Farm. (Div. Res.)
6—Marched to Estrée Cauchie. (Corps. Res.)
31—To Camp (S.E. of Berthonval Farm).

June
1—To Paynesley Area. (Div. Sup.) To S. of Vimy Station at night. (Brig. Res.)
5—Into the Line. Quebec Trench.
10—Relieved. To Thélus Cave. (Brig. Sup.)
17—To Mont St. Eloy. Winnipeg Huts. (Div. Res.)
25—To Thélus Cave. (Brig. Sup.)
26—Forward to Close Support.

July	4—Into the Line. Acheville Sector. 12—Relieved. To Paynesley Area. (Brig. Sup.) 13—To Fraser Camp. (Div. Res.) 14—Marched to Gauchin Légal. 17—Marched to Braquemont. 22—Marched to Ruitz.
August	3—Marched to Mazingarbe. (Brig. Res.) 5—Into the Line. Loos Sector. 9—Relieved. To Noeux les Mines. (Div. Res.) 10—Marched to Fosse 7, Barlin. (Div. Res.) 13—Marched to Mazingarbe. (Brig. Res.) 14—Into the Line. Hill 70 Sector. **BATTLE OF HILL 70** (15/20 August). 20—Relieved (2.15 a.m.). To Les Brebis. (Brig. Res.) 20—Marched to Fosse 7, Barlin. (Div. Res.) 21—Marched to Marles les Mines. (Corps Res.)
September	2—Marched to Bouvigny Huts. (Div. Res.) 3—To Cité St. Pierre. (Brig. Res.) 4—Into the Line. 10—Relieved. To Marqueffles Farm. (Div. Res.) 16—Forward to Cité St. Pierre. (Brig. Res.) 22—To Marqueffles Farm. (Div. Res.) 23—To Estrée Cauchie. (Corps Res.)
October	4—Marched to Gouy Servins. 5—To Zouave Valley. (Brig. Res.) Into the Line, Avion. 10—Relieved. To Tottenham Huts. (Brig. Res.) 13—Marched to Gauchin Légal. 20—Marched to Bruay. 21—Marched to Ham-en-Artois. 22—Marched to Thiennes. 23—Marched to Staple. 31—Train to Ebblinghem. Marched to St. Jean and Wieltje. Two companies forward into support. **SECOND BATTLE OF PASSCHENDAELE** (31 October/10 November).

ITINERARY

November   1—Forward to Capricorn Keep. (Brig. Sup.)
2—Into the Front Line.
4—Relieved. To Wieltje. (Brig. Res.)
7—Forward to Bellevue Spur. (Brig. Sup.)
9—Relieved. To Capricorn Keep. (Brig. Res.)
10—To Camp "C", Wieltje.
11—To Ypres. Train to Brandhoek Area.
12—Bus to Merville.
13—Bus to Bethune.
14—Bus to Hersin Coupigny Area.
17—Marched to Marqueffles Farm.
19—Marched to Alberta Camp. (Brig. Res.)
25—Into the Line. Avion Sector.

December   3—Relieved. To La Coulotte. Train to Chateau de la Haie. To Vancouver Camp. (Div. Res.)
11—Forward into Support. Lens Sector. Liévin.
15—Into the Line. Moulin Sector.
19—Relieved. One-half Battalion in Support (Liévin) and one-half in Brig. Res. (Souchez Huts).
23—Battalion to St. Lawrence Camp. (Div. Res.)

1918

January   7—To Reserve Area. Houdain.
23—Marched to Bully Grenay. (Div. Res.)
31—Into the Line. Hill 70 Sector.

February   7—Relieved. To Village Line. (Brig. Res.)
16—To Bully Grenay. (Div. Res.)
24—Into the Line. St. Emile Section.

March   6—Relieved. To Cité St. Pierre. (Brig. Sup.)
13—To Bois de Froissart. (Corps Res.)
20—Marched to Bully Grenay. (Div. Sup.)
23—At Bully Grenay. (Army Res.)
27—Marched to Chateau de la Haie. Marched (11.45 p.m.) to embussing point.

March	28—Bus (3.20 a.m.) to Marieux. March to Famechon. Bus (4.00 p.m.) to Agnez-les-Duisans. 29—Forward (3.55 a.m.) to Ronville (S. of Arras). (Brig. Sup.)
April	5—Into the Line. Telegraph Hill. 8—Relieved. To Agny. Train to Berneville. Bus to Feuchy-Fampoux Sector. (Support.) 11—Into the Line. Feuchy-Fampoux Sector. 13—Relieved. To Aubrey Camp. (Corps Res.) 21—Into the Line. Gavrelle Sector. 28—Relieved. To Gavrelle Section (Brig. Res.)
May	6—To " Y " Huts. Etrun. (Corps Res.) 19—To Manin. (Army Special Res.) 21/22—Battalion in manœuvres. 25—To Ostreville. (Army Special Res.)
June	30—Marched to Frévillers. (Army Special Res.)
July	1—Battalion to Corps Sports. Tinques. 6—Battalion to Highland Gathering. Tinques. 13—Marched to Anzin St. Aubin. (Div. Res.) 18—Into the Line. Telegraph Hill. 26—Relieved. To Achicourt. (Div. Res.) 31—To Fosseux (3 a.m.).
August	3—Bus to Frévent (9 p.m.). 4—Train to Vieux-Rouen-sur-Bresle. Marched to Avesne. 5—Bus (all night) to near Amiens. 6—Marched to Boves. 7—Forward to N. of Gentelles (12.15 a.m.). Forward at dusk to Assembly Positions. **THE BATTLE OF AMIENS** (8/11 August). (See text.) 9—Marched to Cayeux. Forward to Assembly Positions. Forward in Support.

ITINERARY

August
12—To Beaufort Area. (Reserve.)

ACTIONS AROUND DAMERY (15/17 August).

15—To Parvillers Sector.
21—To Beaufort Area.
23—To Hangard Wood.
24—Marched to Boves.
25—Marched to Saleux (12 p.m.).

BATTLE OF THE SCARPE, 1918. (Capture of Monchy le Preux, 26/30 August.)

26—Train to Aubigny. Bus to Dainville. Marched to near Arras.
27—To near Tilloy Wood.
28—Into the Line (East of Arras).

September
1—**BATTALION IN ATTACK (Crow's Nest Operation).**

BATTLE OF THE DROCOURT-QUEANT LINE (2/3 September). (See text.)

3—Moved back to Drocourt-Quéant Line.
4—Marched to Chérisy. Bus to Warlus. Marched to Berneville.
19—To old trenches near Telegraph Hill.
24—Marched to Arras to entrain.
25—Train to Bullecourt. Marched to Hendecourt. Forward to Buissy Switch.
26.—Forward to Assembly Positions.

27—**BATTLE OF THE CANAL DU NORD.** (Capture of Bourlon Wood, 27 September/1 October). (See text.)

30—Forward to N. of Bourlon. Forward to Assembly Positions (11.45 p.m.).

October
1—**BATTALION IN ATTACK** (5 a.m.). Relieved at night and to Marquion. (Rest Billets.)

5—March to Vis-en-Artois.
6—Forward to Monchy le Preux Area. (Brig. Res.)

| October | 9—Forward 2,000 yards. (Brig. Res.) |

12—Forward (4 a.m.) to near Sailly-en-Ostrevent. Relieved and to S. of Eterpigny.

18—Marched to Gœulzin (7 a.m.). Marched to Erchin (4.30 p.m.).

19—Forward to E. of Helesmes.
20—Forward to E. of Wallers.
21—Forward to Raismes.
22—Relieved. To Fenain.

November 11—**THE ARMISTICE.**

13—Marched to la Sentinelle (19 kilometres).
14—Marched to Elouges (25 kilometres).
15—Marched to Quaregnon (11 kilometres).
18—Marched to Hubermont and Neufvilles (27 kilometres.
21—Marched to Braine le Comte (8½ kilometres).
24—Marched to Ways (25½ kilometres).
25—Marched to Cortil Noirmont (16 kilometres).
27—Marched to Leuze (24 kilometres).
28—Marched to Petit Waret (14 kilometres).
30—Marched to Belle Maison (20 kilometres).

December 2—Marched to Bonsin (20½ kilometres).
4—Marched to Bra (42½ kilometres).
6—Marched to Neuville (19 kilometres).

7—**ACROSS THE GERMAN BORDER.** To Deidenberg and neighbouring villages (21½ kilometres).

8—Marched to Murringen and Hunningen (16 kilometres).
9—Marched to Sistig (31½ kilometres).
10—Marched to Euenheim (27½ kilometres).
11—Marched to Bruhl (25 kilometres).
12—Marched to outskirts of Cologne (12½ kilometres).

13—**ACROSS THE RHINE.** To Volberg (25 kilometres).

14—Marched to Unter Eschbach (5 kilometres).

ITINERARY

1919

January 5—Marched to Hoffnungsthal to entrain.
6—Arrived Huy (Belgium).

February 1/28—Month spent at Huy.

March 5—Left Huy by train (11 a.m.) for le Havre.
7—Arrived le Havre (Canadian Embarkation Camp).
14—Embarked *(S.S. Queen Alexandra)* and crossed to England. Weymouth.
15—Disembarked (Weymouth). Train to Liphook. Marched to Bramshott Camp.

April 10—Train to Liverpool. Sailed for Canada on *S.S. Carmania*.
18—Arrived Halifax. Entrained.
20—**ARRIVED MONTREAL.**

APPENDIX F

The Royal Montreal Regiment

14th Battalion, C.E.F.

STATISTICS

Total of the Nominal Roll	6,270
Individual names on Nominal Roll	5,603
Number of officers who served	**246**
Officers killed	47
O.R. killed	1,077
O.R. died, or killed accidentally	68
Total killed	1,124
Total dead	1,192
Officers wounded	141
O.R. wounded	3,136
Total wounded	3,277
Total casualties (as above)	4,469

SERVICE BY YEARS

1914	149 days
1915	365 days
1916	366 days
1917	365 days
1918	365 days
1919	111 days
Total	1,721 days

Days spent in Canada	60
Days spent at Sea	27
Days spent in England	147
Days spent in France and Belgium	1,458
Days spent in Germany	29
Total	1,721

www.ingramcontent.com/pod-product-compliance
Lightning Source LLC
Chambersburg PA
CBHW071810230426
43670CB00013B/2412